EXPLORATIONS
IN CREATIVITY

EXPLORATIONS IN
CREATIVITY

EDITED BY ROSS L. *Lawler* MOONEY

AND

TAHER A. RAZIK

HARPER & ROW, PUBLISHERS

NEW YORK, EVANSTON, AND LONDON

FIRST EDITION

LIBRARY OF CONGRESS CATALOG CARD NUMBER: 67–22532

H-R   *32478*

Contents

Part III. CREATIVITY: MEASUREMENTS

Contributors

FRANK BARRON, *Research Psychologist,* Institute of Personality Assessment and Research, University of California, Berkeley, California.

KENNETH R. BEITTEL, *Professor in the Visual Arts,* Pennsylvania State University, University Park, Pennsylvania.

W. LAMBERT BRITTAIN, *Professor, Department of Child Development and Family Relations,* Cornell University, Ithaca, New York.

ROBERT BURKHART, *Professor of Art Education,* State University College of New York at Buffalo, Buffalo, New York.

FRIEDA G. COWLING, *Homemaker,* Stillwater, Oklahoma.

RICHARD S. CRUTCHFIELD, *Professor of Psychology,* University of California, Berkeley, California.

IRWIN FLESCHER, *Clinical and Research Psychologist,* Roslyn Heights, New York.

EUGENE L. GAIER, *Professor of Educational Psychology,* State University of New York at Buffalo, Buffalo, New York.

JACOB W. GETZELS, *Professor,* University of Chicago, Chicago, Illinois.

R. J. GOLDMAN, *Principal,* Didsbury College of Education, Manchester, England.

J. P. GUILFORD, *Professor of Psychology,* University of Southern California, Los Angeles, California.

HERBERT GUTMAN, *Marriage, Family, and Child Counselor,* Topanga, California.

WILLIAM D. HITT, *Chief, Behavioral Science Division,* Battelle Memorial Institute, Columbus, Ohio.

JOHN L. HOLLAND, *Vice President, Research,* American College Testing Program, Iowa City, Iowa.

PHILIP W. JACKSON, *Professor of Education and Human Development,* University of Chicago, Chicago, Illinois.

LAWRENCE S. KUBIE, *Consultant on Research and Training,* Spark, Maryland.

CARSON McGUIRE, *Professor of Educational Psychology,* University of Texas, Austin, Texas.

DONALD W. MACKINNON, *Professor of Psychology and Director,* Institute of Personality Assessment and Research, University of California, Berkeley, California.

ABRAHAM H. MASLOW, *Professor of Psychology,* Brandeis University, Waltham, Massachusetts.

MARGARET MEAD, *Curator of Ethnology,* The American Museum of Natural History, New York, New York.

ROSS L. MOONEY, *Professor of Education,* Ohio State University, Columbus, Ohio.

CLARK MOUSTAKAS, *Merrill-Palmer Institute,* Detroit, Michigan.

TAHER A. RAZIK, *Associate Professor of Education,* State University of New York at Buffalo, Buffalo, New York.

KAYLA J. SPRINGER, *Assistant Professor,* University of Cincinnati, Cincinnati, Ohio.

ELIZABETH K. STARKWEATHER, *Associate Professor, Department of Family Relations and Child Development,* Oklahoma State University, Stillwater, Oklahoma.

MORRIS I. STEIN, *Professor of Psychology,* New York University, New York City, New York.

JOHN R. STOCK, *Senior Psychologist,* Battelle Memorial Institute, Columbus, Ohio.

CALVIN W. TAYLOR, *Professor of Psychology,* University of Utah, Salt Lake City, Utah.

E. PAUL TORRANCE, *Chairman and Professor of Education and Psychology,* University of Georgia, Athens, Georgia.

PAUL S. WEISBERG, *Assistant Professor of Psychiatry,* School of Medicine, George Washington University, Washington, D.C.

KAORU YAMAMOTO, *Associate Professor of Educational Psychology,* University of Iowa, Iowa City, Iowa.

Preface

A recent bibliography of writings on creativity and related problems lists 4,176 items.* It covers publications through December, 1964. Half of the entries are dated 1950 or later; half of that half appeared in 1960 or later. The field is rapidly expanding, and it is difficult to keep abreast of developments.

This volume is presented as an aid in gaining perspective on the growing field. In making selections, we have sought to include significant works which, together, show the spread of approaches to the subject.

The entries have been grouped into three sections: Nature, Nurture, and Measurement. Articles which include more than one of the three themes are placed where their main emphasis seems to be. Each section opens with a brief introduction.

The backgrounds of the contributors range through several disciplines: genetic psychology, clinical psychology, educational psychology, child development, art education, teacher education, psychiatry, anthropology, educational and psychological research. Among the contributions, some focus on highly creative adults, some on children, some on adolescents. For some, the aim is to identify the characteristics of known creative persons; for others, the aim is to cultivate the creative characteristics of all persons in a given group; for still others, the aim is to develop tests and procedures which can be effectively used in further research and development. Some seek to improve selection of personnel for given tasks; some to improve education or therapy; some to improve research. Some seek an orientation to nature; some to culture; some to institutional operations; some to family; some to personal experience. Some focus on the person; some on the process; some on the product; some on the environment.

This diversity signifies a widening range of approaches to creativity and

---

* Razik, Taher A. *Bibliography of Creativity Studies and Related Areas,* Creative Education Foundation and State University of New York at Buffalo, 1965, pp. 451.

a widening range of persons concerned with creativity. People are becoming aware of the importance of creativity in many aspects of national life and are taking hold of the subject from their varied points of view.

The future will see still further spread. The problems now faced by mankind are largely due to man's own creativeness. Creativeness will need to account for much more if present problems are to be transcended with solutions. The need is to know more about man's creativeness and to develop his creativeness in ever-increasing proportions of the population.

PART I

CREATIVITY: NATURE

Introduction

There is a sense in which no man can avoid some thought about the nature of creativity. As a living being, he is a creative creature in a world which is creating as it goes along. To live, he is called upon to reason out how he can operate within his world to keep his life intact. When he wants a richer life, he is led to seek the deeper workings in the world and in himself to gain the richer returns. He enters on an ancient quest, continued now, and sure to be the question asked by thoughtful men as long as human living lasts: How *does* creation go? What *is* its structure?

This is the question asked below. In each entry, the contributor takes hold from within the field of work with which he is engaged.

Herbert Gutman, a genetic psychologist, asks how man is made by nature so that he can behave creatively: How did man evolve? What does this mean for cultivating further growth in man?

Lawrence Kubie, a psychiatrist working with adults, asks how the creative system works in man to heal him when he is sick: What is the system the doctor needs to keep in mind when trying to help the healing process work?

Abraham Maslow, a clinical psychologist working with highly developed

1

adults, asks how maturation proceeds when men mature into their best: What is the system that operates in such a case? Wherein lies creativeness?

Donald MacKinnon, a research psychologist working with highly creative adults, asks what the markings are for men who succeed in making of themselves a source for continuing creative work: How is such a man composed?

Frank Barron, a research psychologist working with highly creative writers, asks what the makeup is for those who succeed in making of themselves a creative source for expression in the written word: How are they able to produce a continued flow of fresh and vital stuff?

Carson McGuire, an educational psychologist working with students in schools, asks the form creativeness displays when, in some students, creativeness is found more fully formed than in others: What is the makeup of those students who are more fully formed that those, less so, lack?

Lambert Brittain from the field of child development, and Kenneth Beittel from the field of art education, ask what the distinguishing marks are for those students whose art products are the more creative: What may be inferred as to the nature of creativity when trusting to the product to provide the prime initial cue?

J. P. Guilford, a research psychologist working with adults, asks what "intelligence" becomes when it includes capacity for creative thought: What abilities are then required? Where do they fit in a total system for the intellect?

HERBERT GUTMAN

The Biological Roots of Creativity

Introduction

THE PROBLEM

What is creativity? What is the nature of this trait which distinguishes man most typically from all other living creatures, a trait to which man owes his culture and civilization, which continuously leads him on in his own evolutionary development? This is a burning question which psychologists have largely tended to evade—and for understandable reasons.

Creative behavior, by its very nature, is spontaneous, inner-directed, ordinarily not capable of being elicited at will. Therefore, it is unpredictable and escapes manipulation and control. It is generally not amenable to experimentation.

Modern psychology, being largely empiristic in outlook, having drifted away from the armchair philosophizing of the past, and insisting upon experimental verification, does not feel comfortable with a behavior phenomenon which escapes scientific scrutiny. Instead, psychologists have settled down to the study of adjustive behavior which consists in responses to environmental stimuli or stimulus situations. Here the scientist feels more at home, because the observed phenomena can be treated in terms of a cause-and-effect relationship, the stimulus being the cause, the response the effect.

However, the study of creative behavior has not been neglected completely. Yet, it has been confined to three aspects of creativity: its phenomenal side, productive thinking or problem-solving, and the composition of the trait of creativity. The methods of investigation applied in these studies have been correspondingly descriptive, experimental, and statis-

From *Genetic Psychology Monographs*, 1961, pp. 419–458. Used by permission of the publisher.

tical. Attempts at interpretation are found in all three approaches: in the first, in terms of psychological dynamics; in the second, in terms of mental processes; and in the third, in terms of factor-analysis (Guilford, 1950, 1957).

The approach taken in this article is different from those mentioned above. An attempt is made to establish a link between the creative activities of man and the creative processes inherent in life. The author hopes that such a study may lead to a deeper understanding of human creativity and its products.

HISTORICAL BACKGROUND

The idea of subsuming human behavioral trends under fundamental principles of life is not altogether new. The first systematic attempt in this direction has been made by William Stern in his *opus magnum Person und Sache* (1906, 1918, 1924), of which the first volume appeared in 1906. In this volume, Stern proposed and worked out a conceptual framework within which he then went about to discuss behavioral systems. In the second and third volumes of this significant work, the theoretical concepts developed in the first volume are applied to the problem of human personality and a theory of values respectively.

Stern singles out two fundamental trends which operate in all living organisms: self-maintenance and self-development or self-expansion. According to Stern (1918, p. 34), the principle of self-development has reached the highest level of manifestation in the creative activity of man.

One year after the publication of Stern's first volume of *Person und Sache,* Bergson's *Creative Evolution* (1911) came into print. What Stern called "self-development" Bergson named "élan vitale," a life trend responsible for the creativity of nature as well as of man. Fifteen years later, Morgan (1923) postulated a principle of "emergence" to account for spontaneity and unpredictability in the phenomena of life. A trend toward self-development or creative self-expansion has more recently been emphasized by Allport (1937, 1955), Buhler (1951, 1954), Dobzhansky and Montagu (1947), Dreikurs (1951), Horney (1950), Rogers (1942, 1946, 1951), Russell (1934, 1945), Sinnott (1955, 1957), Snygg and Combs (1949), and others.

The principle of self-maintenance has been more readily accepted by students of behavior than the principle of creative self-expansion. With the publication of Cannon's *The Wisdom of the Body* (1939) it has found general recognition under the new term "homeostasis," which refers to the trend in living organisms to maintain functional balance in their internal environment. The term has lately acquired wider meaning, applying to all self-maintaining activities of organisms. The operation of the principle of homeostasis on the level of behavior can be observed in all activities which aim at the preservation of the status quo or at the restoration of a disturbed equilibrium.

In modern systems theory, which views living organisms as special cases of open systems, the term "homeostasis" has become replaced by "steady state," to stress the fact that the balance in living organisms is in no way a "stasis," a standstill, but a dynamic process aiming at equilibrium, consisting in a perpetual exchange of material with the environment. What leaves the organism during this exchange is called "output," what goes into it "input." Man as an open system, therefore, not only receives from his environment but also makes his contribution to it.

Not all behavior, however, serves to maintain or restore balance. Human behavior in particular not only aims at preserving the status quo but also at producing something new. Man's behavior is not only adaptive but also creative.

The Hierarchy of Behaviors

What is the position of creative behavior among all other behaviors? We can arrange behavior phenomena in a hierarchial order, in which those lower in the hierarchy form the prerequisites for those next higher. The following six levels of behavior may be singled out for convenience: (a) vegetative, (b) reflex, (c) conditioned response, (d) learned behavior, (e) problem-solving, and (f) creative activity. Only the first five levels of behavior have been subjected to extensive study and experimentation, the reason probably being that these levels, standing in the service of the principle of homeostasis, involve an interplay of measurable input and output. They are, therefore, subject to experimentation. By changing the input, the output is altered, and its relationship to the input can be studied.

On the physiological level, the input consists of food, water, and oxygen, the output of various waste products and certain secretions. On the reflex level, the input consists in a well-defined single stimulus in the form of energy of one kind or another; the output, in a single response in which energy is expanded. In simple conditioning, stimuli are paired, associations are formed, and responses are made to stimuli which previously did not have the power to elicit them. In learning, the input is represented either by a series of stimuli or a complex stimulus situation; the output, by a series of responses and a more complex behavior pattern. In problem-solving behavior, the input consists in a situation which constitutes an obstacle to need gratification and requires of the organism cognitive processes for an efficient solution of the problem presented.

The dividing lines between these levels are obviously not sharp, but it can be seen that problem-solving makes use of past learning, learning of conditioning, conditioning of reflexes, and reflexes of physiological processes. The energy generated on the physiological level serves in part to sustain the output on all higher levels.

Creative Behavior

Creative behavior consists in any activity by which man imposes a new order upon his environment. It is organizing activity. More specifically, it is the original act by which that organization is first conceived and given objective expression. It may or may not involve at the same time the creation of an organized structure. The inventor of a machine may end his work with the blueprint for construction. Thus, the actual construction of the machine from the blueprint is no longer a creative act.

Creative output, although contributing something to the environment that was not previously in it, is different from the output phase in homeostasis. What the organism contributes to the environment in creative activity is organization. Although in his creative activity man expands energy and makes a physical impact upon the environment, this energy-expanding component may be looked upon as a carrier for the creative organizational output, just as in broadcasting the radio frequency serves as a carrier for the audio frequency by which it is modulated. The organization which man expresses through his activities is a modulator of this activity.

Although creative behavior often does not appear as a response to external stimuli, it cannot take place without experiences which precede and trigger it. Since creative activity consists in imposing organization upon the environment, it is necessary that man perceives the objects which he transforms and organizes, and that they become represented as percepts or concepts in his own inner world before he can do something with them constructively and creatively.

Because creative behavior is characterized by a unique output of its own which, although utilizing the output forms on all lower levels of behavior, displays an added new dimension—namely that of organization—it is suggestive to assume that the input necessary to feed creative activity likewise is different from all other forms of input on lower levels of behavior by an additional feature which makes this input acceptable to the creative process. The question is: What could this additional feature possibly be? Before answering this question, more needs to be said about the nature of the creative process.

THE RELATION OF CREATIVITY TO GROWTH AND REPRODUCTION

An inherent connection between the creative process and the processes of growth and reproduction has been hinted at not only by creative individuals on the basis of their subjective experiences, but also has been repeatedly stressed by psychologists and biologists who have arrived at similar insights on the basis of studies in their respective fields. Freud claimed that sublimation of the sexual urge "forms one of the sources of artistic activity" (1938, p. 625) and that from it is derived the major part of the energy which, in the history of mankind, has been expanded toward the creation of cultures and civilizations. Otto Rank (1924) sees in the act of artistic creation a reenactment of the process of birth. William Stern (1918) views human creativity as the highest manifestation of the principle of self-expansion which, on the biological level, is expressed in growth and reproduction. Buhler (1951, p. 203) maintains that constructive activity "has its biological substratum in growth and reproduction." A common source for the creative activity of man and the constructive processes of growth is seen by Bergson (1911) in a force immanent in life. This force, the élan vitale, Bergson says, "has the choice between two modes of acting on the material world: it can either effect this action *directly* by creating an *organized* instrument to work with; or else it can effect it *indirectly* through an organism which, instead of possessing the required instrument naturally, will itself construct it by fashioning inorganic matter." Sinnott (1955, p. 146) expresses the same thought thus: "Just as an organism takes random matter and builds it into a living bodily pattern, so the man of art takes meaningless canvas, paint, and marble, musical sounds and the more subtle symbols of written and spoken words, and builds them into patterns. . . ." Coghill (1929, p. 108) claims that the same principle which invented the nervous system is also its operator, and that it is to be identified with the growth potential. He suggests that "growth is one of the means by which the nervous system performs its function in behavior," and states that "the real measure of the individual . . . must include the element of growth as a creative power" (1929, p. 110). Read (1943, p. 192) expresses his views in these words: "The original property in matter and energy which organizes the universe in space and time . . . extends to those forms of energy which we call psychic. Not only are the cosmic and biological processes continuous and co-extensive; the mental processes in man are also part of the same dynamic unity."

The author of the present article shares the views expressed by Stern, Buhler, Bergson, Sinnott, Coghill, and Read. He holds the opinion that all organized and purposive protoplasmic activity deserves to be classified as "behavior," and that constructive or creative activity simply continues where growth leaves off.[1]

The border line between growth and behavior is very thin indeed. Some animals still retain to this day the power of making use of processes of growth for behavioral responses. The amoeba sets a classical example for this mode of behavior. When this protozoon is in need of walking, it gives itself pseudopods; if it has an urge to engulf, it surrounds the food particle with its own protoplasmic mass, thus producing the equivalent of a mouth. This "mouth" closes, and the cavity thus formed assumes the functions of a stomach into which digestive enzymes flow. After the digestion of the food particle is completed, the digestive vacuole moves toward the periphery of the cell body, forming a temporary "anus" for the elimination of the digestive waste products.

Here we have a form of behavior which is expressed through structural

---

[1] Schilder (1950, p. 101), by implication, arrives at a similar opinion when he says: "We may . . . ask what is the psychology of growth, what is the psychology of a reaction of a tissue?"

changes in the body organization. In this case, acting and growing become one and the same process: behavior consists in growing and growth is a behavioral response. Here, the organism creates "at will" structures which it needs for its behavioral or vegetative activities. It uses for this creative process material from its own internal environment.

The ability to express behavior through growth processes is also present in multicellular organisms. Russell (1934, p. 90) cites a case from the phylum *coelenterates,* the hydroid *Antennularia,* which, "if suspended in the water may send out 'roots' or holdfasts to regain contact with the bottom." He comes to the conclusion that "behavior, whether of plants or animals, is thus to be regarded simply as one form of the general directive activity which is characteristic of the living organism."

Behavior such as found in plants, the amoeba, and in *Antennularia* may rightfully be labeled as "growth-behavior."

If it is true that the processes of growth and reproduction and the creative activity of man are expressions of one and the same life principle, a principle of self-expansion through the production of new organization—albeit on different levels of expression—one should be able to find in all these processes a common principle of method by which this creative self-expansion is achieved. The author believes to have found such a common method in the principle of self-duplication. It is the main thesis of this article that the creative activity of man is essentially a reenactment of the biological principle of self-duplication, projected into the behavioral level.

As a first step in the support of this contention, the principle of self-duplication will be traced from the DNA molecule on up to the creative behavior of man.

The Principle of Self-Duplication

BIOLOGICAL SELF-DUPLICATION

It may rightly be said that at the beginning of life stands the principle of self-duplication. This principle constitutes the line of demarcation between inert matter and living things. Dobzhansky (1950, p. 163) states that "self-reproduction is the fundamental quality of life that distinguishes it from inanimate nature."

We find self-duplication on all levels of the organism. It is a theme carried through with many variations in the symphony of life. Organisms reproduce themselves. Their mature offspring may be looked upon as essentially a copy of the parent, in spite of individual variations due to mutation, environmental influences during development, or the shuffling of traits in sexual reproduction.

Growth, development, and reproduction are made possible by the self-duplication of the fundamental building blocks of all organisms, the cells. The most vital part in the cell is the nucleus. It is the home of the chromosomes. An essential part of mitotic cell division is the self-duplication of chromosomes. The self-duplication of chromosomes, in turn, is made possible by the self-duplication of the DNA molecules, which are the active building blocks of chromosomes.

In the process of self-duplication from the DNA molecule to the whole organism, we notice a hierarchy of function. Self-duplication of DNA molecules makes possible self-duplication of chromosomes. The latter are instrumental in cell division, and cell division, in turn, is the prerequisite for reproduction, growth, and development.

A brief description of mitotic cell division is necessary in order to highlight the essential features in the biological process of self-duplication, since their analogues will be traced later in the creative behavior of man.

All organized activities of the cell appear to be directed from the chromosomes in the nucleus. The chemical constituents of chromosomes are protein, desoxyribonucleic acid (DNA), and ribonucleic acid (RNA), of which DNA is now generally believed to constitute the "key to the specificity of the chromosomes" (Crick, 1954, p. 55). The DNA molecules virtually represent the genes and are believed to carry all the genetic information in the form of a "code," a "blueprint" for reproduction and development (Crick, 1954). They are assumed to pass on this information to the RNA molecules in the cytoplasm. The RNA molecules, in turn, serve as templates for the manufacturing of enzymes (Horowitz, 1956).

Mitotic cell division is initiated by a breaking up of each chromosome into two identical chromatids. The chromatids of each chromosome wander off within the cell into opposite directions, forming the nuclear material for the two daughter cells. Before they can assume the role of chromosomes in the new cell, they have to form doubles of themselves in order to be like the original chromosome of which they constituted two identical halves. Instrumental in this process of self-duplication of the chromatids are the DNA molecules. Their self-duplication and the concomitant duplication of structures made of material other than DNA is what constitutes the self-duplication of the chromatids.

How exactly DNA molecules go about duplicating themselves is still a matter of conjecture. But one thing is known, namely, that they construct their doubles from material which they find in their environment. In this process, they do not seem to disband their own organization. The present belief is that DNA molecules are made up of two interlocking chains of DNA, which structure is twisted into a helix (Crick, 1954). During the process of self-duplication, the chains unwind and simultaneously each separated part begins to assemble a complement to itself. The material used in the construction of new chains exists in the nearby environment in the form of free nucleotid units (Horowitz, 1956). The work of construction is performed by the DNA molecules themselves, which use their own structural organization as a template. DNA molecules and chromatids create their like in their own "image."

We can see that the self-duplication of biological structures involves three fundamental procedures: (a) the formation of new structures from material found in the environment of the structuring entity; (b) an assimilation of this material; and (c) the use of the structural organization residing in the structuring agent either as a "template" or as a "blueprint" for the creation of new structures.

In the case of the DNA molecules, the environment exterior to them consists in the interior environment of the cell. The process of assimilation must be sought in the anabolic processes leading to the formation of the free nucleotid units. The process of self-duplication consists in a fitting of these units to the structure of the DNA molecule which serves as a template.

In the case of cell-duplication, the raw material used in the production of new cells comes from the environment external to the cell. Where the cell is part of an organism, this environment is internal to the organism itself. The process of assimilation consists in the processes of digestion, absorption, and anabolism by which the usable components of the raw food are extracted and put into a form suitable for incorporation into the new structure. The process of digestion is performed by the single cell only where it is phagocytic or an independent animal organism. Otherwise, it is carried out by the organism of which it is a part. In the case of green plants, digestion is absent and replaced by photosynthesis.

The assembly of new cell structures takes place inside the cell itself. The "plans" of construction reside in the chromosomes of the nucleus. The construction of the new organism is believed to be directed by the genes, which in this process play the role of "blueprints."

Only in the case of the DNA molecule and the chromosome is the process of self-duplication accomplished by a direct copying of the structure to be duplicated. In all other instances, the process of self-duplication makes use of construction plans which are "decoded" or "translated" into directive "commands" or instructions. In other words, one must assume in these instances a complicated system of information through which the organizing activities are regulated. The "blueprints" residing in the genes are thus analogous to the ideas underlying the creative activities of man.

SELF-DUPLICATION IN CREATIVE ACTIVITY

In the creative activity of man, the material used for the construction of new forms is taken from the environment external to man, and the process of construction takes place in this same external environment. In this respect, man's creative activity resembles the self-duplicating activity of the DNA molecule or the gene.

Since the claim is made here that creativity is a reenactment of the biological process of self-duplication on the behavioral level, it is necessary to demonstrate that in his creative acts man imposes upon his environment an organization which he borrows from himself, and that in this process he resorts to methods analogous to those found on the biological level. What are these methods?

All truly creative activity necessitates, as a prerequisite, a process of identification.[2] The elements used in the creative process must, in some way, become part of what Snygg and Combs call the "phenomenal self"[3] or what Schilder has termed the "body-image," before man can subject them to the process of creative synthesis, because the products of creativity serve to enlarge the phenomenal self or the body-image.[4]

Identification is the psychological equivalent of physiological assimilation: before a material can be incorporated into any organization, it must be assimilated ("ad-similare") to it. Thus, in identification man establishes in his mind a similarity between himself and objects of his environment, or vice versa. This identification does not have to involve the whole of the human organism; it may be a partial one, relating only to parts or specific functions of man.

The similarity which is established through identification is not necessarily a similarity in appearance. In most instances, it is a similarity by analogy.

Although the active phase of the process of creation takes place in the environment external to man, the locus of the "latent" phase which always precedes the active phase is the mind of man, an aspect of his interior environment. During the latent phase, the process of identification through which man enters into a subjective relationship to his environment constitutes the unique input in the creative process which we have been looking for.

In enlarging his body-image, man resorts to the process of self-duplication. It must be pointed out, however, that man's creations are not to be looked upon as copies of himself, but rather as symbolic representations of some of his structural or functional aspects. They are not related to man by identity but by analogy. Therefore, it is more appropriate to speak in this case of self-transformation rather than of self-duplication. In the field of art, poetry, and music, this process of self-transformation is known as self-expression.

In carrying out this process of self-transformation, man employs methods which are analogous to those which we have observed in the self-duplicative activities on the biological level: he either uses his body as a template, or he employs his own inherent structural or functional organization as a "blueprint" which guides him in the construction of his own

[2] Freud, who maintained that sublimation is at the root of creativity, was inclined to believe that "sublimation is always preceded and made possible by identification" (Healy & Bronner, 1930, p. 248).

[3] Snygg and Combs state that "the phenomenal self may include, by identification, persons and objects quite outside our physical selves entirely" (1949, p. 57).

[4] According to Schilder "the body-image can shrink or expand; it can give parts to the outside world and can take other parts into itself" (1950, p. 202).

creations. The amount of self-transformation or self-expression involved in creative acts depends on the product man creates.

In the following classification of man-made structures, those lowest in rank involve the least amount of self-expression or self-transformation in their production, those higher in rank an increasingly larger amount:

1. Existential structures
2. Operational structures
3. Human social structures
4. Artistic and symbolic structures

These structures will now be discussed for the specific purpose of tracing the element of self-duplication in the creation of man-made structures.

Products of Human Creativity

EXISTENTIAL STRUCTURES

The term "existential structures" is applied here to those man-made structures which are of use to man by virtue of their specific construction or form and their availability in a particular location. Instead of actively doing something for man—such as machines and instruments—they *allow* something to be done or *prevent* something from occurring. They facilitate certain activities of man by the mere fact of existing. Their utility consists in passively serving a purpose. Examples of such structures are houses, furniture, bridges, highways, dams, and so on.

Existential structures—with exceptions to be mentioned later—constitute improvements upon man's external environment. They have come into being as a result of man's wish that his environment may contain this or that which it normally does not contain. A chair is an improvement over a tree stump or a boulder. In fact, most likely the first chair has been fashioned from either one of these objects. The hut made of leaves and branches is an improvement over natural tree shelters. The stone house surpasses the cave.

The primary objective for the creation of man-made existential structures is economy in time and energy, and increased comfort. This saving is accomplished through the continuous availability and permanency of existential structures. Thus, to avoid having to cross waterways by wading, swimming, or by means of a boat, man built himself bridges which, in the long run, saved him time and effort and contributed to his comfort.

Existential structures are of three fundamental kinds: (a) those which *allow* man to perform certain activities *on* or *in* them, such as chairs, tables, bridges, highways, houses, etc.; (b) those which *allow* agents other than man to be active *on* or *in* them, such as tubes, and canals through which water is *permitted* to flow, or copper wires which conduct electric currents; and (c) those which *prevent* men, animals, or other agents from acting in certain ways or moving into certain places, such as walls, fences, window screens, dams, and so on.

It is obvious that the border lines between these various kinds of existential structures cannot be drawn sharply, and that a given structure may be grouped with more than one kind. In other words, a structure may serve more than one purpose.

In stating the function of existential structures of the third kind, we generally use a sentence in which the name of the structure appears as a noun and their function is expressed by a verb. Thus, we say anthropomorphically that a dam holds back water, that a window screen keeps out insects, or that these structures prevent this or that.

Existential structures of this kind *do* something for us in the sense that, due to their very structure and strategic position, they relieve man from having to do what they accomplish for him. It is in the invention of these structures where the first traces of a process of identification can be clearly discerned. These structures have evolved from preceding efforts toward the accomplishment of that which these structures accomplish for man. These preceding efforts have been spontaneous, unplanned, and only of passing value. In existential structures, they have been given permanent expression, with a simultaneous increase in efficiency.

It is difficult, if not impossible, to reconstruct the inventive process which produced such structures as dams, walls, fences, which accomplish something for man or relieve him from certain activities. However, two different kinds of experience may be conceived as possible sources for this inventive process. One may assume that, preceding the invention of these structures, man had encountered in his natural environment formations which he experienced as capable of serving him in the satisfaction of certain needs or the achievement of certain ends; and that later, when similar needs or purposes arose in the absence of such natural formations, he copied these in their essential features. One can also take the opposite approach and assume that the experiences which led to the invention of these structures were experiences of man with himself during activities in which parts of his body served the same purpose which later the structures he built came to serve. From this viewpoint, the structures have become substitutes for body parts and their functions on an improved scale. Thus, we may assume that, preceding the invention of a dam, man had succeeded, on a small scale—perhaps as a child in play—to block the flow of water, first with his bare hands and next with the aid of objects manipulated by his hands, and that the extension and amplification of such activity led eventually to the construction of a dam. Likewise, we may assume that, before man invented the fence by which he kept away animals, he drove off unwanted intruders with sticks, and that the fence is simply a duplication and amplification of this effort, crystallized into a permanent structure.

But even where we are forced to assume that such structures are copies of formations which man observed in his natural environment, we still need to account for a psychological link which allows man to take the step of creating that which he has found in nature ready-made. To take the transition from seeing to doing for granted is unjustified, because it does not exist in animals below the level of man. Only when man realizes that he himself can do what he sees done by nature, can he proceed to creative activity. This realization, however, is only possible by a process of identification, in which these structures are seen in relationship to parts of his own body or their functions. Thus, to go back to the example of the dam, it would never have occurred to man to build a dam after having seen a lake surrounded by mountains unless with it has gone an experience that he himself can, with his bare hands or aided by objects, actively hold back water. There must be an association between his perception and his neuromuscular body mechanism in order to produce a creative intuition. Percepts must be translated into motor patterns.

About the intimate connection between perceptive or mental images—which he calls "pictures"—and motor impulses, Schilder (1950, pp. 175–176) has the following to say: "Pictures (representations and perceptions) have . . . an important development in which the psychic tendencies play an enormous part. We have the right to assume that every phase in this development is connected with a particular motility, and is on the other hand directed by the instinctive tendencies. When, therefore, we speak of pictures, we simplify the actual facts. The picture is already the product of varied activities directed toward the external situation." And (Schilder, 1950, p. 176): "There is no picture which is not will, action, and emotion at the same time. When we talk of pictures and contrast them with desires, it should not be forgotten that in the final analysis they form an inseparable unit and are only the two sides of the total human activity."

The translation from percepts into motor patterns is made possible by identification. Schilder (1950, p. 253) stresses that identification may be extended not only to other humans, but to animals or "to everything which is animated, thence to plants, and beyond that to the inanimate world, especially insofar as it moves." We may modify this statement by saying "insofar as it can be related to human activity."

Dams, walls, fences, and other existential structures which relieve man of certain activities may, therefore, be looked upon as distillates of human purposive efforts. In this sense, these structures function as "stand-ins," as substitutes for man. As stand-ins, they may be viewed as man's doubles. In this respect, they are products of a process of self-duplication.

To the extent to which existential structures exceed that which man can do by himself, by doing it more efficiently and permanently, they constitute at the same time enlargements of man's powers or of his sphere of influence. They are, in such cases, not only the outcome of a process of self-duplication but also of self-amplification.

There are some existential structures which have direct reference to man and either serve to protect his body or to enhance his influence upon others. These are the different wearing apparels, ornaments, and masks.

With them, man improves upon his own body or personality.[5] In this respect, they are closely related to tools and weapons, as a subsequent discussion of these implements will show.

OPERATIONAL STRUCTURES

An "operational structure" is here defined as one with which man actively does something or has something actively done for him. They include tools, machines, and instruments.

The line between existential and operational structures cannot be drawn sharply. A structure such as a magnifying glass has no moving parts, and yet it is operational in the sense that it extends the function of the eye. On the other hand, many existential structures have moving parts: houses have doors, some bridges can be raised, dams have floodgates, and so on. Also, many parts of operational structures have existential significance for the function of the whole. This is particularly true of elements in electronic circuits. A wire *allows* current to flow; a switch either *permits* or *prevents* the passage of current; a condenser *prevents* D.C. current from flowing but *allows* A.C. current to flow; and so on.

Operational structures constitute improvements upon man himself. They can be looked upon as extensions of his own powers, skills, and abilities. That some existential structures, such as wearing apparel and ornaments, can be viewed in a similar way has already been pointed out.

Tools

The significance of tools may be illustrated in the hammer. Since a hammer is used for crushing or pounding, man must have invented it when he found that the tools with which nature equipped him, namely his arm and hand, were not always adequate to perform such tasks. He must have felt a need for improving on his own bodily equipment. Thus, with the handle of the hammer, he prolonged his arm; with the head of the hammer, he gave himself a heavier and harder fist.[6] The thus prolonged arm allowed a larger swing; the heavy and hard substitute for the fist increased the efficiency of the force he exerted.

We must assume that the invention of the hammer did not occur at once, but evolved in steps. Experiences with rocks used for pounding and sticks or clubs used for hitting have most likely been the elements which, in a

[5] Schilder (1950, p. 204) states: "The body-image changes continuously and we triumph over the limitations of the body by adding masks and clothes to the body-image."

[6] The following statements by Schilder (1950, p. 202) support the idea expressed here: "The body-image can shrink and expand; it can give parts to the outside world and can take other parts into itself. When we take a stick in our hands and touch an object with the end of it, we feel a sensation at the end of the stick. The stick has, in fact, become a part of the body-image."

process of synthesis, have led to a structure in which the advantages of rock and club have been combined.

There is no doubt that other tools evolved in an analogous way. Nails and teeth were forerunners of and served as models for scraping and cutting tools. Indirect evidence for this claim can be found in mammals who still use claws and teeth for scraping and cutting respectively.

The hammer is a classical example for a product which is the result of a creative process involving self-duplication. Although not identical with arm and fist, it is analogous to these parts of man's anatomy by similarity of structure and function. In extending his own powers and skills by means of the hammer, man has accomplished at the same time an amplification of himself.

The hammer, like other hand tools, is an improved organ which man has added to himself externally. Not being able to grow it, he has lifted the principle of self-duplication to the level of behavior and created for himself an additional organ from material which he found in his environment, using his own body as a template after which he fashioned his creation. What has been stated above about hand tools applies in a similar way to hand weapons.

The symbolic significance of hand tools and hand weapons and also of wearing apparel as extensions of man's body is documented by the very personal attachment which individuals have to these objects and the manner in which they treasure them.[7] This is particularly true with primitive people who fashion such objects for themselves, thus experiencing the gradual "growth" of these objects during the process of creation.

It needs to be stressed that ordinarily man is unaware of the symbolic significance of hand tools and hand weapons as extensions of his anatomy. The invention of these implements involves an intuitive process in which the inventing individual assimilates its simile through identification. He may either find this simile ready-made in his environment or else create it.

Machines

Tools are forerunners of machines. The first machines, tools with movable parts, were hand- or foot-operated and served mainly to increase man's skill. Where they are operated by a multitude of humans, by animals or physical forces, they serve also to increase the power of individual man.

In the machine, many parts do many different things at the same time. How do these parts come to play the specific roles which are assigned to them?

---

[7] Schilder (1950, p. 203) states: "Whatever article of clothing we put on immediately becomes part of the body-image and is filled with narcissistic libido." This statement can be extended to hand tools and hand weapons, in fact, to many other personal possessions.

Related to this concept of an extended self which includes parts of the environment is what Stern called the "Bereich,' or what Snygg and Combs signify by the "Phenomenal Self."

Essentially, the designer of a machine is in the same position as one who organizes a team of humans for the performance of a certain task, such as a general who thinks up a plan of strategy or a motion picture producer who plans the "machinery" for the production of a motion picture. The main difference between the one and the others is that the designer of a machine deals primarily with inert objects and secondarily with humans who operate these, whereas a general or motion picture producer deals primarily with humans and secondarily with objects which are operated by these humans.

Disregarding these secondary aspects in both cases, a comparison shows that, while the general or producer starts out with a plan of strategy or production schedule, respectively, then goes about selecting individuals according to their specific skills and training—or else trains them for the special tasks to be performed—and places these persons into strategic positions where they can play the roles which are assigned to them, the designer of a machine starts out with a conception of what he wants his machine to accomplish, then proceeds to select the suitable parts—or else fashions them—and places these into strategic positions where they can perform the functions which have been planned for them in the overall design. The end result in all these instances is that the members or parts, respectively, contribute collectively to the overall performance of a certain task.

The way in which the role of each member or part is conceived by the one who determines it—be it the organizer of a team or the designer of a machine—is that this organizing individual, in identifying himself with each member of the team or each part of the machine, respectively, vicariously acts out their roles in his phantasy, and then lets these members or parts do what he would do if he were in their place. It is only by this very act of identification that an inventive design can come about. There must be a reference of the creator to himself.

In this sense, it is legitimate to say that a machine, composed of many different parts, is analogous to an organized team of human beings. Even the methods of control employed for the purpose of securing the well-defined functions of the members in a team or the parts in a machine, respectively, are essentially the same in both cases. They are (a) elimination of all courses of action except the one desired; (b) direct guidance; and (c) instruction given ahead of time and to be remembered. The application of the first two methods of control in machines is obvious and does not require special elaboration. The analogy to instruction and memory in machines is to be found in the various automatic control devices. These in themselves constitute structures which are more appropriately called "instruments." The significance of instruments will be discussed later. Where these control devices take into account the preceding performance of the machine, a memory factor is involved.

While the element of "instruction" is at a maximum in the control of humans, it is at a minimum with machines. On the other hand, the control methods indicated under "a" and "b" are at a minimum in human teams—except in slave gangs—and at a maximum in machines. Instruments such as electronic computers, which incorporate the control method listed under "c," are most human-like.

The identification of man with parts of a machine is made possible by the fact that the different mechanical actions which machine parts perform are essentially like those which man is capable of carrying out, by acting either as a unit or by using parts of his body, particularly the bones of his skeletal system. Such mechanical actions performed by the human body as a whole or by its parts are those of pushing, pulling, sliding, rotating, etc. Even the action of springs is exemplified by man when he jumps ("springs").

The important point is that this analogy between the action of machine parts and the acts of man or parts of his body is not just an afterthought, something which we read into it anthropomorphically afterwards, but is the effect of the process of creation through which man projects his own body organization upon his environment. The identification of man with parts of the machine is not something which occurs after the act of creation, but precedes it and constitutes a necessary prerequisite for it.

Therefore, what has been said about tools applies also to machines; their functions are extensions of man's own body functions. Because machines involve a multiplicity of moving parts all of which substitute for activities of man, man is duplicated in each part and multiplied in the machine as a whole. Thus, the machine is the product of a process of self-duplication as well as self-amplification. A self-amplification is further accomplished by the greater power, speed, efficiency, and accuracy which a machine possesses as compared with man. In tools and machines, man is reflected in his mechanical aspects.

We have to keep in mind that a machine is not the creation of one individual alone, but represents the end product of an evolutionary development of technology in which many different individuals made creative contributions. Therefore, we should not assume that every single feature of a new type of machine or instrument designed by a certain individual has to be accounted for by a creative act of that designer. Since all human creations, when made public, become cultural property, they can be used and improved by others. What one inventor contributes may be just one more feature. The creative output of others serves as an input for the creative activity of the one who builds upon it. The more evolution advances, the more any human creation is bound to be the result of a collective creativity distributed over a long period of time.

Instruments

While tools and machines represent extensions of bodily structures or elaboration on his motoric body equipment, instruments constitute improvements upon his powers of observation, his memory, his ability to control, and his mental faculty—in short, his sense organs and nervous system, including his brain. The mother of the invention of the microscope is the wish to see minute objects, of the photographic camera to be able to retain what one or others have seen, of television to be able to see at great distances, and so on. Thus, lenses and microscopes amplify the power of the eye; television improves upon man's range of vision; microphones and sound amplifiers increase the sensitivity of the human ear; all measuring and indicating instruments enhance man's power of observation; recording devices extend the memory; and electronic brains multiply his mental faculties.

It is interesting to notice that many of man's inventions employ organizational and functional principles upon which structures of his own anatomy are based. The photographic camera makes use of principles incorporated in the structure of the eye. The telephone network combined with switchboard resembles the network of neurones with their synaptic connections; cables are structured similar to nerves; flexible tubing makes use of a structural feature embodied in the windpipe; valves are found in the heart and veins; ball-and-socket as well as hinge joints are employed in the appendicular skeleton; dovetail joints are found in the skull. Many more examples could be given.

Musical instruments are more truly machines, and therefore most of them improve upon man's organs suited for the production of sound. The first musical instruments were parts of the human body. Primitive man clapped his hands and slapped his buttocks, legs, chest, and abdomen to produce sounds. Rattles, sticks, and drums became the first substitutes for these parts of the human anatomy and at the same time constituted improvements over them (Sachs, 1940). All wind instruments are substitutes for the human voice. Where they increase the sound amplitude, extend the frequency range, or produce a new tone quality, they also constitute improvements over the voice apparatus of man.

Significance of Operational Structures

A summary can now be given of the significance of operational structures. Operational structures are designed to add to man's energy, skill, and ability. They owe their existence to a drive for self-expansion and are the result of a creative process in which man has externalized an organization which resides within him. They can, therefore, be looked upon as projections or symbolic representations of man's needs, purposes, and organization, structural or functional. The inventor lives in his structures. What they accomplish or perform he accomplished or performed vicariously during the process of design or invention. This process involves a variant of the principle of self-duplication, which may appropriately be called self-transformation or self-translation. Operational structures are, therefore, related to man rather by analogy than by identity. At the same time, in being designed to increase his powers, to improve his skills, and to extend his abilities, they represent amplifications of man.[8] They can be looked upon as improved organs which man has added to himself externally. In the process of self-transformation and self-amplification, man uses himself as a template.

While operational structures serve the principle of self-expansion by extending man's powers, skills, and faculties, existential structures expand the range of man's activities by eliminating conditions which might interfere with these activities or by promoting conditions which may further them. Both classes of structures stand also in the service of self-maintenance by improving man's chances for survival.

HUMAN SOCIAL STRUCTURES

The term "social structures" refers here to organized groups and institutions. Attention will be given here only to those social structures which have grown or evolved, not to those which have been founded—such as clubs, industrial organizations, and the like—because in a founded organization the structural and functional patterns are usually copies or modifications of other already existing ones and, therefore, do not allow a tracing back of the process of becoming.

The elementary social unit of society is the family. It has been often likened to the cell in the organism. From the family evolved the larger social group, comprising a multitude of families. The larger social groups tend to absorb many of the functions of the family in a process of institutionalization. Thus, educational, religious, economic, and self-protective functions of the family are "turned over" to appropriate institutions which have taken over these functions.

The same development is found in the evolution from the one-cell to the multicellular organism. Functions which are performed in protozoa by a single cell are carried out in the multicellular organism by groups of specialized cells combined into tissues, organs, and organ systems.

The functions of the family are largely determined by the parents in it. The parents within the family are analogous to the chromosomes in the cell in three ways: (a) the chromosomes regulate the activities within the cell, the parents those within the family; (b) the chromosomes are instrumental in cell duplication, which is the mechanism underlying the growth processes of the organism; the parents, in exercising their power for reproduction, create the conditions for the formation of new families and thus are responsible for the growth of the larger social group, the tribe or the nation; (c) the chromosomes serve as "blueprints" for the construction of

---

[8] The concept of "amplification" has been applied to processes within the organism by Pascual Jordan (Bavink, 1949) in his "amplifier theory." Brody (1945, p. 260) uses the concept in the same sense as Jordan when he says that "the organism acts as a powerful amplifier which sets in motion large-scale events." The same principle which accounts within the organism for the fact that micro-events on the level of the genes produce macro-events on the level of the organism is assumed, in the present article, to operate between man and the culture he produces.

the organism; the individual parent, through his functional organization, sets the pattern for the organization of society.

This latter point needs elaboration. There is a striking similarity between a social group such as a nation and the human organism in regard to functional organization. All organized social groups have a "head," are "headed" either by a single individual or a specific group of individuals. A head or government operates through executive "branches" which may be likened to the limbs of the body (we speak sometimes of the "arm of the law"); the system of communication in the form of telephone and telegraph lines is analogous to the nervous system; the postal system, through which messages are mailed and delivered to a definite address, is comparable to the endocrine system by which chemical messengers are dispatched to certain organs; the economic system may be likened to the combination of digestive, respiratory, and excretory system, including the metabolic processes; the various transportation systems find their functional counterpart in the circulatory system; the listening and observation posts of a nation in the form of news service, embassies, consulates, spy systems, and radar stations are analogous in their function to the sense organs which bring the organism in touch with its environment and warn it of possible dangers; the boundaries of a nation may be looked upon as its skin.

Like all analogies this one is not perfect, nor does it prove anything in itself. However, if we keep in mind that societies have evolved from family groups and have absorbed—at least to some degree—most of the functions of the family, and if we further remember that the functions of the family are determined by the needs and the functional organization residing within its individual members, it is no wonder that the structural and functional organization of man is in certain respects reflected in the organization of society as a whole.

It may be objected that the similarity between the organization of a social structure such as a nation and the one of the human body is due to the fact that both represent open systems. That open systems do have similarities in functional organization has been pointed out by Bertalanffy (1949, 1952), Miller (1955, 1956), and others. What is here attempted, however, is to show the causality behind such similarities.

It appears then that growth and evolution of social structures such as societies seems to involve the same process which we have observed in the creation of operational structures: self-duplication, self-transformation, and self-amplification on the part of individual man.

ARTISTIC AND SYMBOLIC STRUCTURES

Religious Symbols and Art Objects

The self-expressive and projective processes involved in the creation of religious symbols and objects of art have received wide attention. These objects represent materializations of visions, of ways in which their creator perceives or imagines whatever his creation represents. These objects, therefore, constitute objectifications, projections or expressions of such visions, ideas, perceptual forms and relationships. The organization of these structures reflects an inner organization of man.

Music

Music represents a considerably purer form of creation than art, because what is organized is not matter but energy in the form of sound vibrations. These vibrations are, furthermore, not found ready-made in the environment, but have to be produced by man himself. The vibrations and their physical relationships, however, constitute an organization independent of man. In the composition of a piece of music, the composer utilizes the organization inherent in the laws of harmony to express an inner organization of his own.

Language and Poetry

In language and poetry, the organization is not absolutely dependent on organization of physical sound to express its own organization. The symbols of language may be either auditory, visual, or tactual. Words or phrases make reference to observed objects, events, or relationships between objects and events, and to inner experiences such as feelings and thoughts. What is expressed in language and poetry are organized concepts, ideas, feelings, and values.

Mathematics

In mathematics, creativity appears in its purest form. What is organized is no longer part of the environment but man-created symbols. These symbols, unlike those of language, have no direct reference to objects in the environment. They represent abstract concepts. These concepts are given visual objectification in the form of written symbols for the purpose of communication. The creative process in mathematics is, therefore, a closed circuit, bypassing the environment, whereas in all other creative processes the environment is part of the circuit, in one way or another.

Parallels between Artistic and Symbolic Structures, and Operational Structures

Artistic and symbolic structures, like operational structures, are the result of a process of self-translation or self-transformation. The fact of self-amplification is evidenced in two ways. The particular artistic means of expression provide for a highly efficient transmission of whatever feelings or ideas are to be expressed. Secondly, structures such as objects of art, compositions, books, and the like can be shared by a multitude, can be duplicated, and can be used for enjoyment over and over again.

An Analysis of Creativity

After this survey of man's products of creation, an analysis of the creative process will be attempted. Before entering into a theoretical discussion, a brief review of the literature pertaining to the creative process will be furnished.

THE CREATIVE PROCESS

The creative process is only amenable to experimentation in the case of productive thinking, otherwise called "problem-solving." Attempts toward a systematic study of creative activity have, therefore, been confined to this area. In problem-solving, the objective to be reached by the solution is well defined, and the situation within which the problem is to be solved is definitely structured in regard to certain given conditions or limitations. The problem-solving situation is structured by the experimenter. The subject has no choice in either the structuring of the situation or the objective.

The more the creator has freedom to choose his own objective and to determine the structure of the situation within which he arrives at a solution, the more we can speak of a truly creative process. On the other hand, such a process of creation, because of its very lack of "constants," is not amenable to experimentation. Therefore, studies pertaining to such creative processes consist largely in a compilation of testimonials by creative artists, musicians, poets, philosophers, scientists, and inventors.

All students of productive thinking—with the exception of a few who claim that discovery or invention is due to chance—agree that involved in the creative process is a selection and reorganization of past experiences or acquired bits of knowledge. This fact is accepted by the "associationists" as well as by the "gestaltists," although these schools of thought subscribe to diverging beliefs in regard to the principles and laws at work in this process of organization (Duncker, 1926, 1935; Galton, 1883; Hull, 1943; Maier, 1930, 1931 ab, 1933; Pillsbury, 1910, 1924; Ribot, 1899, 1906; Thorndike, 1922; Wertheimer, 1945). However, very little has been said by these investigators about the motivational aspects of productive thinking. Maier (1931) speaks of a "field of strain." Wertheimer (1945) assumes a perceptual need for "closure" and a "tendency to structural clearness." There is nothing in these explanations which accounts for the organic, compulsory, and strong emotional component that has been observed in all truly creative processes. For a full understanding of the creative activity, therefore, it is necessary to take into consideration not only the reasoning processes involved, but also the dynamic forces which set these processes into motion and direct them toward the production of something new. These we can best observe in "truly" creative individuals,

such as artists, musicians, and poets, and to some degree in scientists and inventors.

The pertinent findings in regard to such creative activity will be discussed briefly for the purpose of highlighting the most salient criteria of the truly creative process.

A spontaneous, involuntary, automatic quality of creative thinking processes has been reported by Hadamard (1949). According to Ghiselin (1952), this quality has been experienced by Spencer, Nietzsche, Gauss, Poincaré, Henry James, and others. In some, this feeling of automatism has been so strong that it was accompanied by an impression that some outside agent had whispered to them the productive ideas which suddenly came to them. Socrates' "demon" is a famous example.

That creative thinking involves subconscious or nonverbal activity is reported almost universally. Rossman (1931, p. 86), who has made an extensive survey of the traits and working methods of inventors, reports that "many inventors attribute the formation of the mental patterns to the subconscious mind." Hadamard (1949), who has studied the psychology of invention in great mathematicians, quotes Poincaré and Einstein in support of the claim that creative thinking involves subconscious or nonverbal mental activity. Evidence for this claim is also given by Maier (1931) in his studies on problem-solving. Ghiselin (1952) comes to the conclusion that "the first impulse toward new order in the psychic life . . . is an impulse away from the conscious activity . . . an impulse toward unconsciousness."

In extreme cases individuals appear to be shut off from reality during these unconscious mental processes, which for this reason have sometimes been likened to states of insanity. Dilthey (1886) quotes Aristotle's statement *"nullum magnum ingenium sine mixtura dementia fuit."*

The withdrawal into the subconscious is usually followed by a sudden flash of illumination. This sequence of incubation and illumination appears to be a universal pattern in the creative process and has been reported by Rossman (1931), Hadamard (1949), Maier (1930), and Ghiselin (1952).

The organic character of this phase of incubation during which the seed of an idea grows in the subconscious until it is born into consciousness has been emphasized by Ribot (1906) and Ghiselin (1952). This phase, often called "gestation period," and the subsequent "illumination" leading to a burst of creativity has been likened to the processes before and during childbirth (Ghiselin, 1952; Ribot, 1906; Wallas, 1926). The birth of an idea or a work of creation is often accompanied by alternating states of pain and joy. The successful completion of the act of creation is experienced as a "satisfaction of being freed from a heavy burden" (Ribot, 1906).

A powerful emotional component in creative artistic and intellectual activity has been reported by Ribot (1906) and Rossman (1931). Ribot

points out that the creative act involves the totality of the individual, the condition of his body, his emotions, his perception, and his conscious as well as unconscious mental processes, including dreams. He states that "all creation . . . implies a unifying, synthetic principle" (1906).

To sum up the most outstanding criteria: In most reported instances, the creative process contains an important phase which is organic in character, having all the earmarks of unconscious growth and development, analogous to processes leading to birth. There is almost universal agreement on an involuntary, automatic, and compelling element in the creative process. The process of creation is accompanied by strong emotions, not only in artists, but also in creative thinkers and inventors, thus involving not only the mental faculties but the totality of the person.

The interpretation of the facts cited is inescapable. Creating is more than problem-solving, although that is certainly part of it. It is more than a rational process. It appears that in the creative process man draws from all departments. As Ghiselin says: "The end to be reached . . . in any creative process is . . . some specific order urged upon the mind by something inherent in its vital condition of being and perception . . ." (1952).

THE SOURCE OF CREATIVITY

What is this vital condition of which Ghiselin speaks? Wherein lies the ultimate source of creative activity? It is the thesis of this article that human creative activity is rooted in the general life principle of self-duplication. This principle accounts for growth and reproduction as well as for man's creative behavior, as we have tried to demonstrate. The subjective experiences of men engaged in creation testify to a link between the process of reproduction and creation, as has been suspected by various philosophers, psychologists, and biologists, such as we have mentioned in the beginning of this article. The link, the common denominator, we claim, is the principle of self-duplication, a principle apparently unique to life, manifested first on the level of the self-duplication of the DNA molecule, finding higher expression on the level of cell-duplication, growth, and reproduction, and culminating in the creative activity of man; a theme played over and over again in the symphony of life.

Seen in this light, creative activity is not merely the result of sublimation of sexual (libidinal) energy, as Freud wanted us to believe; but creative energy and sexual energy spring from the same source, leading merely to expressions on different levels. It is quite conceivable that self-duplicative energy flows with relative freedom between the level of sexuality and creativity, so that energy originally earmarked for the sexual level becomes easily available to creative activity. But where there is an abundance of creative energy and no blocking of expression on the sexual level, this energy may allow creative activity to go on without having to borrow energy from sexuality. Yet, sublimation is not ruled out as a possible dynamism in creative activity, but it does not constitute a necessity for it. It is likely to lead to an extra amount of creative output in cases where a need and an ability for creative expression already exists. Freud, therefore, was right in linking creativity with sexuality, but he was wrong in making the one a derivative of the other.

It is also conceivable that creative or self-duplicative energy may be referred backwards to lower levels of functioning in cases where this energy is prevented from finding free expression on higher levels. Cases of malignant growths in which a psychogenic factor is suspected may involve a release of self-duplicative energy on the growth level where this energy has been blocked on the sexual or creative level.[9]

SOMA AND PSYCHE

If human creativity is an expression of biological creativity on a behavioral level, involving a translation of body organization into organized mental processes—an extraversion of soma into psyche, so to speak—we must assume a system of communication between soma and psyche.

It was relatively easy to show how tools and machines came to represent symbolically certain motor aspects of man, because man can become aware of the movements of his bones and the functions of his muscles. Whatever he does not directly observe with his peripheral sense organs he can experience through the kinesthetic sense. Thus, his own structural or functional organization in its motor aspects can be reported to his mind, and the mind, in turn, can utilize this information in the creation of structures. Communication between soma and psyche is established here through self-observation via perceptual channels.

To demonstrate a similar communicative link in the creative process leading to the invention of instruments is far more difficult, because instruments constitute extensions of man's sensory apparatus and nervous system. The processes involved in the operation of these structures are, however, not within our awareness. We are not directly conscious of the operation of the eye or ear, of the traveling of nervous impulses along nervous pathways, of the activities of brain cells, and so on. Although we can acquire knowledge of many of these structures and their functions by observing them in the bodies of others, it is unlikely that, in all those instances where instruments bear striking similarity in basic design with human organs or are analogous in function to them, the inventor of such an instrument had knowledge of that structure in his body which his creation resembled or is analogous to.

It may be argued that such similarities between man-made structures

---

[9] The idea of "conversion" of psychic into somatic energy is not foreign to psychology. Schilder (1950, p. 178) says that in conversion "a psychic energy, which is prevented from expressing itself, goes into the somatic field. It goes from the psychic sphere into the somatic sphere."

and man-inherent structures are either coincidental or the result of a common dependency of these two kinds of structures upon physical energies of which these structures make use and whose inherent laws determine the design of these structures. Thus, the similarity between photographic camera and the eye is not due to man possessing a knowledge "a priori" of his eye, to an "idea" of the idea in the Platonic sense to which man has access because the eye is part of him, but is due to the properties of light, the laws of optics, etc., upon which both structures depend. Such argumentation certainly has much in its favor, and is doubtlessly valid to a considerable degree. On the other hand, we should not dismiss the possibility of a knowledge of ourselves which comes to us through channels other than our sense organs, peripheral or internal. We have no right to exclude the possibility of other channels of communication between psyche and soma.

The issue becomes confused due to the meaning of the term "knowledge," which is conventionally limited to "conscious awareness." However, if we extend the term "knowledge" to behavior in which an organism acts *as if* he "knows," our difficulty is resolved. The problem of knowledge is a problem of information. I may or may not be conscious of a certain information. If I am, I "know" in the conventional sense. But I may not "know" and still act upon the information. In this case, information influences behavior directly, bypassing conscious awareness.

The assumption is made here that in creative activity man, to some extent, makes use of information which comes to him more directly than through the channels of sense perception. The author believes that, in order to understand human creativity fully, one must assume that somehow man is capable—to some degree—of transforming aspects of his own physical and physiological organization into products of his creation.

The question then is: How is such a direct transformation of man's inner organization into his outer world in the form of his own products of creation possible?

Modern systems theory as applied to man comes here to our rescue. Although still in its prescientific stage, it provides us with concepts which allow us to approach a better understanding of the embedment of psyche in soma. Within the framework of this theory (Grinker, 1956), the human organism is viewed as an intricate system comprising a hierarchial organization of sub-systems with their corresponding levels of functioning: on the physicochemical level, the enzymatic and hormonal system; on the physiological level, the various organ systems involving functions of organs and tissues; on the behavioral level, the nervous system, involving the brain, sense organs, and nervous pathways in conjunction with the muscular and skeletal systems. The higher we go in the hierarchy, the more systems are involved and the larger become the units of functioning. On the behavioral level, the organism functions as a whole, and all levels of functioning are involved in any behavioral act. This requires an intricate system of coordination. To explain this coordination, a system of intra-organic communication is postulated. It is assumed that each level of functioning employs its own special language of "signs" to coordinate its own activities. Thus, the signs on the physicochemical level are hormones and enzymes; those on the level of organ systems, hormones as well as nervous impulses, etc. In order to integrate the functions of a lower level with those of higher levels, in other words to establish communication between various levels, a "decoding" of the language of one level and a "recording" into the language of the next higher level must exist. Thus, the various subsystems are organized into a functioning whole. The translation of signs from one level to another is termed "transformation of information."

Purposeful processes within the organism, however, involve a whole series of discrete events. At each point in time, therefore, there must be available information of what has already preceded. Such availability of information of past events is called "memory." The devices for memory may vary from level to level. On the mental level, memory is assumed to consist in nervous impulses reverberating in circular cerebral pathways. On other levels, structures serve as memory for past processes. Thus, the genes can be looked upon as the memory of the evolutionary processes which led to the organism as it exists today.

How can the concepts of modern systems theory help us to understand the creative process as a projection of man's somatic organization, an extraversion of his inner world onto his outer world? Is it possible to extend the concept of "decoding" and "recoding" to apply to the transition from organic to behavioral functioning? Can we perhaps extrapolate the system of communication, believed to be in operation in a continuous flow from the lowest to the highest level of organization within the bodily confines of the organism, to include creative acts through which, as we have seen, man in effect "adds on" to his body? Must "transformation" be confined to a transformation of signs from level to level of functioning within the organism? Can the concept not be extended to include self-transformation in which organizational patterns inherent in man's soma are transformed in man's creative activities, a translation of the language of soma into the language of the psyche?

From here on, we can only speculate in the vaguest terms. Let us assume that there is a continuous transition from the conscious to the subconscious mind and further to the realm of the unconscious, which latter includes a central representation of all the somatic functions. Where in the brain such representation of the somatic levels takes place can only be conjectured. But in order to understand how the psyche can "know" of the soma, we must assume that the subconscious can establish connection with these brain centers during the creative process. We may assume that, when the mind in the creative process withdraws temporarily from reality, it descends, as it were, into the depths of the subconscious and from there—in rare moments—reaches deeper into the sphere which is in direct contact with the organizational centers of the soma in which all its functional levels are represented. Here are to be found all the "blueprints" and "work-schedules" for self-regulation, growth and development, the secrets of life's creativity. We may say, then, that in creative activity the mind, in its deep recesses, manages to make contact with the soma by taking, as it were, a glimpse at the blueprints of organization and looking into the "memory files" of growth and development, returning from there "illumined" to its conscious state with information pertinent to its purposes. Or, using a different metaphor, we may say that in the creative process there is taking place an extraordinarily close coupling between psyche and soma such that the mind is enabled to tune in on the organismic dynamisms, achieving thus a state of resonance or identification with the whole. In this state of identification, it becomes possible for the mind to operate through the creative energies of life itself, which, although inherent in its own organization, are ordinarily suppressed by the daily demands for adjustive behavior.

At the present time, we stand at the mere beginning of a new medical discipline which studies the interrelation of psyche and soma. We do not yet have the conceptual tools with which we can express and describe a mechanism by which somatic events from the lowest functional level up become represented symbolically in the psyche, so that physical realities can be translated into mental analogues. Let us, however, realize that the processes which we have suggested here are in no way more fantastic than the assumption that genes carry "blueprints" and translate these mental analogues into physical structures, a concept with which geneticists and biologists nowadays operate as a matter of fact, although there exists only the vaguest notion what these "blueprints" consist of, and there is still complete darkness as to how they are used in the construction of an infinitely complex organism. To assume that there exists a process in reverse, a retracing by the mind of "blueprints" underlying structural organization of the soma, is by no means a less reasonable hypothesis.

Summary, Implications, and Outlook

SUMMARY

We have pictured man's creations as objectifications of his own self. Thus, human creativity represents the highest level of manifestation of the principle of self-duplication, which started its evolutionary course with the self-duplicative activity of the DNA molecule.

We have pointed out that in this process of self-projection there is more involved than simple self-duplication. It constitutes a self-transformation, involving at the same time amplification.

The various products of creation thus appear as externalizations of certain aspects of man's self: tools and machines of his body machinery, instruments of his sense organs and nervous system, art of his perceptual images, music of his emotions, language of his conceptualizations, social structures of his functional organization as a whole, physical as well as behavioral.

By involving transformation and amplification, human creative activity is a form of self-expansion. Man creates his outer world not only in his own image but, at the same time, he enlarges this image beyond life-size. As an expression of the principle of self-duplication, creative activity is intimately related to growth and reproduction.

The creative process is made possible by a unification of all the functional departments of the organism, in which the mind becomes identified with the totality of the organism. The mind is thus enabled to benefit from the organizational and constructive energies which work for the maintenance and self-development of the whole. The deep recesses of the subconscious act in this process as intermediaries and interpreters between psyche and soma. Creativity, therefore, is dependent upon a system of communication within the organism from the level of the DNA molecule on up to the conscious mind.

If we see man's creations in this light, the man-made world—culture and civilization in its structural as well as functional aspects—appears as man's exudate, an extension of himself. Man, plus his culture and civilization, then form a large system with its own interactive processes.

FEEDBACK OF MAN'S CREATIONS UPON HIMSELF

The world which man has created becomes part of his environment and, thus, he is in turn influenced by it. In other words, his own creations feed back on him. It is through this process of feedback that cultural evolution has become possible. Whatever cultural products a given generation finds handed down by the preceding generations, it uses as a stepping-stone to build on. Each new creation serves not only as a step forward, but as a platform on which to continue the building process. Thus, man's creations have the significance of memories, of monuments of the ideas and strivings which man has expressed in them and of the purposes which they serve.

Once these creations have been born into man's environment, they have become independent of their creator. They can be used by others for the same purpose for which they were designed. As man's brain children, they begin a life of their own. They can be adopted and socialized. In fact, they can be duplicated, and each copy becomes an equivalent to its original. They can further be improved upon. The social sciences—such as psychology, sociology, anthropology, etc.—occupy themselves largely with the feedback between man and his self-created environment, material and social.

This feedback process becomes more and more important the more civilization evolves. While man, in his own evolution, started out with a nature-made environment, he finds himself more and more surrounded by his own products. In modern present-day urban civilization, nature-made environment has been largely crowded out or has become overgrown by man-made products, a man-made environment. This man-made environment is material as well as social. Man finds himself surrounded not only by a bewildering array of objects and gadgets, but also by complex social organizations manned by a dense population of his own kind. The increased complexity of his environment and the stepped-up interaction with his fellowmen places heavy demands upon his powers of adjustment and, in turn, poses a challenge to his ingenuity and creativity. Thus, a positive feedback circuit has been established in which man is connected with his civilization in a vicious circle. The more man creates the more he has to keep on creating.

THE SIGNIFICANCE OF MODELS

If it is true that man's creative products are the results of a process of self-duplication, self-transformation, and self-amplification, then the reason why so-called "models"—such as "robots" and "electronic brains"—can serve to explain man to himself in his functional aspects is that these structures actually constitute projections or objectifications of his own inner functional organization. The analogous relationship between these structures in their functional aspects and man's own functional organization is not a mere coincidence. It exists by virtue of the fact that "models" as any other creation of man are externalizations of their creator. As such, they can never contain any new principle of functioning that is not already in operation in man. As amplifications, they may have more power, may work with greater speed, or accomplish the work of many different individuals at the same time. They can, however, surpass man only in a quantitative aspect, never in quality.

As objectifications of man, models are nevertheless useful, perhaps even indispensable, to gain understanding of our own structural and functional organization. Material creations of man are a form of self-expression comparable to language and art, except that they reveal to us aspects of our structural organization, while language and art give objective expression to our thoughts and feelings. Thus, through models we can learn about our structural organization, as we can learn through verbal expression about our feelings and thoughts. In this sense, the creation of machines and instruments is a form of projective technique in which we reveal the structural and functional aspects of our body machinery.

We can see that, therefore, a limit is set to the extent to which models can teach us something about ourselves. They will never be able to tell the whole story. They will only be able to reveal to us those aspects of our own organization which are translatable into physical systems. A man-made object is essentially a monument of a behavioral process of man, a distillate of his function. Therefore, we deceive ourselves when we believe that through models we can explain man by something else than man. The machine or instrument is meaningless without taking into consideration its designer. Its purposes and functions are the purposes and functions which its designer gave it. For this reason, no man-made model will ever shed light on the problem of creativity. While human nature represents a whole universe, infinite in its resources, a man-made product is finite and limited. Thus, a machine can never reveal more than we already know about it, whereas in human creativity we have a whole cosmos to draw from, a cosmos vast and infinite, larger than man himself. It is through creativity that we get access to this cosmos.

PHILOSOPHICAL OUTLOOK

We have said that creativity is an expression of the principle of self-duplication, albeit on a higher level of manifestation. The principle of self-duplication, however, while a unique characteristic of the world of living things, in turn, is a manifestation of a still more universal principle, a principle which lies at the base of the whole cosmos. This principle is that of periodicity. A periodic or cyclic process is one which repeats or re-duplicates itself over and over again. Cyclic processes are not only the foundations of life but also of the nonliving world. In the world of living things, we have already pointed out the various self-duplicative processes, from the self-duplication of the DNA molecule on up to the self-duplication of cells and whole organisms. In addition, there is the cycle of life and death, the cycle of fertility periods, the complicated life cycles of certain lower animals, and the various physiological processes of a cyclic nature such as heartbeat, respiration, and the activity of the brain as manifested in the electrical brain waves. Still other cyclic life processes are directly related to the cyclic events of our planetary system, such as the cycle of day and night and the cycle of seasons.

The cyclic processes of the nonliving world range from the macrocosmic events of the rotations and revolutions of heavenly bodies to the micro-cosmic events of vibrations and oscillations of various forms of energy, events which we observe as light waves, radio waves, sound waves, etc. Even matter itself is now understood as a manifestation of cyclic processes in which subatomic entities are involved.

Thus, life may be understood as a unique utilization of the principle of periodicity, turning it into the principle of self-duplication, which is at the root of all creative processes. Through creativity, life "extraverts" cosmic principles, picks up these principles as themes on which it plays a myriad of variations.

Man's creativity is related to his own biological nature, as life is related to the cosmos of the inanimate world. In his creative activity, he extraverts his biological nature and uses the principles he finds in it as themes upon which he elaborates. But, since his biological nature, in turn, is founded upon inanimate cosmos which constitutes the material basis of his soma, he shares in all of cosmos.

It is the realization of these relationships which gives deepest meaning to an insight expressed by Protagoras when he said that "man is the measure of all things."

LAWRENCE S. KUBIE

Blocks to Creativity

The attempt to be creative in any field makes extraordinary demands on the human personality. In science and engineering, creativity demands a flexibility which may be greater than that of almost any other occupation to which man can dedicate himself. The scientist and the engineer must first of all maintain mastery of an enormous, rapidly growing body of data, yet, at the same time, must be as freely imaginative as the poet, the artist, or the musician. He must also possess the capacity to anchor his imaginative flights to reality, to test the degree to which they are consonant with reality, and finally to project them into the future for new uses. Few other occupations demand so much.

I do not deplore the fact that creativity in science makes this demand on us, but only that we do not recognize its implications for the education of the scientist. I deplore the fact that we do so little to help him attain—as a student, and then as a matured scientist—that degree of emotional stability and freedom which is essential if he is to use his intellectual endowments in the most creative and constructive way possible. I am unhappy at our complacency with a primitive educational process which reinforces many of the concealed but universal neurotic ingredients in human nature.

This concern leads to two questions: What is it in the educational process which limits and inhibits creativity? And what can be done to change the educational process so as to lessen its damping action on potential creativity? Even before discussing this, however, we must be clear about the nature of the creative process and its inherent vulnerabilities. This can best be approached through a few examples.

There are scientists and engineers who produce brilliantly as students, and even through their graduate years of study, but then collapse. There are gifted investigators who turn out one or two creative achievements early in their careers, but thereafter are never productive again. Others

From *International Science and Technology*, June, 1965, pp. 69–78. Used by permission of the publisher.

33

seem to acquire creative freedom only slowly and relatively late in life, and therefore fail ever to win security, tenure, or recognition. Others are consistently and repeatedly successful and productive, but notwithstanding become increasingly despondent and dissatisfied. Some young scientists become blocked after marriage, while for others the reverse is true. Many creative minds go through long periods in which they are barren. For some, these prove to be enriching periods of lying fallow. For others, they are years from which their creative talents never recover. For Mark Twain and for Beethoven, such periods were catastrophic.

An early work block may impede a young man's development for years or may destroy him, so that he may never be able to return to his profession. Later in a scientific career, it can turn a promising future into a wasteland. A still later work block may stop a mature scientist so completely that he may have to save himself from scientific oblivion, and his family from want, by turning to teaching, administration, work for a foundation, or even a college presidency.

The outstanding figure in a certain field became scientifically sterile after he had become a full professor and department head. This sterility so embittered him that, although he was a passionately dedicated teacher, he could never allow any student to become creative, to publish, or even to escape from him without a fight. Furthermore, he recommended for important posts only those who were shaped in his own image and were similarly sterile.

How do such work blocks arise? We know from clinical studies of creative individuals from the sciences, the arts, and engineering, that there is no single cause, just as there is no single cause for fever. But we also know that the creative process in each of us is vulnerable to distortion and inhibition by the neurotic process, reinforced by neurotogenic ingredients in the educational process.

The Neurotic Process

What then is meant by the neurotic process? I will not contrast a hypothetical neurotic *man* with an equally hypothetical normal *man*. I will try instead to characterize the neurotic process by pointing out the essential difference between a normal and neurotic *act*. It is important to keep this circumscribed purpose in mind. We must first understand what constitutes the essential disorder of a single act before attempting to characterize a total personality as sick or well.

Every thing which a human being can do can be either sick or well, neurotic or normal. Whether it is feeling, thinking, eating, sleeping, drinking, fighting, killing, hating, loving, grieving, exulting, working, playing, painting, planning, inventing—it can be one or the other. Further, the category to which an act belongs does not depend upon conformity to any cultural norm, nor on whether the act or feeling or thought is intrinsically sensible or foolish, useful or valueless, constructive or destructive. The measure of health is dependent upon none of these criteria. The measure of health is flexibility, the freedom to learn through experience, the freedom to change with changing internal and external circumstances, to be influenced by reasonable argument or by the appeal to emotions and especially the freedom to cease when sated.

The essence of normality is flexibility in all of these vital ways. The essence of illness is the freezing of behavior into unaltering, repetitive, and insatiable patterns. We see examples of such frozen behavior in all creative fields. In painting, we see it in men of worldwide reputations, men who after passing through some inner convulsion of the spirit start on a new "period," dominated perhaps by a new color, or by new subject matter, or a new way of applying the paint, or a new way of stressing outlines, or a new way of distorting proportions, each such innovation soon becoming as rigid as the work of the earlier periods.

Patterns of scientific creativity provide examples of comparable distortions. There is the man whose anxieties compel him always to rush, always to be ahead of time, whose work must always be done long before it is necessary. In his hurry, such a man can barely stop to reflect, to read, to digest, to lie fallow. His opposite number gets to the train only as it is pulling out of the station and can never think about a problem until he is under last-moment pressure. He cannot lie fallow either. In both, the neurotic patterns of behavior exercise distorting influences on the processes of study, of imaginative rumination, of creative experimentation. It cripples the capacity to assemble new data or to arrange old data in new patterns. I think of three scientists of high potential in three different fields whose creative capabilities were distorted by destructive compulsions always and only to criticize. One of the unique honors of science is the humility and honesty with which it tries constantly to correct its own errors. Healthy criticism—of self and of others—is good. But these three men misspent their lives creating nothing, because obsessional mechanisms, driven by unconscious hate and envy, took over the intrinsically useful function of criticism. They did nothing but criticize: today themselves, tomorrow others. The seesaw never ceased.

Another example was a brilliant pharmacologist who tried to establish a hypothesis about drugs and drug action: but his very hypothesis was chosen unwittingly under the influence of concealed neurotic mechanisms, and when he set out to prove it, these same neurotic influences determined the design of his experiments and the techniques he employed. The work on water metabolism of another scientist was skewed by his years of struggle with bed wetting in childhood, and the humiliations to which a scornful father had exposed him.

Neurotic Distortions

What do such observations say to the old cliché, that one must be sick to be creative? Some psychotherapists hold this view, as do many layman; yet this culturally noxious assumption is devoid of truth. No culture known to us has succeeded in bringing up children and adults free from concealed neurotic mechanisms. Therefore, we have never known creative folk in science or the arts who were exempt. The creative capacity of a few has surmounted this obstacle. But it is a fallacious non sequitur to conclude that without the obstacle they could not have been creative.

The creative potential in each of us is *not* dependent upon nor is it derived from the neurotic potential. But the creative process can be distorted by neurotic mechanisms. These arise in early childhood, not out of exceptional circumstances, but out of simple and ubiquitous human experiences. With age, the conflict between the two processes usually is intensified by later stresses, one of which we euphemistically call "education." And when any man succeeds in being creative, he does this *in spite* of this neurotogenic conflict. Indeed, the conflict between his creative process and his neurotic process causes his actual creative productivity to fall far short of his potential productivity. That fragment of his potential creativity which survives the impact of the neurotic process is distorted in content and becomes rigid and stereotyped.

The Communications Machine

Yet there are many complex reasons why the creative person clings to the myth that his neurosis is the source of his creative capacity. Instead of feeling proudly that his creativity is that in him which is unique, he makes light of his extraordinary gift in favor of the rigid, banal, undistinguishing component of his nature: i.e., his concealed neurosis.

I said earlier that the essence of neurotic illness is the freezing of behavior into unalterable and insatiable patterns. This happens whenever a configuration of psychological processes predetermines the automatic repetition of behavior. How this occurs is a complex story.

There is evidence that our psychological processes represent the interaction of concurrent systems. We call them conscious, preconscious, and unconscious. About their continuous interplay we know that man behaves with greatest flexibility and freedom, i.e., most normally, when the preponderant influence is exercised by an alliance of his conscious and preconscious processes. And we know that he operates in the shadow of illness whenever unconscious determinants are dominant. These may strike you as convenient theories rather than as factual, yet they rest firmly on a large array of experimental and clinical data.

In recent years our concepts of the interplay between conscious, preconscious, and unconscious processes in human psychology have changed in a direction which will lead to more precise clinical and experimental work. We now look upon the brain not as a device to do work but as a communications machine to transmit information. At the core of this process is a continuous stream of subliminal, i.e., "preconscious," activity which goes on both during sleep and when we are awake and is carried on without conscious symbolic imagery. Analogous to a computer, it processes "bits" of information by scanning, ordering, selecting and rejecting, arranging in sequences, by juxtapositions and separations on the basis of chronology, by condensations on the basis of similarity, dissimilarity and contrasts, proximity and distance, and finally summating and coding.

This preconscious processing of data proceeds at an extraordinarily rapid rate and with great freedom, as it assembles and disassembles many diverse patterns. The process is both analogic and digital. Let me repeat that none of this preparation of data is conscious, yet this is what implements the processes of thought.

Furthermore, the stream is fed by a continuous bombardment of messages which are signalled from changes in every aspect of the body's functions. It is fed also by an incessant bombardment of signals from changes in the outer world which reach us through our distance receptors. Therefore, we can divide this input into that which comes from the surface of the body—i.e., the bones, muscles, joints, tendons, skin, and apertures— the input from the internal organs, and the input from a distance. Like the central processing itself, the major part of this incessant bombardment is subliminal. Our highly developed symbolic processes *sample* this entire stream of preconscious activity, i.e., the input, the internal processing, and the output. This *sampling* process is conscious: and it is this conscious sampling of the stream of preconscious input, preconscious central processing, and preconscious output which is always miscalled "thinking." This process of conscious symbolic sampling has an important function in mentation; but it is not thinking. Rather, its function is to relate the samples of the preconscious stream to reality, to test them, to ruminate about them, and to communicate them to others. In turn, all of this is fed back into the preconscious stream itself, where it exercises a continuous cybernetic influence. Note again, that learning, thinking, and creating are all preconscious, while this process of sampling, ruminating, testing, and communicating is conscious.

How then do unconscious processes enter this picture? They arise out of distortions of the relationship of conscious symbols to their roots. The symbol itself is never unconscious; it is the link between the symbol and what it is supposed to represent which becomes distorted, displaced, unconscious. This distortion in turn feeds back many secondary disturbances and is an essential ingredient (perhaps *the* essential ingredient) in the neurotic distortion of human nature.

There are many ways of formulating these relationships; but this seems to me to be the one which is most relevant to the problems which confront us here, i.e., the problems of learning and, above all, *the problem of how to protect the freedom of preconscious processing in learning, in education in general, and in creativity.* The freedom which is sought here is freedom from the destructive effects of an "educational" input overload; freedom from excessive anchoring to literal, pedestrian, conscious realities; and freedom from neurotic distortions. This is the great challenge which scientific education (and indeed all education) has never faced in the past but must face now.

Both conscious and unconscious processes are fixed and rigid. The conscious symbol is anchored to literal reality. The symbol whose relationships have become unknown is bound even more rigidly to an unknown. The symbol here is to its hidden root as a delegate who has been sent to a conference table to "negotiate" but with secret orders never to modify his position. We see this stereotyping influence in the works of creative people in many fields—the man who paints the same painting over and over again; the poet who writes and rewrites the same poem; the scientist who grinds the same scientific ax. It is this which leaves its personal signature and accounts for the man who produces only one play, one book, one piece of first-rate scientific work. This is the price we pay whenever unconscious processes hold the upper hand.

The Freedom of Preconscious Functions

How then do creative processes operate between these two rigid systems? This depends upon the freedom of preconscious functions. This is the implement of all thinking, particularly of creative thought. Preconsciously, we process many things at a time. By processes of free associations, we take ideas and approximate realities apart and make swift condensations of their multiple allegorical and emotional import. Preconscious processes make free use of analogy and allegory, superimposing dissimilar ingredients into new perceptual and conceptual patterns, thus reshuffling experience to achieve that extraordinary degree of condensation without which creativity in any field would be impossible.

Creativity and the Free Flow

We must remember always that all three processes act concurrently. Whatever we do, whatever we say, whatever we think—whether we are sick or well—everything is a composite resultant of all three processes. This is true when we dream, when we are creative, or when we are preoccupied with the banal events and affairs of life. The differences are in the relative roles of these components. When a scientist is studying atomic energy or a biological process, when an engineer designs a bridge or a spacecraft, when a classicist studies an ancient language, each deals with his subject on all three levels at once.

On the conscious level, he deals with his subject in terms of communicable literal ideas and approximate realities. On the preconscious level, he deals with swift condensations of their multiple allegorical and emotional import, both direct and indirect. On the unconscious level, without realizing it, he uses his special competence and knowledge to express the conflict-laden, confused, and hidden levels of his own spirit; and to the extent to which unconscious processes dominate his activity, he will use the language of his specialty as the vehicle for the outward projection of his internal struggles. We saw this in the examples cited earlier: The men who did nothing but criticize; the pharmacologist whose hypotheses were chosen under neurotic influences; the scientist whose work on water metabolism was distorted by childhood problems with enuresis. In each of these, the distortions were happening without their knowledge, precisely because unconscious processes had taken over. Each man's creative thinking was being subverted to serve his unconscious needs.

Not only are the products of the preconscious thought stream vulnerable to distortion from unconscious levels, the stream itself must be protected from the same influences, because creativity depends upon its free flow. Let me cite a few examples to reinforce this point: There is the famous reverie by Kekulé of the six snakes in a ring, each swallowing the tail of the one ahead, an image which illuminated for him the structure of the benzene ring. There is Otto Loewe's account of the derivation of the whole neurohumoral concept from a dream. There is Poincaré's solution of a mathematical problem during a state of reverie on a bus.

Such experiences indicate that new syntheses occur when preconscious processes can operate without the restrictions of conscious processes and without interference from unconscious determinants. I deliberately plan my work to capitalize on it. I usually work on a problem until I am tired late in the evening. The moment my head touches the pillow I fall asleep with the problem still unsolved. Frequently, I will awaken two or three hours later—sometimes to find myself in the middle of the very sentence on which I was hung up as I went to sleep—but my head now filled with a rushing tumult of ideas and phrases, a new assembly of the material. I have learned by sad experience that I will have forgotten most of this by the next morning unless I dictate or write a note about it *at once*.

The Demands of Research

Creativity in technical fields puts many special demands on the individual. In the exploratory phase, i.e., while gathering data, one's observations should be free from preconceptions and preferential biases—and, above all, free from any drive prematurely to systematize the data or to formulate hypotheses prematurely. The work of this exploratory phase requires a free, imaginative, flexible, uncommitted attitude of fact gathering, i.e., the attitude in which preconscious functions predominate.

Later steps of scientific or technological investigation demand that this material be subjected to more rigidly organized psychological processes, which enable one to test and then to doubt, then to test and doubt again, and then to rearrange the data into new systems. This requires a personality which can doubt on a consciously self-critical level, yet which will not be caught up in obsessional indecision.

The work of the man who becomes trapped may suffer in various ways. One man cannot rest until a pseudo solution is in his hand. Like the kleptomaniac, he may be forced by phobic and unreal anxieties to attempt to increase his feelings of certainty by falsifying data even after fully convincing evidence is already in hand. Another is afraid to find answers, his terror increasing as he approaches any solution. This forces him to postpone endlessly any definitive conclusion of his work. Or he chooses problems which will take a lifetime to solve. Or he clouds his findings in obscure terminology. Or he refrains from publication altogether.

Clearly, creativity in science and engineering demands flexibility and imaginativeness, but also tightly organized thought processes, matched by a high degree of emotional and psychological freedom. In science, the moment of apparent illumination is never the end of a search. It is always the starting point for new investigation. It provides the scientist with a beckoning goal and an incentive, without which nothing new is ever discovered.

Thus the impact of unconscious conflicts on the creative process are many. If conflicts are buried under distorting disguises, they block the flow of preconscious analogic processes which are essential to scientific creativity. If, on the other hand, a scientist understands his conflicts, if they are out in the open, he can use them. They may spur him on. They become a supplement to, but not a substitute for, his fundamental biogenetic and instinctual processes. He guides them, instead of being enslaved by them. The man who lacks such insights is enslaved by his unconscious conflicts and drives. He lives on a treadmill, for he can never finish one piece of research without being seized with terror that he will never be able to complete another. He can never lie fallow, never rest. Without work he is in a torment of anxiety; and complex compulsions take over his normal creativity. "Success" always cheats him, because success never enables him to attain the unconscious goals of his activity. To him, it is not the need to solve his chosen problem which drives him, but an unknown necessity. His consciously chosen goal is merely a substitute for these unconscious and unattainable goals. Therefore, even when he reaches some consciously chosen goal he feels defeated. He may achieve success by many standards but can never enjoy the achievement. Unless he resolves his inner conflicts, he can never get off the treadmill. In his middle years, such a man is likely to become angry and depressed. Indeed, even in spite of any degree of careeristic success, the likelihood of middle-year depressions is greater with him than with others among his peers who were less "successful." And a "nervous breakdown" in such cases is not a result of overwork, but a consequence of a life driven blindly and without sufficient insights.

The Educational Grind

I spoke sharply of our "primitive" educational practices. I shall make only a few tentative suggestions as to how the educational process might be changed, because I have no easy solutions. My central thesis suggests general lines of research which might lead to new methods.

In varying degrees, individuals need help in acquiring the tools of communication—how to read and listen to words, how to speak and write them. And everyone needs to learn how to resolve unconscious needs and conflicts so that they will not distort the work of the educated eye and ear and tongue and hand. But we do not need to be taught to think. In fact, thinking cannot be taught. The function of education is rather to show us how not to interfere with the thinking capacity which is inherent in the human mind.

The free creative velocity of our thinking apparatus is continually being braked and driven off course by the play of unconscious forces and, unhappily, by conventional educational practices as well. This is because we still try to educate largely by varying degrees of overemphasis on drill and grill, which interfere with the free play of preconscious processes both in the acquisition of new data and in the free utilization of that data.

When educators challenge us to tell them better ways, our only answer is that we can help them to undertake basic research on the educational process. This can lead to new practices which will leave our basic tools free for spontaneous use; basic research on how to impart new information without crippling the mind's creative potential.

This is a general educational problem; the fact that it has not been solved does not imply that we know nothing. We know, for instance, that thinking and learning are not performed consciously. Let us not minimize the importance of this fact, which challenges all traditional approaches to teaching—approaches based on the misleading assumption that we think and learn consciously.

The truth is that we learn preconsciously. The input of fragmentary perceptual data from the world around us is overwhelmingly preconscious. This constitutes an incessant subliminal bombardment which goes on when we are awake and when we are asleep. The same is true for the most highly organized material. This has been demonstrated by experiments on the learning process under hypnosis, which indicate that our conscious intake is only a small fragment of our simultaneous preconscious intake, i.e., that process of intake and recall which occurs without conscious awareness. Furthermore, we know now that what the brain acquires preconsciously it also "processes" preconsciously, which is just another way of saying that all learning and thinking are preconscious rather than conscious processes.

This is not to say that our conscious processes are unimportant. They are important for sampling, checking, correcting, communicating, etc. But this is not thinking. The information we acquire consciously is never more than a weighted sample of the total input. This is one of the most basic facts of psychophysiology; and it has relevance for all educational processes. Yet it is a fact which is largely ignored by educators. So long as conscious sampling is mistaken for thinking, education will continue to neglect the great preconscious instrument of creative learning. Though we know that all effective recording, processing, and creating occurs pre-consciously, we still must learn how to use this instrument. This is the major challenge which psychiatry brings to education.

We can learn new ways of educating only in schools which are both schools *and* laboratories. Just as research is an accepted function of every teaching hospital, research facilities must be attached to all leading public and private schools. The best schools of tomorrow, those which provide the best education, will be those which carry on research every day and all the time in every detail of the educational process. I would like to see such research schools established first in some of our schools of science and engineering, because I believe that the unsolved problems of education can be studied with greater precision here than in other areas of education. Furthermore, if we can solve these problems in technical education, we will spark similar developments in every other kind of education.

Perhaps there should be a National Institute for Educational Research, paralleling the National Institutes of Health, with experimental schools and laboratories and funds for research. Toward that objective, for which there is an urgent need, the nation's leading schools of science and engineering now have an opportunity to provide a first step—by serving as laboratories in which this work can begin. Perhaps at the same time our technical schools can use this as an opportunity to do something about their high rates of attrition. Also it might help to solve a harder-to-measure problem, to which many engineering educators attest, namely, the fact that creativity so rarely survives the educational grind. If we succeed here, the technical schools will be the site of the discovery of new educational processes by which to protect the free use of our preconscious without crippling our creative potential.

I will conclude with an analogy. The freely gifted athlete can imitate with his body anything he sees anyone else do even once, and sometimes do it better than his experienced model. He will pick up a tennis racket, or skip rope, or put on skates, and in a moment will show natural precision and grace, better than the person whom he has been watching. He has a freedom to move and to put new movements together into new combina-tions. He does this with confidence, with bodily imagination, and without anxiety. He is like the naturally gifted artist who barely glances at something casually, and then with a piece of charcoal reproduces it automatically and faithfully. Then he can go further: He can take it apart into fragments and play with it, elaborating out of the initial stereotyped and literal image a new production out of the free play of his own creative fancy. There is much evidence that such effortless learning is the best, whether in graduate study or in our first days at school. We should search out methods by which to enable us to acquire our basic tools in this way. This is the challenge which psychiatry brings to technical education.

ABRAHAM H. MASLOW

The Creative Attitude

This article is a slightly modified version of a lecture presented by the author in October, 1962, to the 8th National Assembly of the Canadian Society for Education through Art, held at the University of Saskatchewan in Saskatoon.

My feeling is that the concept of creativeness and the concept of the healthy, self-actualizing, fully-human person seem to be coming closer and closer together, and may perhaps turn out to be the same thing.

Another conclusion I seem to be impelled toward, even though I am not quite sure of my facts, is that creative art education, or better said, Education-Through-Art, may be especially important, not so much for turning out artists or art products, as for turning out better people. If we have clearly in mind the educational goals for human beings that I will be hinting at, if we hope for our children that they will become full human beings, and that they will move toward actualizing the potentialities that they have, then, as nearly as I can make out, the only kind of education in existence today that has any faint inkling of such goals is art education. So I am thinking of education through art not because it turns out pictures but because I think it may be possible that, clearly understood, it may become the paradigm for all other education. That is, instead of being regarded as the frill, the expendable kind of thing which it now is, if we take it seriously enough and work at it hard enough and if it turns out to be what some of us suspect it can be, then we may one day teach arithmetic and reading and writing on this paradigm. So far as I am concerned, I am talking about all education. This is why I am interested in education through art—simply because it seems to be good education in potential.

Another reason for my interest in art education, creativeness, psychological health, etc., is that I have a very strong feeling of a change of pace

From *The Structurist*, 1963, No. 3, pp. 4-10. Used by permission of the publisher.

in history. It seems to me that we are at a point in history unlike anything that has ever been before. Life moves far more rapidly now than it ever did before. Think, for instance, of the huge acceleration in the rate of growth of facts, of knowledge, of techniques, of inventions, of advances in technology. It seems very obvious to me that this requires a change in our attitude toward the human being, and toward his relationships to the world. To put it bluntly, we need a different kind of human being. I feel I must take far more seriously today than I did twenty years ago, the Heraclitus, the Whitehead, the Bergson kind of emphasis on the world as a flux, a movement, a process, not a static thing. If this is so, and it is obviously much more so than it was in 1900 or even in 1930—if this is so, then we need a different kind of human being to be able to live in a world which changes perpetually, which doesn't stand still. I may go so far as to say for the educational enterprise: what's the use of teaching facts? Facts become obsolete so darned fast! What's the use of teaching techniques? The techniques become obsolete so fast! Even the engineering schools are torn by this realization. M.I.T., for instance, no longer teaches engineering *only* as the acquisition of a series of skills, because practically all the skills that the professors of engineering learned when they were in school have now become obsolete. It's no use today learning to make buggy whips. What some professors have done at M.I.T., I understand, is to give us the teaching of the tried and true methods of the past, in favor of trying to create a new kind of human being who is comfortable with change, who enjoys change, who is able to improvise, who is able to face with confidence, strength, and courage a situation of which he has absolutely no forewarning.

Even today as I read the morning newspaper before coming here, *everything* seems to be changing; international law is changing; politics are changing; the whole international scene is changing. People talk with each other in the United Nations from across different centuries. One man speaks in terms of the international law of the nineteenth century. Another one answers him in terms of something else entirely, from a different platform in a different world. Things have changed that fast.

To come back to my title, what I'm talking about is the job of trying to make ourselves over into people who don't need to staticize the world, who don't need to freeze it and to make it stable, who don't need to do what their daddies did, who are able confidently to face tomorrow not knowing what's going to come, not knowing what will happen, with confidence enough in ourselves that we will be able to improvise in that situation which has never existed before. This means a new type of human being. Heraclitian you might call him. The society that can turn out such people will survive; the societies that *cannot* turn out such people will die.

You'll notice that I stress a great deal improvising and inspiration, rather than approaching creativeness from the vantage point of the finished work of art, of the great creative work. As a matter of fact, I won't even approach it today from the point of view of completed products at all. Why is this? Because we're pretty clearly aware now from our psychological analysis of the process of creativeness and of creative individuals, that we must make the distinction between primary creativeness and a secondary creativeness. The primary creativeness or the inspirational phase of creativeness must be separated from the working out and the development of the inspiration. This is because the latter phase stresses not only creativeness, but also relies very much on just plain hard work, on the discipline of the artist who may spend half a lifetime learning his tools, his skills, and his materials, until he becomes finally ready for a full expression of what he sees. I am very certain that many, many people have waked up in the middle of the night with a flash of inspiration about some novel they would like to write, or a play, or a poem, or whatever, and that most of these inspirations never came to anything. Inspirations are a dime a dozen. The difference between the inspiration and the final product, for example, Tolstoy's *War and Peace,* is an awful lot of hard work, an awful lot of discipline, an awful lot of training, an awful lot of finger exercises and practices and rehearsals and throwing away first drafts, and so on. Now the virtues which go with the secondary kind of creativeness, the creativeness which results in the actual products, in the great paintings, the great novels, in the bridges, the new inventions and so on, rest as heavily upon other virtues—stubbornness and patience and hard work and so on, as they do upon the creativeness of the personality. Therefore, in order to keep the field of operation clean, you might say, it seems necessary to me to focus upon improvising, on this first flash and, for the moment, not to worry about what becomes of it, recognizing that many of them do get lost. Partly for this reason, among the best subjects to study for this inspirational phase of creativeness are young children whose inventiveness and creativeness very frequently cannot be defined in terms of product. When a little boy discovers the decimal system for himself, this can be a high moment of inspiration, and a high creative moment, and should not be waved aside because of some a priori definition which says creativeness ought to be socially useful, or it ought to be novel, or nobody should have thought of it before, etc.

For this same reason, I have decided for myself not to take scientific creativeness as a paradigm, but rather to use other examples. Much of the research that's going on now deals with the creative scientists, with people who have proven themselves to be creative, Nobel prize winners, great inventors, and so on. The trouble is, if you know a lot of scientists, that you soon learn that something is wrong with this criterion because scientists as a group are not nearly as creative generally as you would expect. This includes people who have discovered, who have created actually, who have published things which were advances in human knowledge. Actually, this is not too difficult to understand. This finding tells us something about the nature of science rather than about the nature of creativeness. If I wanted to be mischievous about it, I could go so far as to define science as a technique whereby noncreative people can create. This is by no means making fun of scientists. It's a wonderful thing, it seems to me, for limited human beings, that they can be pressed into the service of great things even though they themselves are not great people. Science is a technique, social and institutionalized, whereby even unintelligent people can be useful in the advance of knowledge. That is as extreme and dramatic as I can make it. Since any particular scientist rests so much in the arms of history, stands on so many shoulders of so many predecessors, is so much a part of a huge basketball team, of a big collection of people, that his own shortcomings may not appear. He becomes worthy of reference, worthy of great respect through his participation in a great and respect-worthy enterprise. Therefore, when he discovers something, I have learned to understand this as a product of a social institution, of a collaboration. If he didn't discover it, somebody else would have pretty soon. Therefore, it seems to me that selecting our scientists, even though they have created, is not the best way to study the theory of creativeness.

I will make one last point before I get to my paper proper. I believe also that we cannot study creativeness in an ultimate sense until we realize that practically all the definitions that we have been using of creativeness, and most of the examples of creativeness that we use, are essentially male or masculine definitions and male or masculine products. We've left out of consideration almost entirely the creativeness of women by the simple semantic technique of defining only male products as creative and over-looking entirely the creativeness of women. I have learned recently (through my studies of peak experiences) to look to women and to feminine creativeness as a good field of operation for research, because it gets less involved in products, less involved in achievement, more involved with the process itself, with the going-on process rather than with the climax in obvious triumph and success.

This is the background of the particular problem I'd like to talk about today.

The puzzle that I'm now trying to unravel is suggested by the observation that the creative person, in the inspirational phase of the creative furore, loses his past and his future and lives only in the moment. He is all there, totally immersed, fascinated and absorbed in the present, in the current situation, in the here-now, with the matter-in-hand. Or to use a perfect phrase from *The Spinster* by Sylvia Ashton-Warner, the teacher absorbed with a new method of teaching reading to her children says, "I am utterly lost in the present."

This ability to become "lost in the present" seems to be a sine qua non for creativeness of any kind. But also certain *prerequisites* of creativeness —in whatever realm—somehow have something to do with this ability to become timeless, selfless, outside of space, of society, of history.

It has begun to appear strongly that this phenomenon is a diluted, more secular, more frequent version of the mystical experience that has been described so often as to have become what Huxley called *The Perennial Philosophy*. In various cultures and in various eras, it takes on somewhat different coloration—and yet its essence is always recognizable—it is the same.

It is always described as a loss of self or of ego, or sometimes as a transcendence of self. There is a fusion with the reality being observed (with the matter-in-hand, I shall say more neutrally), a oneness where there was a twoness, an integration of some sort of the self with the non-self. There is universally reported a seeing of formerly hidden truth, a revelation in the strict sense, a stripping away of veils, and finally, almost always, the whole experience is experienced as bliss, ecstasy, rapture, exaltation.

Little wonder that this shaking experience has so often been considered to be superhuman, supernatural, so much greater and grander than anything conceivable as human that it could only be attributed to trans-human sources. And such "revelations" often serve as basis, sometimes the *sole* basis, for the various "revealed" religions.

And yet, even this most remarkable of all experiences has now been brought into the realm of human experience and cognition. My researches on what I call peak-experiences (1962 ab), and Marghanita Laski's on what she calls ecstasies (1961), done quite independently of each other, show that these experiences are quite naturalistic, quite easily investigated, and, what is to the point right now, that they have much to teach us about creativeness as well as other aspects of the full functioning of human beings when they are most fully realizing themselves, most mature and evolved, most healthy, when, in a word, they are most fully human.

One main characteristic of the peak-experience is just this total fascination with the matter-in-hand, this getting lost in the present, this detachment from time and place. And it seems to me now that much of what we have learned from the study of these peak-experiences can be transferred quite directly to the enriched understanding of the here-now experience of the creative attitude.

It is not necessary for us to confine ourselves to these uncommon and rather extreme experiences, even though it now seems clear that practically all people can report moments of rapture, if they dig around long enough in their memories, and if the interview situation is just right. We can also refer to the simplest version of the peak-experience, namely fascination, concentration or absorption in *anything* which is interesting enough to hold this attention completely. And I mean not only great symphonies or tragedies; the job can be done by a gripping movie or detective story, or simply becoming absorbed with one's work. There are certain advantages in starting from such universal and familiar experiences which we all have, so that we can get a direct feeling or intuition or empathy, that is, a direct experiential knowledge of a modest, moderate version of the fancier "high" experiences. For one thing, we can avoid the flossy, high-flying, extremely metaphorical vocabulary that is so common in this realm.

Well then, what are some of the things that happen in these moments?

Giving Up the Past

The best way to view a present problem is to give it all you've got, to study *it* and its nature, to perceive *within* it the intrinsic interrelationships, to discover (rather than invent) the answer to the problem within the problem itself. This is also the best way to look at a painting or to listen to a patient in therapy.

The other way is merely a matter of shuffling over past experiences, past habits, past knowledge to find out in what respects this current situation is similar to some situation in the past, i.e., to classify it, and then to use *now* the solution that once worked for the similar problem in the past. This can be likened to the work of a filing clerk. I have called it "rubricizing" (1954). And it works well enough to the extent that the present *is* like the past.

But obviously, it *doesn't* work insofar as the matter-in-hand is different from the past. The file clerk approach fails then. This person confronting an unknown painting hurriedly runs back through his knowledge of art history to remember how he is supposed to react. Meanwhile, of course, he is hardly looking at the painting. All he needs is the name or the style or the content to enable him to do his quick calculations. He then enjoys it if he is supposed to, and doesn't if he is *not* supposed to.

In such a person, the past is an inert, undigested foreign body which the person carries about like keys in his pocket. It is not yet the person himself.

More accurately said: The past is active and alive only insofar as it has re-created the person, and has been digested into the present person. It is not or should not be something *other* than the person, something alien to it. It has now become Person (and has lost its own identity as something different and other), just as past steaks that I have eaten are now me, *not* steaks. The digested past (assimilated by intussusception) is different from the undigested past. It is Lewin's "ahistorical past."

Giving Up the Future

Often we use the present not for its own sake but in order to prepare for the future. Think how often in a conversation we put on a listening face as the other person talks, secretly, however, preparing what we are going to say, rehearsing, planning a counterattack perhaps. Think how different your attitude would be right now if you knew you were to comment on my remarks in five minutes. Think how hard it would be then to be a good, total listener.

If we are totally listening or totally looking, we have thereby given up this kind of "preparing for the future." We don't treat the present as merely a means to some future end, thereby devaluating the present. And obviously, this kind of forgetting the future is a prerequisite to total involvement with the present. Just as obviously, a good way to "forget" the future is not to be apprehensive about it.

Of course, this is only one sense of the concept "future." The future which is within us, part of our present selves, is another story altogether (1962 a).

Innocence

This amounts to a kind of "innocence" of perceiving and behaving. Something of the sort has often been attributed to highly creative people. They are variously described as being naked in the situation, guileless, with a priori expectations, without "should's" or "ought's," without fashions, fads, dogmas, habits or other pictures-in-the-head of what is proper, normal, "right," as being ready to receive whatever happens to be the case without surprise, shock, indignation, or denial.

Children are more able to be receptive in this undemanding way. So are wise old people. And it appears now that we *all* may be more innocent in this style when we become "here-now."

Narrowing of Consciousness

We have now become much less conscious of everything other than the matter-in-hand (less distractible). *Very* important here is our lessened awareness of other people, of their ties to us and ours to them, of obligations, duties, fears, hopes, etc. We become much more free of other people, which in turn, means that we become much more ourselves, our Real Selves (Horney), our authentic selves, our real identity.

This is so because *the* greatest cause of our alienation from our real selves is our neurotic involvements with other people, the historical hangovers from childhood, the irrational transferences, in which past and present are confused, and in which the adult acts like a child. (By the way, it's all right for the *child* to act like a child. His dependencies on other people can be very real. *But,* after all, he *is* supposed to outgrow them. To be afraid of what daddy will say or do is certainly out-of-place if daddy has been dead for twenty years.)

In a word, we become more free of the influence of other people in such moments. So, insofar as these influences have affected our behavior, they no longer do so.

This means dropping masks, dropping our efforts to influence, to impress, to please, to be lovable, to win applause. It could be said so: if we have no audience to play to, we cease to be actors. With no need to act we can devote ourselves, self-forgetfully, to the problem.

Loss of Ego: Self-Forgetfulness, Loss of Self-Consciousness

When you are totally absorbed in non-self, you tend to become less conscious of yourself, less self-aware. You are less apt to be observing yourself like a spectator or a critic. To use the language of psychodynamics, you become less dissociated than usual into a self-observing ego and an experiencing ego; i.e., you come much closer to being *all* experiencing ego. (You tend to lose the shyness and bashfulness of the adolescent, the painful awareness of being looked at, etc.) This in turn means more unifying, more oneness and integration of the person.

It also means less criticizing and editing, less evaluating, less selecting and rejecting, less judging and weighing, less splitting and analyzing of the experience.

This kind of self-forgetfulness is one of the paths to finding one's true identity, one's real self, one's authentic nature, one's deepest nature. It is almost always felt as pleasant and desirable. We needn't go so far as the Buddhists and Eastern thinkers do in talking about the "accursed ego"; and yet there *is* something in what they say.

Inhibiting Force of Consciousness (of Self)

In some senses, consciousness (especially of self) is inhibiting in some ways and at some times. It is sometimes the locus of doubts, conflicts, fears, etc. It is sometimes harmful to full-functioning creativeness. It is sometimes an inhibitor of spontaneity and of expressiveness (*but* the observing ego is necessary for therapy).

(And yet it is also true that some kind of self-awareness, self-observation, self-criticism, i.e., the self-observing ego, *is* necessary for "secondary creativeness." To use psychotherapy as an example, the task of self-improvement is partly a consequence of criticizing the experiences that one has allowed to come into consciousness. Schizophrenic people experience many insights and yet don't make therapeutic use of them because they are too much "totally experiencing" and not enough "self-observing-and-criticizing." In creative work, likewise, the labor of disciplined construction succeeds upon the phase of "inspiration.")

Fears Disappear

This means that our fears and anxieties also tend to disappear. So also our depressions, conflicts, ambivalence, our worries, our problems, even our physical pains. Even—for the moment—our psychoses and our neuroses (that is, if they are not so extreme as to prevent us from becoming deeply interested and immersed in the matter-in-hand).

For the time being, we are courageous and confident, unafraid, unanxious, unneurotic, not sick.

Lessening of Defenses and Inhibitions

Our inhibitions also tend to disappear. So also our guardedness, our (Freudian) defenses, and controls (brakes) on our impulses as well as the defenses against danger and threat.

Strength and Courage

The creative attitude requires both courage and strength, and most studies of creative people have reported one or another version of courage: popularity becomes a minor consideration, stubbornness, independence, self-sufficiency, a kind of arrogance, strength of character, ego-strength, etc. Fear and weakness cast out creativeness or at least make it less likely.

It seems to me that this aspect of creativeness becomes somewhat more understandable when it is seen as a part of the syndrome of here-now self-forgetfulness and other-forgetfulness. Such a state intrinsically implies less fear, less inhibition, less need for defense and self-protection, less guardedness, less need for artificiality, less fear of ridicule, of humiliation and of failure. All these characteristics are *part of* self-forgetfulness and audience-forgetfulness. Absorption casts out fear.

Or we can say in a more positive way, that becoming more courageous makes it easier to let oneself be attracted by mystery, by the unfamiliar, by the novel, by the ambiguous and contradictory, by the unusual and unexpected, etc., instead of becoming suspicious, fearful, guarded, or having to throw into action our anxiety-allaying mechanisms and defenses.

Acceptance: The Positive Attitude

In moments of here-now immersion and self-forgetfulness, we are apt to become more "positive" and less negative in still another way, namely, in giving up criticism (editing, picking and choosing, correcting, skepticism, improving, doubting, rejecting, judging, evaluating). This is like saying that we accept. We don't reject or disapprove or selectively pick and choose.

No blocks against the matter-in-hand means that we let it flow in upon us. We let it wreak its will upon us. We let it have its way. We let it be itself. Perhaps we can even approve of its being itself.

This makes it easier to be Taoistic in the sense of humility, noninterference, receptivity.

Trust vs. Trying, Controlling, Striving

All of the foregoing happenings imply a kind of trust in the self and a trust in the world, which permits the temporary giving up of straining and striving, of volition and control, of conscious coping and effort. To permit oneself to be determined by the intrinsic nature of the matter-in-hand here-now necessarily implies relaxation, waiting, receiving. The common effort to master, to dominate, and to control are antithetical to a true coming-to-terms with or a true perceiving of the materials (or the problem, or the person, etc.)—especially, if this is true with respect to the future. We *must* trust our ability to improvise when confronted with novelty in the future. Phrased in this way, we can see more clearly that trust involves self-confidence, courage, lack of fear of the world. It is also clear that this kind of trust in ourselves-facing-the-unknown-future is a condition of being able to turn totally, nakedly, and wholeheartedly to the present.

(Some clinical examples may help. Giving birth, urination, defecation, sleeping, floating in the water, sexual surrender, are all instances in which straining, trying, controlling, have to be given up in favor of relaxed, trusting, confident letting things happen.)

Taoistic Receptivity

Both Taoism and receptivity mean many things, all of them important, but also subtle and difficult to convey except in figures of speech. All of the subtle and delicate Taoistic attributes of the creative attitude which follow have been described again and again by the many writers on creativeness, now in one way, now in another. However, everyone agrees that in the primary or inspirational phase of creativeness, some degree of receptivity or noninterference or "let-be" is descriptively characteristic and also theoretically and dynamically necessary. Our question now is how does this receptivity or "letting things happen" relate to the syndrome of here-now immersion and self-forgetfulness?

For one thing, using the artist's respect for his materials as a paradigm, we may speak of this respectful attention to the matter-in-hand as a kind of courtesy or deference (without intrusion of the controlling will), which is akin to "taking it seriously." This amounts to treating it as an end, something per se, with its own right to be, rather than as a means to some end other than itself, i.e., as a tool for some extrinsic purpose. This respectful treatment of its being implies that it is respectworthy.

This courtesy or respectfulness can apply equally to the problem, to the materials, to the situation, or to the person. It is what one writer (Follett) has called deference (yielding, surrender) to the authority of the facts, to the law of the situation. I can go over from a bare *permitting* "it" to be itself, to a loving, caring, approving, joyful *eagerness* that it be itself, as with one's child or sweetheart or tree or poem or pet animal.

Some such attitude is a priori necessary for perceiving or understanding the full concrete richness of the matter-in-hand, in *its* own nature and in *its* own style, without our help, without our imposing ourselves upon it, in about the same way that we must hush and be still if we wish to hear the whisper from the other.

This cognition of the Being of the other (B-cognition) has been fully described by Maslow (1954, 1962 ac).

Integration of the B-Cognizer (vs. Dissociation)

Creating tends to be the act of a whole man (ordinarily); he is then *most* integrated, unified, all of a piece, one-pointed, totally organized in the service of the fascinating matter-in-hand. Creativeness is therefore systemic; i.e., a whole—or Gestalt—quality of the whole person; it is not added-to the organism like a coat of paint, or like an invasion of bacteria. It is the opposite of dissociation. Here-now-allness is less dissociated (split) and more one.

Permission to Dip into Primary Process

Part of the process of integration of the person is the recovery of the unconscious and preconscious, particularly of the primary process (or poetic, metaphoric, mystic, primitive, archaic, childlike).

Our conscious intellect is too exclusively analytic, rational, numerical, atomistic, conceptual, and so it misses a great deal of reality, especially within our selves.

Aesthetic Perceiving Rather Than Abstracting

Abstracting is more active and interfering (less Taoistic); more selecting-rejecting than the aesthetic (Northrop) attitude of savoring, enjoying, appreciating, caring, in a noninterfering, nonintruding, noncontrolling way.

The end product of abstracting is the mathematical equation, the chemical formula, the map, the diagram, the blueprint, the cartoon, the concept, the abstracting sketch, the model, the theoretical system, all of which move further and further from raw reality ("the map is *not* the territory"). The end-product of aesthetic perceiving, of nonabstracting is the total inventory of the percept, in which everything in it is apt to be equally savored, and in which evaluations of more important and less important tend to be given up. Here greater richness of the percept is sought for rather than greater simplifying and skeletonizing.

For many confused scientists and philosophers, the equation, the concept, or the blueprint have become more real than the phenomenological reality itself. Fortunately, now that we can understand the interplay and mutual enrichment of the concrete and the abstract, it is no longer necessary to devalue one or the other. For the moment, we intellectuals in the West who have heavily and exclusively overvalued abstractness in our picture of reality, even to the point of synonymizing them, had better redress the balance by stressing concrete, aesthetic, phenomenological, nonabstracting, perceiving of *all* the aspects and details of phenomena, of the full richness of reality, including the useless portions of it.

Fullest Spontaneity

If we are fully concentrated on the matter-in-hand, fascinated with it for its own sake, having no other goals or purposes in mind, then it is easier to be fully spontaneous, fully functioning, letting our capacities flow forth easily from within, of themselves, without effort, without conscious volition or control, in an instinct-like automatic, thoughtless way; i.e., the fullest, least obstructed, most organized action.

The one main determinant of their organization and adaptation to the matter-in-hand is then most apt to be the intrinsic nature of the matter-in-hand. Our capacities then adapt to the situation most perfectly, quickly, effortlessly, and change flexibly as the situation changes; e.g., as a painter continuously adapts himself to the demands of his developing painting; as a wrestler adapts himself to his opponent; as a pair of fine dancers mutually adapt to each other; as water flows into cracks and contours.

Fullest Expressiveness (of Uniqueness)

Full spontaneity is a guarantee of honest expression of the nature and the style of the freely functioning organism, and of its uniqueness. Both words—spontaneity and expressiveness—imply honesty, naturalness, truthfulness, lack of guile, nonimitativeness, etc., because they also imply a noninstrumental nature of the behavior, a lack of willful "trying," a lack of effortful striving or straining, a lack of interference with the flow of the impulses and the free "radioactive" expression of the deep person.

The only determinants now are the intrinsic nature of the matter-in-hand, the intrinsic nature of the person and the intrinsic necessities of their fluctuating adaptation to each other to form a fusion, a unit; e.g., a fine basketball team, or a string quartet. Nothing outside this fusion situation is relevant. The situation is not a means to any extrinsic end; it is an end in itself.

Fusion of the Person with the World

We wind up with the fusion between the person and his world, which has so often been reported as an observable fact in creativeness, and which we may now reasonably consider to be a sine qua non. I think that this spider web of interrelationships that I have been teasing apart and discussing can help us to understand this fusion better as a natural event, rather than as something mysterious, arcane, esoteric. I think it can even be researched, if we understand it to be an isomorphism, a molding of each to each other, a better and better fitting together or complementarity, a melting into one.

It has helped me to understand what Hokusai meant when he said, "If you want to draw a bird, you must become a bird."

DONALD W. MacKINNON

The Highly Effective Individual

In discussing the highly effective individual, I shall be focusing upon one of the least understood phenomena in the whole field of human behavior.

It is, of course, understandable that for so many years study of the effective person was slighted. It was inevitable that when psychology sought to cut its affiliation with its parent discipline philosophy toward the end of the last century and attempted to become a science, it turned its attention to simple problems—partial responses, simple sensory, perceptual, and motor responses, simple learning, and the like—for the study of which manageable techniques were available.

When, somewhat later, there developed a concern with the whole man rather than with his simple and isolated reactions, it was not the academic and experimental psychologist who pioneered this new field of inquiry. Instead, it was the physician, the medical psychologist faced with the practical problem of alleviating the suffering of patients. Thus it was that when man as a whole came under scrutiny and investigation, it was the ineffective rather than the effective person who was first probed and studied. Psychopathology is vivid; it cries out for treatment and care. So, understandably, over the years there has been a continuing emphasis upon research into the nature of human emotional and mental distress in the attempt to find some cure for them.

Still another reason why ineffective and sick persons have been more intensively studied in psychology than effective and healthy individuals is that they have been motivated by their distress and suffering to reveal themselves, to let the psychiatrist or medical psychologist find out as much as he could about them. But what are the motivations for a person getting along well in life to reveal himself and his innermost secrets to anyone?

From *Teachers College Record*, April, 1960, *61* (7), no pages given. Used by permission of the publisher.

The great pioneer in the investigation of the sick and disturbed individual was Sigmund Freud, founder of psychoanalysis, and it was Sigmund Freud more than anyone else who gave modern psychology its major notions about human development. The picture he painted was one in which only the direst consequences could be expected to follow marked frustrations of human needs, deprivation of individual requirements, and traumatic experiences. As a result of this, the view concerning the development of human personality which for many years was rather uncritically accepted, and which influenced very much the preachings and preachments of the mental hygiene movement, was that the individual would have to enjoy a loving, supportive, and permissive home and life situation during the early formative years if he was to grow up to be an effectively functioning person. This view might still be very generally and uncritically held were it not for certain psychological investigations that were carried out during World War II.

During this war two major and in many respects novel psychological programs were developed for the selection and placement of personnel. One was conducted by the Army Air Corps, and its objective was the development of tests to pick out individuals who would have the abilities to be trained as pilots, navigators, bombardiers, etc. This program, like the earlier work of experimental psychologists, focused sharply upon partial responses rather than upon man as a whole. It looked for the particular, rather specialized skills and abilities, especially psychomotor skills, which enter into the complicated tasks of flying and navigating an airplane. It was not particularly concerned with the total complexly motivated individual.

Study of Man as a Whole

The other program, in contrast, was forced to focus its attention upon the whole man. This program was developed in the Office of Strategic Services. As is now well known, the Office of Strategic Services was set up to engage in irregular warfare. Its task was to recruit and train individuals to operate as spies, counterespionage agents, leaders of resistance groups behind the enemy lines, creators of black propaganda designed to destroy the enemy's morale, and so forth; and it was clear that, if individuals were to engage successfully in such operations, they had to have rather unusual traits and abilities. Not infrequently, they would be on their own in a foreign country, speaking a language which was not their native tongue. Essential in most OSS operations were an unusual degree of adaptive flexibility, a willingness to assume responsibility for rather unusual actions, loyalty to the cause and to the particular mission. A premium was placed upon independence of judgment as well as good judgment, if one was to operate successfully in OSS assignments.

The group of psychologists and psychiatrists which was asked to set up a program which would assess the qualifications of individuals for the OSS type of activity was faced with the task of measuring the very complex and for the most part positive aspects of personal functioning. It seemed clear to them that no single test would serve the purpose; that it would be necessary to observe, and to measure, just as many aspects of personality as possible; and that their observations should be made in a social situation, because that is where most human behavior actually does occur. The program of testing which resulted from the application of those principles was the assessment program of the OSS. Its essential feature was that the candidates to be evaluated were brought together for several days at an assessment center—a country estate outside of Washington, D.C.— where they lived with one another and with the assessment staff. There they were studied by a variety of means, ranging from a real-life problem situation (the total assessment situation itself) to specially contrived problem-solving experiments; from unstructured projective tests of personality to emperically derived questionnaires and tests of personality traits, attitudes, interests, and values; and from search interviews covering the life history to formal social situations of a stressful character in which the subjects' best behavior was called for in a socially defined role.

It was in the OSS assessment program that, for the first time, large numbers of highly effective individuals were intensively studied by psychologists and psychiatrists who, to their surprise, discovered again and again that persons of the most extraordinary effectiveness had life histories marked by severe frustrations, deprivations, and traumatic experiences. By all generally accepted theories of personality development, they should have been psychiatric casualties, but they were not.

Those of us who were members of the OSS assessment had it vividly impressed upon us how little we knew about the development of personality and how great was the need for research in this field.

Assessment Method in Personality Research

To meet this need there was established in 1949 on the Berkeley campus of the University of California, through a grant from the Rockefeller Foundation, an Institute of Personality Assessment and Research. Its express purpose was to develop further the assessment method for basic research into problems of personality development and dynamics, with special focus upon the characteristics of the effectively functioning person and the life history determinants of such effectiveness.

Assessment involves both intensive and extensive study of persons who have been nominated by experts for their outstanding qualities of originality, personal soundness, creativity, or some other agreed-upon criterion. There are usually ten persons assessed at one time by a staff of roughly the same number; and since in a typical research program subjects are brought to the Institute for study over a period of three days, during which time hundreds of measures, scores, and ratings are obtained for each subject, assessment is an expensive method of personality research. Consequently, there is an obligation upon assessors to record their more or less clinical impressions of each of the assessees in some quantified form which will permit them to be analyzed along with all other assessment data by various statistical operations.

Three methods of recording staff insights have been repeatedly employed in our researches. One consists of checking on an alphabetically ordered list of 300 adjectives those which best describe a given subject (Gough, 1960). A second method, the Q-sort method (Block, to be published), requires the observer to sort into nine piles for each subject 100 statements of personal functioning, distributing them in a forced normalized distribution from those five at one end which, in the observer's judgment, are most descriptive of the subject to those five at the other end which are least applicable to him. The larger number of items, neither so clearly applicable nor so clearly nondescriptive, is sorted in the larger intermediate categories, the total distribution of the Q-items being 5-8-12-16-18-16-12-8-5. The third method involves rating each subject on some 20 to 30 traits of personality (Woodworth & MacKinnon, 1958).

The checking of adjectives, the sorting of Q-items, and the rating of traits may, of course, be made on the basis of observations of the subject's behavior in a number of assessment situations or on the basis of observations made in only one situation, for example, by the life-history interviewer, who sees the subject only during the interview.

By averaging the ratings made by all staff observers, and by compositing their adjective checks and Q-sorts, it is possible to obtain a quantitative expression of staff impressions and relate these mathematically to the more objective measures obtained in our assessments. It is thus possible to state what adjectives and what phrases as well as what objectively measured characteristics differentiate those subjects who score high from those who score low on any given variable, among them the independently rated criterion variables of effectiveness, personal soundness, and originality.

Perceptual Performance

Special attention has been given in our assessment programs to the development of relatively simple and quickly administered tests of perceptual and cognitive abilities. Preliminary work in this area suggested that such tests might turn out to be surprisingly good measures of more subtle and more complex aspects of personality. Success in this direction would be a significant extension of quantitative method to the testing of complex functions of personality.

In a test modeled after Witkin's of the perception of the vertical under the distorting influence of a tilted frame, a subject is brought blindfolded into a dark room (Crutchfield, Woodworth, & Albrecht, 1958; Starkweather & Crutchfield, 1954). When the blindfold is removed, he sees before him the illuminated outline of a square (3′ by 3′) which is tilted 28 degrees to the right from the true vertical. Centered within the area of the square is an illuminated rod. By remote control the experimenter can move independently the illuminated square and rod any desired number of degrees from the vertical. The task of the subject is to adjust the remote control so as to bring the rod into a truly vertical or truly horizontal position, overcoming the distorting influence of the only visual frame of reference in an otherwise completely dark room.

Trials are made alternately with the square tilted 28 degrees to the right and 21 degrees to the left of vertical. Under these conditions, in our investigations the mean displacement of judgments in the direction of the tilted frame may for a subject be as great as 28 degrees.

Now let us examine the correlates of this measure of an individual's tendency to be thrown off balance by a distorting visual frame of reference. We have found that those who performed better on this test also earned higher scores on several measures of intelligence. On tests of the ability to reorganize spatial materials and patterns, they scored higher too, and they had more analytical interest and ability. Those who placed the rod most accurately were shown to be the more original, more complex, and more spontaneous subjects on several other tests. They gave evidence of greater ego strength and independence, while those who were most influenced by the distorting frame of reference showed a greater tendency to be involved with and oriented toward others, desiring relatedness with them.

In the test of the perception of the vertical under a distorting visual frame of reference, as in the case of all our tests, we have an opportunity to discover the way in which high and low scorers are differentially perceived by professional psychologists, by examining our adjective and Q-sort descriptions of the two groups. A survey of the Q-items, which statistically differentiate (at better than the 5 percent level of confidence) the twenty subjects with the smallest displacements from the twenty subjects with the largest displacements, confirms and extends the picture which is obtained from an examination of the test correlates of high and low scores.

Q-ITEMS MORE DESCRIPTIVE OF THOSE WITH
LARGE DISPLACEMENTS

Would become confused, disorganized, and unadaptive under stress.

Undercontrols his impulses; acts with insufficient thinking and deliberation; unable to delay gratification.

Is gregarious; prefers interpersonal and group situations to intrapersonal circumstances; seeks relatedness to others.

Is pedantic and fussy about minor things.

Emphasizes oral pleasure; self-indulgent.

Is concerned with making a good impression.

Q-ITEMS MORE DESCRIPTIVE OF THOSE WITH
SMALL DISPLACEMENTS

Is an effective leader.

Manipulates people as a means to achieving personal ends; opportunistic.

Takes an ascendant role in his relations with others.

Highly values intellectual activity.

Is masculine in his style and manner of behavior.

Is self-reliant; independent in judgment; able to think for himself.

Is cold and distant in his relationship with others.

Is concerned with philosophical problems.

Is unaware of his social stimulus value.

The patterns are clear. Subjects who are more influenced by, which is to say thrown off balance by, a distorting visual field are more likely to reveal themselves as weak, dependent, susceptible to stress, and overly concerned with others. Conversely, subjects who are little influenced by the tilted frame are more likely to appear in assessment as intelligent and analytical, capable of insightful reorganization, cognitively rather than socially oriented, spontaneous, independent, and self-contained.

From such findings as these, and from similar results with other techniques of this kind, we are encouraged to believe that we shall eventually be able to tap and to measure complex functions of personality with relatively simple tests of perceptual and cognitive processes, for it is clear that such processes, rather than being purely perceptual or cognitive in character, are vitally embedded in the total complex of personality and can be utilized to reveal significant aspects and dimensions of it.

A Technique Described

As an example of another kind of procedure with which we have worked in our assessment studies, I shall describe a quasi group-interaction technique or situational test designed to study the personality correlates of cooperation.

It is necessary in such expermentation to create a group situation in which the pressures to cooperation are kept constant for all individuals, so that differences in speed and degree of cooperating can be clearly related to personality variables rather than to factors in the group situation.

To this end, a situational test developed by Crutchfield presents to a group of five subjects what appears to be a genuine group-interaction problem requiring the cooperation of all, but is, in fact, a situation completely controlled by the experimenter (1951).

The task is a group bingo game. The subjects sit in chairs facing outward around a circle approximately 16 feet in diameter. A screen prevents each subject from seeing any bingo other than his own. Each is presented with a bingo card and a supply of numbered counters. The group goal is for all subjects to achieve bingos by distributing the numbered counters among themselves; but all requests for counters and all exchanges of them are made through the experimenter who, moving from subject to subject, acts as an intermediary.

The experimenter carries a tray on which subjects can indicate their request for that numbered counter which they may desire on any trial and from which numbered counters, ostensibly placed there by subjects in response to requests from other subjects, can be taken if desired.

Actually, the numbered counters which are indicated as requested as well as the numbered counters which are avaliable are manipulated, without the subjects' knowledge, so that on each round every subject is presented with exactly the same situation.

By manipulation, it is arranged that on the sixth round every subject achieves a bingo, but none knows that the others have. On the next round, each subject is put in a conflict situation which is identical for all. He is asked to give up one of his essential numbers, which presumably some other member of the group needs in order to complete his bingo. He may yield to this request or ignore it. If he ignores it, the request is presented on every successive trial until he finally yields, or, if he never yields, until the experiment is over.

The conflict is obvious: on the one hand, the subject wishes to maintain his own bingo, for with it he has accomplished his part of the group task; on the other hand, he feels obligation to aid other group members in achieving their bingos, without which the group task is unsolved. But the situation is complicated by the fact that the subject cannot be certain that by yielding to the request the problem will indeed be solved, or that by refusing to yield the solution will be blocked.

This artificially created conflict situation reproduces very neatly the dynamics of real-life situations of group cooperation, which typically involve conflicting pressures on the individual.

A subject's score in this situation corresponds to the number of times the request for a numbered counter is made before he yields. Scores range from 1 to 10, the tenth request being the last that is made. Those who have not given up the requested counter by the tenth trial are scored as "never yielded."

There are large individual differences. In one rather typical group of adult subjects, all of whom held positions of considerable responsibility, one-sixth yielded on the first request, but one-quarter never yielded within the allotted ten trials. The rest fell in between these extremes, with a piling-up of yielding on early rather than on late requests.

Our findings with this procedure have been confirmed with many groups.

Those who respond immediately to the request tend to be impulsive, hasty, social and outgoing, undercontrolled, and generally fluid in personality. Those who yield slowly, or not at all, tend to be excessively deliberate, asocial and withdrawn, overcontrolled, and generally rigid and inflexible in personality. Indeed, all of our investigations with this technique indicate that the optimal performance in this situation is to cooperate neither too quickly nor too slowly but to "strike a proper balance between the tendency to defer too readily to the demands of others and the tendency to be stubbornly resistant in the face of group requirements" (Crutchfield & Woodworth, 1954).

Here we have found, as with many other measures, that the best performance and the most desirable traits are not associated with either the extremely high or the extremely low scores on an inventory or in a test situation, but with some range of intermediate scores. Where such curvi-linearity of relationship does exist, any attempt to predict performance in a criterion situation by computing the usual product-moment correlation between test score and performance rating is bound to fail. The lack of recognition of this fact has, in my judgment, contributed to the dismal showing of so many selection and placement programs.

Dimensions of Personal Effectiveness

Turning to a consideration of some substantive findings in our assessment programs, I would first note that to ask what are the characteristics of the effective person is to raise too general a question. More specific questions must be asked: Effective in what way? Effective for what? Effective in what field or profession?

Oversimplifying what is clearly a tremendously complicated set of relationships, we have, as a first approximation, conceived of two variables as centrally determinative of effective functioning: (a) emotional stability or personal soundness, and (b) originality or creativity of thought and action.

Determinants of Personal Soundness

Let us look first at the factors which distinguish those high on personal soundness from those low on this dimension, as summarized by Barron (1954a). Seven main findings emerge.

1. *Health of the subject during childhood.* To a striking degree, the emotionally sound subjects had been healthy in childhood. Their parents were also reported as having excellent health. Subjects low in personal soundness revealed a greater frequency of childhood illnesses and accidents. Barron concludes that "to a certain extent unsoundness in adulthood seems the consequence of tragic circumstance in childhood" (1954a).

2. *Integrity and stability of the home.* The life histories of the Highs tended to be characterized by the continuing presence of both parents with the children in the home during the subject's childhood. The Lows more often had had homes broken by divorce, death, or illness, or by the absence of the father for long periods of time. The Highs tended to come from economically secure homes and from stable communities. The emotional, social, and physical integrity of the family in the case of the Highs appears to have provided them with "the psychological basis for the creation of the most important inner certainty: that both the world and oneself are stable and worthy of trust" (1954a).

3. *Imagery of the father as a respected, successful person.* The Highs almost always described their fathers as having been respected citizens and persons in all ways worthy of emulation. The fathers of the Lows were more often described as failures or not described at all, since they were unknown to the subjects. It appears that the Highs "had throughout their childhood the continuing presence of a model on which they could base their own conception of potent masculinity," while the Lows were "unable to take over the adult masculine role largely because no image of it existed for them to emulate" (1954a).

4. *Affection and close attention from the mother.* Mothers of the Highs appear to have been loving and solicitous of their sons, closely controlling them at home when they were young. Mothers of the Lows appear, as described by them, to have been seductive, demanding, and overprotective. In the lives of the Lows, the mother had been the dominant parent; in the case of the Highs, the strength of the father appears to have been most determinative. In the interview, the Highs often described incidents in which they had rather strikingly emerged from dependence on the mother. Lows, on the other hand, more often appeared to be still dependent to a considerable degree upon the mother.

5. *Presence of other siblings and positive relations with them.* Highs tended to have more siblings and to report more friendly relationships with them than did the Lows. It would appear that, as Barron has concluded, "the family is a community in microcosm, and fullest participation in the larger community in later life should be facilitated by richness of interpersonal experience and flexibility in role-taking, determined in large part by the roles available in the family circle" (1954a).

6. *Athleticism and competitive play.* The Highs were more inclined to be athletic and to enjoy participation in competitive sports. The Lows were less athletic and less interested in competition. In general, the Highs were more robust and vigorous, more physically courageous and characterized by greater stamina than were the Lows.

7. *Sexual expression.* Both Highs and Lows among the Ph.D. candidates had come to sexual expression somewhat later than the subjects in other groups we have studied. At the time we saw them, the Highs more often than the Lows were either married or had maintained for at least a year a steady, intimate sexual relationship with one woman. "In general," Barron concludes, "the Highs were characterized either by mature, easily achieved masculinity or by a solution in which femininity was sublimated, and masculine sex drives were

satisfied in a stable marriage marked by close dependency on the wife; the Lows were characterized either by manneristic femininity—resulting either in homosexual relations or minimal sexual 'outlet'—or by a 'masculinity' which protested too much" (1954a).

These are general trends. They deserve emphasis. Yet we must not overlook the exceptions to them; and it must especially be stressed that, in this study, the final conclusion was that personal soundness is not an absence of problems but a way of reacting to them.

Life History of Creative Subjects

A quite different picture of the early life history appears when we examine the reports of highly original and creative persons. In one group of subjects, an item analysis of the questionnaire responses of those who scored higher on a composite index of originality revealed that they tended to answer "Yes" to the item, "As a child, my home life was not as happy as that of most others," and to say "No" to the statements, "My father was a good man," "I love my mother," "As a child I was able to go to my parents with my problems," "My home life was always happy."

A glance at the life history interview protocols for several of our samples of highly creative subjects reveals that certainly not all of them had the kind of happy family situation and favorable life circumstances so generally thought to be conducive to sound psychological development. Some endured the most brutal treatment at the hands of sadistic fathers. These, to be sure, constitute the minority, but they appear today no less creative than those whose fathers offered them quite satisfactory male figures with whom easy identification could be made. There is, however, some evidence that those who were harshly treated in childhood have not been so effective or so successful in their professions as those who were more gently treated; and there is more than a hint that these subjects have had some difficulty in assuming an aggressive professional role, because, through fear of their fathers, their feminine identifications were emphasized.

It must be stressed that we are here dependent upon the self-reports of our subjects. Those of superior emotional stability tend to report happy early life circumstances, while those outstanding in originality and creativity more often describe a less harmonious and happy atmosphere within the family circle. We know nothing with certainty about the true state of affairs for either group. In reality, the family situations of the two groups may have been indistinguishable. The differences may have resided only in their perceptions and memories of childhood experiences, and yet it is difficult to think that this alone explains the differences in self-report of the more emotionally stable and the more original and creative.

If, as there is some reason to believe, our more creative subjects have overcome adversities and in some instances even profited from them, what, we may ask, are some of the factors determining such favorable outcomes?

Briefcase Syndrome of Creativity

One of the most striking observations we have made is that the creative person seldom fits the layman's stereotype of him. In our experience, he is not the emotionally unstable, sloppy, loose-jointed Bohemian. More often, it is the unoriginal and uncreative person who appears to be artistic, clever, emotional, whereas we discover ourselves using such adjectives as deliberate, reserved, industrious, and thorough to describe truly original and creative persons. Among ourselves, we have jokingly described this cluster of traits characteristic of the creative person as "the briefcase syndrome of creativity"—closer, if you will, to the notion of professional responsibility than to the Greenwich Village Bohemian or the North Beach Beatnik.

The truly creative individual has an image of himself as a responsible person and a sense of destiny about himself as a human being. This includes a degree of resoluteness and almost inevitably a measure of egotism. But over and above these, there is a belief in the foregone certainty of the worth and validity of one's creative efforts. This is not to say that our creative subjects have been spared periods of frustration and depression when blocked in their creative striving, but only that overriding these moods has been an unquestioning commitment to their creative endeavor.

Some Qualities Related to Creativity

Closely related to the above observation is our finding that although both introverts and extraverts are to be found among creative persons, they tend as individuals to be self-assertive and dominant and possessed of a high level of energy. Whether persons recognized as highly creative would show such energetic assertion and dominance in all societies, we cannot say, but in mid-twentieth century in the United States, they do. If such assertiveness is not a prerequisite for their creativeness, it would appear to be at least necessary, if their creativity is to merit recognition and acclaim. But what is most important for their creative accomplishments is the persistent high level of energy with which they work. And this seems possible because their work is also their play. They do not need to retreat from work to be refreshed, but find refreshment and recreation for themselves in it.

Our creative subjects are in the main well above average in intelligence. Their brains have an unusual capacity to record and retain and have readily available the experiences of their life histories. The intelligent person is more discerning (more observant in a differentiated fashion), more alert (can concentrate attention readily and shift it appropriately), and more fluent in scanning thoughts and producing those which meet some problem-solving criterion. Such a person will generally have more information (in the most general sense of the term) at his command.

Furthermore, items of information which he possesses may more readily enter into combinations among themselves, and the number of possible combinations is increased for such a person because of the greater information and the greater fluency of combination. Since true creativity is defined by the adaptiveness of a response as well as its unusualness, it is apparent that intelligence alone will tend to produce greater creativity. The more combinations that are formed, the more likely it is that some of them will be creative.

But intelligence alone does not make for creativity, especially in the arts. Some of our most creative subjects score lower on measures of intelligence than do less creative ones. What seems to characterize the more artistically creative person is a relative absence of repression and suppression as mechanisms for the control of impulses and images. Repression operates against creativity regardless of how intelligent a person may be because it makes unavailable to the individual large aspects of his own experience, particularly the life of impulse and experience which gets assimilated to the symbols of aggression and sexuality. Dissociated items of experience cannot combine with one another; there are barriers to communication among different systems of experience. The creative person, who does not characteristically suppress or repress, but rather expresses, has his own unconscious more available to him and thus has fuller access to his own experience. Furthermore, because the unconscious operates more by symbols than by logic, the creative person is more open to the perception of complex equivalences in experience, facility in poetic metaphor being one consequence of the creative person's greater openness to his own depths.

We have discovered that our creative subjects have interests and hobbies in common with individuals in certain professions and quite unlike those of persons in other fields of endeavor (these being interests and hobbies unrelated to the field of work). For example, creative subjects in a wide range of fields share common interests with such professional people as architects, authors, journalists, and psychologists but have interests rather unlike those of office men, purchasing agents, and bankers, and, understandably enough, quite unlike those of policemen and morticians.

These patterns of interests and hobbies suggest that original and creative persons are less interested in small detail, in facts as such, and more concerned with their meanings and implications, possessed of greater cognitive flexibility, and characterized by verbal skills and interests in, as well as accuracy in, communication with others.

Invariably, we find our creative subjects entertaining both theoretical and aesthetic values, although for many people, perhaps most, there is some incompatibility and conflict between a cognitive and rational concern with truth and an emotional concern with form and beauty. When there is conflict, it would appear that the creative individual has the capacity to tolerate the tension created in him by strong opposing values, and in his life and work, he effects some reconciliation of them.

In the realm of sexual identifications and interests, our creative male subjects appear to give more expression to the feminine side of their nature than do less creative persons. On a number of tests of masculinity-femininity, they score relatively high on femininity, and this despite the fact that, as a group, they do not present an effeminate appearance or make frequent reference to homosexual interests or experiences in their life histories. In assessment, they appear to be quite masculine, though at the same time showing an openness to their own feelings and emotions, an understanding self-awareness, and wide-ranging interests including many which in our society are thought of as feminine.

If one were to cast this into Jungian terms, one would say that these creative persons are not so completely identified with their masculine *persona* roles as to blind themselves to or deny expression to the more feminine traits of the *anima*. For some, the balance between masculine and feminine traits, interests, and identifications is a precarious one, and for several, it would appear that their present reconciliation of these opposites of their nature has been barely achieved and only after considerable psychic stress and turmoil.

This openness to experience, this wide perceptiveness appears, however, to be more characteristic of those with artistic creativity than of those with scientific creativity. If—grossly oversimplifying psychological functioning —one were to say that whenever a person uses his mind for any purpose he performs either an act of perception (he becomes aware of something) or an act of judging (he comes to a conclusion about something), then we might interpret out findings as follows: our artistic creative subjects are predominantly perceptive, while our scientific creative subjects tend to be more evaluative and judgmental in their orientation to life.

In his perceptions, both of the outer world and of his inner experience, a person may tend to focus upon what is presented to his senses—the facts as they are—or he may focus upon their deeper meanings and possibilities. Now there is no doubt that we would expect creative persons not to be stimulus- and object-bound in their perceptions but ever alert to the as-yet-not-realized, and that is precisely what we find to be true of all our creative groups.

The Jungian distinction between introversion and extroversion is well known: the extravert's primary interests lie in the outer world of people and things, while the introvert's primary interests lie in the inner world of concepts and ideas.

It will come as no surprise, I believe, that the majority of our creative subjects are introverts: 80 percent of the female mathematicians, 68 percent of the architects, 65 percent of the writers, and 60 percent of the research scientists whom we have tested are introverts.

Settling upon their life careers came early for some of our creative subjects, one whom at the age of four had decided he wanted to be an architect. Others were slow in coming to a professional identity, not deciding until several years past college upon a professional career. In the case of several of these, the choice of a life profession was made the more difficult by the fact that they possessed so many skills and interests, providing them with the possibility of many quite different careers.

The independence in thought and action which all our creative subjects have tended to show is well illustrated, for example, by the architects' reports upon their college careers.

Academically, they did quite well, averaging about a B. In work and courses which caught their interest, they could turn in an A performance, but in courses that failed to strike their imagination, they were quite willing to do no work at all. In general, their attitude in college appears to have been one of profound skepticism. They were unwilling to accept anything on the mere say-so of their instructors. Nothing was to be accepted on faith or because it had behind it the voice of authority. Such matters might be accepted, but only after the student on his own had demonstrated to himself their validity. In a sense, they were rebellious, but they did not run counter to the standards out of sheer rebelliousness. Rather, they were spirited in their disagreement, and one gets the impression that they learned most from those who were not easy with them. But clearly, many of the architects as students were not easy to take. One of the most rebellious, but, as it turned out, one of the most promising, was advised by the dean of his school to quit because he had no talent; and another, failed in his design dissertation which attacked the stylism of the faculty, ended up by taking his degree in the art department.

Summary

To summarize what at this stage of our researches strikes me most forcibly about the creative persons whom we have assessed, it is their openness to experience, and the fact that they, more than most, are struggling with the opposites in their nature, striving ever for a more effective reconciliation of them, and seeking to tolerate and to bind increasingly large quantities of tension, as they strive for a creative solution to ever more difficult problems which are not set for them but which they set for themselves.

FRANK BARRON

The Psychology of the Creative Writer

I shall present some observations drawn from a study of fifty-six professional writers and ten students in a creative writing course. Of the professional writers, thirty were persons of high reputation as creators of literature, while the other twenty-six were successful commercial writers of lesser reputation. The groups differed not only in reputation, however, but probably also in intent; in general, though certainly there were exceptions, the members of the distinguished group were consciously seeking to create imaginative literature, while the members of the less distinguished group more frequently chose their themes and shaped their compositions for the market.

In this paper, I shall draw upon data primarily from the study of the thirty distinguished writers, most of whom participated in the research as subjects in so-called "living-in" assessments at the Institute of Personality Assessment and Research. Each assessment subject spent three days at the Institute, usually in company with four other writers.

This study was part of a continuing program of research into creative functioning in a variety of professions, and, in fact, was the first study in the series, which now includes mathematicians, physical scientists, architects, and innovators in industry, as well as groups less professionally defined.

Writers were chosen for study for several reasons. First of all, writing is probably the most prevalent and most widely understood form of communication of creative interpretations of experience. Then too, the social impact of writers in disseminating information, influencing public opinion, forming public taste, and advancing culture, is very great. Finally, language itself is so much an expression of culture that a study of its use in any particular society provides a unique field for observation of creative forces in the culture itself.

Creative writing was defined for the purpose of the study as the composition of phrases, essays, stories, poems, and plays which communicate a single individual's interpretation of experience in an original manner. The primary aim of the study was to characterize creative writers in terms of abilities and personality, in order to compare them with various other groups of creative individuals, as well as with less creative writers and with people in general. A secondary aim was to investigate the process of creation in writing, through careful study of an author's work, through intensive interviews with him about his work, and through tests calling for composition, or providing an opportunity for creative perception and expression. Process was taken to include these as the most prominent aspects of the act: the conscious intention of the writer; preconscious or unconscious intentions, and determinants of the conscious intention (such as the psychic needs being served, the origins of fantasy, the meaning of the work in relation to the total life cycle of the writer); the choice of form; significant revisions, discarded beginnings, final self-criticism; unexpected or unplanned changes in intention or form, sudden inspiration; temporal and emotional phases in the process (intensity of work and feeling, blocks, distribution of attention, periods of easy flow, alternation of convergent and divergent phases); feeling of completion or incompletion; attitude toward the work when it is finished.

As you might imagine, trying to do justice to these aims proved a large order. Trying to express the conclusions in appropriate detail has proved also to be a difficult task. In what follows, I shall have to depend on summary statement a great deal, with just a few examples. For most of the statements based on psychometric evidence, the detailed documentation can be found in various publications, particularly my book *Creativity and Psychological Health,* and my essay in the recently published *New Directions in Psychology II.* Material from the projective techniques, the interviews, and uncodified observations in the assessment setting itself cannot so easily be marshalled in the form of evidence that can be checked in other studies, but I shall nonetheless venture a few generalizations from those sources.

Let me begin by presenting a composite Q-sort description of the writers who were assessed. This composite was arrived at in the following fashion: each member of the assessment staff, without discussing the person with any other member of the staff, employed a 100-item set of sentences to describe each subject at the end of three days of assessment. The Q-sort deck was constructed especially to allow the expression of clinical inference. Sorting was on a 9-point scale with forced-normal distribution. Item placements were then averaged for the staff as a whole to arrive at a composite description of each subject, and these item placements were in turn averaged to arrive at a composite description of the group.

When this was done, the five items most characteristic of the group of 30 creative writers were these:

Appears to have a high degree of intellectual capacity.
Genuinely values intellectual and cognitive matters.

Values own independence and autonomy.
Is verbally fluent; can express ideas well.
Enjoys aesthetic impressions; is aesthetically reactive.

The next eight more characteristic items were:

Is productive; gets things done.
Is concerned with philosophical problems; e.g.,
  religion, the meaning of life, etc.
Has a high aspiration level for self.
Has a wide range of interests.
Thinks and associates to ideas in unusual ways; has
  uncoventional thought processes.
Is an interesting, arresting person.
Appears straightforward, candid in dealings with
  others.
Behaves in an ethically consistent manner; is con-
  sistent with own personal standards.

The student writers, as perceived by the assessment staff, differed from these mature creative writers in several important respects. For them, the second most characteristic item was: "Concerned with own adequacy as a person, either at conscious or unconscious levels." Also, highly characteristic were these items: "Is basically anxious"; "has fluctuating moods"; "engages in personal fantasy and daydreams, fictional speculations." One might put this down simply to their youth and the problems of ego-identity with which they were grappling, but I am inclined to think that something more was involved. From subsequent observation of these student writers, I believe that for them writing was much more a form of self-therapy, or at least an attempt at working out their problems through displacement and substitution in a socially acceptable form of fantasy. They fit closely to the sort of picture Freud gives of the poet in his essay, *The Poet and Daydreaming;* the true artist, however, is of another breed, whatever troubles he may have. Of this I shall try to say more later.

Turning now to the psychometric data from the study of the 30 mature creative writers, we find independent confirmation of several of the staff Q–sort descriptions, which had, of course, been given before the tests were scored. The creative writers earned an average score of 156 on the Terman Concept Mastery Test; the mean score of the Stanford Gifted group in adulthood is 137, and the mean score of 343 captains in the United States Air Force is 60, where the standard deviation for the general population is about 30. These values cannot be translated precisely into IQ terms, but I think we can say with assurance that distinguished writers possess quite superior verbal intelligence. This perhaps deserves emphasis, for there has been some tendency to misinterpret one of the findings of several studies by the Institute of Personality Assessment and Research. The finding is that when ratings of the creativity of individuals relative to one another are obtained for all members of a very highly selected and distinguished group of creators, the correlation with measured verbal intelligence is zero, as was true in our study of creative architects. It should not be forgotten that the mean score for the group as a whole is quite high, however. And, of course, because of the extreme restriction of range on the creativity variable, one must expect considerable attenuation in the correlation coefficient. Probably a more accurate estimate of the true degree of relationship between creativity and verbal intelligence is given in the military officer sample itself, where scores on a set of creativity measures correlate .35 with scores on the Concept Mastery Test.

Creative writers also obtain very high scores on the Barron-Welsh Art Scale, their average score being two standard deviations higher than the population average, though nearly a sigma lower than that of successful painters, and lower also than creative architects. Like artists, they prefer figures that are free-flowing, asymmetrical (or at least not boringly balanced), and visually arresting or challenging.

One of the tests constructed especially for this study is the Symbol Equivalence Test, in which the subject is given a stimulus image (verbally) and asked to think up a symbolically equivalent image. "Leaves being blown in the wind," for example, might suggest "a civilian population fleeing chaotically before armed aggression" (i.e., powerless particles blown by the winds of war). Ten test images were presented, and three responses sought to each. The test was scored by typing each response on a separate card for each of the several hundred subjects who took part in the creativity studies, with the name of the respondent removed, and then having three raters independently rate all responses to a given item relative to one another on a 9-point scale on the variable "originality." This was an onerous procedure, requiring more than ten thousand judgments from each rater, but it served to ensure that the results would be free of bias, since neither the identity of the subject nor the sample of which he was a member would be known to the rater. In this test, creative writers proved significantly more original than any other group of creative individuals we studied.

I have reported elsewhere in detail on the results obtained with the Minnesota Multiphasic Personality Inventory and the California Psychological Inventory. To me, the most interesting aspect of these results was the combination of high scores on the pathological indices of the MMPI with a high average score on Ego-strength and high scores also on such CPI variables as Flexibility, Self-acceptance, Social Presence, Achievement through Independence, and Psychological-mindedness. Creative writers scored low on Good Impression, which is to some extent a conformity scale, and below the mean also on Achievement through Conformance, on Communality, and on Socialization.

The really striking differences between writers and other groups, however, lies in the general area of fantasy and originality of perception. One of our interviews was devoted especially to the fantasy life, from day-dreams and night dreams and hypnagogic experiences to transcendental experiences in full and acute consciousness. An unusually high percentage (40 percent, in fact) of creative writers claimed to have had experiences either of mystic communion with the universe or of feelings of utter desolation and horror. The prologues to these experiences were frequently described with considerable vividness in the interview, and this statistic does not represent a checking of "Yes" or "No" to a question such as, "Have you ever had a mystical experience?" Other experiences of an unusual sort were also described, such as being barraged by disconnected words as though one were caught in a hailstorm, with accompanying acute discomfort, or seeing the world suddenly take on a new brightness. A high frequency of dreaming was also reported, as well as a high frequency of dreaming in color, as compared with student groups we have studied.

Most impressive of all, however, was the extent to which motivation played a role, both in the writer's becoming a writer, and in the way in which creative writing served a more general philosophic purpose. Almost without exception, the successful creative writer had had to suffer considerable hardship in holding to his calling. The hardships included criticism from family and friends, periods of intense self-doubt, financial adversity, sacrifice sometimes of important personal relationships, and even public censure or ridicule. By the time the writer got to us, he was past many of these adversities, although poets, even internationally famous ones, were generally living in very modest circumstances, and there were some surprising, to us, instances of distinguished writers of fiction who still had to take other jobs occasionally to stay afloat. One of the poets in our sample, whose work was reviewed recently in the London *Times Literary Supplement* and was hailed as "the most remarkable body of poetry to come from America in the past decade," was earning his living working in a gymnasium and occasionally as a dock worker, while still another was typing term papers for undergraduates. At the other extreme, there were several novelists whose earnings were in the millions of dollars. Yet to all of them the economic question was of secondary importance; this is true of all of our groups of creative individuals. On the Economic value scale of the Allport-Vernon-Lindzey scale of values, creative individuals consistently earn their very lowest score. It is quite apparent that they are playing for other stakes. What then are the stakes, and if there are stakes, just what is the game?

The game, I believe, centers upon the nature of intellect itself and upon the meaning of human life. In reviewing the performance of creative writers on the Symbol Equivalence test, I was struck by the rapidity with which they moved from the commonplace stimulus image to the cosmic metaphor. Their concerns, as shown in projective tests like the Thematic Apperception Test and the Rorschach, are with mythical themes, with death, with great inanimate forces, with the symbolic rather than the literal meaning of shapes and colors. The freedom-determinism question arises again and again, both in their work and their fantasies. The nature of man in relation to the cosmos is the engaging problem.

Here again, however, a difference must be noted between the mature creative writers and the students, who, as I have indicated, I consider to have been using writing for another purpose. The most intolerable of all forms of banality is cosmic banality, and mooning around about death and the cosmos can be a cheap way of getting out of working. Sharpness of detail, validity of characterization, discipline of form, tireless rewriting and shaping up, a touch of the old shoemaker in finding pride in the craft and even in keeping trade secrets; these were among the characteristics of these creative writers, and when I say that their concern is with cosmic issues, I should add that the issues are brought to life in characterization and in language, so that to the reader is given an opportunity to experience through *his* own nature the reality that the writer perceives.

My own conclusion, then, is that creative writers are persons whose dedication is to nothing less than a quest for ultimate meanings. Or perhaps it is not so much that they are dedicated as that they understand themselves to have been elected and have accepted the office. What is enjoined upon them, then, is to listen to the voice within and to speak out. What they speak is to be truth, but it need not be everyone's truth, or even anyone else's. In these essentials, omitting writing as the specific form, I believe creative writers are no different from creative individuals in all walks of life, including those whose business it is to be silent.

CARSON McGUIRE

Creativity and Emotionality

Two years ago, in explaining the transition from infant organism to human being, my task was to account for some of the foundations of emotional development (McGuire, 1960b). The thesis was that we learn emotional reactions in our relationships with significant cultural agents. Close-tied parental figures, mothers and fathers, can be consistent and supportive so as to encourage basic trust, relative independence, increasing competence, warm intimacy, and a sense of "who I am." On the other hand, they may be inconsistent and manipulative to the point that dependence and hidden or thinly-veiled feelings of hostility emerge in the young person. Equally important are the influences of one's peers, persons of about the same age, beginning in the neighborhood play group and extending through the children's world and the age-graded adolescent societies. Being recognized, accepted, and respected as an effective person by one's age-mates seems to lead to a freedom of emotional expression and a self-discipline which are less seldom found among youngsters who are avoided, rejected, or isolated by peers (McGuire, 1956a; McGuire & White, 1957). Finally, teachers and other more remote adults are cultural agents who are relatively impersonal, yet, consciously or unconsciously, have an impact upon young people. They can coerce the young into being passive conformists in

This paper is based upon research findings in the Human Talent Research Project, supported since 1957 by the Cooperative Research Program of the Office of Education, United States Department of Health, Education, and Welfare, and the Mental Health in Teacher Education Project, funded since 1958 by Grant No. 2M–6635 from the Training Branch, National Institute of Mental Health. These and related earlier projects also have been supported by the University Research Institute, the Hogg Foundation, and the Excellence Fund of the University of Texas. In each undertaking, the writer has been associated with Professor Robert F. Peck and a number of other colleagues, especially Earl Jennings and Donald J. Veldman, to whom he is deeply indebted for ideas and findings which have been incorporated in the present paper. (Written 1962)

75

acquiring academic and other kinds of competencies, running the risk of alienating many boys and girls. On the other hand, responsible individuals in the schools, the church, and other youth-serving agencies may encourage some kinds of creativity, even originality, which mark various types of talented behavior (McGuire, 1961a). The influences of these three sets of cultural agents determine whether or not a young person accurately perceives the world about himself or herself, acquires some degree of personal stability with freedom to express feelings, copes with objects and persons as well as ideas in a realistic manner, and eventually achieves personal integrity (McGuire, 1956b).

My contention then, as now, was that the three essential steps in becoming a human being are loaded emotionally. Through self-other relationships, beginning with mother, an infant and child learns to antici- pate the supportive or nonsupportive (rewarding or punishing) responses of the persons to whom he or she relates. By learning a language, the child communicates his expectancies, and, in turn, experiences verbal directions and control by others. Then, instead of acting in terms of feelings of gratification (reward) and fear of deprivation or separation (punishment), the young person acquires more complex motivations. He or she begins to value approval rather than disapproval. Mood states and concepts of self (Orzeck, McGuire, & Longenecker, 1958), as well as observed behavior, begin to be influenced by experiencing some valued kinds of acceptance instead of frequent avoidance, rejection, and isolation. Lack of acceptance, recognition, and respect as a person often brings about a sense of aliena- tion together with antisocial attitudes. Most important are the learning opportunities which establish a sense of identity. They are essential to establishing a personal integrity which fends off the mistrust, self-doubt, pervading anxiety, and guilt feelings of borderline or ineffectively function- ing individuals. Thus, the learning experiences which shape the psycho- social development of the individual in the family, among peers, at school and other places all combine to influence the development of a personality. They shape the delicate balance of amorality, expediency, conformity, irrational-conscientiousness, and rational altruism which not only moti- vates but makes up the character of each person (Peck, 1958; Peck & Havighurst, 1960).

Recent work (McGuire, 1961a; Veldman, Peck, & McGuire, 1961; Peck, 1962) has confirmed and clarified our emerging ideas about the complexities of human behavior, especially the relationship between cre- ativity and emotionality. Apparently, there are at least three separate aspects of intellectual functioning. One of them is divergent thinking, the acquired ability to think of objects, persons, and ideas in new ways, the basis of creativity. All aspects of intelligent behavior, especially creativity or talented behavior, appear to be influenced in unexpected ways by the dynamic elements of our personality makeups which shape our values and attitudes. Not the least important is the alienation syndrome (mistrust, loneliness, pervading anxiety, resentment, pessimism, and self-centeredness). These hidden elements of an unhealthy emotionality may appear not only in antisocial attitudes, often marked by withdrawal or aggressive behavior, but also lowered intellectual performances. Moreover, the ways in which young people respond to pressures placed upon them by parents, peers, and more remote cultural agents in schools, colleges, and other settings has much to do with both intellectual functioning and mental health. The individual who reacts as an effective person, gaining acceptance and maintaining independent action rather than being passively conforming, not only achieves academically and in a later career but also usually turns out to be a healthy human being.

Factors in Persons

What is the evidence for the assertions just made? Some comes from the Human Talent Research Project (McGuire, Hindsman, King, & Jennings, 1961; McGuire, 1961a) and analyses of data just completed. There are at least three dimensions of intelligent behavior which reappear again and again in our computer analyses of the many kinds of tests administered.

1. *Convergent Thinking*—This is the ability to give the appropriate response, to acquire habits of thought and action which are most acceptable within a culture or subculture—for example, lower-class as compared with middle-class value systems (McGuire & White, 1957). Measures of performances on tests of intelligence, abstract reasoning, space relations, and the ability to listen combine to yield this "factor in persons."

2. *Divergent Thinking*—Some, more than others, acquire a capacity to devise new forms, come up with fresh ideas, and see deeper meanings in objects, events, interpersonal relationships, and symbolic materials. Measures, such as identifying unforeseen consequences, seeing unusual uses or problems, and sensing new meanings in common situations, now are used to identify the creative person. Although some teachers and parents value creative children and adolescents, many are uncomfortable with them and prefer a degree of conformity (Getzels & Jackson, 1960).

3. *Symbol Aptitude*—Through familiarity with books and having stories read to them, middle-class children acquire the ability to recognize verbal and printed symbols rather early. Only among underprivileged lower-class boys and girls who stay in school until the ninth grade does this "factor in persons" appear as a common attribute (Duke & McGuire, 1961). Recognition of mutilated words, identification of short words, and ability to make rhymes are three means used to measure aptitude with symbols.

These three "factors in persons," representing relatively independent elements of intelligent behavior, now can be measured with scores from a limited number of tests whose weights are determined by using an electronic computer. Then three composite "factor scores" for each individual may be obtained as the next step. But there seems to be another dimension, *effective intelligence,* which is not as yet directly measurable. Three lines of evidence bear out this proposition. In their sociometric assessments of one another, adolescents clearly respect behavior that is characterized by intelligent action (Peck & Galliani, 1962). Four experienced judges of human behavior, in assessments of projective and self-report data from over 100 college students, each have identified a factor of "creatively intelligent autonomy" (Veldman, Peck, & McGuire, 1961; Peck, 1962) discussed later in this paper. Finally, the most recent analysis of the Human Talent Research Project shows a pertinent "factor in persons" derived from ninth-grade valuations:

4. *Effective Achievement*—Persons high in values for this "factor in persons" are regarded by their peers as individuals "who try to do all kinds of difficult things quickly and well" (works effectively). Moreover, they are regarded as "sort of brains," "have a lot of ability in dealing with words" (verbal), and "put lots of effort into everything they have to do and keep working until successful or realize that things can't be done" (avoids failure).

The many kinds of personality instruments and attitude scales which were administered to the same ninth-grade boys and girls yield only three "factors in persons." Of these, a dimension that corresponds to the alienation syndrome (Davids, 1955) seems to interfere with efficient cognitive processes. The earlier findings in the prediction of talented behavior (McGuire, 1961a) indicate that antisocial attitudes explain lowered academic achievement. This is more evident in the areas involving language and communication than in science and mathematical thinking. In the ninth grade, too, the alienation syndrome appears to have more impact upon academic attainments or forms of creativity than the other two aspects of emotionality, sensitive conformity, and personal stability.

5. *Alienation Syndrome*—Mistrust, pessimism, loneliness, resentment, anxiety, and self-centeredness are revealed in responses to a number of instruments and scales. The most effective combination of self-reports are those wherein the boy or girl favors statements such as "strict discipline develops a fine strong character" (Authoritarian Discipline), "teen-agers gossip too much about one another" (Criticism of Youth), and "when you get right down to it, no one is going to care much what is going to happen to you" (Negative Orientation to Society).

6. *Sensitive Conformity*—Persons high on this dimension respond in ways indicative of emotional sensitivity rather than being tough-minded (JPQ 1), anxiety about achievements expected of them, and acceptance of school and cultural standards (JPQ 8). On the other hand, such individuals are low in aggressive impulses and are neither dominant nor competitive (JPQ 9).

7. *Personal Stability*—Boys and girls high on this "factor in persons" respond negatively to statements like "sometimes I feel things are not real" (Personal Maladjustment), "I don't feel sure how to act on dates" (Social Inadequacy), and "I sometimes feel nervous and ill at ease" (CMAS Anxiety).

Being accepted by age-mates, as well as recognized and respected as an effective person, apparently leads to a freedom of emotional expression. Those who are neither accepted nor respected, who are set back repeatedly by disapproval of elders as well as rejection by or isolation from their peers, frequently acquire feelings of alienation. In general, they do less well than expected in school. Moreover, they less often show the kinds of culturally-valued behavior which are termed talents. Academic achievement and signs of creativity also are inhibited by the development of anti-academic attitudes. On the other hand, a quiet dependent boy or girl who does not acquire an antisocial outlook may be quite successful scholastically. This is most often true, at least in the judgment of many teachers, when he or she conforms and does what is expected. All too frequently, some teachers (and college professors) expect memorization of facts and "regurgitation" of recalled information at examination time. The preferred alternative, of course, is mastery of underlying principles of "generic learning" wherein the learner grasps the structure of what is being taught (Bruner, 1960).

Each of the foregoing additional "factors in persons" appear when age-mates are asked to evaluate one another in terms of sociometric nominations. For example, in our recent analyses of some fifty kinds of such valuations among boys and girls in the ninth grades of four Texas cities, the computer programs grouped together the three overall attributes in addition to what has been described as "effective achievement" above.

8. *Peer Acceptance*—Individuals with high "factor scores" for this dimension most frequently are nominated as "the ones to be with" (peer affiliation), "a person I would like to be like" (behavior model), and "persons who enjoy everything they do and welcome the chance to do new things" (outgoing optimism). These boys and girls, however, do not necessarily "see things to do, and go ahead and do them on their own initiative" (personal initiative).

9. *Antiacademic Attitude*—The young people who are evaluated as having this underlying attribute most often are named as persons who would *"not* ask for help on a school problem" (negative academic model). They are reputed to "find school work a disagreeable chore and resent any kind of study" (dislikes school) as well as "do enough to get by but resent doing anything extra" (gets by). Moreover, such individuals frequently are nominated as one "you might not prefer to be with" (peer rejection) and "not like to be like" (negative behavior model).

10. *Quiet Dependency*—For this underlying element of age-mate assessments, three sociometric descriptions cluster together. Persons generally regarded as high in the attribute are "sort of quiet and they're often forgotten or just not noticed" (quiet ones), "left out of things and often make other people feel uncomfortable" (isolated ones), and "depend upon their parents or older people for advice and look to them for approval" (adult-oriented).

The ten "factors in persons," or underlying dimensions of human behavior, have been extracted and measured by programming a high-speed electronic computer (the CDC 1604 at the Computation Center of The University of Texas) to "boil down" large masses of data on many boys and girls. As indicated in the foregoing descriptions, the data range from different kinds of performances on intellectual tests, to various kinds of self-reports indicative of emotionality and attitudes, to appraisals of one another made by age-mates. The ones summarized in this report have just been derived from analyses of data gathered in the ninth grade from boys and girls in four participating school systems. Nevertheless, they bear a striking resemblance to the "factor variables" developed in the seventh grade to predict various kinds of talented behavior in grade nine (McGuire, 1961b). The research team expects that they are going to combine in a number of ways to predict teacher evaluations (GPA), performances on objective tests of achievement in different subject-matter areas, and different types of talents in the twelfth grade. In some cases, however, school people are undertaking something out of the ordinary to provide new kinds of learning opportunities (educational telesis). Our hope is that the modifications in school organization and in teaching, especially those directed to encourage creativity and reduce the alienation syndrome as well as antiacademic attitudes, are going to "upset" out predictions in such instances. Then, we are going to have evidence that something can be done to encourage talented behavior and individual mental health.

Dimensions of Mental Health

A parallel study of "factors in persons" which appear to describe essential dimensions of the ineffective, borderline, or effectively-functioning individual (McGuire, 1956b) has been undertaken in the Mental Health in Teacher Education demonstration-research project at The University of Texas. Using seven-point rating scales, four psychologists who were experienced in personality assessment analyzed self-report and projective responses of more than 100 college sophomores. The appraisals were based upon data gathered by the Biographical Information Form, the Peck Sentence Completion Instrument, a group Thematic Apperception Technique (stories to 8 pictures), the Bown School Situations Analyzer, and an Educational Issues Questionnaire. Details of the analyses may be found in an article (Veldman, Peck, & McGuire, 1961) and a chapter of a book (Peck, 1962) published by the Hogg Foundation.

Three dimensions of personality, derived from computer analyses of the foregoing assessments, each appear to have a bearing upon overall estimates of mental health. Briefly described, they are:

1. *Relaxed Outgoing Optimism*—Individuals high on this "factor in persons" respond in ways that reveal hopefulness, rather than depression; the capacity to be outgoing with people, instead of being withdrawn or isolated; relaxed composure and comfortable feelings about oneself, in the place of tenseness and pervading anxiety. A few such people may be somewhat proud and self-satisfied, as well as being aware of some difficulties in interpersonal relations. The negative pole of this dimension might be described as *anxious, self-preoccupied pessimism*.

2. *Creatively Intelligent Autonomy*—By and large, persons high on this dimension are capable of expressing deeply-felt emotions, instead of being mild or shallow in their feelings. Moreover, they usually are highly intelligent in their thoughts, judgments, and behavior. This permits them to be self-directing, relatively independent, and creatively productive, rather than dependent persons with low initiative who show little original expression. They are fully aware of reality and able to "be different," in place of being lacking in perception and tending toward conformity. The other pole might be interpreted as *dull, unthinking dependence*.

3. *Self-disciplined Stability*—For this underlying element of mental health, a number of scales go together in the personality analyses. Most important seems to be a controlled, restrained emotionality, in contrast to a loose impulsiveness. Internalized moral principles, together with restrained, calculated evaluations are found, instead of irresponsible actions and impulsive, snap judgments. Feelings tend to be stable and seldom shown, rather than changeable, or even hostile. The opposite pole could be termed *unprincipled impulsiveness*.

These dimensions may combine in several ways to describe the ineffective, borderline, or effective person in elementary and secondary schools as well as colleges.

Personality, Achievement, and Creativity

Studies in secondary schools (McGuire, 1956b, 1960, 1961a) and at the university level (Peck, 1960, 1962) reveal a complex distribution of types of personality in student bodies. In general, ineffectively-functioning individuals have some common characteristics. Intense self-centered desires and conflicting emotions which stem from a hunger for affection, or loneliness, or feelings of hostility arising out of isolation or rejection by parents and peers are common. These young people often show little foresight and self-discipline. Beginning with the family, and then among age-mates and with teachers, they often withdraw from, antagonize, or otherwise alienate both peers and elders. In high school, and especially in college, they encounter academic as well as personal difficulties. Few, if any, show any evidence of creativity other than escapist fantasy or bizarre activities, neither being accepted as talented behavior. The older person who tries to help them to learn a healthier, more productive way of life has to give a great deal of detailed guidance, and, at the same time, provide a sense of security. This can be done with time and perseverance by establishing a sense of trust, listening instead of telling, making sense to them, and providing guidance when the person "rehearses" and tries out new ways of thinking, feeling, valuing, and acting.

The borderline and average types of personalities often tend to be rather dependent, conforming individuals. Some are expedient in gaining their own ends; others, however, blindly act in terms of habits, avoidances, inhibitions, substitute forms of behavior, beliefs, and prejudices rather than thinking and acting for themselves. Although they may be anxious and not see too much meaning in life, these young people seem to have the incentive to keep going, and they have some vision of what a fully realized life might be. Their persistence makes for achievement, but hardly for creative accomplishments. This "middle-majority" of students, to quote Professor Peck (1962), tend to ask overly simple questions of life and expect similar answers. They memorize and recall knowledge rather than attempt to understand underlying principles. Nevertheless, they can be approached on an individual level by genuinely concerned persons, who may awaken a strong response in them. With patience, such young people slowly can be nudged into assuming increasing responsibilities for independent thought and achievement. Some, when their problems are clarified to them and they have opportunities to express themselves, may learn to be creative and certainly quite talented in various areas of behavior.

The effectively-functioning kinds of individuals are not as often found as one might expect. They are strongly-motivated but diversified personalities, whose interpersonal relationships often are as important to them as their intellectual performances and creative acts. In many of them, there are repressed needs and unused potentialities. Some even show signs of unhappy frustrations and conflicting emotions. Nevertheless, the majority gladly experience powerful emotions and find life richer for them. They think clearly and with foresight, show a richness of imagination, and an active creativity which rarely is found among the less effectively functioning young people. By and large, these individuals are predominately rational and altruistic in outlook and action. They are strongly motivated to learn and benefit by a rich library and other resources, enough guidance to put them on the track of information they seek, and the support of at least a few inspiring teachers and (later) professors. When challenged and given the opportunities, they can be, and usually become, really creative individuals who are not afraid of their complex emotions and the problems of living.

Conclusion

Findings to date in our several research programs indicate that an outgoing optimism, creatively intelligent independence, and a certain amount of self-discipline are essential elements of emotional learning, as well as being free to become a creative or talented individual. Of course, some persons develop certain culturally-valued talents in order to compensate for perceived deficiencies or feelings denied to awareness. But this seems to be the exception rather than the rule. In general, the ineffective person not only has conflicting feelings and little foresight, but also exhibits a lack of effective achievement—often accompanied by some kind of alienation syndrome and/or antiacademic attitudes. The "middle majority" tend to memorize and recall rather than think deeply and work and play effectively. The effective person often is characterized by a creative imagination and the ability to display his or her emotions. With further work on the current projects, we intend to untangle some of the complex relationships among dimensions of human behavior which have only been sketched in this report. Then some concrete recommendations can be made.

W. LAMBERT BRITTAIN
KENNETH R. BEITTEL

Analyses of Levels of Creative Performances in the Visual Arts

Introduction

The report which follows is a by-product of a study dealing with creativity in art and the sciences (Lowenfeld & Beittel, 1959). This study made use of controlled performance tasks in the visual arts which were designed for college students who were upper-class and graduates in art and in art education. These performances were to be the criterion against which paper and pencil tests purporting to measure creativity would be screened. In the process of judging the art performances, various levels of quality appeared. These became the data for the discussion which follows.

It might be helpful to describe a theoretical model for research in creativity in the visual arts. This model has five major dimensions, designating in rough manner the kinds of variables felt to be important to the study of creativity. These are: (1) *person variables,* dealing with personality, a past history, etc., of the artist; (2) *process or medium variables,* dealing with attitudes, self-concepts, roles, decisions while working, recall of thought processes, etc.; (3) *environmental variables* including teacher and teaching processes, since the setting is seen largely from an art educational viewpoint; (4) *product and judgment variables,* dealing with the aesthetic quality of art products, etc.; and (5) effect or *outcome variables,* dealing with behaviors attendant on or influenced by the creative process or product in some way. In light of this model for the study of creativity in the visual arts, the present paper must be seen as dealing only with qualitative levels resulting from the judgment process—in other words, only with product and judgment variables.

From *Journal of Aesthetics and Art Criticism,* Fall, 1960, pp. 83–91. Used by permission of the publisher.

Procedure

From a beginning population of sixty-five upper-class and graduate students in the Art Education and Applied Art Departments of The Pennsylvania State University, fifty complete cases emerged on which the following data were collected: fifteen paper and pencil tests attempting to measure creativity, and three performance tasks produced under standardized conditions. The performance tasks were as follows:

1. The graphic interpretation of a suggestive line from a poem. The following instructions were put on tape, as follows: "You will hear a line of poetry. Use the materials you have—black crayon and two sizes of paper, whichever size you would like to use. Express your own reaction or interpretation in any way you wish. Now listen carefully: 'They came slowly up the road through the colorless dawn like shadows left behind by the night. (Pause) They came slowly up the road through the colorless dawn like shadows left behind by the night.' Now begin."

2. A three-dimensional construction from a standardized kit of various materials, such as strips of cardboard, wire screen, yarn, tongue depressors, tooth picks, etc. The student was told he could reshape any material or use any joining of materials he pleased. A piece of corrugated cardboard was designated the base, and participants were asked to make their constructions solid enough so that they could be transported and stored.

3. An unstructured creative project. The instructions were as follows: "Express in two contrasting versions your interpretation of anything you wish, such as lightness and darkness, happiness and sadness, expansion and contraction, high and low, or anything you wish. Your material for this creative performance will be red and black crayon and a choice of two sizes of paper. If the contrast idea can be verbalized, jot the key words on the back of your paper." This performance required two drawings from each participant.

An assumption underlying the use of performance tasks such as these was that they would be reliably representative of an individual's level of creative achievement in the visual arts. A further assumption was that limitation in medium would elicit creative solutions by making it difficult to depend on sensuous appeal or intrinsic worth of materials. Still a third assumption was that a study of creativity in the visual arts would be unreasonably vague or subjective unless it were based on actual performances under aspects of standardization. Every effort was made to give each participant as much time and privacy as he wished while he was working. Participants were assured of anonymity through the use of a code. Prior to the study, the importance of research in creativity was discussed with all participants. The motivation of the group seemed high. Further evidence of this was given by voluntary attendance at the three evening sessions which the study required.

The problem of judging the level of quality of the performance tasks had to be faced. A team of ten judges was used in this study. The judges were either doctoral candidates in Art Education (with a background of experience in teaching and in evaluating art objects, and practice in one or more art media) or were members of the faculty of the Art Education Department at Penn State. There was a general method of judging used throughout the study. Specific criteria were not applied, since previous studies—e.g., Burkhart (1957), and Lansing (1959)—had shown separate criteria for evaluation to be highly interrelated.

The authors are aware of the many problems and dimensions inherent in the judgment problem. Any art judgment takes on itself risk—not of being wrong, since that cannot be demonstrated, but of being relative. This relativity extends to judges, art objects, criteria, environmental conditions, methods of judging, etc. It is part of the concern of the study of creativity in the arts and sciences, of which this report is a by-product, further to investigate judgment variables. Three different judgments of the art performances were made. Judges discussed sensitivity to materials, quality levels, organization and form, flexibility in theme and handling, originality, fluency of ideas, redefinition of materials and viewpoints. The judgments were (1) an overall appraisal of the aesthetic quality of each single art product compared with every other product under the same performance task; (2) an overall appraisal of the degree of creativity shown in the combined set of three performance tasks for each individual; and (3) an overall appraisal of the aesthetic quality of the combined set of three performance tasks for each individual. In addition to these data, assessments of the creativity of the individuals themselves, as evidenced generally in their studio and class work, were obtained from their teachers wherever possible.

INTERRELATIONSHIPS OF JUDGMENTS
OF ART PERFORMANCE TASKS

1. Sum of a person's score of three products judged singly for aesthetic quality
2. Score of a person's three products judged as a unit for creativity
3. Score of a person's three products judged as a unit for aesthetic quality

$$r\,12 = .744 \qquad r\,13 = .843 \qquad r\,23 = .888$$

The average relationship of these judgments is .83. This figure is so high that it was decided to merge the three judgments as the criterion on which level of performance would be based.

Before leaving the process of judging, it should be reported how the judgments were made. The works to be judged were randomly distributed so that they could easily be seen, both singly and in comparison with others. The judges roughly categorized them as high, average, or low. Judges were instructed not to neglect the extremes and to restrict the comparison to the works before them. After this rough grouping, each judge then rechecked his first judgment and further divided each level into three sublevels. Thus a high-high, medium-high, and low-high were obtained for the high level. In all, nine scale points were thus derived.

These scale points became the basis for judges' scores. By summing judges' scores, an ordering of fifty participants from high to low were obtained. The art products of the five individuals ranking highest, of the five ranking lowest, and of the five ranking closest to average, were set aside for intercomparison in the description of levels of performance and "creativity" in the visual arts. These divisions were not set up as standards but to aid in further theory-building and research into creativity. Such a method, it was felt, also centered attention on art expression itself and made it the base for any comparison of creativity in the visual arts. It potentially frees one for nonevaluative descriptions, since the judgment process itself has done the evaluating. It is the reverse, too, from a priori designation of levels. Here objects felt to be capable of comparison fall into levels which one can attempt to describe.

Description of Three Performance Levels

An examination of these three levels showed some surprisingly marked differences. These differences were primarily intangible, yet a more intensive examination revealed certain characteristics typical of each level. For greater clarity those characteristics which tend to be more objective will be listed first—(1); those qualities which were more subjectively arrived at will be listed next—(2); and last will be mentioned the overall atmosphere which permeated each of the three groups—(3). This last is the most difficult to describe.

1. A cursory examination of the three levels showed that the products of the low level appeared at once simpler and more sparse in feeling, as compared to the more complicated and fuller products of the high level. The drawing examples of the "lows" tended toward a linear quality. That is, the objects and forms depicted were identified from the rest of the area of the paper by a constant though not necessarily continuous line. In the "highs," this linear quality was not evidenced, although it did appear at the middle level.

The low level was also characterized by a symmetrical arrangement of shapes on the drawing surface. In contrast, the high level's drawings appeared lacking in any attempt to equibalance areas. The "highs" had a variety between the performances of one person; that is, the organization of the drawings differed, the pressure of the crayon was not consistent, and each drawing had textural quality which differed from drawing to drawing. The "lows" in some cases not only lacked this variety, but tended to repeat an almost schematic quality.

The three-dimensional constructions of the "lows" were primarily composed of flat shapes. These shapes were used with a minimum of cutting or reshaping from the materials as originally received. The total construction appeared to have no discernible principle of organization, and the spaces between the forms were randomly distributed. The middle level showed some distinctive characteristics in the three-dimensional performance. The forms, somewhat more redefined, were clustered into one unit, or what might be called a monumental form. This appeared in contrast to the "highs," who tended to have several related subsections; at first glance, this type of organization appeared more closely related to the more disorganized constructions of the "lows." However, the "highs" altered the materials; in some cases, there was a consistency of shapes: that is, a penetration of forms—a principle which was not seen in any example on the lower levels. The spaces between forms were utilized by being drawn within, or organized as empty shapes between forms. This awareness and use of negative space was one of the clearly observable differences between the high level and either of the other two levels.

2. Some of the differences between levels are less discernible. These differences are not as concerned with the physical use of materials and the shape of the forms, but rather reflect differences in the organization, requiring a more subjective analysis. For example, the middle level had a lack of spontaneous feeling, a sense of tightness in the forms, as though these had been learned and were being reapplied in a new situation. The "lows'" products had an empty feeling, a feeling of impoverishment, a sparsity of ideas; in contrast, the "highs" had neither the empty feeling, nor the presentation of tight or learned forms, but rather a spontaneity of expression.

A spontaneity of expression could be seen in the use of materials, where the high level tended to exploit the medium. For example, the drawings of crayon were obviously crayon; the crayon was used as a waxy drawing substance which responds well under pressure. There was use of other than the point, and the ability of the crayon to glide over the surface easily lent a sense of movement. The middle level seemed to understand the medium and utilize it to some extent for expressive purposes; but the "lows" were in great contrast in their use of materials. The crayon could have been *any* drawing material for these pictures, for it was used merely as a means to put the object portrayed down in visual form; a substitution of pencil or chalk for the crayon would probably not have affected the drawing very much. It seemed as if the artist were unaware of his instruments.

In the "lows," the principal subject tended to be isolated from the portrayed environment and did not seem to be affected by it. For example, in one picture, miners and houses were somewhat removed one from the other; the miners were marching down the center of the paper and the houses were going about their own business of standing in straight rows. Not only was the principal subject not affected by the environment, but the environment was not affected by the subject—that is, either the subject or its environment could be replaced by other objects in the composition and there would be no resulting confusion. It was as though the person or persons did not count in the environment.

The principal subject among the "highs" was less distinctly portrayed, and the figure or figures tended to be a part of the environment. For example, one drawing of faces was not faces as isolated objects but rather a pattern of faces in which the negative space was utilized as both background and as a shape holding more eyes.

The "highs" also had some characteristics along the same vein in the three-dimensional constructions. There was a tension between forms: in some cases, actual tension, with string or wire strung between shapes; in other cases, the tensions were created purely visually, as with forms in opposite planes or at divergent angles. Some of the shapes of this level were pierced by other shapes, or areas were cut out so that other forms could be seen through them, giving a sense of transparency.

The "lows," in their three-dimensional constructions, paid most attention to positive form: that is, the spaces between the shapes tended to be nonintegrated, free floating, and unused. This related rather closely to the use of space as seen in the two-dimensional work of this level.

3. Differences between the three levels—high, average, and low—were also sensed in ways which could not be attributed as easily to the use of the materials. Whether these differences were essentially in the observers and not in the products could be argued; but at any rate, it may be important for the purpose at hand to attempt analysis of this mood or atmospheric quality.

The "lows'" products gave a feeling of being depersonalized. The self seemed removed from involvement with that which was portrayed. It seemed almost as if the pictures were drawn without any feeling for that which was being drawn, as if the artist were using these forms and shapes as schema to evade the issue of facing one's self. This evasion gave the drawings a cold, empty, shallow atmosphere which was not evident in either of the other two levels.

The middle level's drawings included the self. Here there was evidence of direct experience with the subject matter. Their drawings clearly showed an attempt at putting a direct experience on the paper, and the observers could clearly identify the mood, whether gay, sad, stormy, or gloomy. In some cases, what might be identified as the artist himself was drawn involved in the struggle with passion or walking down the road to happiness.

The "highs" were quite different from the other two and almost on a different plane. Here the artist no longer seemed to be portraying a mood;

but rather the picture, or possibly the artist himself through his medium, was the mood. Here there seemed to be no attempt to portray an event, such as a casket with a candle at each end for death as seen in the lowest level, or even narrowing black circles enveloping the self as in the middle level, but rather the essence of death seemed to be on the paper itself.

To illustrate this point a bit further, a tree in the low level would be portrayed as a general tree, a schematic tree, a tree which looked like a tree; the middle level's tree would be a particular tree, one with which the artist had had some feeling of involvement, with the leaves singled out for careful study, or the patterns of branches most significant; the high level's tree would not be a picture of a tree but would be "treelike" in itself, the surface of the paper giving a feeling of roughness as in bark or being leaflike in quality.

The low level's products were situational, sentimental. There seemed to be no feeling of excitement in them, there was no sense of exploration with either the subject matter or the materials, no risks were taken nor was there any risk even sensed. The middle level's products gave a feeling of a limited awareness of discovery in exploring materials. Their products relied heavily upon learned "good" forms or "proper" methods. It was as though a risk was sensed, but very little risk was taken. The top level seemed to give up visual controls of the materials, but rather the motivating idea and the materials freely influenced the product. Experimentation and exploration with the medium and probing, feeling, and weighing its uses for expressing the theme seemed foremost. In the high level, then, risk was taken openly.

Inferences from the Three Performance Levels

In the description of levels above there was no consideration given to whether the products were done abstractly, conventionally, or naturalistically. The type of art was not considered in either the judging of the art products or in the analysis of these levels of performance. However, an examination of the levels showed that the "highs" tended toward a more abstract type of art. In terms of what we know historically about the field of art, those artists who stand out as being exceptionally creative were not traditionalists in their own time. For example, Courbet, Constable, and Manet were *avant-garde* in participating in the conquest of natural realism in painting. It would seem logical, then, that the type of representation which characterized the high level would tend toward the *avant-garde* within our own society. Although the bases for judgment of creative products may change from culture to culture or from time to time, the essence of these judgments or their comparative positioning might remain much the same.

It might then follow that the products of an artist are only a reflection of his thinking and that the creative artist will question the established standards of his time, will stretch the limits of acceptance, and may be responsible for a new direction. The assumption that art products are an indication of the thinking of the people involved is not a new notion; certainly, the behavior and expression of any person is the outward manifestation of inner compulsion and mental processes. The field of projective psychology relies heavily upon isolated samples of behavior and the transferral of thought to object. In this light, a comparison of the three levels of performances within our study, and the use of these performances as an indication of differences in inner compulsion and mental processes between the levels, may be of help in assessing what basically differentiates them. Following this line of reasoning for purposes of theory-building, the drawings and the three-dimensional construction take on new meaning, and the comments relative to the differences in the three levels of performances now might be related to differences in behavior of the artists.

1. As mentioned in the "Description of Three Performances Levels" above, the high level's products were more complex, asymmetrical, containing shapes within shapes, and having a lack of sameness between products. The artist then might be characterized by a liking for variety and change. He may be one who is not happy within a static balance but seeks disorder, strives to change the status quo, does not conform easily to restrictions. He may also enjoy remaking his environment, both physically and socially. He can function with a number of different goals in mind, and may enjoy the pursuing of an idea or notion beyond the obvious solution, and feels free to function when there are no restrictions to his thinking or behaving.

One of the clear differences between the products of the three levels was in the use of negative space by the "highs." Their three-dimensional constructions utilized transparencies, and there was tension, either visual or actual, between the related forms. In terms of the artist, this might indicate that he is more aware of all aspects of a problem, more sensitive to the intangible and to the effect of the unconscious. He is probably not two-value-oriented, but is sensitive to the intervening shades fluctuating between black and white or can see good in bad. He may be aware of others' feelings and not be afraid of "silence." He probably is unwilling to rule on what is or what is not significant beforehand or even during the process of any action. His values tend to emerge within the context of a situation rather than be predetermined by tradition. He does not like authoritative action by others nor by himself, but can tolerate divergent opinions and unrelated goals.

The products of the "highs" showed a greater spontaneity and an inter-relationship of various parts of a composition. A person from this level might be spontaneous in other ways in his behavior, expressing himself freely without fear of consequences, be able to talk about a subject without a prepared speech. He is not upset by disarrangement and enjoys the unexpected.

2. The middle level gives us a different picture and should, on the basis of our analysis, show some rather sharp contrasts in theoretical behavior on the part of the artist. His three-dimensional construction tended to be monumental or forced into a unit. This attempt at fitting artistic behavior into a predetermined form might show a fear of letting parts have their own autonomy. The forcing of action into a pattern may cause certain rigidity in thinking, a striving toward one goal, or forcing attention toward one answer and ignoring side issues or other contributions.

The middle level's drawings showed a sense of self-involvement by the inclusion of what could be surmised as the artist in the drawings. In other types of behavior, this might show up as a person getting personally involved in issues and problems, possibly at times to the extent of losing the central theme of a problem or the seeing of alternatives, and taking successes or failures personally and blaming himself for actions beyond his control. The drawings of the middle level had a tightness of form and a repetition of learned shapes. This reliance upon "safe" patterns showed a certain fear of exploring the unknown. It may be that the external accoutrements of status within our society become important, and a pattern of proper behavior or accepted behavior is expected. Prestige becomes important, as does finding one's own cog in the wheel.

3. The low level's drawings showed a strong reliance on outline and a literalness of theme. The strong linear quality itself might suggest a liking for distinct limits to problems or actions, a liking for responsibilities and for jobs to be clearly defined. Feeling more comfortable working within restrictions or under authority might relate to the literalness or obviousness of theme. Both are conditions where clear purposes or limited concepts or ideas can be dealt with, one at a time.

The "lows'" products tended to be symmetrical, with attention paid to equibalancing areas. This liking for balance, or order, for everything in its proper place, may tend to close off the influences of accepting the accidental or tend toward the repression of natural impulses.

This level tended to use materials unchanged as they were presented to them for the three-dimensional construction, and in their drawings seemed totally unaware of the background areas or negative space within their compositions. The acceptance of materials, events, objects, or positioning as unalterable or uneffected by an individual's effort seems to relate to some points above. The unawareness of negative space or less conscious ideas in the artist's mind could relate to a clear differentiation between that which is important and that which is not, or that which is good and that which is bad. This may be a fear of examining the intangibles, or of allowing one's self to think beyond the immediate problem, or of considering the "irrelevant" as important.

The low level's products were sparse, lacked spontaneity, and the principal subject matter was isolated from the rest of the composition. This may show a lack of many ideas or the fear of committing one's self beyond the limits of a problem. Such a person would not be able to express himself easily or spontaneously, but would hesitate to let his inner feelings be known and might revert to accepted patterns or behavioral clichés to hide his emotions. Except on a superficial level, there is little real interaction between the self and the environment, and this may be related to a fear of taking or accepting risk, a fear of others' opinions and criticism so that these are avoided, and even the possibility of a fear of the self.

Discussion

In the above material, there are striking similarities to some of the writings of others bearing upon the characteristics of creative people. Barron (1958) gave a series of tests to doctoral candidates who had been rated as to their originality. In making selections from various drawings, the people judged as original were inclined to like the apparently unbalanced. In completing line drawings and in constructing mosaics, these same original individuals tended to introduce asymmetry and complexity into their drawings and mosaics. He concludes that creative individuals are more at home with complexity and disorder than other people are.

Burkhart (1957) and Michael (1959) give some support to the assumption that the highly creative are more process- and medium-oriented. Burkhart found that the self-concept of the highly creative student included self-descriptive words like: free, involved, self-seeking; whereas such words were lacking in the low student. Michael found trial-and-error, instead of a predetermined approach, typical of those students producing works of high quality.

Maslow (February, 1958) describes creativeness in what he calls self-actualizing people as being spontaneous, effortless, a kind of freedom from clichés and stereotypes. His subjects differed from the average in not being frightened by the puzzling or the unknown, and were often attracted by it. Maslow claims that the basic difference between creative people and average people is that the more creative lacked fear of the unknown or of themselves. Average and neurotic people, he believes, control and suppress much that lies within them.

Ehrenzweig (1953) believes that the source of inspiration for the creative person is stored in his unconscious. In terms of our description, the high level tended to be more sensitive to the unconscious while the low level reverted to patterns of behavior and had fear of their own feelings.

Although this study is theoretical in nature, it may have some practical value in helping establish some bases for an operationally feasible research project into creativity in the arts. Terms coming from the performance levels directly may have more relevance to artistic creativity than those borrowed from research in other disciplines. In essence, the subjects for the larger study of which this is only one portion, were already demonstratively creative; that is, they would tend to cluster at the upper end of the normal curve because of natural forces operating to discourage the less artistically creative before they reached upper-class and graduate level. It is quite interesting, then, to see that even in this limited range such marked differences were discernible. We are, of course, making several assumptions which we are in no position to defend. The first is that a small sample of performances under controlled conditions with limited materials would indeed be a stable index of creative output. It may be that less controlled conditions or a larger sample of products over a greater period of time would add to the study. Another basic assumption is that the products are only an indication of the thinking of the people involved. Longitudinal studies within the arts and relevant research outside the arts may clarify the operational and theoretical value of these assumptions.

J. P. GUILFORD

Intellectual Factors in Productive Thinking

Two years ago, at the first Conference of Productive Thinking, I proceeded on the assumption that productive thinking should be defined in terms of the two categories of productive-thinking abilities in the structure-of-intellect model (Guilford, 1959a; Guilford & Merrifield, 1960). In the context of intellectual abilities, productive thinking seemed to be well defined in terms of the factors in the areas of divergent production and convergent production, the abilities within those two categories differing in terms of the basic *kinds* of information involved, on the one hand, and in terms of the kinds of *products* of information generated, on the other.

I still think that, for a defensible *psychological* definition of productive thinking, this conception is sound. From a scientific point of view, it is a good definition, because it is empirical, since each factor is empirically based and can be defined by pointing to a unique class of tests measuring ability in common. In the course of the Conference, it became apparent that in the context of education, a broader conception was not only current but also necessary. And there is the much larger context of everyday life, in which a broader conception of productive thinking is also needed.

During the past two years, in part due to the stimulation from the first Conference, I have given considerable thought to questions of how the concepts in the structure-of-intellect model might serve to illuminate some of the problems connected with thinking and learning in general. I have tried to integrate the information and thinking derived from the factorial point of view with the contributions from other sources. One result has been a long chapter on theory of creative thinking, to appear in a book entitled *Theory and Data in Psychology,* edited by Helson (Guilford, in press, a). What I have to present to you here is in part a preview of that chapter, with some appropriate modifications.

A paper prepared for presentation at the Second Conference on Productive Thinking, conducted by the Project on the Academically Talented Student, of the National Educational Association, May 2–4, 1963, in Washington, D.C.

95

Creative Thinking and Problem-Solving

In these days, "creativity" is a magic word; it catches immediate attention. Inevitably it comes up in the context of the subject of productive thinking. I note that it was not used in the title for this Conference, for which some commendation is perhaps in order, for the term is a kind of "catchall" label, much too loosely employed. Only when we break it down into its several manageable implications are we able to do much creatively about it.

We gain some degree of clarity by discriminating among several things that come under the label. We can define "creative potential" as a collection of abilities and other traits that contribute toward successful creative thinking. Creative thinking is distinguished by the fact that there is something novel about it; novel, that is, to the thinking individual. The degree of creativity shown is directly proportional to the degree of novelty.

Another very common use of the term "creativity" means creative production. Production is output. In this connection, we can make two further distinctions. Output may be in the form of tangible products, such as a poem, a scientific theory, a machine, a musical composition. Some writers also insist that the tangible product be socially worthy or useful. This adds the requirement of value judgments, something that is outside the scope of basic science, but is significant in the spheres of technologies that deal with human affairs.

To the psychologist, there can be creative thinking even when there is no tangible product. There are always some products of thought, and it does not matter whether they are expressed or not. They can still be detected in a number of ways. In the approach of behavioristic psychologists, there has been a great reluctance to tackle the important problems of implicit behavior, but that is precisely what we have to do, in order to discover the most important things that occur in the form of behavior, in the human organism, at least. Our approach must be largely indirect and inferential. This does not mean that we cannot make observations, for we can. If we cannot get a look inside the organism's psychological functioning, it must be remembered that the physicist is no more able to get a look inside the atom. The observation can be as objective in the one case as in the other.

The "products of thought" come in six varieties, as recognized in the structure-of-intellect model—units, classes, relations, systems, transformations, and implications. Incidentally, there are a number of ties to the conclusions of Piaget at this point. Piaget insists that the laws of thinking are the laws of logic, and his link with logic is through the concepts of classes, relations, and implications. As is true in logic, he more or less takes units for granted. When he speaks of schemata and groupings, he is probably referring to a number of the six kinds of products that I mentioned, including systems. There is nothing that I see in Piaget's reporting that corresponds to transformations, although some of you who are better acquainted than I am with Piaget's work may find a parallel.

STAGES OF CREATIVE PRODUCTION

Beginning with Graham Wallas (1926), we have had a commonly accepted, general description of a complete act of creative production in terms of four familiar stages—preparation, incubation, illumination, and verification. Wallas was not intending to make a serious contribution to the theory of creative thinking; his objective was to help his readers think more creatively. The breakdown was a matter of convenience in dividing up the total chain of events for the purposes of closer examination and discussion.

Another breakdown in the form of a temporal sequence of events was proposed by Rossman (1931), after his study of over 700 productive inventors. His seven stages are:

1. Observation of a need or difficulty
2. Analysis of the need
3. Survey of all available information
4. Formulation of objective solutions
5. Critical analysis of the solutions
6. The birth of the new invention—the idea proper
7. Experimentation to test out the idea

Except for the reference to incubation in the Wallas list, the two lists are very similar. For our purposes here, the most striking thing about them is their resemblance to a number of sets of hypothetical descriptive stages proposed for the rough description of problem-solving, from that of John Dewey (1933) on down to the present. Dewey recognized five stages:

1. Recognition of a problem
2. Analysis of the problem
3. Suggestion of possible solutions
4. Testing of the consequences
5. Judgment of the selected solution

The similarity between the stages in problem-solving and those in creative production are sufficiently similar to justify the expectation that the same theory will just about cover both. After all, there is no problem for an individual unless he appreciates the need for thinking that has some novel aspects. If he is completely ready to cope with a situation, of either internal or external origin, there is no problem; no change in behavior is needed to cope with it. The change in behavior is the novel aspect of his response.

Changes in behavior that come about through coping efforts and that endure for any appreciable length of time are in the category of learning. Thus, we have some logical, intimate psychological connections between creative production, problem-solving, and learning (Guilford, 1960). I think it is safe to say that all problem-solving that is genuinely problem-solving is creative. It is not so clear that all creative thinking is problem-solving, although a very high percentage of it can be so interpreted. At any rate, the expression "creative problem-solving" seems to be redundant.

Problem-solving is creative; there is no other kind. Only if we are in the habit of restricting creative thinking to the select few individuals who have socially recognized talents for creative thinking would this proposition not be true. To make such a restriction goes against the principle that abilities and other traits are commonly distributed in the general population; that there is continuity of talents from great to small; and that the psychology of thinking has one set of principles that applies quite generally.

As we consider the operations of creative thinking and of problem-solving at closer range, it is even more clear that the two phenomena are made of the same cloth, as I hope to show. Understanding the one helps to understand the other. Although the traditional steps of Wallas and of Dewey and others take us only a very short way toward the understanding of either phenomenon, it is convenient to follow those steps, or stages, in further discussions. The two phenomena can be conveniently embraced in the single term "productive thinking."

At the Conference two years ago, I was struck by the fact that considerable productive thinking was recognized as playing a potential role in the process of understanding. This conception was notable, because I have often defined the intellectual abilities concerned with the operation of cognition as those pertaining to understanding or comprehension. I have sometimes said that a cognitive ability (using the term "cognition" in the narrower sense, in the structure-of-intellect theory)[1] is an ability to know or to recognize or to discover a kind of information, where the kind of information is specified by its kind of content and its kind of product. The use of the term "discover" in this connection should be restricted to instances of prompt or immediate discovery. Where cognition is not immediately forthcoming, some productive operations, in the form of divergent or convergent thinking, or both, may well be required. Realizing that one needs a better understanding of something is in itself a recognized problem. Hence, the productive thinking that is aimed at improved understanding also comes under the general heading of problem-solving.

MOTIVATION FOR PROBLEM-SOLVING

Behind all problem-solving, as behind all behavior, there are motivating influences. Sometimes the problem appears to arise entirely from within the motivating condition of the individual; the state of his needs and his drives. In psychoanalytical contexts we are told that a poet, painter, or other artist is trying to solve a personal problem (Kris, 1953). His art product expresses both his conflict and his solution to his problem. Other problems arise by virtue of the interaction of the individual with his environment. Any utilitarian motive whatever may be the source of recognition that there is a problem and of the effort directed toward solving it.

From different sources among writers there is a growing recognition that

---

[1] In contrast to the usage of some writers, who refer to any intellectual ability as a cognitive ability.

in addition to the more obviously utilitarian motives, there is a unique source of drive for problem-solving; a drive of an intellectual nature; a drive that appears to reach its fulfillment merely through the mastery of problems. E. L. Thorndike (1931) suggested that, in general, satisfaction comes from normal functioning of any of our equipment, including our brains. From questioning his inventors, Rossman (1931) concluded that for many of them a dominant driving force was the thrill of surmounting difficulties or solving tough problems. More recently, White (1961) makes a case for the existence of a drive for gaining competence. Maslow (1958) and Carl Rogers (1962) speak less definitely of a very pervasive drive that they call "self-actualization." From all this there comes, like a welcome breath of fresh air, a belief that children and others can be motivated by needs other than those of hunger, thirst, pain, and sex; that they can learn to know and to value the sweet taste of intellectual achievement.

A Transfer Theory of Productive Thinking

Although a theory of productive thinking must give due attention to the motivational aspects, the understanding of the nature of productive thinking must come largely through the study of its intellectual aspects. It is these aspects that we must know about, if we are to bring about the conditions that encourage development of the skills involved in productive thinking, and if we are to be able to tell others how they may improve in productive-thinking operations. In this paper, most of my attention is, therefore, given to the intellectual aspects, attempting to see just where the factors of intelligence fit into those operations, and how the illumination that they provide dovetails with information from other sources.

The Wallas and Dewey stage concepts were obviously designed to describe productive thinking that deals with problems of major importance and that require a relatively large amount of time for solution. Such problems are not typical, for in everyday life many problems are solved in very short times. In the latter instances, there is usually no opportunity to observe anything like the successive steps. Perhaps they do occur, but in greatly telescoped form. At any rate, it would seem desirable to have a theory of productive thinking that takes care of all instances, whether of short, medium, or long temporal length. The steps observable in slow motion pictures, so to speak, are implied in cases of much shorter duration. With this assumption, I shall follow the typical steps as a principle of organization of my discussion, with the belief that it has wide application.

THE ROLE OF INFORMATION

The stage of preparation, as Wallas calls it, includes the first two steps, recognition of a problem and analysis of the problem, in Dewey's conception, and includes Rossman's first three steps: observation of a need or difficulty, analysis of the need, and survey of information. In line with the very first steps of Dewey and Rossman, factor analysis shows a unique ability that has been called "sensitivity to problems." In the structure of intellect, the factor has been defined as the evaluation of semantic implications. The notion that an operation of evaluation comes first is congruent with a major thesis of Miller, Galanter, and Pribram (1960) to the effect that in any units of behavior, first comes a test of the situation, in which the organism finds that the situation calls for action or it does not. If it calls for action, a problem is sensed.

Wallas regards the stage of preparation an information-gathering period, and Rossman speaks of the survey of information. These statements properly imply the importance of information in the creative process. Although we may agree with Einstein to the effect that imagination is more important than knowledge, we are forced to admit that information is essential. The information that we can use is offered to us by the immediate environment, is sought after by us in the environment, or is recalled or retrieved from our memory storage. The chances are that the retrieved information is not exactly in the same form or is not recalled by the associated context in which it was learned or committed to storage. At this point, association principles become inadequate, if we think only in terms of contiguity. Novel thinking means that the retrieved information is to be used in a new form or in new connections, and this means transfer learning. This line of thinking is the key to what I call the "transfer theory" of productive thinking. Information recalled for use in new form or a new connection is a phenomenon of transfer. A thing learned in certain connections is torn out of the context in which it was learned, for use in some new context.

Psychologists' and educators' attitudes toward the phenomenon of transfer have gone through many swings of psychological fortune and misfortune, as we all know. From the extreme position of "formal discipline," there was a swing almost to the opposite extreme of belief in specific learnings only, some sixty years ago. Gestalt psychology brought us back from this extreme position, but has failed to exert much influence on the matter. In spite of much research in recent years showing much evidence of transfers of relatively broad scope, learning psychologists have more or less turned their backs on the evidence, largely because the findings play havoc with their neat S-R theories.

Taking a cue from factor-analytic theory, I should say that in most learning there exists different levels of actions on the specificity-generality continuum. There are general, transferable aspects, at different levels of generality, and there are specific, nontransferable aspects. Among the transferable aspects are the unique, generalized, intellectual skills, which become known as factors or "primary mental abilities," to use Thurstone's terminology. Also, among the transferable components are particular products of information, which I substitute for the time-honored concept of association, in my informational point of view in psychology (Guilford, 1961 ab).

IDEA-GENERATING PHASE OF PRODUCTIVE THINKING

The most interesting and sometimes the most spectacular phase of problem-solving is that during which possible solutions are generated. The flashes of genius that occur during this phase catch the popular eye. Insights of lesser glamour are numerous and also need to be accounted for. The vast majority of generated ideas are insights of such insignificant note that only the thinker himself can appreciate them. They hardly justify Wallas's label of "illumination"; but this is a matter of degree.

In jumping to the solution-generating phase, we have passed over the stage of incubation, which only Wallas mentions. The rather unexpected and sudden emergence of some of the best ideas after periods of little or no work and no apparent progress has naturally led some theorizers to say that we have unconscious minds or preconscious minds that work things out unbeknownst to us. This is a charming but futile substitute for an explanation. It tells us nothing about how the thinking was actually executed. The problem of discovering what happens is still with us, if we have an ounce of scientific curiosity; we cannot dodge the responsibility that easily.

It is logically possible to treat problem-solving during rest intervals in the same category with spaced practice in learning, especially when we regard problem-solving as learning. It may be that the same hypotheses that account for the effects of spaced learning in memorizing or in sensori-motor practice will also account for the effects of incubation in productive thinking. Space will not be taken to go into those hypotheses here; they are discussed in standard textbooks on learning (McGeoch & Irion, 1953). The phenomenon of incubation in problem-solving is also probably in the same category as the experience everyone has in trying to recall a person's name that refuses to come. It comes very readily an hour or a day later, even in the absence of any immediate cue.

THE ROLE OF FLUENCY

Factor analysis indicates three kinds of fluency. In the verbal or semantic category of the structure of intellect are ideational fluency, associational fluency, and expressional fluency, which represent efficiency of calling out of memory storage items of information to fulfill certain specifications. The kind of products retrieved are units, related correlates, and systems, in relation to the three types of fluency, respectively. There are also three parallel fluency abilities for dealing with figural information and three for dealing with symbolic information predicted by the model, all but one of which have been demonstrated by factor analysis.

In connection with problem-solving, Duncker (1945) and others propose that the problem, as understood, sets up a search model or models. The problem is recognized as calling for information meeting certain specifications. A fluent thinker can run through the logical possibilities or logical alternatives in quick fashion. His process of retrieval works efficiently. In a test of ideational fluency, the search model is provided by the item, for example, the instruction to name things that are white, soft, and edible. In a test of associational fluency, an item may ask the examinee to produce words that mean almost the oppostie of the word "dry." In a test of expressional fluency, the search model calls for the production of sentences that meet certain restrictions. The search model is thus a good self-cueing device of a kind that we use constantly.

In spite of the fact that we often hear disparaging remarks about persons who have good memories, in view of the need for stored information we see the importance of having good retention as well as good retrieval of information when we want it. From the structure of intellect, we expect to find as many as 24 different memory abilities. These have to do with goodness of retention. The production abilities, divergent and convergent, have to do with the ease of retrieval of stored items of information. If we would improve this aspect of problem-solving, we need to find the conditions during the committal to storage and also during retrieval from storage that facilitate operations in idea generation.

Historically, most of the experimental work on memory has been on the learning stage. By contrast, very little has been done on recall of information. In view of the importance of recall for productive thinking, it is time that more concentrated effort be given to that phenomenon. Some principles of recall have been derived from research by Bousfield and his associates (1954), and they have some interesting parallels in connection with performance of examinees in taking fluency tests. There is not enough space to go into those parallels here.

THE ROLE OF FLEXIBILITY

Factor-analytic studies have revealed three distinct types of flexibility vs. rigidity in thinking. In the divergent-production category, along with the fluency factors, there are two kinds of flexibility; one is flexibility in the production of classes, and the other is flexibility in the production of transformations. In seeking from storage some items of information in a potentially large, unrestrictive class, for example, naming uses of a common brick or a common wire coat hanger, one examinee will roam about from one subclass to another, covering a wide variety of classes; another will apparently try to work each class for all it is worth before shifting to another. The number of shifts from one class to another is a score for what has been called "spontaneous flexibility." A high degree of this kind of flexibility also means low degree of perseveration within classes. The thinker who will permit himself to roam widely, when the information called for may possibly be in a number of different classes, has a greater probability of coming upon the needed idea.

When Wm. J. J. Gordon (1961) advises us to begin problem-solving at a high level of abstraction, he may be saying, in effect, that we should allow our search to roam over a very broad class of possibilities. Ann Roe (1952) may have been talking about the same phenomenon when she reported that many of the top scientists she studied were generalizers. Too much concentration on particulars is often detrimental to creative progress. Arnold reported (1962) that employees dealing with spark plugs had difficulty in making lists of attributes of a spark plug, but could readily do so for a bicycle. It is said that Einstein would often deny his understanding of the obvious, in order that he might gain new looks at things. All of these phenomena may be related to spontaneous flexibility, or the divergent production of varied classes of information.

The other two types of flexibility are similar in that the key in either case is believed to be ease of producing transformations, for purposes of divergent thinking in the one case and for arriving at a convergent answer in the other. Abilities of this type in the category of divergent production have been called "adaptive flexibility." Those in the category of convergent production have been called "redefinition" abilities. In either case, conceptions are readily modified or redefined in order to use them in solving problems. In either case, we have a diversity of trials as in trial-and-error behavior. The individual who can revise his trial attempts more readily has an advantage; he is not limited to futile repetitions of the same failing approaches.

The redefinition abilities can be logically affiliated with the well-known phenomenon of "functional fixedness." In this application, functional fixedness reflects low status with respect to redefinition ability. You are probably familiar with the famous Maier string problem (Maier, 1930). In a relatively bare room, two strings hang at some distance apart from the ceiling. The subject is told to tie the two free ends of the strings together. He cannot succeed until he hits upon the idea of first tying pliers that lie on a table to one of the strings, and swinging the pendulum he has thus made, so that both strings are within his reach at the same time. He redefines the pliers from the conception of their use as a handy tool to the conception of their use as a weight in a pendulum.

Quite a few experiments have been done to determine under what conditions an individual will quickly make the transformation and under what other conditions he will be retarded. Using an implement just previously for its customary purpose retards the redefinition; using it in one or more unusual ways facilitates the redefinition. Using other objects in unusual ways just before the string problem is presented is of some help to the subject (Maltzman et al., 1956). Even seeing someone use the object in an unusual way also helps (Bond, 1955). The effects of applying the common use of the object prior to the string problem wear off with time, in accordance with normal forgetting principles (Adamson & Taylor, 1954).

THE ROLE OF INSIGHT

The sudden transformations, such as are observed in solving the string problem, are sometimes described as "insights." This is not to say that all insights are transformations. The sudden arrival of any new product may be given the same description, and this may occur in the area of cognition as well as in the areas of divergent or convergent production. It may be that some degree of insight, however infinitesimal, is involved in all learning. Sometimes it is of such an extent as to be observable; usually it is not. The most spectacular instances come to the creative thinker in what Wallas called the stage of illumination. In such instances, the size of the intuitive leap is simply extraordinarily great.

Since it was pointed out and emphasized by Gestalt psychologists, the phenomenon of insight has been very much downgraded and shunted aside by stimulus-response psychologists, because they have not known what to do with it. Their disposal of it is often with the usual cliché, "It's all a matter of past experience." It is true that experiments show that conditions in past experience can be favorable to the occurrence of an insight; but they never fully account for it. There is always something added; something new. And it is the business of the psychologist to find out what that "something new" is and how it comes about.

From the point of view of informational psychology, learning is the gaining of new information in the form of new or revised products. The crucial problem is to find out how new products come into being, whether they come by large, spectacular jumps or by small accretions. We shall not understand insight, and we shall not understand learning, until we know how products of information are formed.

Among the products of information that are important in major creative productions is the product of system. The significant step in creation is often in the form of a system of some kind. For a visual artist, it is a motif or a conception for a painting or a mural. For a writer, it is a story plot or a theme. For a planner, it is a scheme. For a scientist, it is a model or a theory. Writers who describe the behavior of outstandingly creative people almost invariably report such a step early in the solution of the problem. To say that the formation of the system proceeded unconsciously is of no help whatever; it should be a challenge to the scientist to find out what happened. A few experiments on such problems have already appeared.

THE ROLE OF EVALUATION

Wallas's stage of verification appears to involve two aspects that can be illuminated by structure-of-intellect concepts. On the one hand, the creative thinker, having adopted his general schema, proceeds to give flesh and skin to the skeleton by adding detailed information. At this point, the elaborative abilities of the divergent-production category come into special significance. Elaboration abilities are defined as pertaining to the divergent production of implications. The schematic outline calls for certain extensions or completions rather than others; additions implied by the structure itself.

The other important aspect of verification is that of evaluation. The structure of intellect provides for a whole set of evaluative abilities; abilities pertaining to sensing what is proper and what is not. I have proposed elsewhere (1961) that evaluation is the general basis of reinforcement in learning. It is sufficiently broad in conception to embrace other conceptions, including Hull's drive-reduction hypothesis, Thorndike's confirming reaction, and even Neal Miller's pleasure-pain hypothesis. All of these are potential sources of information that can be useful and probably is used in the operation of reinforcement. We need to know more about the psychology of evaluation. There must be discoverable laws of congruity vs. incongruity of information, as there are laws of cognition, memory, and of production of information.

My chief objection to Wallas, at this point, is that the operation of evaluation is by no means confined to the last stage of creative production; it undoubtedly occurs all along the way. It operates at the first moment in sensing the existence of a problem. It helps sift information during the analysis of the problem. It comes into the picture during the stage of idea generation, although we are told by Osborn (1957) and others that this is no time for evaluation; that we should generate ideas with suspended judgment. There is much evidence to show that evaluation is often detrimental to free flow of ideas, either for the lone thinker or for group thinkers. There is also evidence that it is more detrimental to the appearance of low-quality ideas than it is to the appearance of high-quality ideas.

It is interesting that Rossman, in his seven stages of invention, does not confine evaluation to a final stage. In fact, of his seven stages, the odd-numbered ones, especially, could be the locus of considerable evaluation. His whole list of steps is reminiscent of the TOTE pattern proposed by Miller, Galanter, and Pribram (1960) as the basic unit of behavior, where the letters TOTE stand for test, operate, test, and then exit from the pattern, respectively. Their "test" can be interpreted as evaluation. The paradigm for the Rossman steps would be TOTOTOTE, with E added as an eighth step.

But it must be recognized that we have problems within problems. There are sub-problems and even sub-sub-problems. Sub-problems are solved in turn, on the way to the solution of a major problem. Miller, Galanter, and Pribram point out that within the major strategy, with its overall TOTE pattern, we have a number of tactics or minor TOTE patterns. Thus, testing or evaluation occurs all along the way, so long as there is any concern about standards of correctness or excellence. Whether or not the thinker is hungry for feedback information, he is bound to have much of it as he goes along, which he may use or not in evaluation.

Summary

In this relatively condensed presentation of views on productive thinking, I have attempted to set forth at least the general scheme of a theory. The theory borrows ideas from a number of sources, but primarily from the structure-of-intellect model and its category concepts. There has been an effort to employ such concepts to help illuminate many of the phenomena that have already been observed in the course of productive thinking.

The first general observation that was made concerns the high degree of similarity between steps in problem-solving and steps in creative thinking that leads to an end product. It was suggested that all problem-solving involves creative thinking because of some degree of novelty shown by the problem solver. The same general theory should account for both. Both are properly regarded as instances of learning, because of the changes they bring about in behavior.

In both, there is an initial sensitivity to a problem, for which there is a corresponding type of ability in the structure-of-intellect model. There is next an analysis of the problem, which involves primarily cognitive abilities. The way in which the problem is comprehended sets up search models, which serve as cues for the retrieval of stored information. Stored information involves a set of memory abilities. The generation of ideas by recall from storage is likely to be by way of transfer, because the information is retrieved by a new cue in connection with which it had not been learned. The theory of productive thinking here proposed is, therefore, given the label of a "transfer theory."

Facility of information retrieval depends in part upon certain abilities for fluent information production, of which there are three. They differ in terms of the product category in which the items of information belong: units, related correlates, or systems. Three kinds of flexibility factors help to keep the search from becoming too limited in scope and to transform the nature of a product or to redefine it for new uses and new connections. Elaboration abilities help to make additions and to achieve completions.

At all stages of problem-solving, evaluative abilities contribute to the selection of the best information and the rejection of unsuitable information. The initial step of sensing a problem is itself an act of evaluation. The final step of accepting the finished product is also an act of evaluation. At any step of the way, although there are times when judgment should be relaxed for the sake of idea production in large quantity, evaluation provides guiding influences.

Thus, although the most obvious aspects of creative thinking appear to depend upon the abilities to do divergent-productive thinking and the abilities to effect transformations of information, with the abilities of fluency, flexibility, elaboration, and redefinition playing significant roles, with creative thinking put in its larger context of problem-solving, we see that any or all kinds of abilities represented in the structure of intellect can play their useful roles, directly or indirectly.

PART II

CREATIVITY: NURTURE

Introduction

By necessity, man has long been involved in the nurture of creativity, both within the world around him and in himself. Within the world around him, he has had to nurture the creative in the simple task of growing food to feed his appetite. He has had to confront nature and ask how good things grow, where and when, and what efforts of his own fit best to net the best return. He has made his gardens, cultivated his fields, raised his livestock, learning, all the while, that his life depends on fitting his creative work to the way creation goes when nature is creator.

He has been involved in the nurture of creativity again, when, in giving birth to offspring of his own, he has recognized himself as source and has wanted to know what nurturance serves best to bring his young along. Once grown to manhood, men have the question still to face, since maintaining life and bringing it to flower still requires creative nurturance. The "good life" for man is a life rich with nutriment of varied kinds, well balanced, fresh and freshly realized. Cultivation is required; there is no end.

So men have long concerned themselves with the nurture of creativity, though they may not have been so explicitly concerned as we are now. We are explicitly concerned to nurture creativity where we can.

In the selections which follow are found a number of engagements with the theme.

Morris Stein identifies the creative person and then asks what a culture needs to nourish him: What role do critics serve? What place do patrons have? And peers? What psychic soil is best?

Paul Weisberg and Kayla Springer proceed from a psychiatric base to analyze results that come from studies of home environment to ask how the gifted child is dependent on what his home provides: What do parents do that has a bearing on the case? What attitudes do they express? With what effect?

Jacob Getzels and Philip Jackson identify two sets of very able adolescents, one at the top on creativity (but not on IQ), and the other on the top on IQ (but not on creativity), asking, then, what difference appears in the homes of these two sets: Is it a difference in the education of the parents? In their occupation? In their age? In what they read? In the way they rear a child? In the way they were reared themselves? What is a home that nurtures best the creative growth of youth?

Irwin Flescher identifies four groups of students (creatively-talented, intellectually-talented, twice-talented, and non-talented) to sort out what then appears as connection to performance tasks in school: What children are best served by the environment the school provides? Who has success? Is it the more creative ones? Or less?

Margaret Mead puts anthropology to work in sizing up the place the culture gives to the teacher's art and makes it plain that there needs be a social source from which creative growth can come into a teacher's life.

Clark Moustakas shows us what the clinician sees when he looks beneath the surface of school life to note the lessons taught by the way the schooling system operates. These are not the lessons which are put into the curriculum but the lessons that come through, nonetheless, to teach the child how he is to live his life.

Paul Torrance points out that varied cultures form a varied source for creativeness, that our culture has its effect through attitudes we take, and then goes on to lay out concrete ways in which teachers may be led to become more creative in themselves and in what they offer to children.

Richard Crutchfield gives a creative answer to the structure of creative nutriment by devising programmed learning tasks which, when used in teaching children of grades five and six, net growth in the capacity of the children to respond creatively to problem-solving tasks. He seeks the order of creative problem-solving thought and shows that growth occurs when teaching follows an order which is appropriate.

Ross Mooney seeks an integrative theme. He turns to nature for his clues to how creative systems work and finds, within their form, a common mode of working which then serves as base for conceiving how creation goes when it occurs in the relationships of men to men in teaching-learning tasks: What does creativity become when it serves as integrative theme, education's final base and aim?

MORRIS I. STEIN

Creativity and Culture

In this paper[1] a series of hypotheses will be discussed regarding the personality of the creative individual, his work, the process through which he achieves it, and some of the relationships between these and the culture in which they appear. These hypotheses were developed in the course of studying the personalities of a small number of Chicago artists.[2] The tentative nature of the hypotheses should be emphasized—their validity is still in question. They are now being subjected to test in a study of chemists.

Let us start with a definition. The creative work is a novel work that is accepted as tenable or useful or satisfying by a group in some point in time. Each of the parts of this definition will be considered separately.

By "novel" I mean that the creative product did not exist previously in precisely the same form. It arises from a *reintegration* of already existing materials or knowledge, but when it is completed it contains elements that are new. The extent to which a work is novel depends on the extent to which it deviates from the traditional or the status quo. This may well depend on the nature of the problem that is attacked, the fund of knowledge or experience that exists in the field at the time, and the characteristics of the creative individual and those of the individuals with whom he is communicating.

Often, in studying creativity, we tend to restrict ourselves to a study of the genius because the "distance" between what he has done and what has existed is quite marked. Such an approach causes us to overlook a necessary distinction between the creative product and the creative experience.

[1] Adapted from a paper presented at the Northwestern University Centennial Conference on Anthropology and Psychiatry, May, 1951.
[2] The study of artists was supported by a grant in 1950 from the Social Science Research Committee of the University of Chicago. The study of chemists was supported by the Research Division of Armour and Co., Chicago, Illinois.
From *Journal of Psychology*, 1953, *36*, pp. 311–322. Used by permission of the publisher.

109

The child who fixes the bell on his tricycle for the first time may go through stages that are structurally similar to those which characterize the work of the genius. His finished product, however, is a return to a previously existing state of affairs. The product of an inventor's labor, on the other hand, may strike one as creative immediately because it did not exist previously. In speaking of creativity, therefore, it is necessary to distinguish between internal and external frames of reference.

Turning to the characteristics of the creative experience or creative process and the personality of the creative individual, we adopt a bipolar point of view, in which there is an *interaction* between the creative individual and the problem on which he is working, or, in broader terms, and the environment in which he exists. To speak solely of the existence of the stresses and strains in the environment without due consideration of the individual, as some investigators do, or to deal primarily with the stresses and strains in the individual and to overlook the nature of the problem or the environment as other investigators do, is an arbitrary approach which is a consequence of the specialization in our profession today. Such separate emphases, however, can yield only partial insight and understanding.

The first question that arises in analyzing the creative process is the question of motivation: Why does the individual create? This does not differ from any other motivational problem. Therefore, in the early stages of the creative process, the individual experiences a state of disequilibrium —one might say that homeostasis is disturbed, or that there is a lack of closure, or, from a hedonistic point of view, that the individual experiences a lack of satisfaction with the existing state of affairs. On probing more deeply into the roots of the individual's personality, one may realize the historical factors and personal needs which determine the subject's *sensitivity* to such states. The creative person has a lower threshold, or greater sensitivity, for the gaps or the lack of closure that exist in the environment. The sensitivity to these gaps in any one case may stem largely from forces in the environment or from forces in the individual.

Associated with this sensitivity is the creative individual's capacity to *tolerate ambiguity* (Frenkel-Brunswik, 1949). By "capacity to tolerate ambiguity," I mean that the individual is capable of existing amidst a state of affairs in which he does not comprehend all that is going on, but he continues to effect resolution despite the present lack of homeostasis.

To summarize this early stage of the creative process: the creative individual may be characterized as a system in tension sensitive to the gaps in his experience and capable of maintaining this state of affairs. Some individuals go no further than this point in the creative process. Their creativity is manifested in the fact that they have played a critical role in calling the attention of others to the gaps that exist. But for others, the creative process continues to the next stages—hypothesis formation and hypothesis testing. These individuals seek various solutions that would close the gap or that would effect closure.

To be capable of developing such hypotheses, it is suggested that just as there need be some communication between the individual and his environment (i.e., that which was termed sensitivity previously), so there need be communication between some or all of the inner personal regions. Stated somewhat differently, the creative individual is characterized by permeable boundaries that separate the self from the environment and that separate some or all of the regions within the self. At times when this permeability does not exist, it may be induced by the taking of drugs or alcohol, as we find to be the case in many creative persons. Or it may exist when the person is distracted or devoting himself to other works.

The character of the inner personal region obviously varies with the nature of the work that is undertaken. For persons in one area (physics, for example), it may mean greater flexibility in the intellectual sphere, while for others (the artist), it appears as a greater flexibility in the emotional or affective sphere. To be sure, there is an interaction between the two spheres, and rigidity in one area may well impede developments in the other and sidetrack the creative process.

This interaction and some of its hazards are well illustrated in Schiller's response to a friend who complains of his lack of creative power. He says:

The reason for your complaint lies, it seems to me, in the constraint which your intellect imposes upon your imagination. Here I will make an observation, and illustrate it by an allegory. Apparently, it is not good—and indeed it hinders the creative work of the mind—if the intellect examines too closely the ideas already pouring in, as it were, at the gates. Regarded in isolation, an idea may be quite insignificant, and venturesome in the extreme, but it may acquire importance from an idea which follows it; perhaps, in a certain collocation with other ideas, which may seem equally absurd, it may be capable of furnishing a very serviceable link. The intellect cannot judge all those ideas unless it can retain them until it has considered them in connection with these other ideas. In the case of a creative mind, it seems to me, the intellect has withdrawn its watchers from the gates, and the ideas rush in pell-mell, and only then does it review and inspect the multitude. You worthy critics, or whatever you may call yourselves, are ashamed or afraid of the momentary and passing madness which is found in all real creators, the longer or shorter duration of which distinguishes the thinking artist from the dreamer. Hence your complaints of unfruitfulness, for you reject too soon and discriminate too severely (Freud, 1938, p. 193).

The "momentary and passing madness" is, I believe, a function of the permeability of the boundaries in the inner personal regions that are usually blocked from consciousness. The intensity of the "momentary and passing madness" is correlated with the depth to which the experience goes. For the artist, it may go deeper into subjective experience than for the scientist. Instances of such experiences are described by many creative persons. Thus Zervos, in discussing Picasso's creative process, says:

His only wish has been desperately to be himself, in fact he acts according to suggestions which come to him from beyond his own limits. He sees descending upon him a superior order of exigencies; he has a very clear impression that something compels him imperiously to empty his spirit of all that he has only just discovered, even before he has been able to control it, so that he can admit other suggestions. Hence his torturing doubts. But this anguish is not a misfortune for Picasso. It is just this which enables him to break down all his barriers, having the field of the possible free to him, and opening up to him the perspectives of the unknown (Read, 1948, p. 109).

For some persons, the creative process may stop during the stage of hypothesis formation. They develop too few hypotheses because of intellectual or emotional reasons; or, in the process, they become sidetracked by considering a specific intellectual matter that is not relevant to the demands of the moment; or they come upon a previously unresolved emotional difficulty that forces its attention upon them.

The process of hypothesis formation in the creative person is not a haphazard nor rigid process. It is a flexible one that is often characterized by either implicit or explicit direction. The creative individual's time perspective is oriented toward the future. He senses in the present how some aspects of the final form of the product are to appear. Thus Wertheimer, in discussing Einstein's thought processes while he was working on the theory of relativity, says:

Before the discovery that the crucial point, the solution, lay in the concept of time, more particularly in that of simultaneity, axiom played no role in the thought process—of this Einstein is sure. (The very moment he saw the gap, and realized the relevance of simultaneity, he knew this to be the crucial point for the solution.) But even afterward, the final five weeks, it was not the axioms that came first. "No really productive man thinks in such a paper fashion," said Einstein.

Later he added:

During all those years there was a feeling of direction, of going straight toward something concrete. It is, of course, very hard to express that feeling in words; but it was decidedly the case, and clearly to be distinguished from later considerations about the rational form of the solution. Of course, behind such a direction there is always something logical; but I have it in a kind of survey, in a way visually (Wertheimer, 1945, p. 183).

It has been observed by some that, in the course of the creative process, the creative individual experiences depression. The hypothesis is suggested that this depression arises as a result of anxiety that is brought forward by the lack of direction just mentioned. The creative person no longer feels that he is going forward, and still he cannot enjoy the present state. The lack of direction may be a consequence of an excessive number of hypotheses that occur to the subject and the feeling of inadequacy as to the possibilities of testing any of them. It may also arise as a result of his inability to communicate his ideas to others. Finally, as the result of the relaxation of the inner personal barriers, old unresolved tensions are brought to the surface which are the residues of earlier life experiences wherein the individual was realistically inadequate—thus, there is a process of reinforcement. Indeed, for the creative individual, this is only one point in a sequence of events; but for others, it may be the end.

After the development of a series of hypotheses, or even simultaneously with them, there is testing of the hypotheses. The testing may vary with the area of the work. For one person, it may involve the construction of practical models, while for others, it may involve changing the features of a painting. In any case, it is suggested that when the final solution is attained, that is, when there is closure for the individual, he experiences a feeling of satisfaction with the final work, a feeling of exhilaration with the good gestalt. It is this feeling that is manifest in "Eureka" or "This is it!"

Some investigators in the area of creativity who have relied primarily on the Rorschach test have remarked, with some degree of dismay if not disturbance, that the records of their subjects contain responses that are to be found in the records of severely disturbed persons. These responses apparently occur in sufficiently large numbers so that the emotional stability of the subjects is questioned. I would like to suggest that this finding may result from any one or a combination of the following factors. It may, indeed, be an accurate reflection of the creative person's instability, and it is this instability which may result in the subject's being sensitive to the lack of closure in his environment. It was, therefore, suggested previously that in the inner personal regions there is communication between *some* or *all* of the regions. The creative person may not necessarily be completely integrated. Some of the factors that differentiate him from the neurotic or the more severely disturbed person, such as tolerance of ambiguity, direction, and a time perspective oriented to the future, have already been discussed. He is also different from the neurotic or psychotic in the next stage—that of communication, which will be discussed below. Furthermore, the Rorschach finding may be a manifestation of the extent to which the creative individual differs from others, and is congruent with his tendency to perceive accepted reality in a manner that differs from most people. By deviating from the traditional and status quo, the individual has achieved the first stage in arriving at the novel work. Furthermore, since many of the so-called "bad" signs in the Rorschach are inadequately formed *Gestalten,* his responses may reflect his ability or capacity to tolerate ambiguity in one area—the perceptual area. The Rorschach responses are then only a sample of an individual's behavior in one area, from which we may infer his behavior in other areas. Finally, to fixate completely on the disturbed aspects of a creative individual's personality is to emphasize a finding that may be an artifact of our present theory, which is oriented, possibly much too heavily, toward psychopathology, and an artifact of the experimental design, which does not take into account aspects of the personality for which the Rorschach is not necessarily the best. Mind you, it is not suggested that the Rorschach finding is invalid, but that it is only part of the story. The part that is not considered sufficiently is the creative person's ability to convey or to communicate his personal experiences to others so that they may react to it.

This brings us to the second part of the definition suggested above: that the creative work is tenable or useful or satisfying. These terms were selected to cover the areas of ideas, things, and aesthetic experiences, respectively, although they may well be replaced by other terms. My essential purpose here is to develop the thesis that the results of the creative process must be communicated to others. Communication with the self alone is insufficient. The creative person must achieve, as Sullivan says in another context (1940, 1945), "consensual validation." This may be clearer if we take the case of the psychotic person. Much of what the psychotic does has significance only within a narrow idiosyncratic framework. At times, he may not even be able to communicate his experiences adequately, as one finds in the "word salads" and neologisms of the schizophrenic. And further, the ideas he has do not stand up under test. But the creative person is able to convey his experiences so that they can be tested, or, if he has tested them, so that they may be reacted to by others.

Suggesting that the creative work may be regarded as an element in communication implies at least two factors: (a) The creative person must have available to him means or media through which he can express himself. Just as each of us required training in language to convey our ideas, so it is obvious that to be creative in painting the artist needs some experience in the use of pigments, charcoal, and other media. Such a study might well reveal the congruence that exists between the personalities of the subjects and the areas in which they have selected to work. (b) In the course of communicating his ideas, the creative person needs to abstract or eliminate certain aspects of his work which are completely of himself. In the final stages of communication, the individual must, as Mead would say, bear in mind the "others" with whom he is communicating. The extent to which this occurs varies with the area of work. Thus, it is more prevalent in science than in art. But in either case, there is a process of evaluation in which completely autistic factors, or the difficulties that were experienced in the course of arriving at a solution, are eliminated. Thus, in Einstein's work:

The way the two triple sets of axioms are contrasted in the Einstein-Infeld book is not at all the way things happened in the process of actual thinking. This was merely a later formulation of the subject matter, just a question of how the thing could afterwards best be written. The axioms express essentials in a condensed form. Once one has found such things one enjoys formulating them in that way; but in this process they did not grow out of any manipulation of axioms (Wertheimer, 1945, p. 183).

Similarly, we find that Zervos reports on Picasso's work:

I see for others, that is to say that I can put on canvas the sudden apparitions which force themselves on me. I don't know in advance what I am going to put on the canvas, any more than I decide in advance what colors to use. Whilst I work, I take no stock of what I am painting on the canvas. Every time I begin a picture, I feel as though I were throwing myself into the void. I never know if I shall fall on my feet again. It is only later that I begin to evaluate more exactly the result of my work (Read, 1948, p. 109).

It should be indicated that at times the creative person may present his work so well after his evaluation that others regard it as "simple," and wonder why they never thought of it.

The next major portion in the definition of the creative work is acceptance by a group. It is suggested that the creative product is congruent with the needs or experiences of a group. It strikes a chord for the group as it does for the individual. The creative product "resonates" with the needs or experience of a group. The use of this word with regard to creativity reminds one of the resonance theory of hearing, in which it is postulated that different wave lengths of sound are heard because they strike different parts of the basilar membrane. To make an analogy between this and creativity, one might say that creative products resonate all along a responsive membrane. Thus, certain art works resonate with feelings, while inventions resonate because they fulfill practical needs. In the case of art, it should be pointed out that there is not always a one-to-one relationship between what the artist attempted to express and what it resonated in the group. The conditions under which this does or does not occur is a matter for further investigation.

Acceptance by a group is significant. It provides the creative worker with his final test of reality, if you wish. The size of the group may vary. At times, it may be only those on the "left bank," Greenwich Village, or the small number of persons who first gathered around Freud and Einstein. Individuals may seek out the creative person, or he may have to proselytize them. The group provides the individual with necessary feedback so that he can clarify, alter, or make progress in his future work.

Finally, we arrive at the last point in our definition that the creative work is accepted at some point in time. The historical point of view reflected by the phrase "some point in time" is inserted in the definition to account for the fact that some men, like Van Gogh, may not be considered creative in their own lifetime; as a matter of fact, some, like Socrates, pay dearly for their ideas. Yet when the works of art or the ideas are rediscovered or are brought to attention at some future date, when the forces of society have changed, it is only then that these persons attain their rightful places in history. Indeed, in some areas of creativity, there may be "universals," e.g., form and use of space in art with only content varying in time. But in determining the validity of such universals, one needs to be aware of the hazard that what we regard as the critical elements in the universals today is a function of ourselves, and it may not necessarily be congruent with the manner in which these works were regarded in their own times.

The discussion, up to this point, has been limited primarily to the creative individual and the creative process. Let us now turn to a consideration of the interaction between the processes described and culture.

If what was said previously regarding the sensitivity of the creative individual in relation to both his external and internal environments is valid, then it may be said that a culture fosters creativity to the extent that it provides an individual with the opportunity to experience its many facets. A culture that limits the freedom of a person to study in one area, or a variety of areas, cuts down his opportunity to pick out the gaps that exist in the culture and also keeps him from learning the necessary media of communicating his feelings or ideas.

A culture also fosters creativity to the extent that its parent-child relationships and child-rearing techniques do or do not result in the setting up of rigid boundaries in the inner personal regions.[3] Techniques that result in excessive repression or guilt restrict internal freedom and interfere with the process of hypothesis formation. Attention must also be directed toward the broader aspects of education. For example, does the culture tolerate deviation from the traditional, the status quo, or does it insist upon conformity, whether in politics, science, or at school? Does the culture permit the individual to seek new experiences on his own, or do the bearers of culture (parents, teachers, and so on) "spoon-feed" the young so that they constantly find ready-made solutions available to them as they come upon a situation that is lacking in closure? Furthermore, to what extent do the adults accept or reward and thus reinforce the creative experience that the individual has had? For example, in the case I spoke of earlier—the child who fixed his tricycle bell—his experience could have been handled either by a depreciation of his experience and verbalized as, "Oh, anyone could have done that!" or the magnitude of his experience for himself could have been recognized, and he could have been encouraged to seek similar experiences in the future. Experiences of this kind should be studied both in the home and in formal educational systems.

The stage of development of a culture obviously influences the means available to the individual for creative progress. Thus, the modern physicist has new vistas open to him as a result of the recent developments in nuclear physics. From the experience in this area, it may be said that the variety of creative works that occur in a culture vary with the number of works that deviate markedly from the traditional and are accepted. Only with the acceptance of the theory of relativity and other findings was the

---

[3] Indeed, certain cultures set up rigid boundaries in certain regions and not others. This will no doubt affect the areas of creative work.

present development of physics possible, and we may well expect many new discoveries and applications in this area.

The culture may be marked by strict adherence to a specific philosophy, and this too influences progress in the arts and sciences. Giedion (1948) suggests how a mechanistic view of the universe has affected the work in many areas of inquiry. And, in the course of modern history, we have seen how various political and religious movements have at times stimulated and then markedly limited progress. Points of view which are developed in one area and studied by a worker in another way may aid the latter in sensitizing him to the gaps in his fund of knowledge. This is manifest in the recent developments in communication theory in the social sciences which were stimulated by the physicists. The extent to which progress is made in the new area of application may well depend on the rigidities of the philosophy that is adopted and/or the manner in which it is interpreted and followed by those who accept it. For example, present-day mechanism and materialism has caused Giedion to suggest that we have been overlooking humanism, and he highlights the need for a man who can live in "equipoise."

Furthermore, philosophies of life undergo cyclic change as a result of a multitude of factors. When a "valley" appears, the extent to which a culture comes out of it depends on the extent to which it is capable of tolerating ambiguity and encourages and tolerates a diversity of viewpoints as a new philosophy is developed. Further research might, therefore, be centered around the comparison of creative works when there is a consistent *Weltanschauung* and when one is lacking, or when there is a conflict of philosophies.

Finally, we come to a specific aspect of the culture—the audience with whom the creative person communicates—the critic, the patron, the followers, and the population at large.

The critic plays a very significant sociological role in determining what the larger population has available to it as instances of creativity. When we started our study of creative artists, we had a difficult time in getting critics to agree on who was a creative painter. Reputable persons in the art world disagreed with each other. Now let us assume that one of the critics, as was the case, is the curator of a gallery. That person would hang the works of one artist and not the other. For some people, because of the prestige of a museum, this work now becomes a "creative" work. But what of the others? They have to wait to be "discovered" by other critics, and this may even happen, if they are fortunate, in their own lifetime. It might be wise, therefore, to study the personalities of critics or the supporters of scientific research, since they play such important roles in determining what is creativity.

In some respects similar to both the critic and the supporter of scientific research, is the patron of arts. He, by virtue of the fact that he contributes financially to the artist's support, must be communicated with. How much of the patron's needs enter into the artist's evaluation of his final work depends on the relationship that exists between the two. The patron, just as was said of the broader culture, may well direct and restrict the content of his artist's work, if not the manner in which he works, because of his financial position. This raises a more crucial question in our own time, when there are few, if any, patrons of the arts who are comparable to the Medicis, let us say. Is there anything to the hypothesis that *one* of the factors resulting in the development of nonobjective art is the fact that the artist no longer is subservient to a patron, and he can therefore express himself as he wishes.

In considering the final stages of the creative process, it was suggested that the creative work must strike a chord or resonate in some manner with the group that accepts it. If this hypothesis is valid, then it would follow that the personalities or the experiences of the group are in some manner similar to those of the creative individual. It may be further suggested that studies of creative products provide some data for making inferences regarding the needs of the group that are being satisfied. Thus, it may be suggested that one of the factors involved in the acceptance of modern art today is that it represents a retreat or a rebellion, if you wish, against the materialism and intellectualism that has marked much of our time. It is a voice speaking against a period in which there is a denial of certain feelings. To be sure, to make similar interpretations of previous cultures may be hazardous, if this is accepted as the only evidence. We cannot completely put ourselves in the place of primitive man.

Finally, one must also consider the problem of communication between the creative individual and the population at large. In some areas of works, such as practical inventions, communication may exist with an extremely large portion of the population because they are aware of an invention's demonstrated usefulness. Indeed, communication may stop when it is necessary to understand the thinking that has gone into the development. Modern artists have been most vociferous in asking why their art is not appreciated more widely than it is, especially when they as individuals feel that they have captured the spirit and problems of the day. This raises the question whether, in an "age of anxiety," some individuals do not find it safer for themselves not to be aware of the problems that exist around them. Just as society affects the creative process by developing individuals who cannot relax the boundaries in the internal and external regions, so the extent to which an audience does resonate with an art product is a reflection of the extent to which they as perceivers are capable of relaxing their defenses. Thus, by studying the "nonappreciators," we can also learn a great deal of the culture.

In summary then: A definition of the creative work was presented. A creative work is a novel work that is accepted as tenable or useful or satisfying by a group in time. In line with this, it was hypothesized that studies of the personality of the creative individual may reveal a sensitivity to the gaps that exist in his own culture, and his creativity may be manifest in calling attention to these gaps or in finding a means of effecting closure, or his sensitivity to certain facets of this may result in his desire to communicate to others. In addition to sensitivity, attention was called to the creative individual's ability to tolerate ambiguity and to maintain direction as he develops and tests his hypotheses. The final product, considered as an element in communication, resonates with the needs or experiences of a group at some point in time. In considering cultural factors, it was hypothesized that the extent to which a variety of creative products are developed depends on the extent to which cultural influences permit the development of both freedom between the individual and his environment and freedom within the individual; on the extent to which the culture encourages diversity and tolerates the seeming ambiguity that such diversity suggests. We also considered certain aspects of the audience, specifically the critic, the patron, the appreciators, and the population at large with whom the creative person communicates. The experimental problems involved in testing the hypotheses mentioned are numerous, but they are not insurmountable.

PAUL S. WEISBERG

KAYLA J. SPRINGER

Environmental Factors in Creative Function

We are reporting here a psychiatric and psychological study of gifted children, which attempts to elicit significant and relevant factors in family life contributing to functional creativity. Application of the principles of dynamic psychiatry to the area of creative functioning has, in the past, been limited in scope. Kubie's recent book (1958) on the subject, for instance, is still basically addressed to the question that has been embarrassing psychiatrists for half a century: Does analysis, in modifying the conflict areas of the personality, quell inner tensions that are necessary to the creative act? Some interest has been expressed in the nature of creativity as an intrapsychic process, but there has been little agreement and no clear formulation (Anderson, 1959; Bergler, 1947; Grotjahn, 1957).

One implicit assumption that has been shared by many psychologists and psychiatrists working with creativity has been that creative function is a constitutional variable, much as is intelligence. It is only in recent years, as a matter of fact, that the differentiation between creativity and intelligence has been clearly established. The main concern of the professional has been to find ways to preserve creativity, or at most, to release it from its shackles.

We felt that the environmental aspects of creativity had been neglected. It is, after all, valid to ask whether a certain set of circumstances early in an individual's life may not only sustain creativity but may actually "create" it. To that end, an experiment was designed, the purpose of which was to find whether particular sorts of families had children with particular levels of creative function, and if that turned out to be the case, whether a formulation could be arrived at as to what the connection might be.

Before the research design and procedure can be described meaningfully, one definition must be stated. Functional creativity, then, for the purposes

---

From *Archives of General Psychiatry,* December, 1961, *5,* 64–74. Used by permission of the publisher.

of this study, is defined as the ability to produce, in a given situation, compositions, products, or ideas which are essentially new or novel, and previously unknown to the producer. It can be imaginative activity, or thought synthesis, where the product is not a mere summation. It may involve the forming of new patterns and combinations of information derived from past experience, and the transplanting of old relationships to new situations, and may involve the generation of new correlates. It must be purposeful or goal directed, although it need not have immediate application or be a perfect and complete product (Drevdahl, 1956).

Method and Design

A sample was sought of children who were still intimately involved in the home environment. At the same time, it was sought to avoid contamination of the data by the extraneous factor of intelligence. It has been found that creative function varies significantly with the IQ up to the very superior range of intelligence; above that level, there is no correlation between the two factors (Meir & Stein, 1955). It was decided, therefore, to choose the sample from children whose intelligence was in the gifted range.

In Cincinnati, the first formal intelligence testing in the Public School System is the administration of the Kuhlmann-Anderson group test in the spring of the third grade. It was felt that the closer to puberty the children in the sample were, the greater would be the danger that a withdrawal from the family environment on their part might cloud a view of any relationship between that environment and the level of creative function they exhibited. It was decided, therefore, to work with fourth graders, most of whom would be nine years old at the time of our study.

From the more than 7,000 public school children to whom the Kuhlmann-Anderson test had been administered the previous spring, the fifty children with the highest scores were chosen. Several further limitations were put on the sample: Families in whom the parents of the child were divorced from each other, or in whom one or both of the natural parents were deceased, or in whom the child was adopted after early infancy, were excluded.

Letters were sent to the families of the children chosen for the study, asking their cooperation. Each set of parents was asked to set aside an evening for their interviews, and to bring the child to be tested about a week afterward. More than 80 percent of those contacted indicated a willingness to take part. Having excluded a few families for reasons noted above, and having adjusted the sample in a random fashion so that an equal number of boys and girls participated, we retained thirty-two families for the study. All thirty-two of the participant families completed the procedures of the study.

The aims of the testing and interviewing were threefold. First, we wanted to obtain as broad and extensive a picture of the personalities and attitudes of the parents as possible from a relatively brief contact. Second, we wanted objective evidence as to the level of creative function in the children. And third, we wanted information about the basic personality structure of the children, which we hoped might be usable as a link between family patterns and creative function.

The contacts with the parents were conducted as semistructured psychiatric interviews, lasting between an hour and an hour and a half with each parent. Emphasis was placed on the marriage, family patterns, and attitudes toward the particular child in the study. The interviews were written up in a standard way, with categories under which verbally communicated data were recorded, and categories which called for the impressions of the interviewer. These categories were scored immediately after each set of interviews, without waiting for all other interviews to be completed.

Raw data obtained from the interview were used as the basis for judgments as to the parents' personality qualities, particularly those which applied directly to the family interaction. The judgments were made without the interviewer knowing the level of performance of any of the children on the creativity testing. Conversely, the data on the parents was unknown to the researcher who tested the children until after all the test data were gathered and scored.

The criterion tests of creativity used in this study are a selected portion of a battery designed by E. Paul Torrance of the Bureau of Educational Research, University of Minnesota (Bowers, 1960; Torrance & Michie, 1959; Torrance, Palm, Palamutlu, & Radig, 1959; Torrance & Radig, 1959; Torrance, personal communication to author; Yamamoto, 1960). The tests, derived from Guilford's factor analytic studies of creative adults (Guilford, Wilson, Christensen, & Lewis, 1951), are designed to elicit certain thinking abilities which have been shown by Guilford to be related to the creative process. These tests have been modified and augmented by Torrance for use with children in the early school years. While still in various stages of revision, they have been applied to large numbers of children, so that norms and other data regarding them are available. As far as could be ascertained, there are no other tests designed specifically to assess creative thinking in children about which large amounts of data have been gathered. The thinking abilities sought are: Ideational Fluency—the number of ideas which can be produced; Flexibility—the ability to shift from one idea to another; Originality—ability to produce uncommon ideas; Curiosity—sensitivity to problems in the environment; and Hypothesis Development—ability to make solutional guesses about environmental problems. Further aspects of thinking which have been felt to be related to creativity are: Irrelevance—the lack of a logical relationship between the response and the stimulus; and Fantasy—an unrealistic or unreal response, although there might be a logical connection between the response and the stimulus.

The specific tests used in the study are described as follows: *The Tin*

Can Test requires the child, within a time limit of 5 minutes to think of as many different uses as possible for tin cans. This test was scored for Ideational Fluency—that is, the number of uses mentioned; and for Flexibility—that is, the number of different categories of uses. For example, responses such as: use as a pencil holder; put mail in; hold nails; would each get one score for Ideational Fluency, but all three would total only one score for Flexibility, since they all fall into the category of use as a container.

The Circles Test consists of a series of circles on which the child is required to draw, in ten minutes, as many different objects as he can which have a circle as their basic formal element. The test was scored for Ideational Fluency and Flexibility, both as described above, and also for Originality, with norms for the latter provided by Dr. Torrance (personal communication to author), and, in some cases, created by the group under study. For example, "clock," "watch," and "button" each received one score for Fluency, but totaled only two for Flexibility, since "watch" is only a variation of "clock." Original responses included: "bicycle," using two circles as wheels; "stoplight," using three vertical circles; "whirring propellers of an airplane," using more than one circle.

The Ask and Guess Test, composed of three parts, presents the child with a picture; in this instance, representing the nursery rhyme "Peter, Peter, Pumpkin Eater." The child is required first, to ask as many different questions as possible about the picture; second, to make guesses as to what led up to, or caused, the situation depicted; and third, to make guesses as to possible outcomes. Five minutes is allowed for each subtest, or fifteen minutes in all. Responses to these tests were scored for variety and adequacy. Variety refers simply to the number of different responses produced, while adequacy refers to the appropriateness of the responses to the specific requirements of each section of the tests. The latter two sections of the test were further scored for Irrelevance and Fantasy.

Psychological tests, other than the criterion tests, were Rorschach and Draw-a-Family. The Rorschach was included to provide information regarding the child's personality structure and functioning. The Draw-a-Family, for which the child was asked to draw a picture of himself and his family, was expected to yield information regarding the child's conception of his relationship to the family unit.

In addition to the psychological testing of the children, the interviewer of the parents had an interview with each child, the purpose of which was twofold: First, it was felt that certain impressions might be gained which could supplement the more objective personality data from the Rorschach and Draw-a-Family tests. Second, the parents' opinions about their children could be compared to the impressions of the interviewer, thus providing a measure of parental attitudes. This interview was slightly more structured than that with the parents, and was aimed at relationship patterns, fantasy and dream material, image of self, fears and ambitions, and methods of handling anxiety. These interviews, like those with the parents, were then written up on a standard form, including categories both for objective data, and for impressions of the interviewer. The categories, again, were scored immediately, without reference to the patterns shown by any of the other children in the study.

The interview data was used as basis for judgments of various aspects of the personality structure of the children. These judgments were then compared with the Rorschach and Draw-a-Family material, and with the appropriate references in the parental interviews.

The material thus obtained was processed as follows: Criterion creative function tests were scored, interest correlations were checked, and raw scores were converted to standard scores. Parents or children were rated in each judgmental category in six gradations ranging from strongly present to strongly absent. The data were then evaluated by a two-tailed "student" t-test on each judgmental category, comparing the criterion test scores of individuals rated strong to those rated weak in that category. From the relationships thus derived, family patterns were pieced together which differentiated the children showing more functional creativity from those showing less. The Rorschach and Draw-a-Family findings, as well as the child interview, were then used to attempt to show the operations by which the family patterns might influence the level of creative function in the child.

Results

CRITERION TESTS

The raw scores of the criterion tests are tabulated in Table 1. The productivity of the group, it may be noted, is highly variable, even though the group tested is a homogeneous one as to race, intelligence, and in the main, sociocultural status. The tests thus differentiate well between members of the group. We felt justified in weighting the raw scores as to the time allowed to perform the subtest for two reasons: First, the intertest correlations were found to be 0.82 or higher. It was felt, therefore, that a reasonably representative sample of the whole test battery had been given. Second, since only selected portions of Torrance's battery were used, this weighting would not appear to violate any structural scoring considerations.

Table 1. RAW SCORES ON CREATIVITY TESTING

	Tin can	Circles	Ask and guess	Adjusted totals*
Range	0 to 46	16 to 94	0 to 160	32 to 330
Mean	18.2	52.0	65.7	157.0
Median	13.0	49.0	64.5	147.0

* "Adjusted totals" refers to the weighting of the raw scores as to the time allowed for each subtest.

The distribution of the group is depicted in Figure 1. Standard scores varied from +2.6 to −1.8 standard deviations. The shape of the curve of distribution is seen to be approximately rectangular. It may be noted that one member of the group has a standard score about one standard deviation above that of anyone else. A question is raised as to whether this performance falls within the normal curve of distribution, or whether it may not represent a capacity different in kind from that of the other members of the group.

Fig. 1   Creativity Test Score Distribution

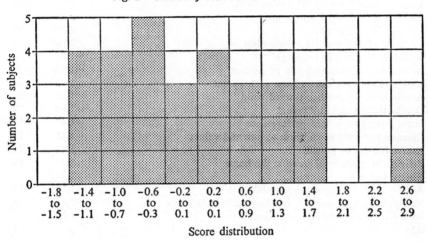

INTERVIEWS WITH PARENTS

Except in a category such as religion, where no such division is possible, every category was judged on a 6-point scale, ranging from markedly present to markedly absent. Those in the top two classifications were then compared to those in the lower two in terms of the criterion test scores of the child of the family in question. The listing of the categories, in Table 2, is arranged in the approximate order of the degree to which they turned out to correlate with the criterion scores.

It will be noted that there are three kinds of categories: Those in which an objective judgment can be made, such as Age of Parents; those in which only a first level of inference is necessary, such as Stress Placed on School Performance; and those which require secondary inferences, such as Hysteria in Mother. The question arises as to how accurately the interviewer was able to judge the data, particularly in those categories which require secondary inferences. When discussing those categories for which secondary inferences were necessary to rate the parents, therefore, an attempt will be made to clarify the evaluation process, so that credence may be lent to the validity of the category.

As seen from Table 2, a few of the categories correlated highly with performance on the criterion testing. In each case, the difference between the criterion scores of the children in those families judged high in the quality, and those judged low, was significant at the 0.01 level of confidence.

Table 2. CATEGORIES OF JUDGMENT FROM INTERVIEWS WITH PARENTS; CORRELATIONS WITH CRITERION TESTING PERFORMANCE

Category	t	d.f.
Expression without domination in parent of same sex as child	4.65*	13
Parental acceptance of regression in the child	4.10*	18
Father's occupational autonomy	3.20*	22
Compulsivity in mother	−2.30†	16
Intensity of father-child relationship	2.26†	14
Sexual satisfaction in marriage	−1.86	18
Acceptance of maternal role in mother	−1.80	17
Variation between stories from each parent	1.72	14
Ambivalence of mother toward child	1.63	22
Domination of child by parent	−1.62	20
Stress placed on school performance	−1.47	17
Demand for child to conform to parental values	−1.46	19
Expressiveness of parent	1.44	14
Religion as a powerful force in the home	−1.36	18
Sibling status	1.35	19
Ambivalence of father toward child	−1.16	18
Variation between parents in characteristic defenses	1.06	18
Intensity of mother-child relationship	1.06	16
IQ	n.c.	19
Hysteria in mother	n.c.	14
Family income	n.c.	19
Age of parents	n.c.	18
Religious affiliation	n.c.	29
Parental estimation of child's ability	n.c.	16

* Significant at the 0.01 level of confidence.
† Significant at the 0.05 level of confidence.
d.f. = degrees of freedom in determination of t.
n.c. = no correlation (t less than 1.00).

Expressiveness, which was judged by the openness of interchange during the interview, failed to attain statistical significance because the expressive parents had children who were either in the top, or the bottom, group in terms of the criterion testing. When it was combined with the category Domination of the Child by the Parent, however, it became highly significant. This latter category was judged by estimating how extensively the parents described themselves as participating in the child's development and current interests, how confidently the parents assumed themselves to be the child's favorite parent, and how anxious the parents appeared to be made by independent strivings in the child. Those parents who were expressive and did not dominate their children had children who did significantly better on the criterion testing than parents who were not expressive, *or* were dominating in their attitudes toward their children. This correlation was particularly marked in the parent of the same sex as the child, as noted in Table 2.

A second category which correlated highly with children's test scores relates to the parental attitude toward regression in the child. Parents who were acceptingly indifferent to their children's regressive tendencies had children who did significantly better on the criterion testing than children whose parents either regularly suppressed regression, or else actively encouraged it in them. The judgment was made by evaluating the parents' answers to questions about regression in the child, as to candor and self-awareness.

The final category that attained a 0.01-level correlation with the criterion test results was Father's Occupational Autonomy. The thirty-two fathers were rated as to their role in decision-making which could influence the nature and condition of their work. A physician or attorney in private practice, or the owner of a repair shop, would rate high, while a bus driver or civil servant would rate low. There was a significantly positive relationship between the level of Father's Occupational Autonomy and the level of performance of the child on the criterion tests.

Several other categories had a tendency to relate to the test performance, without that relationship reaching the 0.01 level of confidence. The mothers of the high-ranking children tended to be more ambivalent toward their child than the mothers of the low-ranking children, but the fathers of the high-ranking children tended to be *less* ambivalent toward their child than the fathers of the low-ranking children. The fathers of the high-ranking children thus tended to have a more positive relationship with their child than did the mothers, while the reverse was true with the low-ranking children. This tendency was even more marked for high-ranking boys than girls. Both parents of high-ranking children tended to have greater intensity in their relationships to the child than did the parents of the low-ranking children, with the tendency more marked in the father-child relationship. The mothers of high-ranking children tended to be less compulsive, and to accept their maternal role less, than the mothers of low-ranking children. There was a tendency for parents of the high-ranking children to demand conformity to parental values less than parents of the low-ranking children. There was a tendency for religion to be a less powerful force in the homes of the high-ranking children. The variance between the stories the parents told during the interview, particularly as those stories applied to the marriage and the family, tended to be greater in the families of the high-ranking children. The parents of the high-ranking children, further, tended to vary more between themselves in the defensive techniques that appeared to be characteristic of them, than did the parents of the low-ranking children. The eldest child tended to do better in the criterion testing, and being a middle sibling in a sib line longer than three seemed to be a disadvantage, although the number of children in our sample fitting the latter description was too small to be treated statistically. Sexual satisfaction in the marriage tended to be lower in the families of the high-ranking children than in the families of the low-ranking children. Sexual dissatisfaction stemming from frigidity in the wife correlated better with high criterion test performance, particularly in the boys, than dissatisfaction stemming from the overtly inadequate performance of the husband.

The only category of those that did not relate to the criterion test scores that will be noted is that of IQ. The method of choosing the sample successfully eliminated intelligence, in the group tested, as a differentiating factor in creative function.

Placing the categories which are, or tend to be, correlated with the criterion test scores together, an optimal family pattern emerges. It is not an overly close family unit, with little clinging to each other for support. Conformity to parental values is not stressed in the child, for instance. Nor is it a particularly well-adjusted marriage. The sexual adjustment in the marriage is mediocre, and each parent sees the marriage, and family life, in terms somewhat different than does the other. It is a family in which there is open, and not always calm expression of strong feeling, without that expression being used to bind the child to the values of the parents. Father interacts strongly and positively with the child. Mother interacts with the child quite strongly, but tends often to be ambivalent in her maternal feelings. Father is a man who exercises some authority, both at work and at home. And in this optimal family, when the child regresses, the behavior is accepted by the parents without discomfort, but the parents do not use the child's regression as a crutch by which they can reinforce their own self-esteem. The creative child is often an elder sibling, but is not a particular favorite, in that there is no overevaluation of his or her abilities by the parents.

The family described above is, obviously, an artificial construct. None of the families tested satisfy all its criteria. All the families of the top-scoring children in the study, however, fit most of the patterns outlined.

PROJECTIVE TESTS

The Rorschach was used, initially, to make a total evaluation of each child's personality organization and functioning. It was found, however, that the individual patterns provided by this kind of analysis obscured any group patterns relating to achievements on the criterion tests. It was decided, therefore, to attempt to assess more circumscribed aspects of Rorschach behavior. Since the criterion scores were known to the authors at this point, other clinicians to whom such knowledge was not available were requested to make certain of the judgments.

The significance of the Rorschach factors noted below in terms of the psychological health of the child was not considered. With the exception of a very few, these children were considered to be without marked emotional disturbance.

While most of the children in the sample responded to the Rorschach in ways far beyond their age level expectations, there were some qualitative characteristics of Rorschach behavior which differentiated the group scoring high on the criterion tests from the rest of the group. These were: first, a tendency toward unconventional responses; second, a tendency toward unreal percepts; and third, a tendency toward fanciful and imaginative treatment of the blots. Both the unconventionality and some of the unreality arose from the interpretation of unusual areas of the blot in an attempt to make an inclusive, total response to the whole card. Some of the combinations so formed had no positive referent in reality. It appeared characteristic of these children that they tried to attain a synthesis; in this case, an interpretation of the whole card, by relating disparate elements in the card, and considerable fancy in interpreting those elements. The fanciful treatment of the blots consisted not only in the conventionally accepted use of ghosts, fairy-tale figures, or people from outer space, but more strikingly, in the imaginative themes by which they interwove the objects of their perception. Despite these unusual characteristics, the number of popular responses did not differ between the criterion groups, nor were they less than to be expected in a normal population of adults. Further, these high-ranking children accepted their own percepts easily, despite the somewhat strange and unreal world they depicted.

One cognitive process thought to be necessary to creativity is the ability to dissolve already formed boundaries, and to re-form new organizations or thought products. This factor was analyzed by an approach to the Rorschach devised by Friedman (1953), which describes the organization of the blot on a developmental continuum from primitive to highly complex organizations. The normal population falls primarily in the middle to high range, while persons with thought pathology tend to fall at the lower end. The developmental theorist's hypothesis that the creative individual would show both extremes of the primitive-mature continuum was confirmed in a study by Hersch of adult artists (1957). The application of this scoring system to the present study indicated that the children who had high scores on the criterion tests gave a preponderance of responses at both extremes. The proportion of their total responses, which were either vaguely defined or highly organized compared to those which were organized on a very simple level, was signficantly greater than among the rest of the children.

The children were further compared on the basis of formal Rorschach scores. While there was no significant relationship between the total number of responses and scores on the criterion tests, a significant positive relationship was found between the production of both human movement (M) and color (C) responses and scores on the criterion tests. The former relationship was significant at the probability level of less than 0.005. Human movement responses have traditionally been considered to represent movement and activities that the individual is carrying on within his mental life. Developmentally, the presence of movement responses signals a stage at which the child internalizes behavior patterns and sets up in fantasy certain roles, largely unconscious, which may or may not be acted out in his actual relationships. The internal locus implied by M, further allows for greater independence from environmental influence.

The number of C responses was significantly related to criterion scores at a probability level of less than 0.01. Color responses are considered to reflect the affective life. Thus, a sensitivity to color on the Rorschach represents a readiness to respond emotionally to the environment. It is worth noting that the balance of M to C responses, a relationship which is considered to reflect a basic inward versus outward orientation of the individual, was totally unrelated to the criterion scores. Thus, the children who scored high on the criterion tests produced significantly more of both kinds of responses than did the other children. Furthermore, their production of both kinds of responses was greater than that expected from a normal population of adults.

The children are, theoretically, in the latency age range. They might, thus, be expected to show an increase in attention to reality and tangibles in their environment and a decrease in fantasy, emotionality, and concern with affective relationships. These trends would follow from the heightened use of repression characteristic of latency. In the high-scoring children, however, no such evidence of latency functioning was apparent. The high production of M and C responses suggests that, as a group, they show a relative lack of dependence on repressive techniques. Further, the content of their productions indicates that oedipal, or heterosexual, problems were as important to them as problems of environmental mastery.

The drawings of the family, included for information regarding the child's conception of the family unit, were classed in two major categories. The larger classification included those drawings in which all members of the family were presented on one page, and in relatively true age-size perspective. The other category included any deviation from this presentation. The deviations took the following forms: exclusion of the self; placement of the self on another page; isolation of the self from the rest of the family spatially or in body orientation; disproportionate size of self relative to other members; division of the family unit so that some members were on one page and some on another. It was felt that, whatever the personal relevance of the specific form of the deviation, they all reflected some feeling of apartness, of disunity, rather than an anonymous inclusion within the family group. Deviations were noted in over half of the drawings of the highest criterion group; in the lowest group the figure was less than 20 percent.

INTERVIEWS WITH CHILDREN

The judgments concerning the children made from the interviews with the child were on a 6-point scale, as were those made from the interviews with the parents. Those children in the upper two classifications were then compared to those in the lower two, in terms of criterion test scores. The listing of the categories in Table 3 is arranged in the approximate order of the degree to which they turned out to correlate with the criterion scores.

A few categories correlated highly with the criterion testing. Of these, Humor was one. The correlation between humor and creative function in children has been noted previously (Getzels & Jackson, 1959). Lack of humor, in our series, correlated extremely well with low criterion test performance; a markedly developed sense of humor was less constantly present in the high-scoring children.

Two other categories which correlated very well with test performance were Ease of Early Recall, and, particularly, Strength of Self-Image. Early recall could be objectively judged, at least in terms of the interview situation. Strength of self-image, like humor, required an inference by the interviewer. But whereas the inference necessary to the judgment of the child's sense of humor was a secondary one, requiring an evaluation of the approach to the question stimulus taken by the child, the inference necessary to the judgment of the child's strength of self-image was based more on the manifest content of the response. The child was asked to describe himself in terms of height and weight, reaction to environmental changes, family, the school situation, and so on. The children who put themselves somewhere definite in each of these frames of reference were ranked high in strength of self-image, even though that somewhere might not always be a pleasant place.

The final two categories that correlated significantly with the criterion

Table 3. CATEGORIES OF JUDGMENT FROM INTERVIEWS WITH CHILDREN; CORRELA-
TIONS WITH CRITERION TESTING PERFORMANCE

Category	t	d.f.
Strength of self-image	4.14*	14
Ease of early recall	3.20*	19
Humor	3.16*	16
Availability of oedipal anxiety	2.61†	15
Uneven ego development	2.56†	18
Strong sexual identification with parent of same sex	1.81	16
Overt upset at loss of dependency gratification	1.80	19
Aggressiveness	1.66	18
Opinion that parents view them as people rather than things	1.52	16
Lack of constricting anxiety	1.36	18
Self-respect	1.28	17
Omnipotent fantasies	−1.01	20
Internalized decision-making	n.c.	18
Underlying depression	n.c.	16
Actively seeking independence	n.c.	19
Identification with defensive patterns of either parent	n.c.	13
Sex	n.c.	30

* Significant at the 0.01 level of confidence.
† Significant at the 0.05 level of confidence.
d.f. = degrees of freedom in determination of t.
n.c. = no correlation (t less than 1.00).

test scores were associated with the level of psychosexual maturity in the child. Oedipal anxieties were closer to the surface in the high-ranking than the low-ranking children, as judged by fantasy, content of early memories, and dream material. There was, also, more unevenness of ego development in the high-ranking children. Interests in Shakespeare and in dolls might peacefully coexist in these children, and controls appropriate to adolescence or even adulthood might alternate with impulsive, almost infantile, behavior during the interview. In the high-ranking children, the placations of latency seemed to be ineffective.

Certain other categories tended to separate the high scorers from the low, without this tendency reaching statistical significance. The high-scoring children, more than the low-scoring ones, tended to see their parents as viewing them as people rather than things. The high-scoring children also tended to be more outwardly upset about loss of dependency gratifications than the low-scoring ones.

The high scorers tended to have fewer omnipotent fantasies than the low scorers, although the difference was slight. The nature of the fantasies varied, incidentally; those in the lower groups had fantasies primarily concerning mastery of the physical environment; while those in the high group had, as well, fantasies concerning their status in a peopled world. The high-scoring children tended to be more aggressive than the low-scoring ones, and finally, to have a stronger sexual identification with the parent of the same sex than did the low-scoring children.

Constricting anxiety tended to depress performance, but some children who were anxious and constricted in the interview were able to do very well on the criterion tests. It may be noted here that one aspect of the design which appears suspect is that one is not, by the design used, determining base-line creative ability, but rather creative function under a special, and specific, set of circumstances. The circumstances can be assumed to stimulate the performance of some of the children, while depressing that of others. We now feel the problem to be less of a major obstruction to valid findings, however, than we had at first feared; for the creative solution implies response to a problem stimulus. It is not found by withdrawing from the stimulus. The response to the test situation, therefore, would tend to improve the scores of the more creative children. As noted above, constricting anxiety in the interview sometimes accompanied high criterion test performance. The children showing such a pattern refused to block out the stimulus, even though it was anxiety-producing.

One category that did not correlate with the test findings will be noted briefly. In spite of the popular image of the creative person as being independent-minded, the tendency for the child to make up his own mind instead of following the parental lead did not correlate with high-test performance. It may be that the stubbornness and independence of thought characteristic of some creative adults may be only facultative, a necessary implementation of creative thinking if the new idea is to survive an initially hostile, or at least inert, response.

Comment

The first purpose of this study is to gain evidence as to possible environmental factors in the development of creative function. It appears from the data that there are certain family characteristics correlated with creative performance in the children. These are, in summary, expressiveness without domination, acceptance of regression, and a lack of dependency of each parent on the other, or on the marriage or family as a means of reinforcing their own individual status. Actually, in no case among the children who ranked high on the criterion testing was a family pattern found which differed markedly from that described above. The suggestion is thus strengthened that environmental factors may be essential in the development of creative function.

Using the above hypothesis, the second purpose of the study is to attempt to formulate from the data the ways in which the family setting might facilitate the creative response. The characteristic pattern found in families of creative children is an openness of exchange and active interaction between two well-defined adult personalities, with the better defined personality of the two tending to be that of the parent of the same sex as the child. The parents express emotionally laden material, both toward each other and toward the children. It is as if these parents have in large part settled the question of who and what *they* are, and although the knowledge is painful and anxiety-provoking at times, they do not turn aside from it. Instead, they may overreact to it, and thus there is likely to be considerable open hostility from time to time in the homes of the high-ranking children. Along with a less marked dependency of each marital partner on the other, these parents depend less on the parent-child relationship as a means of reinforcing their own security as individuals than do the parents of the low-ranking children.

It is hypothesized that the effect of such a family pattern on the children is, first, because of the expressiveness and lack of family interdependency, to impose a chronically anxiety-provoking situation in the home. Along with the threat to the child, however, comes a security, introjected in part from the parents, who are sure of themselves as individuals, and in part resultant from the lack of threat of domination. The child, then, has conflicts brought into the open, which need not be completely repressed. Both the security of the child's personality alluded to above, and the expressiveness encouraged in the home assure this. The findings from both the psychological testing and the interview with the child that the child is actively involved with oedipal or heterosexual problems, has good early recall, and has a strong self-image support this part of the formulation.

A second effect of the family pattern is to allow the child comfortably to regress. This calls for parental qualities similar to those noted above. The parents are sure enough of *themselves* to regress at times, without being afraid of losing control, thus relieving the child of guilt over its own immature behavior. They need not, further, demand constant maturity of behavior in the child, in order to bolster their own picture of themselves as parents. As has been pointed out in the psychological tests, the high-scoring children extensively used regressive modes of organization, as well as mature ones; and in the child's interview, the high-scoring children's behavior vacillated rapidly between adult and infantile.

A third effect of the high-scoring child's typical family pattern is that it does not inhibit the child in the development of his individual patterns of viewing the world. The family stimulates but does not dominate. This is supported by the parents' lack of insistence that the child accept their values, the child's strong self-image, the child's acceptance of his unreal percepts on the Rorschach, and the "different" Draw-a-Family picture.

A fourth effect, implied by some of the above comments, is that the identification patterns of the creative child favor reliance on other defenses than withdrawal and repression. This is supported by the expressiveness of the parent of the same sex, and the child's strong sexual identification with that parent.

The psychological testing showed the high-scoring children to be less reality bound than the low-scoring ones. The anxiety experienced by the high-scoring children is not characteristically handled by repression, but rather by a fantasied restructuring of the environment. These restructuring fantasies tend to be concerned with human interactions, and tend not to be flamboyantly omnipotent. They are not particularly strongly held, in that fantasy can rapidly change, but they are held with the temporary suspension of disbelief essential to the creative act.

Creative function is the product of the creative mind. A definition of the creative mind proposed here is that it is one in which a problem stimulus easily evokes material from various experiential areas. This mind is able to regress in terms of organization so that the material from those experiential areas has free access to the problem. It is, further, able to accept a resulting synthesis apart from any apparent illogical quality that synthesis may have. The development of such a mind, it is hypothesized, proceeds from an adaptive, reconstructive technique learned early in childhood, in which the child regresses comfortably, and does not use repression or withdrawal as primary means of dealing with a chronically anxiety-producing environment. Finally, the learning or adoption of such a technique depends largely on family patterns which favor its emergence. The elucidation of some of those patterns has been attempted in this study.

Summary

From a study of intellectually gifted fourth graders and their parents, a hypothesis is developed as to the nature of the creative response and its relationship to various factors in the home environment.

JACOB W. GETZELS
PHILIP W. JACKSON

Family Environment and Cognitive Style:
A Study of the Sources of Highly Intelligent
and of Highly Creative Adolescents

From the time Binet first constructed his intelligence test with the resulting ubiquitous IQ metric to the present, the problem of intellectual ability and giftedness has remained largely a psychological issue. The important question has been a psychometric one: how can we obtain a precise measure of the general ability called intelligence or of a group of factors comprising so-called mental capacity? When sociologists have attempted to deal with differential cognitive functioning and giftedness, their efforts have most frequently been restricted to relating social class or ethnic variables to *amount* of mental ability as represented by the aforementioned IQ.

As we have had occasion to remark elsewhere (Nov., 1959), involved in the IQ conception of intellectual functioning are several types of confusion, if not outright error. First, there is the limitation of the single metric itself, which not only restricts our perspective of the more general phenomenon, but places on the one concept a greater theoretical and predictive burden than it was intended to carry. Second, within the universe of intellectual functioning, we have behaved as if the intelligence test represented an adequate sampling of *all* functions—the "gifted child," for example, has become synonymous with the "child with a high IQ." Third, we have so emphasized the measuring of different *amounts* of intellectual ability that we have neglected the understanding of different *kinds* of intellectual ability.

Despite its longevity, there is nothing inevitable about the use of the IQ in defining intellectual ability and potential giftedness. Indeed, it may be

From *American Sociological Review,* June, 1961, *26* (3), pp. 351–359. Used by permission of the publisher.

argued that in many ways this metric is only an historical accident—a consequence of the fact that early inquiries in the field of intellectual functioning had as their social context the classroom and as their criterion academic progress. If the initial context of inquiry into mental ability had not been the classroom, other qualities defining intellectual functioning might have been identified just as the qualities measured by the IQ apparently were in the classroom. Indeed, even without shifting the context of inquiry from the classroom, if only the original criterion of learning had been changed, the qualities defining intellectual functioning and giftedness might also have been changed. For example, if we recognized that learning involves the production of novelty as well as the remembrance of course-content, then measures of creativity as well as the IQ might become appropriate defining characteristics of mental ability and giftedness. It is, of course, a commonplace to recognize people who seem to be highly "intelligent" (as measured by the IQ) but apparently not "creative" (whatever that seems to mean in any particular case), and people who are "creative" but not necessarily "intelligent" (at least as measured by the conventional IQ).

The research project from which we are drawing our present report was directed toward the following three related tasks:

1. To identify two groups of subjects differing significantly in *kind* of intellectual functioning—in this case, "intelligence" and "creativity."

2. To examine the personal-social behavioral concomitants of the two kinds of intellectual functioning—for example, would the groups also differ in levels of achievement, patterns of interpersonal relations, types of career aspirations, etc.?

3. To study in some depth the family environment of the two groups.

Differentiating Cognitive Style:
Subjects, Methods, Findings

The methods and findings with respect to the first two tasks have already been reported in detail elsewhere (1959; July, 1960; 1960), and will be presented here only insofar as is necessary to clarify the issues and findings with respect to the third task—determining the relationship between type of intellectual functioning and family environment—which is the focus of this report.

The experimental groups were drawn from 449 adolescents constituting the total population of a Midwestern private secondary school[1] on the basis of performance on the following instruments:

[1] The children in this school come in large measure from families who are in the employ of an urban university, or from families who, although not employed by the university, prefer to reside in or near the university community, and to send their children to its school because of its presumed excellence. The children are much above average in ability, the mean IQ of the total school being 132, with a standard deviation of 15.1.

1. Standard IQ tests, most usually the Binet itself.

2. Five creativity measures, taken or adapted from Guilford and Cattell, or constructed especially for the study, as follows:

a. Word association. The subject was asked to give as many definitions as possible to fairly common stimulus words, e.g., "bolt," "bark," "sack." His score depended on the absolute number of definitions and the number of different categories into which his definitions could be put.

b. Uses for things. The subject was required to give as many uses as he could for objects customarily having a single stereotyped function, e.g. "brick," "paper clip." His score depended on the number and originality of the uses he mentioned.

c. Hidden shapes. The subject was required to find a given geometric form hidden in more complex geometric forms or patterns.

d. Fables. The subject was required to provide a "moralistic," a "humorous," and a "sad" ending to each of four fables in which the last line was missing. His score depended on the number, appropriateness, and originality of the endings.

e. Makeup problems. The subject was presented with four complex paragraphs, each containing a number of numerical statements, e.g., "the costs in building a house." He was required to make up as many mathematical problems as he could that might be solved with the information given. His score depended upon the number, appropriateness, and originality of the problems.

What most of these verbal and numerical tests had in common was that the score depended not on a single predetermined correct response, as is frequently the case of the common intelligence test, but on the number, novelty, and variety of responses.

On the basis of the IQ measure and a summated score on the creativity measures, the two experimental groups were formed as follows:

1. The high-creativity group. These were subjects at the top 20 percent on the creativity measures when compared with same-sex age peers, but *below* the top 20 percent in IQ. Their mean IQ was 127, with a range from 108 to 138. N = 26 (15 boys, 11 girls).

2. The high-intelligence group. These were subjects in the top 20 percent in IQ when compared with same-sex age peers, but *below* the top 20 percent on the creativity measures. Their mean IQ was 150, with a range from 139 to 179. N = 28 (17 boys, 11 girls).[2]

[2] The initial samples of highly creative and highly intelligent subjects were larger than the final experimental groups. Because of the goals of the overall project, students who were also especially outstanding in qualities such as psychological health or morality were the subjects of independent study. In a sense, the present experimental groups may be said to represent relatively "pure" types, since they do not include adolescents gifted as well in a number of these other characteristics. There were also students who were at once both "highly intelligent" and "highly creative." These too are not included in the present study.

Having thus identified two groups differing (at least by test score) in style of intellectual functioning—in effect, the objective of the first research task—we were ready to turn to our second task, which may now be put in the form of a direct question: What is the nature of the performance of the groups on the following personal-social variables: school achievement, perception by teachers, production of fantasies, and choice of adult career? The findings were quite straightforward:

1. *School achievement*. Although there is a 23-point difference in average IQ between the high IQ's and the high creatives, the school achievement of the two groups as measured by standardized achievement tests was *equally superior* to the population from which they were drawn.

2. *Perception by teachers*. The teachers were asked to rate all students in the school on the degree they enjoyed having them in class. The high-IQ student was rated as more desirable than the average student; the high creative was not.

3. *Fantasy production*. Six thematic apperception test-type pictures were shown, and the subjects were required to write four-minute stories to each of the pictures. The stories of the two groups were found to be strikingly different, the creative making significantly greater use of stimulus-free themes, unexpected endings, humor, and playfulness.

4. *Career aspirations*. The two groups were asked to indicate their career aspirations and occupational choices. When these were analyzed into "conventional" (e.g., doctor, lawyer, engineer) and "unconventional (e.g., adventurer, inventor, writer) categories, it was found that 16 percent of the high IQ's and 62 percent of the high creatives had made "unconventional" career choices.

In short, two conclusions seemed clear from studying the children themselves: First, they could be differentiated by kind of preferred intellectual functioning, i.e., into high-IQ and high-creativity groups. Second, when they were so differentiated, the two groups were equally superior in achievement to the population from which they were drawn, and they themselves differed significantly in a number of personal-social variables, including perception by teachers, fantasy production, and choice of career.

Family Environment and Cognitive Style: Methods, Subjects, Findings

The central issue of the present report is: Do the two groups also vary systematically in the nature of their family environment? Accordingly, family inventories and two- to three-hour interviews were obtained from approximately 80 percent of the mothers of the two groups. The analysis of these data may be discussed with respect to each of the following family variables.

1. Education and occupation of the parents.

2. Age of the parents.

3. Mother's recollection of her own family situation when she was her child's age.

4. Reading interests in the family, at least as represented by the number and type of magazines taken.

5. Parental satisfaction and dissatisfaction with the child and his school.

6. Parental satisfaction and dissatisfaction with their own child-rearing practices.

7. Mother's description of the kinds of friends preferred for her child.

EDUCATION AND OCCUPATION OF PARENTS

Educational data were available for the parents of twenty-four of the twenty-eight high IQ's and for twenty-four of the twenty-six high creatives. When these data were analyzed by simply dichotomizing college graduates versus others, the result obtained could be summarized as in Table 1.

Table 1. NUMBER OF COLLEGE GRADUATES AMONG FATHERS AND MOTHERS OF THE TWO EXPERIMENTAL GROUPS

	IQ (n = 24)	Creative (n = 24)	χ^2	p*
Father	21	15	4.00	0.05
Mother	16	12	1.37	N.S.

* Because of the exploratory nature of this phase of the research, many of the comparisons presented here were derived from the obtained data. Therefore, the probability values attached to the chi-squares in this and the following tables must be viewed with caution.

The data were also dichotomized by parents having at least some graduate training as against those having no graduate training. The results of this analysis are given in Table 2.

Table 2. NUMBER OF PARENTS HAVING SOME GRADUATE TRAINING

	IQ (n = 24)	Creative (n = 24)	χ^2	p
Father	19	13	3.38	0.10
Mother	13	5	5.69	0.02

Whichever analysis is undertaken, it seems that the parents of the high-IQ child tend to have higher educational status than the parents of the high-creativity child. But what is perhaps more noteworthy is the *greater specialized training* of both the mother and the father of the high IQ's. The essential difference is probably not so much in the general level of cultivation, which is very high for both groups when compared to the general population, but in the significantly greater specialization of training or, if one will, "professionalization of education" of the high-IQ group.

In this connection, the occupational data are relevant. The data for fathers are presented in Table 3, and for mothers in Table 4.

It appears that we are dealing not only with two different types of children but with two different types of parents. As might be anticipated from the data on educational status, a greater proportion of the high-IQ fathers than of the high-creativity fathers are found in the academic or educational occupations. But it is noteworthy that, despite their greater professional training, a greater proportion of the mothers of the high-IQ children than of the high-creativity children are exclusively housewives, and do not hold other full- or part-time jobs. It would seem that the mothers of the high-IQ subjects have more time to devote to their children than do the mothers of the high-creativity subjects. In this connection, it will be shown from other sources of data that the high-IQ mothers are, in fact, likely to be more vigilant about the "correct" upbringing of their children than the high-creativity mothers.

Table 3. OCCUPATIONAL STATUS OF THE FATHERS OF THE TWO EXPERIMENTAL GROUPS

Occupational status	IQ (n = 24)	Creative (n = 24)	χ^2	p
University teaching, research, editing	15	7		
			6.15	0.02
Business	4	11		
Medicine, law	5	6	—	—

Table 4. OCCUPATIONAL STATUS OF THE MOTHERS OF THE TWO EXPERIMENTAL GROUPS

Occupational status	IQ (n = 24)	Creative (n = 24)	χ^2	p
Housewife only	18	11		
			4.27	0.05
Full- or part-time employment	6	13		

AGE OF PARENTS

The mean age is almost exactly the same for the two groups of mothers, and although the age of the fathers tended to be slightly greater for the high-IQ group than for the high-creativity group, it was not significantly so. The significant and striking difference between the two groups was in the discrepancy or congruence between the age of the father and mother. If the data are dichotomized as one year or less age difference and two years or more age difference, the results may be summarized as in Table 5.

We may only conjecture at this time about the reasons for the age discrepancies or similarities between the parents of the present sample, and about the effects of these age factors on the family environment. But two reasons for a number of the discrepancies seem relevant: waiting to finish

Table 5. AGE DIFFERENCE BETWEEN PARENTS FOR THE TWO EXPERIMENTAL GROUPS

Age difference between parents	IQ (n = 24)	Creative (n = 24)	χ^2	p
0 to 1 year	4	13		
			7.38	0.01
2 or more years	20	11		

advanced academic training before risking marital responsibilities, and waiting to be satisfactorily "settled" to maintain a family in the "right" style. Both reasons suggest an apparently greater insecurity among the high-IQ parents than among the high-creativity parents, a suggestion that is also supported by subsequent interview data.

MOTHER'S MEMORIES OF OWN HOME

The relevant interview question was: How would you describe the home you lived in as a child? The responses were long and detailed—the mothers seemed to enjoy relating their own real or imagined childhood experiences to their children's present situation. Here, for example, is a fairly typical response by one of the high-IQ mothers:[3]

It was as typically Midwestern middle class American as one could find. Neither rich nor poor . . . The family belonged to important people in town. Father was the principal of the school, active in church and in the literary group. His was a large family, and there were many homes we could go to. Father died when I was thirteen. Mother began teaching school. We thought more about money. Then I worked while in college. I have some doubt about that—traumatic insecurity, especially financially. So abnormally thrifty ever since—keeping magazines. . . . I hope children won't miss these highlights of our life even if disasters. . . .

The problem of quantifying this kind of material is of course formidable, and many differences that one "feels" as one reads the complete sets of interviews "wash out" as one attempts to categorize. Nonetheless, certain categorical differences may be noted. For example, seven of the twenty-two high-IQ mothers for whom interview material is available say specifically of their home that it was "middle class," and only one of the eighteen creative mothers for whom interview material is available says this. Eight of the twenty-two high-IQ mothers describe their family in rather global-emotional terms; twelve of the eighteen creative mothers seem to do this. That is, the high-IQ mothers tend to be more "stereotypic" in their descriptions (they tend to put themselves in "classes"); the creative mothers attempt rather more rounded descriptions.

[3] Here and throughout the paper the mothers' statements are taken from notes recorded during the interview. At the time these interviews were made, the parents of five other experimental groups were also being studied. The interviewers did not know into which of the seven groups any mother belonged. The present quotations have been altered in irrelevant details to maintain anonymity.

But the chief categorical difference—and a very relevant one—lies in their reference to the financial status of their home and childhood. As the data in Table 6 show, the high-IQ parents tend not only to mention finances significantly more often than the high-creativity parents, but to emphasize financial hardship more often. Whatever else these responses imply about the different remembrance of things past and areas of latent concern, they do tend to support the suggestion of greater insecurity among the parents of the high-IQ children than among the parents of the high-creativity children.

Table 6. MENTION OF FINANCIAL STATUS AND OF POVERTY IN DESCRIPTIONS OF OWN HOME LIFE BY MOTHERS OF THE TWO EXPERIMENTAL GROUPS

	IQ (n = 22)	Creative (n = 18)	χ^2	p
Mention of finances	16	7	4.64	0.05
Emphasis on poverty, financial hardship	9	1	4.84*	0.05

* Yates correction applied.

READING INTERESTS IN THE HOME

It is almost impossible to obtain an exact measure of the reading habits of a family. Nonetheless, an attempt toward a partial assessment was made by asking the following interview questions: What magazines and newspapers do you subscribe to or buy regularly? What magazines do you read just once in a while?

Professional or scholarly journals, which would have increased the count for the high-IQ parents, were omitted in the analysis. Despite this, there was a difference in the number of magazines coming into the homes of the high-IQ and high-creativity subjects, a difference that is quite illuminating.

The twenty-two high-IQ families reported reading "regularly" a total of 125 magazines, and "sometimes" 54 magazines. The eighteen high-creative families reported reading "regularly" a total of 107 magazines, and "sometimes" 30 magazines. The respective means were 8.14 for the high IQ's and 5.94 for the high creatives. If the families are divided into those mentioning six or fewer and those mentioning seven or more magazines, the relationship portrayed in Table 7 is observed.

Table 7. NUMBER OF MAGAZINES "TAKEN" OR READ IN HOMES OF THE TWO EXPERIMENTAL GROUPS

Number of magazines	IQ (n = 22)	Creative (n = 18)	χ^2	p
6 or fewer	7	12		
			4.34	0.05
7 or more	15	6		

There seem to be significant quantitative differences between the two groups. There are also some noteworthy qualitative trends in the data. For example, twenty-one of the twenty-two high-IQ mothers report taking or reading fifty "mass media magazines" (*Time, Life, Newsweek, Reader's Digest*). This is about 28 percent of their total. Sixteen of the eighteen high-creativity mothers report taking or reading twenty-seven "mass media magazines," which is about 19 percent of their total. Conversely, five of the twenty-two high-IQ mothers mention seven "magazines of liberal political comment" (*Reporter, Nation, New Republic*)—about 3 percent of the total—but seven of the eighteen high-creativity mothers mention ten magazines in this category, i.e., about 7 percent of their total. Perhaps the most noteworthy difference is in the number of children's magazines (*Boys Life, Junior Natural History Magazine,* etc.) mentioned by the two groups. Ten of the twenty-two high-IQ mothers mention seventeen such magazines, three of the eighteen high-creativity mothers mention five such magazines.

5. *Parental satisfaction and dissatisfaction with the child and with his school.* A crucial issue in the present study of family environment and giftedness is the reaction of the parent to any unusual qualities in the child and the type of education the child is getting. Two interview questions are relevant here:

a. During your child's earliest years in school, did the teachers call to your attention or did you yourself notice anything unusual about him and school?

b. As far as the present school is concerned, what are the things you like best about the education your child is getting? Is there anything about your child's education at this school that you are not satisfied with?

The replies to both questions are quite consistent and informative. They will be discussed in turn.

a. Although the high-IQ and the high-creativity parents report the same number of total observations and the same number of favorable and unfavorable qualities in their children as seen by *teachers,* the high-IQ parents report both a greater number of total observations (fifty-nine against thirty-one) and a greater number of unfavorable qualities as seen by *themselves.* When the latter data are dichotomized into "not more than one unfavorable quality" and "more than one unfavorable quality," the result is the relationship presented in Table 8.

Table 8. NUMBER OF UNFAVORABLE QUALITIES OBSERVED IN THEIR CHILDREN BY MOTHERS OF THE TWO GROUPS

Number of unfavorable qualities observed	IQ (n = 23)	Creative (n = 19)	χ^2	p
Not more than one	13	17		
			5.53	0.02
More than one	10	2		

What is noteworthy in these data is the greater "vigilance" and "critical" or at least "less accepting" attitude of the high-IQ mothers—they both observe *more* about their children and they observe a greater number of *objectionable* qualities. It is as if they were on the lookout for things to improve about their children. (In this connection, the greater number of children's magazines the high-IQ parents take is perhaps relevant.)

b. The same "vigilance" and critical attitude is seen in their attitudes toward the school their children are attending. Here again, the high-IQ parents report a greater number of total observations (138 against 95), and a significantly greater number of dissatisfactions, as shown in Table 9.

Table 9. NUMBER OF UNFAVORABLE SCHOOL QUALITIES OBSERVED BY MOTHERS OF THE TWO EXPERIMENTAL GROUPS

Number of unfavorable school qualities observed	IQ (n = 23)	Creative (n = 19)	χ^2	p
Not more than one	7	12		
			4.5	.05
More than one	16	7		

6. *Parental satisfaction with their child-rearing practices.* Despite the apparent greater misgiving and uncertainty of the high-IQ mother toward her child and toward the school, she expresses fewer misgivings and uncertainties than does the high-creativity mother regarding her own child-training practices. It is almost as if she were critical of others but "smug" about herself. The relevant interview question was: As you look back on the ways you have tried to make your child responsible to you as far as bedtime, playing outside, leaving the house, homework, and so forth were concerned, would you say you were too lenient, not lenient enough, or what? The results are presented in Table 10.

Table 10. MOTHERS' SATISFACTION AND DISSATISFACTION WITH THEIR OWN CHILD-TRAINING PRACTICES

Opinion of own child-training practice	IQ (n = 23)	Creative (n = 19)	χ^2	p
Satisfied	17	8		
			4.37	0.05
Dissatisfied	6	11		

7. *Kinds of friends preferred for their children.* There is one final set of data that rounds out the differences between the family environment of the high-IQ and the high-creativity families, at least as represented by the mothers' attitudes. The interview question was: What qualities do you like to see in your child's friends?

Again, the high-IQ mothers had somewhat more to say. But the striking finding was the difference in what they said. When the qualities mentioned are divided into two categories, the one relating to "external" character-istics (e.g., "good family," "good manners," "studious"), the other to "internal" characteristics (e.g., "sense of values," "interest in something," "openness—not secretive"), the result is the relationship summarized in Table 11.

Table 11. CHARACTERISTICS PREFERRED FOR CHILDREN'S FRIENDS BY MOTHERS OF THE TWO GROUPS

Characteristics	IQ (n = 23)		Creative (n = 19)			
	X̄*	S	X̄	S	t	p
External—Specific, e.g., good family, manners, studious	2.48	1.20	1.58	1.07	2.56	0.02
Internal—General, e.g., sense of values, interests, openness	0.91	1.12	1.79	1.47	2.13	0.05

* These means refer to the average number of characteristics mentioned.

Several sample responses may give some greater substance to these tabular differences. Here, for example, are two high-IQ mothers describing the qualities they would like to see in their child's friends: (a) "Sunday school children, religious, go to church every Sunday, of parents whose standards are ours. Honest, sincere, clean-minded, and clean-mouthed. Studious." (b) "Right between the eyes—aware of my own inadequacies. Intelligence is certainly foremost—admit to my snobbism. Kind of cultural background, not money. A level of family. What I don't like—wild kid who doesn't know how to behave in a house—dirty talk—I've put up with it—a certain amount is acceptable—outside can use up energies. Neither extroverted nor introverted." Here are two high-creativity mothers describing the qualities they would like to see in their child's friends: (a) "Like what I want to see in E [her child]—it's the same thing. Valid sense of values—what a person is rather than what he appears to be. Satisfaction in creative constructive activity. Balance and maturity in interpersonal relations. Interest and enthusiasm for learning and reaching out beyond it to greater understanding." (b) "Openness—not secretive that old folks won't understand. Interest in something to do—not bored expression. Temperate in manners and habits. Frankness and honesty. Interest in living." It is here in the projections of desirable traits for their children's friends that we may perhaps see the most honest aspirations for their own children. As the high-creative mother says, "It's the same thing." And it is here, as we have seen, that we again find some very striking differences indeed.

Discussion and Summary

It is clear that the intellectual functioning of adolescents can be differentiated, not only into quantitative categories of high and low IQ, but also into
qualitative categories among which are "high IQ without concomitantly
high creativity" and "high creativity without concomitantly high IQ." The
intellectual functioning represented by these two categories bears resemblance to Guilford's factors of "convergent" and "divergent" thinking
(April, 1957). When adolescents representing these qualitative categories
are identified, it is found that they also differ on a number of significant
personal-social variables. For example, although both are equally superior
to the average student in school achievement, they are perceived differently
by teachers, they differ in the nature of their fantasy productions, and they
aspire to different career goals.

With respect to these initial findings, and before a study of the family
environments was undertaken, we suggested that,

the essence of the performance of our Creative adolescents lay in their ability
to produce new forms, to risk conjoining elements that are customarily thought
of as independent and dissimilar, to go off in new directions. The creative
adolescent possesses the ability to free himself from the usual to "diverge" from
the customary. He seemed to enjoy the risk and uncertainty of the unknown.
In contrast, the high IQ adolescent seemed to possess to a high degree the
ability and the need to focus on the usual, to be channelled and controlled in
the direction of the right answer—the customary. He appeared to shy away
from the risk and the uncertainty of the unknown and to seek out the safety
and security of the known (1959, p. 56).

In an attempt to relate the differences in intellectual behavior to a
broader psychosocial context we found fruitful Maslow's formulations of
Defense and Growth (Getzels & Jackson, July, 1960, p. 122). He writes:

Every human being has both sets of forces within him. One set clings to safety
and defensiveness out of fear, tending to regress, hanging on to the past . . .
afraid to take chances, afraid to jeopardize what he already has, afraid of independence, freedom, separation. The other set of forces impels him forward
toward wholeness of self and uniqueness of self, toward full functioning of all
his capacities, toward confidence in the face of the external world at the same
time that he can accept his deepest, real, unconscious Self. . . . The basic
dilemma or conflict between the defensive forces and the growth trends I conceive to be existential, imbedded in the deepest nature of the human being,
now and forever into the future. . . . Therefore we can consider the process of
healthy growth to be a never-ending series of free choice situations, confronting each individual at every point throughout his life, in which he must choose
between the delights of safety and growth, dependence and independence. . . .
Safety has both anxieties and delights; growth has both anxieties and delights
(1956, pp. 37–38).

In these terms, the high-IQ adolescent may be seen as preferring the anxieties and delights of "safety," the high-creativity adolescent the anxieties and delights of "growth."

We would maintain that the intellectual differences between these groups and the underlying psychosocial orientations have their source not only in the immediate school experience but in the family environment in which the adolescents grew up. The family environment of these students, at least as portrayed by the mothers' interviews, is consonant with the psychosocial formulations applied to the groups. The parents of the high-IQ student tend to recall greater financial difficulties during their own childhood and hence, at least by inference, may be said to have experienced in the past, and perhaps the present, greater real or imagined personal insecurity than is true for the parents of the highly creative students. The high-IQ parents seem to be more "vigilant" with respect to their children's behavior and their manifest academic performance. As compared with the parents of the highly creative adolescents, the parents of the high-IQ students tend at once to be more critical of both their children and the school; it is as if their standards were always just one step ahead of attainment. Nor is their vigilance limited to concern for their child's educational progress. They appear equally concerned with the desirable qualities possessed by their children's friends. The qualities they would like to see in their children's friends, which may in a sense be conceived as projections of the qualities they would like to see in their own children, focus upon such immediately visible virtues as cleanliness, good manners, studiousness. In contrast, the parents of the creative adolescents focus upon less visible qualities such as the child's openness to experience, his values, and his interests and enthusiasms.

When these differences in the parents' attitudes and aspirations are combined with differences in educational specialization, the age discrepancy between father and mother, and the kind of reading material available in the home, the overall impression of the high-IQ family is one in which individual divergence is limited and risks minimized, the overall impression of the high-creativity family is one in which individual divergence is permitted and risks are accepted. In this sense, the concepts of Defense and Growth, which were used to distinguish the high-IQ adolescent and the high-creativity adolescent, seem also useful in distinguishing between their family environment.

Conclusion

Several concluding comments seem in order, particularly since the type of data presented here lends itself rather easily to misinterpretation and overgeneralization. First, in describing the high-IQ and the high-creativity adolescents, we do not intend to give the impression of the one as representing "good guys" and the other "bad guys." The distinction we are making is analytic, not evaluative. Both convergent and divergent thinking are valuable in their separate ways. Second, in discussing the greater "vigilance" of the parents of the high-IQ group, we do not intend to give support to the current unfortunate dichotomy between "bad" authoritarianism and "good" permissiveness. The issue is not all-or-none, either-or, but appropriate emphasis. Third, in adducing evidence for the greater "specialized education" and "bookishness" of the parents of the high-IQ children as against the parents of the high-creativity children, we do not intend to suggest that the presence of books or specialized knowledge in the family leads inevitably to high-IQ, the absence to high-creativity. It is not the presence of books or specialized knowledge but their use and meaning that make the difference. Finally, we should like to point out that, at least as much by the issues raised as by the nature of the preliminary findings we have presented, the question of how types of cognition are shaped by types of family environment is a fruitful area for sociological examination.

IRWIN FLESCHER

Anxiety and Achievement of Intellectually Gifted and Creatively Gifted Children

Introduction

An immediate concern with regard to recent explorations of the creative process is the limited generalizations that can be made from the findings. The discovery (Getzels & Jackson, 1960) that creativity is an important determinant of academic achievement, although there is a relatively low correlation between creativity and intelligence, appears destined to have far-reaching educational implications. In view of this, the atypical nature of the selected sample in the aforementioned study necessitates scientific caution in interpreting the significance of those results. The demonstration of equal superiority in scholastic achievement between a highly intelligent and a highly creative group was based on the failure to reject the null hypothesis. It is noteworthy that, although the mean IQ scores were disparate, both groups represented an exceptionally high order of intellectual potential. There is a question as to whether differential achievement expectations were realistic in that situation, particularly since standardized achievement tests are deficient in measuring gifted vertical and horizontal development in areas beyond the normally prescribed curriculum. In a series of replicated procedures (Torrance, 1960) with a variety of school populations, it was found that the Getzels-Jackson phenomenon is likely to occur under certain conditions but not under others. However, the reasons for the failure to reproduce the results in certain samples are not clearly evident.

The intent of the present study was to pursue the validity of implications concerning the comparative influence of unusual creative thinking and exceptional intellectual endowment on the learning process. It was felt that more meaningful observations and increased confidence in the findings

From *Journal of Psychology*, 1963, *56*, pp. 251–268. Used by permission of the publisher.

149

would derive from research involving an adequate control group characterized by nonextraordinary intelligence and creativity. Furthermore, these indices would need to be respectively equated with nontalented intelligence as found in a creatively-gifted group, and nontalented creativity as found in an intellectually-gifted group. Scientific inquiry warrants inclusion of still another group in which subjects are simultaneously gifted in intelligence and creativity. It was stipulated in the previously cited studies (Getzels & Jackson, 1960; Torrance, 1960) that individuals outstanding in both respects were eliminated from the design. This omission assumes critical importance in the light of the theoretical proposition (Guilford, 1959a) that general intelligence and creativity may be respectively conceptualized as convergent- and divergent-thinking processes which represent two apparently antithetic factors of intellect. How formalized intelligence and creative ability interact to affect school achievement is a necessary dimension to examine.

Explanations regarding complex cognitive functioning inevitably lead to the search for intervening variables. The Getzels and Jackson study revealed that achievement motivation was not a distinguishing factor. In seeking clarification of the intelligence-creativity-achievement relationship, the present investigation was designed to determine to what extent the personality variable of anxiety is a mediating influence.

The degree to which operational anxiety may be a hidden selective factor when groups are constituted by levels of intelligence and creativity is of crucial importance in contrasting achievement measures. The interfering and the facilitating effects of differential anxiety on academic achievement have been established (Sarason, Davidson, & Lighthall, 1960). There is reason to suppose that the effects of inordinate anxiety are no less disruptive and restrictive in relation to the elusive and fragile gift of productive creativity. Evidence of an inverse relationship between the personality trait of attitudinal rigidity and verbal creativity (Fleming & Weintraub, 1962) supports this position. The converse proposition logically follows that a low anxiety level is a necessary correlate of unhampered and spontaneous psychological processes characteristic of creative endeavor. This assumption is in keeping with the neopsychoanalytic formulation (Kubie, 1958) that creativity depends on an inner freedom from distortions and obstructions of neurotic origin. The dependence of divergent-thinking operations on personality dynamics is further suggested by the finding that ". . . creative persons are especially disposed to admit complexity and even disorder into their perceptions without being made anxious by the resulting chaos" (MacKinnon, 1962, p. 489).

Method

MEASURES

In the early part of 1962 a variety of creative aptitude tests was administered to the sixth-grade population of the East Williston School

District. These divergent-thinking tasks were modeled after the theoretical constructs developed by Guilford (1950, 1956). The creativity battery included five separate tests; two of these were scored twice, for independent criteria of creative thinking. The seven subscores were converted to standard scores, and a composite measure was computed which yielded an index of Total Creativity.

A brief description of the divergent-thinking tasks and scoring procedures is presented below.

A word association test was given in which the children were required to respond to each of a list of twenty stimulus words. The test items were selected from a compilation of the 570 most commonly used words in the English language (Lorge, 1949). For every stimulus, after discounting irrelevant and bizarre answers, a statistical count was made of the frequency of mention of each association. The only responses credited were words or phrases that were one of a kind. The score for each child gave a measure of Remote Associations.

As a measure of nonverbal creativity, the students were instructed to "draw an old man." Inspection of the projective material revealed a consensus in the modes of expressing this concept, e.g., a high frequency of beards, canes, and eyeglasses. Productions which digressed from the standard perspective, and which were judged to be novel or clever, were given appropriate credit as Divergent Drawings.

A test requiring the designation of different uses for each of six familiar objects was administered. Common and unusual uses were determined by statistical frequency. Two scores were derived from this test. The crediting of unusual evocations yielded a score for Unique Uses. In addition, the test replies, exclusive of the unusual answers, were re-evaluated. The enumerated common responses to each stimulus were inspected to ascertain for each child the number of changes in *set* from one type of content category to another. This supplied a measure of Spontaneous Flexibility.

A task of devising diversified titles for a given story plot was included in the battery. Rare and clever titles provided a score for Original Titles. In addition, after discounting original responses, the number of obvious or ordinary titles offered determined the degree of Ideational Fluency.

The final test in the creativity series was a written composition. The children were requested to project themselves into the future and write an account about themselves as ladies or gentlemen twenty-five years hence. The entire set of future autobiographies were reread many times to establish stereotyped content and the incidence of repetitive themes. Uncommon and original ideas, and novel reorganization of familiar experiences, were the criteria used in identifying Imaginative Compositions.

Subsequent to the presentation of the divergent-thinking tests, the pupils were required to respond to two anxiety inventories (Sarason et al., 1960). The General Anxiety Scale for Children (GASC) and the Test Anxiety Scale for Children (TASC) were administered in that sequential order. Scoring was in accordance with the standardized procedures, and the resultant ratings gave evidence of the extent of General Anxiety and Test Anxiety for each child. The two scales were also combined into a Total Anxiety score.

Aside from the obtained information of creativity and anxiety, the current results of the routine school testing program were made available. These included data on intelligence and scholastic achievement.

The California Test of Mental Maturity (CTMM) supplied the measure of intellectual potential (IQ). It is noteworthy that the mean intelligence level of the available student population fell within the upper segment of the above-average range, and therefore, the incidence of high IQ scores was comparatively greater in this sample than is found in a nationally average population.

Achievement indices were derived from the results of the Metropolitan Achievement Tests (MAT). The Intermediate Battery yielded standard scores for Word Knowledge, Reading, Spelling, Language, Language Study Skills, Arithmetic Computation, Arithmetic Problem Solving and Concepts, Social Studies Information, Social Studies Study Skills, and Science. A composite score for Total Achievement, based on the ten subscores, was also computed.

GROUPS

The assembled data on IQ and Total Creativity were the indices used in the selection of four subsamples from the tested population. The stringent selection criteria precluded the formation of adequate subsamples by sex. Boys and girls were approximately equal in number in each group, thereby minimizing sex differences as a source of variation.

The groups were constituted as follows:

Ss characterized by high intelligence as defined by an IQ of 130 or above, but who were not in the top quartile in creativity, comprised the *Intellectually Talented* (N = 28). Conversely, Ss who scored in the top quartile on tests of creative thinking, but whose IQ scores fell below 130, represented the *Creatively Talented* (N = 29). A third group of Ss, identified by IQ scores of 130 or higher, and by creativity scores ranging within the top quartile, was designated the *Twice-Talented* (N = 24).

The procedure in the formation of the fourth group included additional criteria. This group represented Ss with IQ scores below 130 and creativity scores below the top quartile. After the selection of the three talented groups on the basis of exceptional intelligence and/or exceptional creativity, the entire remaining population sample fell into the nontalented category. Since the intent was the establishment of a representative control group in accordance with a balanced design, the array of nongifted scores in the two singly talented groups had to be accounted for. Hence, each S was selected from the remaining nonexceptional population whose IQ score exactly matched or closely approximated one IQ score in the group designated the *Creatively Talented,* and who simultaneously possessed a creativity score which exactly matched or closely approximated the creativity measure of one individual in the group representing the *Intellectually Talented*. The resultant group was the Nontalented (N = 29), a subsample characterized by means and standard deviations for intelligence and creativity which were of the same magnitudes as their corresponding nonexceptional counterparts in the two otherwise gifted groups.

ANALYSIS

In accordance with the plan of the investigation, the four counterbalanced groups were combined into a two-way classification system. Figure 1 illustrates the scheme of the 2 by 2 factorial design. Each of the two independent variables, intellectual endowment and creative thinking, is represented by two complementary aptitude levels (relatively defined as *high* and *low*). The arrangement provided for the simultaneous evaluation of differences between the row means and between the column means. Furthermore, the factorial approach permitted comparison of the two variables in all combinations, allowing the determination of whether there was an interaction between the row and column components, or whether each exercised an influence apart from the other. Thus, the design yielded estimates of the variance due to each of the main effects, *intelligence* and *creativity,* and to the *intelligence* X *creativity* interaction. A series of two-way analyses of variance and their corresponding F ratios were computed for the various measures of anxiety and achievement.

The analysis of variance provided the method of assessing differences in anxiety and in achievement between groups of children classified by levels

Fig. 1   2 × 2 Factorial Design

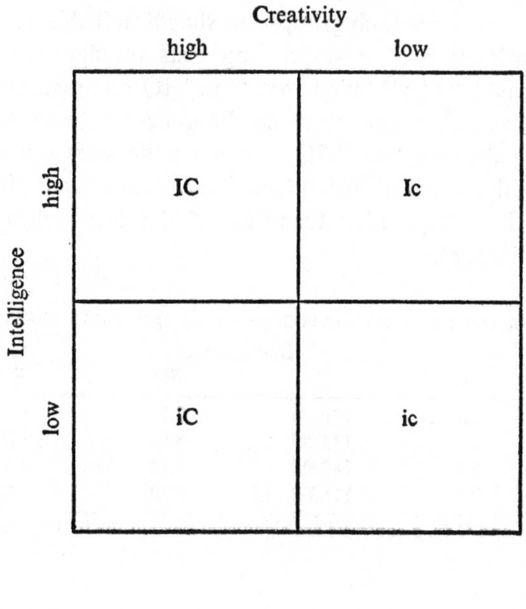

Creativity

	high	low
Intelligence high	IC	Ic
Intelligence low	iC	ic

of intelligence and creativity. In order to pursue relevant implications of the present research, it was also important to investigate similarities and differences between various sets of tests for the combined study sample. This was accomplished by the technique of multiple-factor analysis.

In the factor-analytic method, only such factors emerge as are entered in the battery. In the present design, the various anxiety, intelligence, and creativity measures, by virtue of the assumption of their relationships with achievement, were alleged to be determinants of scholastic performance. Inclusion of the achievement tests provided the criterion (academic success). The major purpose of the factor analysis was to see which of the other tests in the battery were loaded with the same factors with which the criterion was heavily loaded. It was felt that multiple-factor analysis would lend additional meaning and clarification to the outcome of the two-way analysis of variance.

Accordingly, product-moment correlations were computed among twenty-three variables, including all the available scores of anxiety, achievement, intelligence, and creativity. Prior to the derivation of the factor-analytic data, the composite measures of Total Anxiety and Total Achievement were removed from the correlation matrix, since whatever factors they represented were already present in their corresponding subtests. The matrix of intercorrelations for the remaining twenty-one variables was factored by the centroid method, and the extracted factors subsequently rotated to simple structure by the varimax procedure.

Results

Measures of central tendency and variability for the IQ and Total Creativity scores of the four research groups are shown in Table 1. A preliminary analysis of variance and corresponding tests of significance for paired contrasts indicated that all "high" vs. "low" IQ contrasts differed beyond the 0.01 level, and that there were no differences between the two "high" IQ or between the two "low" IQ measures; the very same relationships were established when the Total Creativity means were similarly scrutinized. Thus, the comparative identities of the four select groups were statistically delineated.

Table 1. MEANS AND STANDARD DEVIATIONS OF IQ AND TOTAL CREATIVITY MEASURES

Group	N	Intelligence		Creativity	
		$\bar{X}$	SD	$\bar{X}$	SD
Ic	28	140.46	7.70	5.89	2.35
iC	29	115.55	8.98	13.28	2.59
IC	24	142.08	8.71	13.58	2.15
ic	29	115.68	8.81	5.82	2.19

Note: All I vs. i and C vs. c contrasts are significant beyond the 0.01 level.

Table 2. SUMMARY OF ANALYSES OF VARIANCE FOR ANXIETY DATA

Variable	Source	df	MS	F
General anxiety				
	Intelligence (IQ)	1	10.17	0.24
	Creativity (Cr)	1	28.18	0.67
	IQ × Cr	1	34.41	0.82
	Within (W)	106	42.07	
Test anxiety				
	IQ	1	19.95	0.74
	Cr	1	29.65	1.10
	IQ × Cr	1	0.00	0.00
	W	106	27.01	
Total anxiety				
	IQ	1	58.65	0.54
	Cr	1	115.61	1.08
	IQ × Cr	1	31.92	0.30
	W	106	107.48	

Note: None of the F ratios approaches significance.

ANALYSIS OF VARIANCE

Table 2 presents the results of the analyses of variance for the three anxiety indices. The findings were uniformly negative, since nonsignificant results were obtained for both main effects and their interaction. In no instance was the null hypothesis in danger of rejection. This indicates a lack of supportive evidence that either of the two levels of intelligence or of creativity, or any combination of these factors, had a differential effect on the degree of measured anxiety. It was established that any concomitant differences in achievement in this research may not be ascribed to the mediating influence of anxiety.

The analyses of variance for the ten subscores of achievement and the total composite score are summarized in Table 3. The findings were consistent in all cases; the main effect of intelligence was highly significant beyond the 0.01 level of confidence, while the effects of the creativity factor and the interaction were nonsignificant. As anticipated, intelligence is portrayed as a powerful determinant of academic achievement. However, the data did not allow the inference to be drawn that creativity is significantly related to scholastic aptitude. The Getzels-Jackson phenomenon was not evidenced.

INTERCORRELATIONS

The intercorrelation coefficients for the twenty-three variables are arrayed in Table 4. Anxiety is seen as inversely related to achievement, but the low negative correlations were only evidenced in a few of the achievement variables. The data suggest a slight tendency for manifest anxiety to intrude on academic achievement. Anxiety appeared for the most part to

Table 3. SUMMARY OF ANALYSES OF VARIANCE FOR ACHIEVEMENT DATA

Variable	Source	df	MS	F
Word knowledge	Intelligence (IQ)	1	2569.26	49.65*
	Creativity (Cr)	1	82.41	1.59
	IQ × Cr	1	30.58	0.59
	Within (W)	106	51.75	
Reading	IQ	1	2337.05	41.42*
	Cr	1	27.47	0.49
	IQ × Cr	1	18.59	0.33
	W	106	56.42	
Spelling	IQ	1	2669.05	37.61*
	Cr	1	0.85	0.01
	IQ × Cr	1	3.12	0.04
	W	106	70.97	
Language	IQ	1	3899.48	59.25*
	Cr	1	75.44	1.15
	IQ × Cr	1	25.14	0.38
	W	106	65.82	
Language skills	IQ	1	1919.14	28.45*
	Cr	1	44.79	0.66
	IQ × Cr	1	7.16	0.10
	W	106	67.45	
Arithmetic computation	IQ	1	5620.03	82.88*
	Cr	1	0.11	0.00
	IQ × Cr	1	1.48	0.02
	W	106	67.81	
Arithmetic conceptualization	IQ	1	4310.33	85.00*
	Cr	1	5.06	0.10
	IQ × Cr	1	16.43	0.32
	W	106	50.71	
Social studies	IQ	1	1941.64	40.31*
	Cr	1	26.10	0.54
	IQ × Cr	1	46.08	0.96
	W	106	48.17	
Social studies skills	IQ	1	2780.13	37.72*
	Cr	1	35.75	0.48
	IQ × Cr	1	49.01	0.66
	W	106	73.70	
Science	IQ	1	2258.11	51.28*
	Cr	1	32.06	0.73
	IQ × Cr	1	118.65	2.69
	W	106	44.03	
Total achievement	IQ	1	293622.32	100.61*
	Cr	1	1493.66	0.51
	IQ × Cr	1	2190.03	0.75
	W	106	2918.55	

* Significant beyond the 0.01 level.

Table 4. 23 × 23 INTERCORRELATION MATRIX

(N = 110)

Variable	2	3	4	5	6	7	8	9	10	11	12	13	14	15	16	17	18	19	20	21	22	23
1 General anxiety	57	91	-17	-06	-09	-03	-06	-08	-08	-21	-22	-23	-15	-11	06	04	05	-01	04	16	-17	10
2 Test anxiety		86	-28	-18	-15	-14	-12	-09	-07	-22	-11	-30	-20	-16	03	07	14	06	-18	27	-12	12
3 Total anxiety			-25	-13	-13	-09	-10	-09	-09	-24	-19	-29	-19	-15	05	06	10	03	-06	23	-17	12
4 Word knowledge				76	73	70	64	53	59	64	53	65	83	63	-24	-04	24	14	13	02	30	12
5 Reading					66	68	68	49	54	63	58	64	82	61	-24	-04	22	09	19	05	20	12
6 Spelling						69	56	51	57	55	45	55	78	59	-23	-03	13	00	15	-04	11	01
7 Language							71	67	68	53	57	60	85	68	-27	01	15	16	13	09	23	14
8 Language skills								57	65	55	56	66	81	56	-28	03	19	13	07	07	26	15
9 Arithmetic computation									84	54	60	51	79	74	-30	-07	21	-03	00	11	15	04
10 Arithmetic conceptualization										63	62	60	84	76	-25	02	22	03	00	12	17	09
11 Social studies											63	62	77	57	-17	02	12	00	02	08	24	08
12 Social studies skills												60	76	59	-19	08	20	07	-05	02	28	07
13 Science													79	62	-24	-02	09	-05	06	-15	20	-07
14 Total achievement														79	-30	00	22	06	08	05	26	09
15 IQ															-28	01	16	02	16	02	21	04
16 Remote association																18	06	05	15	-05	-19	37
17 Divergent drawing																	05	23	-07	-01	19	36
18 Unique uses																		36	16	14	26	62
19 Spontaneous flexibility																			01	35	25	65
20 Original titles																				-15	18	35
21 Ideational fluency																					19	43
22 Imaginary compositions																						41
23 Total creativity																						

Note: Decimal points have been omitted.
r = ±.19 required for significance at the 0.05 level.
r = ±.25 required for significance at the 0.01 level.

be unrelated to intelligence or creativity, with the one exception that Ideational Fluency was correlated with Test Anxiety. Apparently, the presence of anxiety in examination situations is somewhat influential in stimulating the number of answers or ideas on tests where multiple responses are encouraged.

The intercorrelations among all eleven achievement categories were high positive, and all the MAT subscales were just as closely associated with intelligence. There were some meager positive relationships between various achievement measures and certain creativity subtects, notably Unique Uses and Imaginative Compositions. Of interest were the consistently low negative correlations between the achievement scales and Remote Associations.

IQ was also found to be inversely related to Remote Associations; however, the CTMM scale was discovered to be unrelated to the other creativity measures, with the further exception of a slight positive correlation with Imaginative Compositions.

The intracreativity correlations indicated moderate relationships between certain subscales, and no apparent relationships between others. The range of these subtest correlations (not including the composite Total Creativity variable) was from $-.19$ to $+.36$, with four rs significant at the 0.05 level and four rs significant at the 0.01 level. The presence of thirteen nonsignificant rs implied that the creativity battery may have been measuring several unrelated elements, an observation which was subsequently confirmed by the factor-analytic data.

FACTOR ANALYSIS

Six independent factors were isolated as a result of factor analyzing the intercorrelations among twenty-one scales. The rotated factor matrix is given in Table 5. The factors are presented in the traditional manner, listing each of the six in order of magnitude. Tests with loadings of $\pm.30$ or more were considered significant in naming a factor with confidence. Analysis of the loadings in each column resulted in the following factor identifications.

Factor I is a substantially loaded factor. All ten achievement subtests had loadings of $+.67$ or higher, and this cluster represents the criterion of academic success. The high loading of $+.81$ for IQ reflects the validity of the synonymous reference to intelligence tests as measures of scholastic aptitude. Conversely, the achievement tests are seen as measuring a large component of formalized intelligence. This factor may, therefore, be appropriately described as learning ability or *general intelligence*. A moderate loading of $-.34$ for Remote Associations on Factor I is the only suggestion of an antithetic relationship between convergent thinking and an alleged creativity variable. The loadings of the other creativity scales on this factor were negligible.

Factors II, III, and VI are specific factors relative to divergent thinking.

Table 5. ROTATED FACTOR LOADINGS

Variable	I	II	III	IV	V	VI	h²
General anxiety	−.08	.02	−.02	.75	−.07	.08	.59
Test anxiety	−.19	.16	.00	.64	.09	−.14	.50
Word knowledge	.82	.14	.00	−.20	−.20	.08	.78
Reading	.82	.09	−.01	−.07	−.20	.11	.74
Spelling	.79	−.04	−.05	.00	−.16	.11	.68
Language	.85	.12	.04	.08	−.03	.00	.75
Language skills	.79	.11	.09	−.02	−.06	−.05	.65
Arithmetic computation	.76	.09	−.04	.04	.49	−.15	.85
Arithmetic conceptualization	.80	.09	.03	.02	.42	−.08	.84
Social studies	.70	.04	.07	−.26	.09	−.03	.57
Social studies skills	.67	.06	.14	−.21	.20	−.10	.56
Science	.76	−.14	.05	−.25	.02	−.01	.66
IQ	.81	.02	.06	−.03	.25	.02	.72
Remote association	−.34	.05	.06	−.03	.11	.49	.37
Divergent drawing	−.03	−.04	.82	.11	.07	.19	.73
Unique uses	.17	.57	.03	.00	.14	.32	.47
Spontaneous flexibility	.03	.68	.16	.01	−.12	.07	.51
Original titles	.12	.08	.02	−.01	−.10	.46	.24
Ideational fluency	.01	.55	−.04	.20	.05	−.24	.41
Imaginary compositions	.21	.41	.56	−.24	−.09	−.15	.62
Total creativity	.02	.77	.32	.10	.08	.49	.95

Note: Loadings of ±.30 or greater are italicized.

Since all the noncreativity variables had insignificant loadings on these factors, the three columns were essentially descriptive of the factorial dimensions of the creativity battery. That several orthogonal factors were observed to contribute to the variance of the Total Creativity scores was already suspicioned from the nature of the creativity subtest intercorrelations. The three creativity factors do not lend themselves to easy interpretation, despite the fact that certain subtests of productive thinking were relatively pure measures of one factor, and entirely unrelated to the factors represented by the other two columns.

The chief loading on Factor II was Spontaneous Flexibility. Of the four variables measuring Factor II, Spontaneous Flexibility and Ideational Fluency were the scales not significantly weighted in the other two creativity columns of the matrix. This permits Factor II to be identified as a *flexibility-fluency* factor. The duality illustrates an interdependence between shifts in thought perspective and the generation of ideas. It is logical to suppose that performance on the tasks representing the other two scales loaded on this factor, evoking unusual uses and writing imaginative compositions, would be determined by the flexibility and fluency of verbal thought processes.

Factor III is somewhat paradoxical in content. Nonverbal and verbal creative productions were both loaded on the same factor. Divergent Drawings and Imaginative Compositions were freer, less structured tests than the rest of the creativity battery, and are representative of clinical projective techniques. The available recourse to inner fantasy activity through the media of imagery or ideas is the distinguishing feature of these tasks. It seems appropriate to refer to Factor III as *fantasy expression*.

Three test variables, Remote Associations, Original Titles, and Unique Uses, were weighted on Factor VI. The principal characteristic of this verbal factor centers about the novel response. Factor VI is, therefore, labeled *originality*.

The definition of Factor IV is relatively clear. Substantial loadings for the two anxiety scales define this factor as *anxiety*. While the analysis of variance negated the hypothesis that anxiety is an intervening influence, it is noteworthy that several achievement scales and the Imaginative Compositions test revealed slight, but probably insignificant, negative loadings on this factor.

Factor V is evidently a subset of achievement. The significant loadings on this factor were the two arithmetic scales. Their quantitative nature leads to the conclusion that this is a *numerical* factor.

Discussion

The delicate complexity of the creative process seems vulnerable to the intrusion of personality dynamics. There is no serious dispute over the contention that nonintellective, personality factors are related to creative potential. However, the specific nature of this relationship is still relatively undefined. The present study explored the reasonable proposition that anxiety plays an intervening role in creative productivity. The results presented no convincing evidence that either general or test anxiety significantly affects performance on certain specified tasks of creativity.

A limiting feature of the present design may have been the use of objective inventories to measure anxiety. The GASC is concerned with diffuse emotionality, while the TASC items deal with physiological concomitants and habitual ways of behaving. The question arises whether an objective approach can adequately assess such an unconsciously determined, ego-involved variable as anxiety, particularly at a level of interaction with unstable creative energy. The depth of measurement of a personality trait is a function of the kind of test administered. It is conceivable that a more indirect, subjective-projective method might have provided a measure with increased sensitivity.

The hypothesis of a creativity-anxiety link is important enough to warrant further exploration. It is not sufficient to discover what level of anxiety is optimally related to creative productivity; an equally significant inquiry is the degree to which disruptive tensions and anxieties are generated by external pressures on the individual to constrict and suppress his creative strivings. The forces at work to redirect divergent processes into compatible, conforming behavior are powerful social motives. That many creative personalities are not readily understood or socially adaptable is suggested by an insightful study of creative scientists (Taylor, 1959a), which described such characteristics as a repression of emotionality and a low level of interpersonal involvement in human relations. Torrance (1962a) has pointed out that creative children are likely to feel isolated and psychologically estranged from parents, teachers, and classmates. If this be true, then many home and school situations must give rise to serious inner conflicts and resultant anxieties in children with exceptional creative potential. A greater psychological understanding of the personality dimensions of creative children is one of the prerequisites for the reduction and prevention of their conflicting social needs and characteristic psychic turbulence. This knowledge is crucial to a rapidly evolving goal in contemporary education—the identification, preservation, and enhancement of creative talent.

Despite the present observation that anxiety was not significantly related to divergent thinking, the importance of creativity for personality-as-a-whole is undeniable; however, the importance of creativity for formal learning and school achievement, as we shall see, must be seriously questioned.

The consistent demonstration in the analysis of variance that the two differentiated levels of intellect yielded highly significant differences on all the achievement subtests is an indication that the academic needs of the intellectually gifted students in this population sample were being met. It should be noted, however, that the correlations between intelligence and all the achievement scales were substantial, and that the factor-analytic data revealed a common loading for both variables. This is not surprising since the same kinds of problems and test items are used on both types of tests; furthermore, intelligence scales are often standardized and validated in terms of scholastic achievement. It is characteristic of both kinds of tests that they involve the logical ordering of many facts in order to "converge" upon a single, correct solution. The present findings provide empirical evidence that performance on standardized achievement tests involves convergent-thinking operations associated with the measurement of intelligence.

There is a sharp contrast between the highly significant main effect of intelligence and the decidedly nonsignificant F ratios regarding creativity. The results did not confirm the hypothesis that creative potential is a determinant of academic achievement. Inspection of the intercorrelation matrix provides additional information relevant to this finding. There was, for the most part, a lack of positive relationships between the creativity measures and intelligence (one creativity scale was inversely related to IQ). Data supplied by Getzels and Jackson (1962, p. 20) show moderate correlations, significant beyond the .01 level, between intelligence and a majority of the five creativity scales employed in their study. It is suggested that one reason for their resultant creativity-achievement relationship was the component of general intelligence selectively operating in their battery of creativity tests. The more "intelligence-free" characteristic of the creativity battery administered in the present study serves to partially explain the obtained negative results. The problem of whether and how creative aptitude influences the learning process bears further investigation.

A compelling question regarding research on creativity is why original thinking should be expected to be a relevant factor in scholastic achievement, the nature of the latter being so markedly convergent in content. Formal learning is very unlike original and creative activity, and convincing evidence of a significant relationship is still wanting. At present, intelligence tests are referred to as tests of *scholastic aptitude*. On the basis of current knowledge, it is an unwarranted assumption to broaden the concept of scholastic aptitude to include creative potential. In fact, an inverse relationship between convergent and divergent processes is just as likely to be the case. It has been shown (Houston & Mednick, 1963) that the individual who avoids improbable associations in preference for the highly probable is not likely to develop highly creative solutions to problems. In the present research, the significant negative loading for Remote Associations on the factor identified as *general intelligence* is further indication of a possible antagonistic relationship.

An important observation concerning the nature of the creativity battery was furnished by the factor analysis. The loadings emphasized the fact that some of the creativity scales were sole measures of one of the three isolated factors of divergent thinking—*flexibility-fluency, fantasy expression, originality*. The intercorrelations also revealed a lack of relationship between various creativity measures. Different subtests were totally independent measures of different things. Apparently, certain divergent-thinking tasks are also widely divergent from each other. The absence of common characteristics in the assortment of scales may serve to explain the inconsistent findings on creativity among different investigators, and is one plausible reason for the nonsignificant findings of the present endeavor. The problem has been clearly stated in a recent analysis of the meaning of creativity measures:

If tests of different "creativity" subabilities show very low correlations, then which children will be identified as creative will depend very heavily upon the particular collection of subtests that is used. . . . That is, one group of "creative" children, identified by one set of tests, may score high on tests of academic achievement, whereas another, chosen by a different battery, may not (Thorndike, 1963, p. 423).

It is obvious that validity for many of the newly devised measures of creative potential is purely an assumption. The investigators of a recent study of divergent thinking concluded that they were "skeptical of research which indicates wide variability among students in creativity, when the variability is inferred solely from information gathered in testing situations of short duration" (Klausmeier, Harris, & Ethnathios, 1962, p. 75). The questionable nature of the creativity indices demands restraint in the categorical labeling of individuals as more or less "creative." Any premature identification is likely to be misleading. There is the urgent reminder that the multiple measures of creativity are still in the experimental stage. It is unfortunate that, because of the high valuation on both intellectual pursuit and creative talent in our culture, doubtful inferences are being eagerly adopted as settled facts.

The nature of original thinking indicates that the newfound techniques of assessment are not sufficiently developed to adequately account for many elusive elements of creative endeavor. It is unlike convergent or rational thinking which conforms to a logical model and is more easily accessible to evaluation. Concerning creativity, what else can we currently uncover about the range and quality of hidden resources and potentialities of the student in the present study who responded that an automobile tire could be used as "a tarnished, oversized halo"? Thinking which diverges poses the riddle of the multiple-headed organism. The very concept of diversity suggests that there are testing innovations yet to come before application to the educative process may be meaningful and valid.

The detection and nurturance of productive originality is a laudable goal, but the practical value of creative development is not easily realized. It is not known, for example, what transfer value a high order of creative aptitude in childhood has for later life. In certain respects, such a gift is not perceived as a particularly advantageous attribute. Getzels & Jackson (1962) revealed that, while parents and teachers ranked creativity among the first three qualities of gifted children, neither parents nor teachers included creativity among the first three qualities needed for success as adults; instead, they stressed personality attributes. The relevance for creativity is apparent, however, since the factors of productive thinking are intimately linked to personality.

The emerging question as to how creative talent may be nurtured in the educational setting should be related to the purpose for which the productive-thinking abilities are being sought. If the specified aim is greater formalized achievement expectations, the results are apt to be disappointing. However, in line with the sound educational principle that learning should be satisfying, there is inestimable value in an educational climate which permits the expression of idiosyncratic needs, maintains a tolerance for innovation, is receptive to divergent-thinking activity, and encourages creative leadership. Such an atmosphere would be psychotherapeutic and growth facilitating, enabling significant development along such behavioral continuums as: rigidity—flexibility; unproductivity—fluency; unimaginativeness—fantasy; generality—originality. This approach is consistent with the idea of teaching the whole child, of meeting the global needs of the student, and of preserving the identity of the individual.

The cultivation of creative potentialities has heretofore been largely neglected by educators. If the ultimate goals are increased capability for personal expression, greater inventiveness, and the blossoming of gifted leaders, the experiences may prove richly rewarding. It follows that out of the dedicated efforts to foster creative talent will come the development of achievement measures specifically designed to evaluate progress in learning to create and think productively. These *divergent achievement* indices would necessarily be based upon empirical developmental expectations regarding each of the significant dimensions of creativity. It is proposed that just as IQ is related to convergent achievement, an analogous relationship exists between CQ (Creativity Quotient) and divergent achievement.

Summary

The comparative effects of exceptional intellectual potential and unusual creative aptitude on academic achievement were investigated. Four groups were constituted by levels of intelligence and creativity; respective sub-samples represented children gifted in either of the two, in both, or in neither variable. Results of a two-way analysis of variance consistently demonstrated the significant role of intelligence in scholastic performance, while creativity was not determined to be related to academic success. The extent of general and test anxiety were also assessed, and found to be unrelated to intellectual ability or productive thinking. A factor analysis revealed the multifactorial nature of the creative battery administered in this study; the loadings further described the various divergent-thinking subscales as bearing little relationship to each other.

Further exploration of the interaction between personality dynamics and creative activity is indicated. The dubious validity of measures of creative productivity suggests the need for establishing rigorous scientific criteria to preclude the spurious identification of "creative" individuals. Efforts should be made to distinguish between convergent and divergent achievement. Future research should focus upon those individuals with concomitant ability of a high order in both intelligence and creativity; it is this group which is perhaps truly representative of genuine giftedness.

Where Education Fits In

How can we keep creativity alive in children—schools and school teachers being what they are? This is a very simple problem but also, on the face of it, an insoluble one. It is, moreover, a problem which confronts the entire modern world.

What models do we have in older traditions? In seventeenth-century Scotland the schoolmaster—the dominie—was one of the brightest boys of the village, sometimes a young man who had prepared for the ministry. According to tradition, he trudged off to Edinburgh, a bag of oatmeal slung over his back, starved, studied and became a scholar, and returned. A stern taskmaster in the village school, he eventually sent off his brightest pupil with another bag of oatmeal, who in turn learned Latin and Greek and returned to the village. This method assured a very high regard for learning in the village school.

In the classical Chinese system poor scholars, and those who had failed to pass the examinations that opened the doors to administrative bureaucratic positions, were the first teachers of the next generation of scholars in the village schools. In eastern European Jewish communities, the teacher who beat little boys with a switch and lashed at them with his tongue was also a man who had aspired to be a scholar and had fallen short of the mark. And, generation after generation among the Chinese and the Jews, the love of learning and the creative pursuit of knowledge emerged. When it came to inspiring generations of small boys, one might almost conclude that the best teacher was a bitter failure, a man held in contempt by a community which nevertheless valued what he was asked to produce: scholars better than he was himself.

In the earlier days of American history, we had our own version of the young male teacher: not the man who had been turned back from his

From *Think*, November–December, 1962, pp. 16–21. Used by permission of the publisher.

chosen way, but the awkward boy whose eyes were turned to the long road to success opening out before him. He was the poor boy who was going on to medicine, to law or politics—to fame. Meanwhile, for a year or two, he taught school, giving the rows of freckled-faced, bare-legged urchins in front of him a glimpse not of an abandoned dream but of a towering ambition that would soon take the young teacher out of the classroom.

In the same little red schoolhouses, the brightest girl, herself just out of the last class, also taught. No whip in her slight hands, she drove the sluggish and quelled the riotous by sheer determination. For her, as well, teaching was an interim occupation.

But where once our schoolchildren were numbered in the thousands, today they are numbered in the millions. The girl teacher who only last year was a pupil and the young man whose firelight studying spilled over into the noisy morning classroom are gone. Even the isolated one-teacher school is fast disappearing. Schools are taught, now, by those who choose teaching as a lifetime profession for which they must have special preparation. While they are still students, they are already set off from their fellows in the liberal arts and the sciences; and they are treated as a group in our population who are, by definition, necessary but not honored, ill-paid and only slightly esteemed, mainly feminine and (in stereotype) unwilling spinsters.

In 1958, we had an estimated 1,237,849 classroom teachers in our public schools. At the elementary school level, 678,478 of these teachers were women and only 99,846 were men. At the high school level, men teachers, of whom there were 231,817, slightly outnumbered women teachers, of whom there were 227,708.

In 1961, despite the great emphasis that was being put on the need for teachers, it was expected that new entries into the field would be less than the 120,000 needed as actual replacements—leaving out of account another 120,000 needed for the functioning of our schools without any special changes.

In general, teaching is still regarded primarily as a career for girls. If men do go into teaching, they should be high-school teachers of science or mathematics or, preferably, principals and supervisors. As it is also regarded as a suitable way—for men and women—to move from lower class to lower middle class status or to cling to endangered middle class status, the profession bears the marks of the ideas and ideals of the lower middle class. This class, which has been described as the core of American culture, has clear, firm, and unadventurous standards of prudence, cleanliness, neatness, caution, carefulness. Its members are the kind of people—safe, careful, respectable—to whom landlords gladly rent houses, who are welcomed as installment buyers, to whose hands civic duties and neighborhood activities can be safely entrusted.

By the hundreds of thousands, young people who, by their choice of profession have bettered themselves and have arrived in a class position in which they are secure and from which they have no driving ambition to move, become the teachers of our children: the children of lawyers and doctors and bankers, the children of recently arrived immigrants, the children of the poor.

They Teach by Choice

In fact, the children we are trying to educate are extraordinarily varied in background, in intelligence, in originality, in their expectations and hopes. But the teachers are remarkably similar, however much they may differ from one another individually. They are not disappointed classical scholars; nor are they aspiring clergymen or clergymen who have lost their faith; nor are they young men who tried to paint and failed, who tried to sing and failed, who tried to be scientists and failed.

They are teachers by choice.

The old prescription for stimulating children and young people was to have them taught by people who were not teachers on purpose but were merely interim teachers, readying themselves to become something else, or else were teachers by default, who might be expected to convey some of their own frustrated ambition to their pupils. Present-day teachers are what they want to be—when we are lucky. When we are unlucky, they are but do not want to be teachers. In this case, the young women want to be wives and mothers with homes of their own; for them, teaching represents a kind of plateau on which they stand (hopefully, only temporarily) between school and marriage. The young men want to be psychologists or educational specialists or administrators; for them, teaching represents a tiring activity which slows down their accumulation of credits and degrees and published papers needed for advancement.

The others, those who really want to teach, usually have had the good fortune of having encountered a good teacher whose enthusiasm for her subject caught their imagination, and they have stood out against all the other life models provided by relatives and friends.

At first glance, this is an uninspiring picture, if we are thinking about encouraging creativity in children. For by creativity we have come to mean originality, spontaneity, freedom to move and to think in unusual ways.

Almost inevitably, creative children are likely to be in some way unusual children, if only because they get bored with the idea of Jack's *always* going up the hill with Jill and of George Washington's *always* appearing as the model for not telling lies. Creative children in general do not accept things as they are; they do not easily settle down to their lessons as they are given to them, no more and no less.

How, then, can we expect a young woman who wants to teach—whose aim is to keep the twenty-five or thirty children in her charge well-disciplined, cheerful and passing, who must concentrate on what all of them must accomplish—to welcome a creative child? Isn't everything she stands for antithetical to the values we now urge her to have?

There are those who think so. Many people insist that a pupil can go through the public school system of any one of our large cities without ever meeting a well-educated person; they point to appalling provincialism of students in teachers' colleges, unacquainted with and unquestioning about the wider world. Supporting their argument by the contention that a stream cannot rise higher than its sources, they ask how a teacher of small horizons can open wide horizons for her pupils and can tolerate the children who dart across every boundary that comes within their view?

Yet I do not think that the situation is anything like as dismal as it can be made out to be.

Neglected Women

True, most elementary schoolteachers are women. Few of them are given a chance to rise in their profession, and they most often obey the dictates of men who may be their intellectual inferiors. The crucial teaching which will release mathematical and scientific creativity is not entrusted even to superior women teachers. Instead, these subjects are assigned to men—and sometimes to men who would rather be football coaches. (It is also true, however, that an admired coach who is also good at science may produce a whole flock of eager young scientists.) And literature, poetry, and art—fields within which creativity can be tested out and explored—are most often taught by women and are presented to boys as feminine preoccupations.

And most truly, we pay our teachers, men and women, so poorly that many good teachers cannot afford to remain in the profession of their choice.

Grant all this, and the argument still misses something.

Rabbits to Tarantulas

In our schools, in every school all over the country, there are teachers who want to be teachers of subjects they care about and know how to teach. And the real teacher, the great teacher, is doing a creative task to which other kinds of creativity in her pupils can respond. As she draws out of her pupils every latent talent, every unguessed act of skill, as she presents ancient history or Latin or earth science as an enthralling subject, she provides a model for the way in which the creative child can explore the natural world, or ideas in books in libraries, or pictures and objects in museums. With the skills at her disposal, the really good teacher can help a pupil find books she herself has never read (nor would ever want to read); she can encourage a pupil to explore conic sections by making new string figures; she can seize upon the most unlikely objects—from homeless baby rabbits to tarantulas—with which her pupils present her and make something of it all.

If we define creativity as an ability to make original constructions in a desired direction, the good teacher should be viewed not as a second-rate literary critic, not as a would-be scientist or artist, but as a first-rate, practicing teacher.

The good teacher may be genuinely searching for creativity in her pupils. But she is continually defeated in her efforts by the demands of her supervisor, the politics of the local school system, the lack of space, the lack of materials, the lack of assistance in doing things she should never have to do, the size of the class, the clash of ethnic and class backgrounds. Given these obstacles, she can encourage the child who responds to her need to discipline first and then to teach with what energy she has left.

But she is unprepared to cope with the child who uses his creativity to defeat her: the child who constructs questions that will arouse the boys to raucous laughter, whose raised hand she must therefore distrust ("Please, what is an Adam's apple?" "Where is Space?" "What is a neutrino?" "What happened to the missing link?"); the child who invents secret clubs and ciphers and signals and ceremonies that turn the classroom into something strange and unpredictable; the child who includes her, in half-recognizable form, in his stories and dreams. With all these children she is at a loss.

We fail to see obstructiveness as an aspect of creativity. Candidates for an award in science must be recommended by their schools, and one of the traits which they must show is *cooperativeness*. Parents attending a Vassar Summer Institute, asked to complete the sentence, *I like children who . . .* , wrote in such words as *obedient, spontaneous, clean, independent, neat,* and so forth. But nowhere does the dilemma show up so sharply as in school. The teacher, however deep her commitment is to her subject matter and to bringing out unusual gifts, cannot risk bringing out gifts that may disrupt the precarious balance of her overcrowded classroom. Under today's conditions, the best teacher has little enough time or energy for any kind of creativity, and none for the disruptive sort.

Yet these conditions, which necessarily turn the teacher against the child whose spontaneity and liveliness upset the class, can be remedied—most of them quite easily and inexpensively.

We can build enough schools.

We can hire clerks and janitors and guards to take much of the burdensome load off the teacher's back.

We can pay our teachers well enough to keep as teachers all those who really want to teach.

But to accomplish this—to insist that the school should be a place where no child and no teen-ager is stifled and dulled out of creativity—another step must be taken. Those who teach future teachers must themselves respect teaching. They must treat it as a fascinating and creative profession. They must be men and women who have sparkling eyes and enthusiastic voices when they teach—and when they talk about education. Just as the painter learns to paint by watching a painter and the young surgeon learns by watching a master surgeon operate, the future teacher can learn only by watching and listening to a good teacher.

A Creative Delight

Teaching is an art that has no appeal when it is described only in words. Books on education are usually as poor substitutes for living models as books on lovemaking are for a lover's gentle hands or as cookbooks are for the sight of a chef actually mixing a sauce. Talk about education is dull. But teaching, practiced as an art by a teacher in love with her subject matter, is a creative delight.

But as long as universities set no premium on good teaching, as long as promotion depends on degrees and publication (as it does at present), all teaching, even for kindergarten children, is automatically downgraded. Styles are, after all, set at the top, not in the small normal school now become a state teachers' college or even a state college or perhaps a state normal university. The more upgrading of this kind takes place, the more glaring the contrasts become. In the old normal schools, there were teachers who did genuinely care about teaching, who still sniffed the smell of the schoolroom, pungent with hidden apple cores, stuffy with the smell of powdered chalk that made everyone sneeze. And when they remembered the smell, their hearts warmed, and children—creative children waiting to be taught—danced through their lectures.

Lost in the Maze

Today, however, these newly-named colleges are looking for ways of acquiring new status. With new funds, they are trying to lure new staff into the new buildings. And the staff come, not because they can teach or because they respect teaching, but because here are well-paid academic jobs in which they will feel free to neglect the creativity of their students, who are learning from them how to be teachers, while they turn out articles to swell their own bibliographies. On such campuses there are bitter feuds between the old-timers, who believe in teaching, and the newcomers, who are avid for academic recognition and degrees and promotion. Too often what could be worked out about new ways of handling new subject matter, where the old faculty and the new could work together, gets lost in the maze of argument.

There are, of course, some supplementary things a community has the capacity to do.

A library, even a small library, can be a center of intellectual exploration. A museum, even a limited one, can provide a setting in which children can wander wide-eyed. When a museum or a library, a zoo or a nature trail is so arranged that there are areas where children are free to hold things in their hands, as well as only look at them, the chances of creativity are higher. For there is good reason to believe that creativity—in the final sense, creative achievement by adults—arises when many senses are stimulated from many layers of the personality at once, when the memory of a cadence combines with the sight of the shape of a hillside and an unsolved mathematical problem which is echoing in one's head.

The more any section of the educational system permits experimentation with all the senses—with movement, writing, painting, constructing, as well as echoed words—the better. And only some of this need be done in school.

But there is a genuine risk that a community may get too fascinated with these adjuncts to the school, and then the school itself will be neglected. Focusing on the possibilities that exist outside the school, we may forget that our children spend thirteen years in school five days a week, nine months a year, sitting still or wriggling miserably, contained, constricted, bored, often in despair, because we do not construct a situation within which good teachers can really teach. The construction of windowless schools may have merits, but not if the primary intention is to keep children from staring out of windows at a world where people move about and things happen.

There is also a temptation to run off in other directions.

It is said that television courses and films will soon solve the problem; and there are the teaching machines. Before long, tests for originality will be programmed into teaching for originality: "How many different designs can you name using these three figures?" How reminiscent this is (in advance) of the old school punishment: "You will stay in school until you have written a list of 100 words made up of some of the letters in *extraordinary*." Such a punishment might locate an original mind, but it would not teach the child how to develop that originality.

Misguided Diatribes

Included in almost all our recent statements of aspiration in education—to educate more scientists and more mathematicians, to teach more foreign languages, to produce will-disciplined, nondelinquent, responsible citizens —are diatribes directed against the school system by professors in liberal arts colleges, irate parents, high military officers, public speakers. But they seldom go to the heart of the matter, and that is the chance we give teachers to teach.

The truth of the matter is that it is not *teachers* we look down on, fail to value, fail to reward—it is *teaching* itself.

More Than Lip Service

Medicine is an art regarded with reverence. Why should the ability to stimulate and shape a well mind be less valued than the surgical skill to remove a tumor from a damaged one? This is itself a measure of our present lip service to creativity. We want people who are original, creative, spontaneous, innovative. But we want them to be produced by teachers whom we condemn in a hundred ways to be overworked and uninspired, unrespected and underpaid. We have seen what a related activity has done in the arts where we overvalue the product while we undervalue the living painter, allowing him to starve or to eke out a miserable living with commercial art, while we auction off the works of his comfortable dead predecessor for $100,000 a painting. So, also, we would like the children of America—as a product—to be creative, to learn about creativity, while we make the best chance they have to learn, to respond to teaching, as uncreative as possible.

There is only one sure way to develop creativity in all the different kinds of children in our schools. We must cherish all the way through—in the normal school and the teachers' college, in the way the teacher's job is set up, in the freedom granted to the teacher to teach while others perform the thousand chores which are no essential part of this task and this art, in the time given the teacher to read and explore and think and plan and search for new materials—the creativity of all those who have elected to become teachers because they want to teach.

If we are to give more than lip service to creativity in children, we must actively support the creativity of the teacher. That is to say, we must come to recognize fully the creativity of good teaching.

CLARK MOUSTAKAS

Creativity and Conformity in Education

War, overpopulation, starvation, and disease are problems easily recognized as severe threats to man's continued survival and destiny. Not so clearly visible but equally widespread are the destructive and evil consequences of self-distortion and alienation. The search for truth, meaning, honesty, the search for authentic life, the hunger for love and communion with others, the struggle for a genuine existence based on real capacities and real talents of real persons—these are not just emotional phrases but signs of disturbance, restlessness, and boredom in everyday life. The deterioration of meaning, the breakdown of values, the increasing substitution of machine for man, of program for person, of mass for individual, of modeling and copying for inventing and creating—all of these threaten the flow of life and the potential richness and beauty of human experience. The deterioration of morals and values and the proliferation of brutality and violence are as serious as the threat of thermonuclear war. There are those who understand and know but pretend not to see; and those who look on indifferently as if it were happening only to others; and some no longer know and no longer care. It is often a clever game of pretenses and exchanges—if we do not see the inhuman, the superficial, the dishonest and false in a tangible way, then they do not exist. If the destructive does not impinge directly upon us, then we can ignore it. For those too burdened already and too removed from hope and courage, life is static and fixed; excitement, vitality, and enthusiasm are gone. For others, it is a matter of calculated planning and managing, modulated gestures and voices, and steady gains in status, prestige, and power; a matter of building better machines and models and performing more precisely defined roles and functions.

Modern life is not centered in genuine interhuman experience between

Sections of this paper are taken from *Essays towards a Humanistic Psychology* (in press b) and *The Authentic Teacher* (1966).

173

real persons, nor does it encourage diversity and individuality. Ambitious adults set up goals and communicate expectations, either indirectly and deviously, so that what they really want and expect from the child registers at subliminal levels regardless of what they say; or, quite openly, adults program the child's life in such a way that he progresses step-by-step toward their definitions, toward their goals, toward their expected achievements. Often the individual is unaware that he, as a unique, growing person, has been cancelled out and what remains is a concept, a definition which has been pieced together by external perceptions and judgments.

In a climate, where freedom and choice are denied, the individual comes to reject his own senses. He does not make full use of his perceptions and faculties in determining which experiences contribute to self-realization and which are irrelevant or impeding; he no longer uses his own organs and powers to create reality and to venture into new life. Since the individual does not trust his own immediate experience, and the response of his senses, to lead him to new experience, he is neither open to himself nor to the world.

The values and resources which exist within the deep regions of the self have not been tapped and explored, and so he becomes one of the sea of faces, one of the modulated and patterned voices. His parents did not love and cherish him as an independent self. They did not help him to discover interests, meanings, and values that would get their initial impetus from him, from the movements of his body, from his growing awareness of life, and from his wish to explore life on his own terms. In short, they have rejected him and, unknowingly, he has come to reject himself.

Thus, the young person searching for identity and self-affirmation, lacking recognition and threatened by the withdrawal of love, launches himself into an alien life. He substitutes the spontaneous, flowing self for a controlled, calculating self-system dominated by the rules and "shoulds" of the adult world. The original self-awareness becomes self-deception and the individual no longer realizes that he has abnegated his real self in favor of a substitute, that alienation has replaced authentic development of the self.

There is much in life to reinforce the inauthentic pattern—the humdrum of everyday activity, drifting with convention; being stuck by rules and regulations, yielding to pressures, compromising, doing the expected, and everything that passes for morality, particularly the superficial clichés and the rules of convention and propriety. Other forces which hinder the development of the self include: playing a role, doing one's duty, and analyzing, interpreting, and intellectualizing experience. In general, all efforts and actions directed toward looking behind reality, explaining and justifying its existence, interfere with direct, primary, authentic experience.

Alienation, which often begins in the home, is further intensified, extended, and reinforced in the school, where the focus is on group standards and group norms, grades, adjustment, and security. Kneller

(1965, pp. 90–91) describes the consequences of treating the individual as a member of a mass society:

In order to get along, he learns to do what his teachers ask of him and what his peers expect of him. This is not faith in the self but self-surrender . . . to have faith in himself, the student must be able to trust his own experiences of life or, if you will, his own verdict on that experience. To this end he must be able freely to respond to life and freely to reflect on his responses.

Does the school allow him this freedom? Hardly! The school screens his experience, determines what aspects of the world he will respond to, and preconsiders how he will behave in regard to them. As a result, the pupil comes to distrust his own response to life and embraces instead the habits conditioned in him by his school.

Blindness and deception exist in schools where alienation is taken as a sign of healthy adjustment; where sophistication becomes a substitute for honesty, simplicity, and sincerity; where assertive individuality creates a battleground for teacher and pupil conflict; where the ones in power defeat a genuine existence through conditioning, use of external symbols of status and reward, authoritarian persuasiveness, and numerous consequences that are employed in order to crush rebellion and resistance, and overwhelm and defeat the stubborn person. The child in the school very soon becomes separated and detached; he becomes alienated from his work. He has no real connection to the activities that are scheduled and programmed for him.

Desensitization is another characteristic of deteriorating life in the school. It occurs through a process of deprivation and separation where one is treated as an object, where skills and subject matter are more significant than learners, where goals must be pursued regardless of the real wishes, aspirations, and capacities of persons, where rationalizing, explaining and analyzing take the place of spontaneity, humanistic experience, and natural feeling. Children catch on quickly to the preferred way. The shrewd child picks up the appropriate form, and begins to ask questions and seek explanations, without any real interest, relationship, involvement, or background. This kind of response is often given status and flatters the teacher. Profound involvement in an area of knowledge, insight, and discovery do not come by seeking or getting explanations. Genuine learning requires a sense of mutuality and a feeling of encounter in learning, an immersion into the subject—labor, exertion, and hours of searching and struggling. And the deeper the perplexity, the more burning the curiosity, the less children will seek explanations. When the learner has exhausted his study from his own searching, when he comes to the end of his own resources, if his search is authentic and self-inspired, only then does he seek additional clarification and help. The creative teacher does not explain, but turns the learner back to his own resources or helps him to acquire new ones (Hawkins, Summer, 1965).

Unfortunately, this is not the process of education in the school of today. Too often the adult observes, manipulates, and directs; the adult notes the child, probes him, writes him up, and breaks him down into specific traits of weakness and strength; the adult treats the child as a thing, and he soon learns to react like one. When the child is perceived as an object for intellectual and social nourishment, when he is treated as a member of group or mass society, without reference to his unique and varying differences, when he is perceived as an empty vessel to be filled with facts and explanations, there is real danger that he will lose touch with his own awareness and response to life. There is real danger that he will begin to build a wall around himself and learn to protect himself against the penalties of being honest and forthright. He will become insensitive to his own bent for inquiry and self-discovery; he will become insensitive to the range of feelings that characterize genuine human existence. In short, he will become alienated and detached from any kind of meaningful endeavor.

The student in the school becomes alienated in the same way that any worker can become alienated from his work. He develops an estranged attitude toward his schoolwork; he is outside of it, he is bored and engages in schoolwork under coercion and compulsion, either from the threat of punishment by the teacher or parent or from the restrictive demands and directives of his "should" system. In the school he is labeled—gifted, average, retarded; and he is classified—fast, average, slow. In many ways he is stereotyped and fixed and expected to play the role defined by professional nomenclature, abstract goals, and unseen faces. He is expected to become a replica of the stereotype and give up his own fresh, spontaneous contact and response to life. He is prodded; he is motivated; he is directed; he is rewarded; and he is punished. He is assigned lessons from a teacher's manual which dictates what he should read, how much, and in what manner. And, he moves from one subject to another by virtue of invisible authorities whom he does not know, would not recognize, and does not ever meet. His education is detached, impersonal, fragmentary, and guided by anonymous hands. No wonder school is a burden and work is a chore. No wonder, more and more, he becomes numb and deadened in the process of moving from grade to grade. No wonder there is no excitement or joy in learning and no involvement. He is denied as a self; *he* does not exist except as the generalized other; his creative energy is restrained, stifled, and almost totally ignored. Kneller (1965, p. 99) has described the deadening impact of hierarchy and organization:

In the schools this energy is frustrated by regulations designed to keep masses of young people in order by making them behave in unison. It is frustrated, too, by tired, overworked teachers, who cannot spare the time to nurture the creativity of the individual student because they must struggle amid the impersonal web of administrative detail and mass guidance and counseling procedures to instill into their swollen classes the basic requirements of a stereotyped syllabus.

And the ultimate result—uniformity of behavior, uniformity of expression, death of individuality, docility, passivity, and conformity. In spite of the eventual capitulation to the system, there are still signs of restlessness, resistance, and boredom, and chaos and disorder; when the teacher's back is turned, there are still signs that the individual is dissatisfied, that he is searching and striving to discover more meaningful avenues of expression and ties to life.

The teacher hangs on—to what—to intellectual values, to scores, to achievements, to whatever facts can be mustered to justify the curriculum and prove that, in the end, the battle to defeat individuality, freedom, imagination, and exploration is worth it; in the end, the scores are higher, and the number of months of upgrading in the subject areas can be pointed to with pride. What has happened in the process? First, the child is further alienated from himself. The activities he engages in have nothing to do with his own integrity, with his own response to life. He is also alienated from his teacher who does not exist as a person and does not recognize his uniqueness, his perceptions of reality, his commitments to life. His own feelings become blunted; his wishes are cut off and rejected as a basis for learning; his sensitivity and awareness are defeated through criticism, through external standards of conformity, and through modes of group life. Finally, the child becomes fragmented in the labels and classifications applied to him. Facts, knowledge, intellectual gains are the important values—in spite of the fact that intellectual values represent only a fragment of human life, only one dimension of existence. Thus, many of today's classrooms carry the banner of M'Choakumchild's Schoolroom (Dickens, 1964, pp. 7–9):

"Now, what I want is, Facts. Teach these boys and girls nothing but Facts. Facts alone are wanted in life. Plant nothing else, and root out everything else. You can only form the minds of reasoning animals upon Facts: nothing else will ever be of any service to them. This is the principle on which I bring up my own children, and this is the principle on which I bring up these children. Stick to Facts, sir!"

"Girl number twenty," said Gradgrind, squarely pointing with his square forefinger, "I don't know that girl. Who is that girl?"

"Sissy Jupe, sir," explained number twenty, blushing, standing up, and curtseying.

"Sissy is not a name," said Mr. Gradgrind. "Don't call yourself Sissy. Call yourself Cecilia."

"It's father as calls me Sissy, sir," returned the young girl in a trembling voice, and with another curtsey.

"Then he has no business to do it," said Mr. Gradgrind. "Tell him he mustn't. Cecilia Jupe. Let me see. What is your father?"

"He belongs to the horse-riding, if you please, sir."

Mr. Gradgrind frowned, and waved off the objectionable calling with his hand.

"We don't want to know anything about that, here. You mustn't tell us about that, here. Your father breaks horses, don't he?"

"If you please, sir, when they can get any to break, they do break horses in the ring, sir."

"You mustn't tell us about the ring, here. Very well, then. Describe your father as a horsebreaker. He doctors sick horses, I dare say?"

"Oh yes, sir."

"Very well, then. He is a veterinary surgeon, a farrier, and horsebreaker. Give me your definition of a horse."

(Sissy Jupe thrown into the greatest alarm by this demand.)

"Girl number twenty unable to define a horse!" said Mr. Gradgrind, for the general behoof of all the little pitchers. "Girl number twenty possessed of no facts, in reference to one of the commonest of animals! Some boy's definition of a horse. Bitzer, yours. . . . Your definition of a horse."

"Quadruped. Graminivorous. Forty teeth, namely twenty-four grinders, four eye-teeth, and twelve incisors. Sheds coat in the spring; in marshy countries, sheds hoofs, too. Hoofs hard, but requiring to be shod with iron. Age known by marks in mouth." Thus (and much more) Bitzer.

"Now girl number twenty," said Mr. Gradgrind. "You know what a horse is."

The exaggerated emphasis on facts, on intellectual accomplishment, is ill-advised in another sense; intelligence is not the highest level of value. In his study of values, Hartman concluded that intellectual values are the least significant in the development of the self. These come from our systemic dimension, the dimension which builds systems, constructs rules and regulations and stresses routine, order, duty, and discipline as maxims of life. An extreme example of how intellectual values can be used destructively and why they can never be the basis for ultimate human values and actions is contained in Hartman's (November 7, 1962) analysis of Eichmann:

Was Eichmann a bad man? Oh, not at all. He did his duty. He said, "I never killed anybody. I am a transportation specialist. My work was to make schedules—railroad schedules. That's all I did. I followed my orders. It wasn't my business to know who was being put into those railroad cars. I never put anybody in. It wasn't my business where they went to. My orders were to make railroad schedules—and that's what I did. I transported people." Well, he transported them to the fire, but that was incidental. He did it with great thoroughness and was proud of it. He was a very systematic man and the system was his life. . . . This is systemic value. It is amoral—as is the law and as is science. Both are systems. This amorality may be immoral and it may also be moral. It all depends on how the system is being used.

Intellectuality, convention, the system is out of focus today; it is over-stressed and overused and in exaggerated forms stifles creativity and spontaneity. When intelligence is used to establish rigid systems and hierarchies, when it becomes a substitute for human concern and human involvement, when intellectual values are more important than self-values, then they become destructive, violating individual integrity and human decency. The system—any system which chooses intelligence over morality

—is rooted in mechanics and laws which, basically, are no more than the values of authoritarian individuals who prefer death to life, submission to courage, routines and habits to inventiveness and ingenuity, and, on the whole, anything that passes for order, efficiency, and organization.

The values and resources of each individual self, the potentialities and talents ready to be formed and shaped, should be recognized, encouraged, and affirmed in our schools. Life comes from life, and the teacher is the living agent in the school. As a living agent, the teacher must not abdicate the human dimensions which he can communicate to the child—respect for his individuality, recognition of his particular interests, needs, and directions, encouragement of his growth in identity. The human talents, the human resources of the teacher are the teacher's primary value in the educative process. As a unique individual, the teacher can be open to new experience, open to emerging life.

Being open to the inherent life in the classroom means first of all being open to one's own inner life as a person; it means centering oneself in evolving perceptions and potentialities which come to fulfillment in living itself; it means being aware of human values as well as intellectual and social values; it means being open to the unfolding process in learning and to values and meanings which include but transcend facts or techniques; it means letting each person be himself, encouraging and valuing individuality and letting it shine forth. It means recognizing the child as a valuable being in his own autonomy and independence, and understanding the child through listening, communion, and genuine presence. It means being open to all experiences, and participating in each experience as a new venture. It means respecting and affirming the validity of the child's perceptions, and accepting as fact the reality of those perceptions for the child.

In the classroom, there are infinite possibilities for life, many directions of choice and self-actualization. Given a chance, content will emerge as the individual engages in meaningful study and work. Then knowledge becomes integral to the individual and is absorbed into the self. It is important to remember: There is no single way but many paths to depth in learning and multiple areas of knowledge and experience. All of life is a potential avenue of discovery and insight. Somehow we have lost touch with the reality of the learner as a person of infinite possibilities for encounter with many, many dimensions of life. The curriculum has been constructed to give single lessons, with single questions and single answers rather than for diversity, variety, and multiplicity.

Genuine relationship between learner and subject takes the form of pattern rather than stimulus-response connections. Even machines are now built to recognize this fact. David Hawkins (Summer, 1965, p. 551) makes the point clearly and strongly:

From what we now know of informational processes, even machines designed for pattern recognition and classification will function most efficiently—when

dealing with a very complex system of data—if they are deliberately programmed for such "non-directive," in some respects even random, "Monte
Carlo" exploratory behavior. In spite of the anxieties about machines in our
culture, it may be that the machine designers are closer to an appreciation of
what is involved in human learning than are those circumscribed by the
simplistic traditions of behavioristic psychology and "programmed learning."

In an authentic education, the emphasis is on direct, primary experience,
using one's own senses, perceiving reality freshly and naively, and spontaneously encountering life.

To illustrate, in Salinger's story "Teddy" (1953, pp. 298–299), Teddy is
asked, "What would you do if you could change the educational system?"
He responds with these drastic recommendations:

I know I'm pretty sure I wouldn't start with the things schools usually start
with. . . . I think I'd first just assemble all the children together and show
them how to meditate. I'd try to show them how to find out who they *are,* not
just what their names are and things like that. . . . I guess, even before that,
I'd get them to empty out everything their parents and everybody ever told
them. I mean even if their parents just told them an elephant's big, I'd make
them empty *that* out. An elephant's only big when it's next to something else—
a dog or a lady, for example. . . . I wouldn't even tell them an elephant has
a trunk. I might *show* them an elephant, if I had one handy, but I'd let them
just walk up to the elephant not knowing anything more about it than the
elephant knew about *them.* The same thing with grass, and other things. I
wouldn't even tell them grass is green. Colors are only names. I mean if you
tell them the grass is green, it makes them start expecting the grass to look a
certain way—*your* way. . . . Besides, if they wanted to learn all that other
stuff—names and colors and things—they could do it, if they felt like it, later
on when they were older. But I'd want them to *begin* with all the real ways of
looking at things, not just the way all the other apple-eaters look at things.

In his encounters with life, the child enlarges his awareness of reality; he
achieves a heightened sense of integration, a meeting of the center of
himself with ongoing life, with wonder, excitement, and mystery. Through
openness, whether in self-dialogue or in communication with others,
creative life emerges. One way in which this openness of being can be
awakened is for the teacher to encourage the child to attune himself to the
intuition of his senses. Kneller (1965, p. 93) suggests the following:

On his way home, should he catch sight of a flock of birds gathering against
a darkening sky or a burst of sunlight flaring upon a garden wall, or should he
hear the cry of traffic swept far off on the evening air, he would take these
impressions to his heart and let them instruct him in their obscure and tongue-
less way of the mystery of things. Life itself, vaster than our expression of it,
speaks to us in countless ways—in the words of a friend, in the movement of a
symphony, in a breath of wind across a bed of flowers, in the sigh of cities, in
the sirens of factories, in the murmur of pain, in the shouts of ecstasy. If our
students are to be creative, let them *listen* to life.

Of course, listening can be part of a process of dialogue, one aspect of self-expression. New creations are formed in the process of creating; conversations unfold in new directions rather than repeating old thoughts; paintings take on unexpected qualities as the painter and the paints are encountered in the fullness of being; a poem *becomes,* even while it is being written. Any expression created in the process of ongoing life may also be a step to new creation. Here are some samples of painting with words which are an outgrowth of authentic life with fifth graders (Goody, unpublished):

Cool morning . . . dawn breaks.
The wind whispers through the trees.
Sunshine warms the earth.
          —*Robin Rosenberg*

Black is the night without moon or stars.
Black is the fuel coming out of a huge rocket,
A small black cat, a man's top hat.

Black is the coal you put in ships,
The watery, slimy, ugliness of oil,
The lining for a beautiful picture of colors,
Or the fall of a shadow on flowers.
          —*Donald Abrahm*

The glow of dawn which is so bright,
A daisy shedding its petals white,
The gulls that fly in the warm twilight,
A furry cat that creeps at night,
The taste of spring that is so light.
Do you know why 'pure' is white?
          —*Susan Helms*

Brown is a beautiful color.
It's the color of chocolate cake,
A baseball mit, a shadow on a lake.

Brown is the color that makes you feel proud,
Also a wheat field that's just been plowed,
The color of rooftops high in the sky
And graceful birds that soar and fly,
The posts that hold up my bed,
And the hair on the top of my head.

The brown of a person who's been in the sun,
The feeling of a child who's having fun.
A beautiful color is brown.
          —*Stefanie Felix*

Silence is a stream flowing to the sea,
A bee gathering pollen from the flowers,

> Lying in a green carpet of grass;
> Watching the clouds drift through the sky,
> The lovely fragrance of flowers.
> —*Susan Goodwin*

The authentic person, rooted in himself and not stuck in a system of fixed procedures, policies, and programs, does not analyze and explain reality; he engages in it freely, openly, immediately, spontaneously.

Related to education, this means the teacher is in the process of becoming himself and thus, catching glimpses of life from the child, opens new pathways for learning and relatedness, new opportunities for authentic experience. Every experience that will enable the child to become himself is authentic. Becoming oneself means freedom to choose, making decisions, and taking responsibility for one's actions. It means commitment and engagement, involvement as a self which leads to culminating, actualizing experiences. In the authentic classroom, the concern of the teacher is not with facts or objects but with the experience undergone, with the process of becoming oneself.

For example, in presenting a poem, the teacher simply presents it—not to teach or instruct but only because it expresses a significant dimension of the teacher's world. It has meaning and value for the teacher. As a poem, it is a real poem, a poem which fills the teacher with an aliveness and an aesthetic feeling, not merely a poem which should be included or taught, but one that compels, invites, and activates the teacher, one that challenges the teacher to new awareness and meaning. The teacher does not paraphrase, explain, guide the pupils, or ask questions. All of these methods would objectify the poem. In authentic experience, the person and the environment are in collaboration; the poem is a primary source of experience and enlists or invites involvement. In the process of relating and experiencing, the individual and the environment become fully integrated, and the distinction of self to universe disappears.

In presenting a meaningful resource, a reading, a play, a poem, a story, the teacher, if authentic, is presenting himself, an aspect of his world. If the presentation engenders life, it is because the teacher believes in it, is filled with it, in such a way that an integration is achieved between the teacher and the source. While presenting the source, a new experience is created, an experience which might serve both in itself as an aesthetic moment of revelation or disclosure for the child and at the same time as the impetus for further inquiry and self-realization. No resource will be experienced in the same way; it has no exclusively objective value, but if it is real, if it is genuine, it can initiate a process of experience in the learner; the experience itself will be personal, subjective, and dependent upon the particular uniqueness of the learner.

In authentic experience, the subject matter is related to the learner. It arouses and sustains his interest. It is not something out there to be memorized and repeated, but rather it is raw material in the form of books, maps, movies, instruments, sounds, colors, shapes, forms, water, earth, sky, people, trees, motions, mechanics, air—any dimension of life that captivates the individual and sustains meaning and value. Any subject matter or environmental resource that extends knowledge, deepens appreciation and understanding, and expands the awareness of the learner is an appropriate source of enrichment and discovery. Hawkins' (Summer, 1965, p. 547) description of the curriculum of the creative kindergarten of the "progressive education" era is the kind of subject matter and life that can be engendered in the modern school:

Here there was not only a style of teaching that involved children deeply in subject matter, but the subject matter grew with the style—water, sand, clay, paint, good infant literature, the cultivation of story and song, carpentry, lenses, prisms, magnets, blocks, the house of packing boxes and orange crates, soil and seed, animals, the dance, and all the rest. I do not believe that this tradition failed at all; its influence has been reduced by erosion (sometimes to the vanishing point), by pressures for thin mechanical programs of "reading readiness," "number experience," and the like, most of which tend to reduce the very readiness they seek to cultivate.

The authentic teacher has few discipline problems (Vandenberg, Spring, 1962). Being himself is the surest way for the teacher to be respected by his students. Students are repelled by alienated teachers. If the teacher is authentic and a disciplinary situation arises, it is either because the student is not being what he can be; in other words, he does not wish to be a troublemaker but becomes one in conflict with himself, or it is the result of his being what he chooses to be, which happens to run counter to prevailing modes of conduct; in other words, he becomes a troublemaker. In either case, the problem can be handled as an existential confrontation. The teacher can face the issue with the student and, through struggle within crisis and compassion, come to a resolution of the problem. In such a conflict, teacher and child can remain together constructively, as real persons, and not resort to destructive powers and tactics (Moustakas, in press a).

What are the conditions which facilitate freedom, openness, choice and responsibility, the conditions which encourage authentic existence in the classroom? Rogers ("Learning to Be Free") has abstracted these conditions from the pioneering efforts of creative educators and from pertinent research in psychotherapy and in the classroom. It is necessary that the individual, at whatever level of education, be confronted by resources, issues, and problems which are meaningful and relevant to him. It is essential that the teacher hold an unyielding and deep trust in the child as a person of value with capacities and talents which, when free to be expressed, will eventuate in positive and constructive experiences. If we trust the capacity of the individual for developing his own potentiality, then we can permit him the opportunity to choose his own way in his learning.

It is important that the teacher be a real person—enthusiastic, sad, angry, joyful, calm, excited, stand out in an honest way with the range of feelings that differentiate the living person from the mechanical role player. It is essential that they teacher prize the child as a person, be aware of and value his feelings and thoughts, convey genuine understanding based on the child's own perceptions, and accept his tempo and pace, his way of perceiving and relating to the life of the classroom. It is also important that the teacher provide resources.

In such a setting, initially the student may experience much frustration, struggle, and disturbance; but gradually he comes to be responsible, creative, and free. He comes to be clearly present as a unique individual, as a genuine and integrated being, as someone who can relate and grow in his life with others.

The moment for initiating an authentic life and departing from alienation and dehumanization is always present. No matter how entrenched a person is in the world of the other, in rationalizing, in analyzing, in intellectualizing, no matter how immersed the individual is in standards and values and goals of the system, he still can, in the next moment, decide to alter the course of his existence. He still can become the one he really is, create meanings and values and actualize potentialities that are consistent with his real self. No one can take this away. And for any particular person, no one can predict what the individual will do (Frankl, 1960). Regardless of his past, in any situation he can choose to activate genuine talents and resources, real directions of the self. It is always true for each person that at any moment he can choose to become himself, which is the only way to authentic existence.

E. PAUL TORRANCE

Nurture of Creative Talents

In ancient Greece, the philosopher Plato declared that "what is honored in a country will be cultivated there." Plato surely must have included creative talents among the things that are nurtured by honoring them in a culture. The prevailing concept, however, is that creativity must be left to chance, and that if one has outstanding creative talent, it will somehow flourish in spite of neglect and abuse. This erroneous idea has dominated thinking even among educators, in spite of the mass of contrary evidence. No one would argue, of course, that hereditary factors do not place limits upon creative development and achievement. Creative abilities are inherited to the extent that a person inherits his sense organs, a peripheral nervous system, and a brain. How these abilities develop and function, however, is strongly influenced by the way the environment responds to a person's curiosity and creative needs.

The historical evidence is compelling. How can one otherwise account for the great number of creative musicians in the period of a single century in Europe between 100 and 200 years ago? There were Handel, Mozart, Chopin, Lizst, Verdi, Schubert, Mendelssohn, Debussy, Dvorak, Berlioz, and Wagner. How can one account for the large number of great artists and sculptors during the period of the Renaissance? Why were there so many inventors in the late nineteenth century? Why does Australia produce so many good tennis players, the United States so many good basketball and baseball players, and Russia so many good women athletes? Why has the past decade produced so many outstanding Negro athletes? As Reynolds (1958) has pointed out, it is doubtful that the basic potentialities of people vary greatly from one century to another. It seems likely that many kinds of talent, including creative talents, exist in most populations at any given time. Reynolds explains this phenomenon by suggesting the principle that "talents will develop most frequently and to the highest level in the fields that are given heroic character"—essentially what Plato said in ancient Greece.

We find further evidence of the power of cultural influences in the nurture of creative development and functioning through the cross-cultural studies my associates and I have conducted (Torrance, 1963b; Johnson, 1963; Prakash, 1966; Torrance & Goldman, 1966). For example, in the United States, after about age ten, girls consistently perform better than boys on almost every kind of verbal test of creative thinking. In India, however, two investigators (Prakash, 1966; Raina, 1966) with independently collected data from different parts of the country and about five years apart found that boys excelled girls on practically all of these same verbal tests. It was also found that children in India perform disproportionately better on verbal than on figural tests of creativity. Children in Western Samoa, Negro children in Georgia, and lower-class children in Pittsburgh, Pennsylvania, performed better on figural than on verbal tests. It is difficult to believe that children in India are born with better verbal than figural creative thinking abilities and that the reverse is true in Western Samoa, among Negro children in Georgia, and among lower-class children in Pittsburgh (Smith, 1965). It is also difficult to believe that in the United States girls are born superior to boys in verbal creativity and that the reverse is true in India. Differences in the nurturing influences of the cultures involved explain the differences cited. In India, especially in cities like Delhi where the data were collected, one has to know several languages to get along. Verbal abilities are given heavy emphasis. Western Samoa has had an alphabet for only a short period of time, and verbal skills are even now not greatly honored. In the United States, schools and middle-class culture reward verbal skills. This has not been true, however, in the Negro and lower socioeconomic class subcultures. The patterns of the developmental curves and levels of creative functioning from one culture to another can be explained logically on the basis of the nurturing influences of the cultures (Torrance, 1963b, 1965a).

If cultural and historical influences are so powerful, is it possible for teachers, educational methods and materials, and parents to make real differences in the creative development and functioning of children? In my opinion, the evidence calls for a definite "Yes." Elsewhere (Torrance, 1965a), I have summarized a variety of laboratory and field experiments that indicate the behavior of teachers can make differences in creative functioning. In field experiments (Torrance & Gupta, 1964), instructional materials designed to provide experiences in creative thinking and with information about the nature and value of the creative process proved to be powerful enough to make differences in creative development. Dozens of experiments from kindergarten through graduate level tell the same story. The history of medical and scientific discovery tells a similar story. How else can one explain why certain teachers produced so many students who made outstanding discoveries (Gibson, 1958; Peterson, 1946)?

I shall attempt now to review some of the cultural influences that seem to be important in nurturing creative talents in the United States and to propose a program for helping teachers gain the insights and skills that seem necessary if teaching is to make a difference.

Cultural Influences That
Affect Creative Development

SUCCESS ORIENTATION

The United States has frequently been characterized as the most success-oriented culture in the world. Our education is said to prepare only for success, not for coping with frustration and failure. Frustration and failure must be avoided either by succeeding or not attempting ventures where failure is a possibility. This inhibition to creative thinking occurs repeatedly in the testing of children with creative thinking tests. Many children refuse to think of what Mother Hubbard could have done when she found the cupboard bare, because "it never could have happened."

Success orientation, when greatly overemphasized, is inimical to creative growth because creative ways of learning involve experimentation, taking risks, making mistakes and correcting them. If making errors is forbidden and results in severe punishment, children soon give up all hope of success and cease efforts to learn. To nurture creativity, teachers may have to modify their concepts of classroom success to permit children to succeed first in ways possible to them and use the resulting growth to motivate them to higher levels of creative functioning. There is a strong need of a greater variety of ways in which children can succeed in school.

PEER ORIENTATION

The United States has also been characterized as a culture in which children and young people are more concerned about the evaluations of peers than of parents, teachers, and other authorities. Evidences of the inhibiting effects of peer pressures to conformity emerge when we conduct sociometric studies, creative writing studies, and the like. It is likely that this powerful peer orientation is responsible in large part for the sharp drops in curves of creative development at about the fourth and seventh grades in most United States schools. Original ideas are common targets of peer pressures to conformity.

The distressing thing is that many youngsters seem to be so concerned about peer pressures that they "give up" all efforts to learn and to think. In an unpublished study of mine concerning forty-five seventh graders nominated by their teachers as likely to drop out of school, 95 percent indicated that they did not think that anyone would take seriously their ideas and suggestions.

Schools can do much to lighten the tyranny of the peer pressures that inhibit creative development. In creative problem-solving experiences respect can be developed for unusual, minority ideas. Ability and interest groupings can lighten these pressures for many children. Arranging for appropriate sponsors or patrons for promising youngsters can be very powerful. The evidence from history seems to indicate that the child who starts earliest in his special efforts has the best chance of developing to the highest level in his special field (Reynolds, 1958). Sponsors can give promising youngsters a chance to develop in creative ways at an early age.

SANCTIONS AGAINST QUESTIONING AND EXPLORATION

Although teachers generally recognize the need for children to ask questions and otherwise inquire about the wonders and mysteries about them, such tendencies frequently are squelched. Forty-three percent of the potential dropouts mentioned above indicated that they were afraid to ask questions in class. Only 17 percent of a large sample of fourth graders indicated that they were afraid to ask questions (Torrance & Gupta, 1964).

MISPLACED EMPHASIS ON SEX ROLES

Boys and girls in different ways suffer in creative development from society's misplaced emphasis on sex role differences. Pressures resulting from this misplaced emphasis needlessly make taboo vast areas of experiencing. Creative behavior, by its very nature, requires both sensitivity and independence in thinking. In the United States, sensitivity and receptiveness and feminine virtues, while independence in thinking is a masculine one. Again, there is much that schools can do to reduce the tyranny of this misplaced emphasis. One way is through activities that approve independence in thinking and judgment as well as sensitivity and receptiveness. Training in the arts for boys and in science for girls, through science and art camps and various kinds of co-curricular and curricular activities, is one approach.

DIVERGENCY EQUATED WITH ABNORMALITY

"Genius" and "madness" have long been associated with one another. Almost all inventors, composers, creative scientists, and other creative persons have been regarded as insane. Although this belief was discredited long ago, there has persisted the idea that any divergence from behavioral norms is unhealthy and immoral and must be corrected. Teachers should be alert to look at behavior disapproved by the norm group for signs of creative potential. Such potentialities may not occur in the kinds of behavior valued by the school, at least not until recognized and given intelligent guidance and direction.

OTHER INHIBITING INFLUENCES

The foregoing are only a few of the cultural influences that seem to affect in powerful ways the creative development of children in the United

States. We might have included emphases upon a work-play dichotomy, a clock-orientation with emphasis on speed, emphasis on appearing to be rather than actually being, and overemphasis on a limited number of talents rather than on the diversity that we need. Instead of discussing these influences, I shall sketch briefly a proposed in-service education program to help teachers achieve the skills and concepts necessary to soften the tyranny of these cultural forces.

Teacher Skills for Nurturing Creativity

Almost any penetrating analysis of what is required for successful nurturance of creative talent leads to a recognition of the need for helping teachers improve certain skills. Through a series of articles in the *Instructor* magazine (1964–65), I proposed and outlined a series of learning experiences through which I believe teachers can improve the skills that seem crucial. This series of experiences is based on an analysis of the skills necessary for nurturing creative talents and the present status of these skills among most teachers. I have suggested that school faculties, groups of interested teachers, or individual teachers work on a different skill or set of skills each month. Participants would try deliberately to practice and improve one skill at the time, gradually integrating all of them into their behavior repertoire.

For this purpose, I have suggested a number of workshops:

WORKSHOP 1.
RECOGNIZING AND ACKNOWLEDGING POTENTIALITIES

One of the most important teacher skills needed in nurturing creative talents is the recognition and acknowledgment of potentialities. This skill is difficult to acquire, because acknowledging the potentialities of another is somehow threatening and requires imagination. One has to see a child or young person, even one who misbehaves, not as he is, but as he could become.

There is little likelihood that teachers will do much to nurture creative talents until they become aware of these potentialities. Standardized tests are useful in becoming aware of abilities that might otherwise remain unnoticed. Teachers need not be dependent upon tests, however. Through the natural learning and problem-solving activities of children, there are many opportunities for observations that make one aware of creative potentialities. Teachers can also plan experiences that call for creative thinking and motivate children to participate in them. One of my classes compiled a list of 230 different observable signs of creative classroom behavior. One workshop experience might be to see how many of the following signs abstracted from this list can be observed in a given classroom and how these signs can be used in furthering the creative development of the children concerned:

Intense absorption in listening, observing, doing
Intense animation and physical involvement
Challenging ideas of authorities
Checking many sources of information
Taking a close look at things
Eagerly telling others about one's discoveries
Continuing a creative activity after the scheduled time for quitting
Showing relationships among apparently unrelated ideas
Following through on ideas set in motion
Manifesting curiosity, wanting to know, digging digging deeper
Guessing or predicting outcomes and then testing them
Honestly and intensely searching for the truth
Resisting distractions
Losing awareness of time
Penetrating observations and questions
Seeking alternatives and exploring new possibilities

WORKSHOP 2.
BEING RESPECTFUL OF QUESTIONS AND IDEAS

A major requirement for creative behavior is the capacity to wonder, to be puzzled, to see gaps in knowledge, and to respond constructively. Children have this capacity, and it impels them to ask questions and seek answers. Being respectful of children's questions is not easy for teachers. It requires the teacher to respond with interest and curiosity rather than with threat and punishment.

To develop the skill of respecting questions and ideas, I propose that teachers begin with the exercise sketched below.

1. Think about what it really means to be respectful of the questions and ideas of children. Make a list of the common ways teachers respect or fail to respect the questions and ideas of children.

2. Try deliberately to be respectful of the questions and ideas of youngsters.

3. Write detailed descriptions of one incident in which an effort was made to be respectful of an unusual vexing question and one incident involving an original idea by a child or young person.

4. Discuss descriptions with one another, with a friend, or with a supervisor, trying to decide how well the effort succeeded and producing a variety of possible ways the teacher could have used.

In workshops, the success of this procedure will depend upon the extent that the participants feel psychologically comfortable and are willing to expose their values and behavior patterns so that perceptions and reactions can be analyzed and changed.

WORKSHOP 3.
ASKING PROVOCATIVE QUESTIONS

Several studies have shown that over 90 percent of the questions teachers ask call only for the reproduction of information in the textbook or presented by the teacher (Sanders, 1966; Torrance & Hansen, 1965; Boesen, 1966). To improve skills in asking provocative questions, teachers need to see what some of the different kinds of questions are. Several available schemes lend themselves to this purpose. One such scheme is presented in the paperback, *Classroom Questions? What Kinds?*, by Sanders (1966), a curriculum researcher who discovered that the teachers in his school system rarely asked anything except memory questions. This book offers suggestions for improving memory questions—questions that emphasize the truly important facts, generalizations, and values. In addition, there are ideas for improving skills in asking questions that call for translation, interpretation, applications of information, analysis, synthesis, and evaluation. This book could be the focus of a series of workshop experiences. One week, practice could be given in making up and trying out translation questions, questions that ask the learner to translate what he has learned from one abstraction level to another, and going beyond the information to determine implications, consequences, and effects. The following week, emphasis could be given to practice with other kinds of questions. Finally, practice could be given in combining and integrating all of the different kinds of questions into a sequence of experiences.

This is one example of a scheme that could be used. Other, perhaps equally useful, schemes would be Guilford's Structure of Intellect Model (Guilford, 1959a, 1966a). Bloom's Taxonomy of Educational Objectives (1956), and Burkhart's Divergent Power Model (Burkhart & Bernheim, 1963).

After trying for a few days to ask more provocative questions, it would be useful to check progress. A class session might be taped and analyzed. Immediately after a session, the teacher could write down all of the questions he can remember asking. One member of a workshop group might write down the questions that another workshop member asks in a classroom session. In classes of older children or adults, the teacher can have a student record the questions he asks. The skill has to be practiced, progress evaluated, and improvements made. Workshop members can analyze one another's questions and discuss possible alternatives.

WORKSHOP 4.
RECOGNIZING AND VALUING ORIGINALITY

Teachers should make deliberate efforts to recognize and value original ideas and solutions, because there is a strong tendency to ignore or discredit all unfamiliar ideas. One good way of helping teachers begin developing this skill is to involve them in the production of original ideas and assessing the degree of originality of a standard set of responses. In such a process, participants can find out why certain responses are obvious and commonplace, being produced by a primitive and easy kind of closure with little expenditure of energy. The mind has not paused long enough to make the mental leap necessary for producing original responses. Such responses are not surprising, do not ring of the essence of the truth, and do not break away from the safe, easy, and ineffective.

In a series of experiences, teachers might try deliberately to recognize and enccurage originality. One useful experience would be to write detailed descriptions of attempts and have them analyzed by the group. The following questions might be used as a guide:

1. In what form did the original idea occur?
2. What was the immediate reaction of the teacher?
3. What were the reactions of other pupils?
4. How was the original idea recognized and respected?
5. What were the immediate consequences of respecting the idea?
6. What do you predict that the long-range consequences will be?

WORKSHOP 5.
DEVELOPING ELABORATION ABILITY

No idea or solution will make much difference unless someone elaborates it and works out the necessary plans for executing it. From several current studies, it appears that the single most differentiating characteristic of the mental functioning of the juvenile delinquent and the school dropout is a serious inability to elaborate. Important scientific breakthroughs have frequently been postponed because the person who produced the idea failed to elaborate it. There is, of course, the danger of too much elaboration.

Workshop participants might focus on encouraging elaboration of some common, specific activity, a reading lesson, a plan for classroom or playground activity, or the like. A workshop group might see how many different and original ideas it can produce to encourage elaboration in connection with a particular curriculum task or area.

WORKSHOP 6.
UNEVALUATED PRACTICE AND EXPERIMENTATION

Periods of unevaluated practice and experimentation have changed tremendously what happens to students in my own classes. They make far greater progress than formerly in applying course content in the solution of personal and professional problems.

Workshop participants could try at least once a week to arrange a time for some kind of unevaluated experience. They should record their experiences, trying to answer the following set of questions and to discuss them with another person, perhaps trying to avoid correcting and evaluating what was done:

1. What was the initial assignment and the nature of the situation in which it was given?
2. How did you communicate that there was freedom to experiment without being evaluated?
3. What happened during the practice period?
4. What happened immediately after the practice period?
5. What was the nature of the similar follow-up task in which the new insights or skills were applied?
6. How was it rewarded, if rewarded?
7. What were the immediate outcomes?
8. What do you predict will be the long-range outcomes?

WORKSHOP 7.
DEVELOPING CREATIVE READERS

It is easier to remember and use information read creatively than things read passively or critically. When a person reads creatively, he is sensitive to problems and possibilities. He searches for new relationships, synthesizes unrelated elements, redefines or transforms known information into new uses, and builds onto what he knows. Thus, he produces multiple alternatives, looks at information in different ways and in greater depth, and fills in the gaps.

It takes effort to change from a passive, absorbent, or critical reader to a creative one. A person can become a creative reader by heightening expectations and anticipations or by doing something with what is read. These two approaches are discussed in some detail elsewhere (Torrance, 1965b) and prove to be as powerful with adults as with children.

Heightening expectations involves the creation of tension or warming up. Doing something with what has been read can occur at any one of four different levels:

1. Reproducing with imagination what is read, making things sound like the thing happening
2. Elaborating what is read
3. Transforming and rearranging what is read
4. Going beyond what is read

In workshop groups, the first week might be spent in helping participants themselves become more creative readers, heightening their expectations and doing things with what they read. Subsequent weeks could be devoted to helping participants help their pupils become creative readers.

WORKSHOP 8.
PREDICTING BEHAVIOR

The work of Ligon (1965) has demonstrated the value of improving the accuracy of one's ability to predict the behavior of others and the practicality of doing so. He has suggested the formation of "Co-Scientist Skills Clubs" and has provided the first edition of a manual for such clubs. The basic skills that would be cultivated are accuracy of observation and prediction of the behavior of others. He suggests three principles for developing improved skills in this area, and a workshop program could be built around them:

1. The desire to be accurate
2. Prediction of what the child will do in a given situation and then observing what he does
3. Use of the child's own words as much as possible in recording observations

WORKSHOP 9.
GUIDED PLANNED EXPERIENCES

Investigators such as Ojemann and his associates (Ojemann, 1948; Ojemann & Pritchett, 1963; Ojemann, Maxey, & Snider, 1965) are finding that mental development is quite different when children are provided with planned sequences of learning experiences rather than when they encounter only what the environment happens to provide. Application of the concept of guided learning experiences represents a deliberate attempt to assist a child in learning by developing from an analysis of the learning task and the nature of the learner, a planned sequence of experiences for mastering the learning task and by motivating him to participate in these experiences.

WORKSHOP 10.
SEARCHING FOR THE TRUTH WITH METHODS OF RESEARCH

Since the very essence of creativity is "searching for the truth," it is important that there be a series of workshops on the development of the basic concepts and skills of searching for the truth. Without these skills, there will be a lack of depth in creative thinking. Attention should be given to the skills and concepts involved in different kinds of research: historical, descriptive, and experimental. For each of these kinds of research, a profitable workshop experience would be the development of at least one lesson through which a deliberate attempt would be made to develop the relevant skills.

WORKSHOP 11.
CREATIVE PROBLEM SOLVING SKILLS

No program to improve the teaching skills needed to nurture creative talents would be complete without deliberate efforts to improve skills in creative problem-solving. There are a variety of approaches that might be used. One of the most productive and widely used of these approaches is one formulated by Osborn (1963), Parnes (Parnes & Harding, 1962), and their associates. It has been demonstrated that the basic concepts and skills can be developed to a useful degree through a series of workshop experiences as brief as two or three days. Such skills, of course, have to be practiced and improved.

RICHARD S. CRUTCHFIELD

Instructing the Individual in Creative Thinking

An educational dilemma facing us today is that we must meet an increasing need for individualized instruction, while the continuing growth of our mass educational system makes individualization less and less possible. I should like first to comment briefly on three sources of the increased demand for individualized instruction—one pedagogical, one motivational, and one social.

The pedagogical reason stems from the enormous effort currently directed at educational reform. The aims of raising academic standards, of maximizing the potential of gifted students, of helping the handicapped and underprivileged, and of stimulating the under-achiever, all point toward the need for improved methods of instruction in which the individual becomes the focus of attention. The widespread movements in curriculum innovation similarly involve a concern with individualization, in their explicit effort to make the developing conceptual structure of the subject matter as congruent as possible with what we are beginning to learn about the orderly developmental structure of the child's cognitive functioning. It is increasingly recognized that, to make the instructional process optimal, account must be taken of the specific background, capabilities, and distinctive cognitive style of the given individual. In order that any bit of instructional information—no matter how small—be properly understood and mastered by the individual, he must be enabled to assimilate it relevantly to his own cognitive structure, to transform it according to his own preferred and distinctive cognitive style, in such a way as to "make it his own." This requires individualized instruction that is geared to the distinctive attributes, needs, and cognitions of the particular person. This does not mean, of course, that individuals must be taught singly, with different materials designed for each alone. It does require that the common instructional

From *New Approach to Individualizing Instruction*. Princeton, New Jersey: Educational Testing Service, 1965. pp. 13–25. Used by permission of the publisher.

methods and materials have such scope and flexibility as reasonably to fit the diverse requirements of the different individuals. This is the pedagogical challenge—to make instruction sufficiently individualized while still maintaining it within the feasible limits of large-scale education.

A second major source of the demand for individualized instruction is motivational. There is acute need for ways to preserve the student's sense of individual identity in the sea of anonymity flooding the large-scale educational institutions of today. The Free Speech Movement at Berkeley is but one dramatic symptom of the widespread disenchantment of college students with the mass educational process in which the individual is drowned. Though these particular protests took the form of demonstrations for freedom of speech and political action, I believe that more basically they derive from the student's feeling of loss of identity in the impersonal educational mill, where he is processed through large lecture classes, tested by objective examinations, and recorded in symbols on computer tape. What he earnestly wants and seeks is the opportunity for learning experiences which are meaningful to *him,* in which *he* is meaningfully engaged with the teacher and the subject matter; in short, he wants individualized instruction.

A third major cause of the increased need for individualized instruction is social. It has to do with the changing nature of man's future world. The aims of educational training today must reflect the needs and purposes of tomorrow. I believe that the nature of man's tomorrow is such as to require greater and greater stress on individualized instruction today. It is a sobering thought that the children we instruct in elementary school today will be only forty years of age by the year 2000. We cannot clearly foresee the state of the world at that time, but we can be certain that it will be vastly different from our current world. We cannot even make sensible projections from the past because the acceleration of change is so much greater now than ever before. We may confidently expect far-reaching breakthroughs of a technological nature long before the year 2000. Automation, the high-speed computer, and other technological advances will render superfluous a great part of today's routine labor and even routine skills and intelligence. Genetical engineering may by that time enable us deliberately to reshape man's biological makeup. Physical immortality may be just around the corner. Many or most of the crucial social problems confronting us today—for example, poverty, prejudice, and overpopulation—may by that time have been virtually solved. The information explosion will multiply the sum total of human knowledge manifold and will make obsolescent many of the facts and concepts of today.

In the face of all this, we cannot now pretend fully to know just what and how the child should be taught in the way of specific facts and concepts, nor even what specific skills he should acquire. What education today must, therefore, seek to do is to bring about the optimal development of the whole individual. He must be equipped with *generalized* intellectual and other skills, skills which will enable him to cope effectively with whatever the state of the world is as he will later encounter it, in the context of rapidly changing facts and concepts. Central among these generalized skills is the capability for creative thinking. The individual will need to be able to think creatively about the yet unforeseen problems of his society and world, in the light of facts and concepts yet to be discovered. And the individual will need to attain a greater degree of self-fulfillment of his unique creative potentialities, because there will be a major shift away from preoccupation with routine work and external achievement toward preoccupation with creative experience and inner satisfaction.

These reflections about the needs for individualized instruction, especially in connection with the training of creative skills, are germane to the program of research on instructing children in creative thinking and problem-solving which my associates and I have been carrying out over the past four years. We have been guided by the belief that virtually *every* child—regardless of his level of intelligence, school achievement, and socioeconomic background—needs and can substantially benefit from explicit training in creative thinking; that there is, in short, an enormous gap between his usual performance on creative thinking tasks and the performance he is really capable of.

Our aim, therefore, has been to strengthen in the individual child certain cognitive skills which are central to the creative process and to encourage in him certain attitudes and dispositions which favor the use of these skills. We have sought to enhance the child's readiness and capacity for fluent generation of ideas, ideas which are unusual and imaginative, yet effectively adaptive to the reality-constraints of the particular creative problem. We have sought to train the child's ability to sense problems and to grasp their essentials, to see them in fresh and insightful ways, to approach them intuitively as well as analytically. We have sought to teach him how better to bring to bear on the problem what he possesses in the way of concrete knowledge, principles, and heuristics which are germane to the solution. And, finally, we have sought to promote and strengthen in him self-confidence about his own abilities for creative thinking and to increase his motivation to engage in it.

To these ends, we have undertaken to develop special new instructional materials and procedures suitable for fifth- and sixth-grade children. Confronted with the dilemma that creativity training must be individualized as far as possible and yet that the materials and methods should be suitable for easy administration to entire classes, we have sought to resolve this dilemma by casting our training materials into what may loosely be called a programmed self-instructional form. It may seem to you paradoxical, if not downright perverse, to seek to use programmed methods for the teaching of creativity. Certainly it would seem likely that programmed instruction, if used in a rigidly orthodox fashion, might be potentially detrimental to the very creative qualities we seek to enhance. For one thing, programmed instruction may tend to produce an excessive homogeneity among the thought processes of the students commonly trained. At the end of what is allegedly a "successful" program, all individuals having been marched through the *same* set of rigidly prepatterned steps will have arrived at the *same* way of looking at the *same* material. Such undue homogenization tends to preclude the diversity in thought processes essential to the promotion of creativity, both in the individual and in the group. For another thing, the "successful" program, by virtue of the very effortless ease of learning that it enables, may fail sufficiently to arouse and engage the individual's own activity of searching and striving after meaning, which is an essential part of creative growth. The goals of efficient learning and the goals of creative growth may thus be in intrinsic opposition. Moreover, a "successful" program through which the individual is marched in an authoritative logical lockstep, may tend to inhibit the questioning and skeptical attitude that is often conducive to creativity. The locus of cognitive initiative and control is thus subtly shifted from the individual to the program; the aim becomes that of tuning the individual to the program rather than the program to the individual. Finally, one of the essentials of creativity would appear to be the ability temporarily to tolerate ambiguity, complexity, and lack of closure while progressing toward solution of the problem. Yet a cardinal aim of programmed instruction is to attain the utmost of clarity, precision, and definiteness at each step. Here, too, we see that there may be an inherent opposition between the aims of orthodox programmed instruction and those of creativity training.

But through more flexible forms and uses of programming we can avoid some of these detrimental aspects and can capitalize upon its positive potential for creativity training. Its features of self-administration and self-pacing, for example, permit the individual considerable latitude in independent regulation of his own preferred rate of work and tempo of thinking on the materials. In order to challenge the student, the size of step can be made substantially larger than it is in orthodox programming, where the monotony of repeated small steps may destroy interest. Thus, a typical frame, or page, may contain much more complex material, require more time for reflection, and call for multiform rather than single responses.

Perhaps the most crucial methodological problem in programming for creativity is how to provide appropriate feedback to the individual's ideas. In more conventional programming having to do with the straight assimilation of subject matter, what is to be reinforced is the giving of the one "correct" answer. But in creative thinking on problems, a great many *different* answers are possible, and one aim of creativity training is to reinforce this diversity, uniqueness, and individuality of response. Thus, we must provide a kind of "creative feedback" that will be relevant and reinforcing for all or most individuals taking the program, regardless of the wide diversity in their responses. Suppose, for example, that we are stimulating the student to think of unusual uses for a particular object. An effective feedback to his responses might be to give him an illustrative set of diverse and unusual ideas that have been, or could have been, produced by others. The set would be intended to broaden the student's vision and limits of acceptance as to what constitutes unusual ideas appropriate to the problem; at the same time, it should contain some illustrative ideas not too far removed in quality from the perhaps more pedestrian ideas that he would have given. In this way his creative sights may be elevated without unduly discouraging him about his own less impressive initial creative attempts.

The auto-instructional materials that we have developed for fifth- and sixth-grade children make use of these various positive features of programming. In their most recently revised form, they consist of a series of sixteen booklets, approximately 30 pages each. The booklets are worked on individually by each student at his own pace. They contain story material in a semicartoon presentation. On some pages the student is asked to write down his ideas on questions that are raised in the booklet; other pages are simply to be read and studied.

The booklets have a continuous story-line which follows the adventures of two school children, Jim and Lila (brother and sister), as they try to solve a series of detective problems and other mysterious and puzzling occurrences under the tutelage of their Uncle John, who is both a high-school science teacher and a spare time detective.

This identification-model approach is intended to introduce the reader gradually into problem-solving activity, without threatening him with feelings of failure. By this means, he can be brought vicariously to experience the vicissitudes of the creative process without himself being plunged immediately and painfully into it. Jim and Lila are school children like himself. In the early stages of the lessons, they are depicted as suffering from the anxieties and ineptitudes concerning creative thinking that are all too common among school children.

As they proceed through the stories, they are depicted as gradually overcoming these handicaps—though with occasional setbacks—until at the end they reach a stage of enthusiastic interest about thinking-problems, and a strengthened sense of competence in dealing with them. The attempt is to maintain a close identification-link between them and the reader; as they move ahead, so does he, with the gap never becoming too large. Indeed, we intend that as many readers as possible will come finally to *surpass* Jim and Lila.

Uncle John is intended as a benevolent authority-figure—demi-parent, demi-teacher—who stimulates and guides Jim and Lila (and the reader) in these adventures in thinking, showing them how to think for themselves. Gradually, as the stories progress, the reader is called upon to take a more and more active role in giving his own ideas, and thus he is meant to be gradually weaned from dependence on Jim's and Lila's ideas, just as *they* are being weaned from reliance on Uncle John's.

Each lesson is a complete problem-solving episode, containing all of the principal steps and processes inherent in creative problem-solving. To begin with, Jim and Lila confront a mysterious occurrence, for example, a puzzling theft and disappearance of money on a riverboat, or strange happenings in a deserted and reputedly haunted mansion. They are encouraged to generate many ideas and to check these possibilities against the facts. With new facts coming in, they revise their hypotheses. When these fail to solve the problem, Jim and Lila are led to reformulate the problem, to see it in a different way, and thus to generate new ideas. As further incidents occur, they are led closer and closer to a solution, until finally things fall into place, and they achieve the solution. The structure of the lessons is such that the alert reader is very likely to discover the solution for himself, a step ahead of Jim and Lila. This deliberately contrived "discovery experience" is thought to be an extremely important factor in the development and reinforcement of creative thinking skills and attitudes in the student.

The lessons are constructed not only to give the reader repeated experiences in the solution of interesting problems, but also directly to instruct him in helpful strategies or heuristic procedures for creative problem-solving, by showing him how he can use them in the concrete problems. The procedures pertain to the formulation of the problem, the asking of relevant questions, the laying out of a plan of attack, the generation of many ideas, the search for uncommon ideas, the transformation of the problem in new ways, the evaluation of hypotheses, the sensitivity to odd and discrepant facts, and the openness to metaphorical and analogical hints leading to solutions.

As we have said, the lessons are also intended to promote beneficial attitudes and motivations in the reader. Mainly, the aim is to build up the child's successful experience in coping with thought problems, thus reinforcing his interest in such activity and his self-confidence in the mastery of creative thinking skills. At the same time, we undertake to instill in him a variety of dispositions which favor the creative process—open-mindedness, suspension of premature criticality of ideas, readiness for the arousal of curiosity, intuitiveness, and the like.

Above all, it is indispensable that the instructional materials actively interest and involve the reader. That they clearly do so in the studies we have made of them is partly owing to the exciting nature of the mystery stories and the maintenance of suspense while on the track of the solution. As the series of lessons progresses, there is a gradual shift from the obvious drama of detective stories toward the subtler drama of more purely intellectual problems. Jim and Lila—and hopefully the reader, too—thus come to discover that creative thinking is exciting, enjoyable, and personally significant.

During the past two years we have carried out two major studies of our instructional materials in sixteen fifth- and sixth-grade classrooms in public schools of Berkeley and vicinity. All together, 481 children have been studied—267 given the training materials, and the remaining 214 serving as control subjects.

First, a six-hour battery of pre-tests was given to all the children. The children in half of the classrooms were then given the series of auto-instructional lessons as part of their regular classroom work. One booklet was given each day over a three- to four-week period. Each child worked individually at his own pace, the average time taken per booklet being about 30 minutes. The control children in the other half of the classrooms, who were comparable to the trained children in intelligence, sex, racial distribution, and creative thinking proficiency, were not given the instructional materials. Some of them were given a short set of booklet materials which contained a serial adventure story in cartoon format. They were required to answer questions about the story in the booklets, but these questions had no bearing on creative thinking. The purpose was to insure a sense of task involvement in these control children and to acquaint them with work in such booklets. Others of the control children were handled in different ways; some of them were given no materials of any kind.

Following the end of the training period, all classes were given an eight-hour battery of post-tests in order to measure changes in creative thinking proficiency occurring between pretest and post-test.

Before turning to an account of the results of the training, we should look briefly at what was included in the pre- and post-test materials. First, there were several measures of intelligence, personality, and cognitive style. Second, there were special inventories designed by us to reveal the individual's attitudes about creative thinking and his self-evaluation as a creative thinker. Third, there were several of Torrance's tests of creative thinking in children, which have been widely used in research of this kind. Finally, and most directly relevant as criterion measures for our purposes, there were a number of tests specially constructed by us to measure creative problem-solving proficiency. Most of the available creativity tests for children, such as those of Torrance, are tests mainly of divergent thinking only. There are few available problem-solving tests of the kind we require, which entail a synthesis of both convergent and divergent thinking. Thus, we undertook to develop our own set of such tests.

The test problems are presented in booklet form, each booklet constituting one entire problem that is worked through on successive pages, with ample time for thinking. The problems are ones which tend to interest children, which minimize the need for special knowledge for the solution, and which have considerable complexity and scope, requiring the child to apply a number of different thinking skills. Each problem lends itself to several alternative solutions, varying in scope and elegance, rather than to a single rigorous solution. Performances on the problems can be scored in a variety of dimensions, most importantly for number of ideas generated, for quality of ideas, and for number of solutions achieved.

Some of the problems are detective puzzles, such as the location of a jewel that has been stolen during momentary darkness at a dinner party, or the explanation of how an entire house mysteriously vanished overnight. Other puzzles are not of a detective nature, for example, how X-ray beams can be used to destroy a tumor without harming the healthy tissue that completely surrounds it, or how a man can get himself out of a deep pit with steep sides without any available tools. The problems are meant to be of general interest, not directly related to schoolwork, though several of them do have closer curricular relevance. For example, it is alleged that an ancient city has been found buried virtually intact in the sandy desert; the problem is to think of possible causes for the apparent sudden demise of the city several thousand years ago.

Our summary account of the results of the two major studies should start with the findings on these various problem-solving tests, which were intended, of course, to be most directly suitable as post-test criteria of effectiveness of the training program. The findings are clear. The trained children showed a marked superiority in performance over the control children. This was true of every one of the test problems without exception, and for each of the main attributes of creative thinking that we measured. The trained children were able to generate about twice as many acceptable ideas as were the controls. The rated *quality* of their ideas surpassed that of the control children by an even greater margin. The trained children proved more sensitive than the controls in noticing significant clues and factual discrepancies in the problems, and were better able to benefit from metaphorical hints to solution that were embedded in the test booklets. The largest differences of all occurred on the most important criterion, namely the achievement of actual solutions of the problems. Here the trained children surpassed the controls by margins ranging up to three to one.

It is manifest then that the auto-instructional program does succeed in improving proficiency in creative problem-solving. We also discover that the beneficial effects *generalize* to types of test materials quite different from the problems. The divergent thinking tasks adapted from Torrance show similar positive results. One of these is the Tin Can test, in which the child is asked to think of as many unusual uses of tin cans as he is able. The trained children markedly outperform the controls both on sheer volume of ideas and on the originality of their ideas, as measured by Torrance's criterion of statistical infrequency. It should be stressed that this test is quite unlike anything included in our training lessons. The same is true of the Dog Improvement test, in which the child is to suggest inventive ways in which a toy dog could be made more attractive as a toy. Here the trained children make far more suggestions than the controls, and the rated quality of their ideas is even more highly superior. In the Circles test, the individual is given several pages printed with empty 1½" circles and is asked to draw as many different objects as he can, using a circle as the integral part of each object. By being told expressly to try to draw objects "that no one else will think of," he is given a set toward production of uncommon ideas. The results are that the trained children complete a somewhat greater number of circles; what is much more important, the ideas they create are far less trite and obvious than those of the controls, as measured both by statistical infrequency of occurrence and by ratings of originality made by independent judges.

We see, therefore, that there is widespread generalization of the effects of the training lessons to the enhancement of imaginative and inventive processes in the individual. However, there are discernible limits to the generalization. For instance, in the Imaginative Story test, the child is to write a short story constructed around a set of five given elements—persons and objects of a somewhat unusual nature, e.g., a "man who always smiles," a "book with black pages." In this demanding test, the trained children perform no better than do the controls. And also on several test problems of a purely *logical* nature, not requiring creative thinking, the trained children show no gain over the controls.

Turning now to the question of attitudes, we find that the training lessons did produce some modest amount of positive change in the child's attitudes toward problem-solving and creative thinking activity, but did not produce significant change in his self-confidence and evaluation of himself as a creative thinker. Clearly, the present version of the auto-instructional materials falls far short of what we had hoped to accomplish in respect to modification of these crucial attitudes, despite the marked effectiveness of the materials in strengthening creative thinking skills.

Some light on the probable persistence of the training effects is given by findings on a further follow-up testing of the children that we carried out five or six months after the end of training. The children were tested by their new teachers on several new criterion tests that we provided. The results are that the previously trained children continue to surpass the control children on some of the criterion tests, by approximately a two-to-one margin. However, it is also notable that the persistence of the original training effects is greatest for proficiency in problem-solving and is less so for performance on the divergent thinking tasks. It would thus appear that what has been most firmly established in the individual is the kind of problem-solving skill with which the training program was directly concerned, and that the more generalized and by-product effects on the individual's creative thinking are not so strongly entrenched by training.

Another issue of paramount importance, of course, is whether the lessons benefit *all* the children or only some of them. For this we must look beyond the simple statistics showing average gains of the trained children over the control children. We must ask how much the comparative gains are for children of varying levels of intelligence, of socioeconomic background, and of initial levels of creative thinking proficiency. We have divided our entire sample of children into three IQ levels—those with IQ's above 115, those ranging from 100 to 115, and those below 100. The results show that for *each* of these three levels the trained children markedly surpass the controls in test performance. There is, by the way, an appreciable correlation between IQ and our criterion test scores, but it is notable that the effect of training overrides the effect of intelligence to such a degree that the low-IQ children after training actually surpass the untrained high-IQ children. A very similar result is found when we compare children of different initial levels of creative thinking proficiency.

The Negro children—predominantly from disadvantageous backgrounds —also markedly gain from the program, though only about half as much as do the white children. But note that even though on pre-tests the Negro children scored appreciably lower than the white children, subsequently the *trained* Negro children gain enough to surpass the *untrained* whites on the post-test creativity measures.

There are, of course, many remaining questions that only further research can answer. We need to know, for instance, what effect, either beneficial or detrimental, the teacher's attitudes toward and method of classroom use of these materials may have. We need to know whether such materials when expanded to full-semester or full-year length will continue to elicit the enthusiasm, interest, and involvement of the child. We need to know whether the effects we demonstrate on our test materials do significantly generalize toward improving the child's regular school performance, increasing his creativity in working on more traditional curriculum materials. And we need to know how these effects may interact with the effects produced by the new experimental curricula that are sweeping the educational system.

Though we have sought to maximize the suitability and relevance of our materials for the individual child, we have made only a short step toward the ultimate goal of individualization. We intend now to construct additional materials which will provide for a considerably larger amount of self-selection and self-guidance by the individual, and which will have greater scope and flexibility in the feedback that is provided to the responses of the individual. One of several technical approaches to this latter problem will be to adapt our methods to the use of computer-controlled feedback, such as is being developed by other investigators for other purposes.

We also now intend to extend our training materials to higher and lower grade levels and to embrace a considerably larger part of the domain of creative functioning. So far we have concentrated mainly on creative problem-solving. Currently, we are writing new materials within the same general format which are more directly aimed at the strengthening of the child's abilities for creative understanding of complex phenomena, for inventiveness and visual imaginativeness, and for the free expression of original ideas in which the problems are themselves created by the individual.

Finally, we are undertaking a more intensive attack on the problem of modifying those attitudes which have special relevance for the encouragement and strengthening of creative drives and expressions in the individual.

Creation in the Classroom Setting

At the root of "the creative" is "creation." Life is creative by its nature, fitting to a universe that moves in its inner composition as creation-in-the-making. Those of us involved in education are involved in working with creation forming in ourselves, in those we serve, and in the world surrounding. This is basic, and the ground in which education is to gain its scientific rooting.

The question is, what is the structure of creation? And, for education, what is the form that education gets when it *is* creation?

These are the questions to which this paper is devoted, the answers given in a distillation of what I have learned to see from my years of searching.

In the first section, I lay open what I see as the structure of creative systems as nature produces them. I look at the elemental structure of the universe, the elemental necessities of living creatures, what growth entails, and evolution. I also look at human beings for the ordering that is revealed in man's perceiving, learning, problem-solving, communicating and educating. In the second section, I lay open what I see as the shape education gets when, in the classroom setting, education takes on creative form—in the way the teaching goes (and learning), and in the way a course of study forms (and the full curriculum). The third and closing section then explains the source from which my thinking stems, and the reasons why I write the way I do when seeking to communicate what I have learned from research on creative systems in the universe and man.

The Nature of Creative Systems

Looking at the *universe* for the elemental, we can see at once that it is composed of many forms of energy (light waves, atoms, molecules, organisms, mountains, seas, human beings, etc.) in interlocked relation, such that, in the passing moments ("now," "now," "now") in succession, they undergo recomposition to net emergent shapings. Creation moves,

206

emergent in the moment, as energies transact with one another to net a transformation in sequential order, ordered in the total. The movement moves. The universal womb is birth-giving. Creation is the context and the continuum. This is the elemental structure.

Looking at *living things in nature,* we can see that they have *existence as a living structure* only as they maintain themselves in an environmental setting with a give-and-take of energy across their borders to sustain an inner composition essential to their natures, each moment netting fittings, in and out, which are freshly forming. In a universe creating, they are creative structures, required to be emergent with the moment in the moving composition. Each moment needs be birth-giving if living things are to continue living.

Growth of living beings requires (1) increase of energies available from outer sources, (2) increase of integration in the inner structure, (3) increase of transactions with the environment to net (4) more fulfilling fittings, fitting to the creature. Growth of living beings is dependent on increase in these basic operations required of creative structures. Increasing life depends on participation in creation in increasing measure.

Evolution of the species follows close on growing. Arrange the species in sequential order from the most primitive to man, and what shows in the progression is increment in the capacity of the organism (1) to reach into the environment to net fresh inclusions, (2) to integrate what then comes in for handling, (3) to sustain a given course of action for the longer spans of time involved in further reaching, and (4) to participate more fully in creating, making more selections, approaching consciousness of self as involved in choosing fittings. Evolution moves in the direction of the increasing role of consciousness in the makings of creation. Creation comes more clearly into knowing.

Looking at *man* to note his psychological structure, we can see that his perceiving functions (1) to increase his reach into his environment for a wider reading, (2) to increase the internal organization of the significances then resulting, (3) to increase the span of controls on action for the further reachings, and (4) to increase the involvement in creation through more selective fittings in creation's moving. Perception was created in creation's womb, and creation is its function.

Learning, in a man, works to extend the value of perception's working. It records and orders what has come as consequence of man's action as he transacts across his borders to effect a fitting union with his world as creation moves in its progression. It forms conceptual structures to serve as means by which to guide a man to more meaningful involvement in creation's making. As learning grows, (1) more meanings are included (2) in more integrative structures (3) to increase the value of predictions guiding actions, (4) seeking resolutions more inclusive of the total composition—of man, himself, and of the wombing universe in which he is emergent creature.

Problem-solving, in a man, extends the work, again, of learning. It is the capacity *to act as if* an act were carried out before, in fact, it is undertaken. It uses past experience, product of prior learning, to predict what may happen if and when certain acts are carried out in conditions given. (1) It multiplies interlocking learnings, (2) seeks their conscious integration, (3) provides a ground for more sustaining action, and (4) sharpens need for evaluations which work out to be productive in their fitting to creation, as acts, in fact, are taken. By means of conscious problem-solving, conscious men increase the range and depth of their conscious knowing of creation's shaping.

Looking at man to note his *social* nature, we can see that *communication* is the crucial function. Communication allows men (1) to be inclusive of one another as members of the species, (2) to integrate their meaning for each other, (3) to order their transactions to be increasingly supportive, and (4) to share more fully in communion with their natures. Communication between two human creatures is an act of interlocking their emergent knowings in the sequence of upcoming moments as they share them. As one speaks, the other listens, receiving what is coming for its meaning in the forming of what he then speaks, while the other listens, thus to form a back-and-forth of intercourse which is no less birth-giving in its basic structure than nature offers, elsewhere, for forming fresh conceptions. Communication, done in tune, is a way to know, profoundly, creation's wondrous, ordered working.

Education builds on communication's structure. Whether taken as the act of teaching in the presence of a learner, or as the system of the schools in the larger social structure, education is the conscious effort of a person, or a people, to afford nourishment for the growth of consciousness in the human species. Humans are caught with the requirement that they consciously cultivate growth of conscious knowing in their kind, derived from the fact of nature that we are each born as a problem-solving system, so broadly open to manifold inclusions that we must take responsibility for teaching one another how to use the system and what to feed it. Taught nothing of this, death ensues. Taught what is ill-fitting, sickness follows. Taught well, the fittings fit to the way creation goes, inside and out, and intercoursing. The discipline is toward ever more conscious knowing of creation-on-the-make, whether it be in nature's forming (as the natural sciences entail), or in society's forming (as the social sciences entail), or in man's forming of himself (as the arts and humanities entail). The aim of education is everywhere the same, and, when fulfilled, productive of a consciousness of creation which (1) includes more, (2) integrates more, (3) guides more, and (4) fulfills more than would otherwise be the case.

In all of this, the *person* is the crucial unit for the human species. It is the person who knows or does not know, who produces or does not produce, who communicates or does not communicate, who solves problems or does not solve problems, who learns or does not learn, who perceives or does not perceive, who grows or does not grow, who exists or does not exist. The human race exists, packaged in its persons. This is the elemental unit, the link to life for human kind. The person's capacity (1) to open himself, (2) to integrate himself, (3) to sustain progressive action, (4) to fulfill himself—these are crucial. These are the necessities for him as for all creative systems.

The demand is *universal:* creative systems operate as systems (1) open, (2) integral, (3) transactional, and (4) emergent in their fittings. Such systems grow when there is increase in each dimension, accompanied by increase in the others.

The *development of a person* consists in his evolving with a mind more open in its searching, more integral in its forming, more sustained in its progressively sequential action, and more selectively refined in its increasing fittings of emergent formings.

This we know, not only from the inner logic, but from our studies of advanced creative persons, matured in cultivation of themselves as creative creatures. Those we have learned to call "great," because of their capacity to give birth to successive works of value, have been persons who, sensing in themselves the operation of a system, have learned to teach themselves how to cultivate its forming. They have learned to cooperate with their inner natures, putting conscious mind to use in supporting what, unconsciously, is given. Taking these men as models, we know to take their teachings and to seek, more consciously, to likewise teach ourselves and others.

We have a guide to educative ventures in the development of persons.

Creation in the Classroom Setting

In the classroom setting, we have, as elemental, the communicative system between a teacher and a student. We know its basic nature: two creative systems intercoursing, feeding one another.

The teacher is a sender and a receiver; the student is a sender and a receiver. What the teacher sends, the student needs be able to receive; what the student sends, the teacher needs to be able to receive. As the teacher receives a particular sending from the student, the teacher needs be able to organize a response which is relevant to what the student can next receive and use; the student, receiving, then organizing his response to be relevant to what the teacher can next receive and use, and thus to continue the sequence of communication. As each receives and sends, he has to be able to project into the inner world of the other and to sense what is forming there. Then his communication can be meaningful (a means) to the sequential and emergent development of the communication. Otherwise, communication fails; education fails. Communication is the center of the educative system.

The teacher, appointed by the culture, is presumed to have ingested into

his system those forms of knowing best designed to feed into the intercourse for germinating growth within the student, as emergent-human-
being-growing-in-his-knowing, of how the fittings go to be more fulfilling of
his nature as creative being in a universe creating.

The teacher, then, needs to know, in broadest compass, how the fittings
go (1) in the communicative structure and its operation, this being means
to his fulfillment as a teacher, and (2) in the way creation goes in human
kind and in the world-creating, this being basic structure for the total. In
lesser compass, focused on the student he is facing and on some aspect of
the world in which the teacher has had most intense engagement, the
teacher needs to know how the fittings go (1) in the mind of each student
there before him, and (2) in the field of study in which the teacher has had
his main encounter. The latter, he has ingested into *his* mind as a major
forming structure, taken as a composition which is more inclusive, more
integral, more sustained, and more fully formed than the students have yet
come to know.

In the emergent moments of his teaching, the task at hand is to guide the
intercourse so that the fittings in the minds of those specifically before him
and the fittings in *his* mind can have a resolution to net, for the student, a
growing comprehension. Development, for the student, proceeds in this
fashion, provided the student, too, is given chance, and takes it, to guide
the intercourse from *his* end of the engagement, so that fittings of his own
may be evident and relevant to the formings of the teacher as grounds for
the progression. Development proceeds only from the base of what's
existent, and the student's base needs be evident and relevant, both to the
student and the teacher, since progress in the student's growth is his base
progressing. The communication needs be mutual, with responsibility
required at both ends of the circuit, focused on emergence of the student's
mind as growing system. The teacher's mind is instrumental.

Though instrumental, the teacher's mind is not without rejuvenation, if
the communicative system is vital in its function. If the teacher gives his
life into his mind when expressing what is forming in him, and the student
gives his life into his mind when expressing his returning message, then the
teacher can receive life for himself from the life the student offers. Life
flourishes in a reciprocating system where one participant, giving life,
receives it from the other, turn about, in communal fashion. The person of
the teacher grows as he finds a fitting with the growth evolving in the varied
persons present in the classroom setting. Communication, vitalized, serves
all of those participating. Each, giving life, receives it when the systems,
interlocked, are open, integrative, sequentially attuned to progressive fittings. Creation, then, is forming, and fresh energy is released for further
making. This is nature's mode of working.

Converse to this, of course, is the path to dying. Death ensues for a
given system when it closes down, disintegrates, or fails to function in
sequential give-and-take with what's around it. In the classroom setting,

teaching dies, and so does learning, when the system of the teacher or the learner closes down, disintegrates, or fails to function in the sequential give-and-take of emergent formings.

On the continuum between death and life in fullest measure, teaching-learning gets its evaluation in the classroom setting. Is the communication vital? Does the teacher come to life in his expression? Is his life renewed by his participation? Is his response freshly formed in resonance with what the students offer? Is he open to the students' sending? Does he watch and listen for the cues upcoming? Does he have a target in the inner world of the students' forming, as he shapes up his expression? Is he open to different minds among them, seeking avenues to each in reciprocating meaning? Is he testing to find the students' openings? Does he know what they are closed to? where they lack an integration? what blocks they have in their expression? how each can best make clear his form of knowing? what past experience has offered each by way of grounds on which to build his further knowing? his stage of maturation as self-teaching person? etc.

What about the students for their end of the communication? Are they free to offer their expression? Are they trying? Are they open to the efforts of the teacher? Are they reaching for connections? Do they come to life when in the classroom setting? Do they put themselves into what they do when seeking meaning? Are their questions vital? Are their questions and expressions relevant in the sequential order? Are they targeting their offerings to meet the forms emerging in the teacher's growing composition? Do they sense their minds are growing?

Thus the questions tumble out to guide evaluation of communication in the classroom setting. There are other matters to which we also need to give attention.

As agent of the culture, what the teacher uses as guide to the progression is "a course of study," derived from his experience in relatively intense engagements with creations in some field of focus. His knowledge, there, is formed in integral connections by which to open out, in sustained extensions, an enlarging net of knowings which comprehend, in increasing measure, how creation goes in his field of focus. As man comprehends his world and comes to form means by which to effect a useful fitting between movements in his mind and in the world surrounding, he takes these means, called "meanings," and forms them into conceptual structures, called "disciplines," by which to discipline his actions when seeking further fittings. The teacher, ingesting one or more of these in concentration, then uses what he knows to form a course of study by which to induct the young ones, coming on, into his world of meaning. Through the teacher as its agent, the culture of a given time thus passes on what men, in that field, then think to be important for perpetuating life in man and opening way to further growth of species.

Teachers then assemble into communities of scholars and take on the name of "school" or "college." Here they map out, not only courses for the students' progressive development in respect to each given discipline, or "field of knowledge," but "curricula" by which to guide the neophyte, when, offered choices among the total courses offered, he has to answer what he wants to give his life to in the time allotted. The "curricula" form answers to what the community of scholars take to be paths to the "development" of its varied students, and each teacher, in his classroom, presumes the students there before him to have a connected way of growing, not only in his class, but in the total setting.

The question is, is the curriculum, in fact, so ordered? What is the connected way of growing in between the courses offered? What forms the basic union for the student as he moves from course to course, seeking integration of himself as he opens out into varied fields of knowing? What is the discipline that disciplines the courses into a union fitted to the growing of a person? What does the teacher do, who, seeking way to make his contribution to the integration, designs his course accordingly? What is the question that is common to each and all the teachers such that, asking it and working toward an answer, the teachers form a community of mind, needing one another, communicating back and forth to effect development within themselves and in the total such that, doing so, they provide a fertile field for growth and integration of the student? What is the fitting question that, integrating and growing teachers, also integrates and grows the students?

We know the answer, having answered for ourselves, what is development? The question is how creation goes, forming on its way to shape the universe and life and man. Creation is not a disordered thing; it has form. Life has form; growth has form; evolution has form; perception has form; learning has form; problem-solving has form; communication has form; education has form; development of persons has form—these are illustrations as we have sketched them heretofore, and the form, at the level of a basic system, is everywhere the same. This appears to me to be the case as creation forms throughout the universe and life and man.

Taken so, we then have a common question for all disciplines, a way to invite integration of the human mind, no matter where it turns. In the natural sciences, it is the question of how creation goes in the workings of nature; in the social sciences, it is the question of how creation goes in the workings of men among men; in the arts and humanities, it is a question of how creation goes in the workings of men when men are creating their own meaning as emergent human beings. The subject matter changes for these fields, but not the basic question. In each case, there is a man (a creative system), using his mind (a creative system) to effect (create) a fitting (a creation) between what is forming in him (being created) and what is forming in his field of focus (being created), thereby to realize creation-on-the-make within his knowing. Past experience forms a ground, or bed, or womb of prior knowings, inseminated, then, with what comes in from present focus to germinate fresh conceptions and give birth to emergent knowings. *There is a creator, creating a creation from the way creation goes,* no matter what the subject matter. The basic process, the basic setting, the basic aim, is everywhere the same, derived from the fact that we are creative systems in a system of creation under way.

Teachers, therefore, have a common quest by which to vitalize communication with each other and form a community in spirit as well as name. A given teacher in a given course can make his contribution to the integration by revealing how it is that, in his field, the prime pursuit is to realize creation as one comes in tune with creation-on-the-make within one's self and what's focused on. The students, then, have a common theme to greet them, a common tune, as they turn from one course of study to another in their weekly regimen and in their full curriculum. Creation is the theme. Integrated thus within their world, the students have a way to their development as integrated men.

These considerations give rise, again, to a set of questions with which to evaluate the classroom setting: Does the teacher know the theme? Does he know himself as a creative being? Does he accept himself as such? Does he reveal himself to students as a man creating? Are his students able, then, to see how creation goes when the teacher does the working? Is the student then invited to do creating in *his* turn? Is the discipline organized to help him? Does it reveal the elemental story in what is focused on? Are its past creations recognized as the product of man's creative work; introduced as such; taken to have value, now, as they serve creation, once again? Is the content opened out so that, taken in, it serves to integrate the student's acts in his *own* sequential runs, forming fittings of his *own* which net the elemental meaning?

Or is the classroom setting the other way around, where the discipline is taken as an end, a product organized as stuff already dead, to be worshipped now, as idols are, by those who are not to touch it so as to leave it just the same? Is the teacher blind to what he needs be focused on in the deeper vein? Is he lacking in the theme? unknowing of *his* nature? afraid of what it means? unavailable as model for the development of men? closed down? unintegrated? unvitalized? ill-fitted as life-giving?

Let this be the end of what I now say on the basic theme. This may be enough, perhaps, to show the mode of my engagement with the problem.

Source of the Struggle

In closing, let me say, lest my language be deceptive, that I have come to this expression from struggle with the elemental question. At age twenty, I left college because it had come to be, for me, death-dealing. I was growing weak and scrawny because I could not get from living there what my life needed for its growing. I was ill-fitted to the setting as I saw it. In nine months out, much of my time was spent in the lap of nature, communicating with that primal structure. This offered ground for giving form to scientific questions. I returned to college, resolved to see, beneath the operation, what was giving life and what was giving death to those within it. With the help of a vital teacher, I found my way to make college life rewarding, determined then to do what I could for others.

This came to be my lifetime struggle, and in the years which followed, I worked at it in varied roles—researcher into student life and problems; student personnel administrator; acting dean of a college; aide to councils, committees, and other academic bodies, too numerous to mention; co-ordinator for research in a complex college—these roles used to teach me the nature of the educative enterprise as it is, and might be, if more fruitful. My search was focused on discovery of ground in nature which would give me way to see beyond the foibles of the moment, the fashions, the superficial clutter, the ingrained habits of tradition, the ignorances that tend to multiply when men meet in groups to form their common ventures.

My answer grew within me from the roots I'd tapped in those nine months with nature. I was then gaining ground for shaping up the elemental questions, and girding for the lifetime struggle. The struggle has been constant. In recent years, when I have found my way into expression of a basic answer, I have found so many of my fellowmen to be without the question. They, seemingly, have little need to fight for life, to know life, to know growth, to know creation, or, indeed, to know education in its primal function, though they are caught up within it.

But there are signs the times are changing. There are many interested in the creative, and well there might be, for the time has come in the life of the human species when the question is badly put before us, do we want life to continue? By conscious choice, we have built the means for ultimate destruction; by conscious choice, we have now to choose life for ourselves or extinction. Choosing life, we need to know, quite consciously, what goes to make it, and this means to know creation in its forming.

Fortified by this observation, I have dared to give expression to my question and its answer, and to do it in a way appropriate to its conception. When one tenders up creation as his answer, he needs be creative in expression or the answer never reaches. There is no way to cheat on nature, and, when human nature is the point of focus, the scientist needs humanist as his integral companion.

So my language breaks into the poetic, and my terms take on a philosophic flavor, but I would not have you think me aiming at either poetry, or philosophy, or even science, if that term is narrowly construed, or any other "discipline" as usually defined, if what this means is less than the primal struggle to gain life-released through the educative venture. My discipline derives from the struggle with the problem; all else is instrumental.

I know the game as it is played in academic circles, having served in varied roles to test its very nature. In these roles, I have been "successful," as success is measured. But I rebel at the puny grasp we have of the educative venture, for the problem now, as I near sixty, is not mine alone, as it appeared to me to be at age twenty; I see it now as the problem of education serving life for the extension of the human species. Without life-released in fullest measure in our educated people, can life itself continue? This is now the question.

PART III

CREATIVITY: MEASUREMENTS

Introduction

When creativity is equated with genius and the process of creation is thought to be wholly mysterious, there is no need to develop the measurement of creativity. But when creativity is taken to be a valued potentiality of all men and its development a valued social aim, then measurement becomes important. The phenomenon of creativity needs to be publicly defined, located, compared and related to other phenomena so that it can be recognized and systematically cultivated by many people, working programmatically in many situations. It is then that measurement develops and serves a basic need.

Measurement of creativity is not easy; to make the effort is to meet, head on, the challenge to convert the mysterious into the concrete, the general into the specific, the unordered into the ordered, the unquantified into the numbered. Possible failures must be faced and successes analyzed with cautious care to get the residues that can be used as core for next developments. Progress is slow if one looks only at the residues; but, now, the major point to note is the quickly broadened range in which encounters with the problem of measurement are carried on.

The following studies show the varied course of work to date:

Calvin Taylor and John Holland review and summarize research studies in which tests are used as measures of creativeness. They emphasize that many factors need to be taken into account, that multivariable approaches are required, and that criteria need to be comprehensive in their range.

Elizabeth Starkweather and Frieda Cowling focus on creativity in the preschool child and work toward a needed clarity in the way conformity is viewed: Is nonconformity, per se, to be included as a criterion, or is the choice to be more restrained than that? Is it necessary to include a measurement, as well, of the time and place where nonconformity appears?

Eugene Gaier screens out studies which have dealt with the relationship between motor skills and creativeness, asking if they correlate. If so, is the relationship direct? Inverse? Significant?

Robert Burkhart is interested to know to what extent IQ tests can be predictors of success in fields of art. He reviews and summarizes studies made of this relationship in students from the early grades through graduate: Can IQ scores be used to judge what youth can do in art? Or not?

William Hitt and John Stock use tests to analyze the temperament of men who daily work at the frontiers of scientific and industrial research, searching for differences in their temperamental tendencies toward originality and logical reasoning: Do these tendencies differ at levels of significance? What do they suggest to management?

R. J. Goldman considers tests which have been developed for use in school programs to cultivate creativeness and describes those produced at the University of Minnesota, under Paul Torrance, for such use: What do they probe into? What do they contain? How promising is this development?

J. P. Guilford uses the frame of reference of his classic work on the structure of the intellect to lay open the range of measurements that need be taken into account to have a comprehensive grasp of creative potential and creative performance: What is this range? What do the measures need to differentiate? How complete is the battery to date? How adequate?

Kaoru Yamamoto is concerned with the validation of creative thinking tests and gives an appraisal of the present status of these tests in this respect: How valid are these tests? What are the problems met?

Taher Razik puts into perspective the major developments which have come about in recent years to strengthen measurements of creativity and to give them a place in the further development of education for creativity: What have been the main developments? Where has progress been attained?

CALVIN W. TAYLOR

JOHN L. HOLLAND

Development and Application
of Tests of Creativity

Research knowledge about creativity is scanty. Some of the best research projects are large ones not yet published or still in process. Until a few years ago, the complexities of creativity discouraged research studies in this area. Recently, increased research activities in creativity, in which the subjects have most often been scientists, have been exploratory in nature; several have been very provocative. Many of the researchers have focused on understanding the nature of creativity and of the creative person, rather than hurriedly trying to build a creativity test to market for widespread use; consequently, a great variety of characteristics has been studied by means of several types of measuring instruments. Research has sometimes focused on a characteristic, such as independence, which has been measured by several separate devices; in other instances, it has focused on possible measures of creative potential—for example, on high-level aptitude-type tests as opposed to personality or motivation-type tests. Much of the research reported was directed toward finding concomitant characteristics of creativity that should eventually permit building tests of creativity potential.

The overall pattern of research measuring creative giftedness has not followed the pattern of research on intellectual giftedness. Moreover, some researchers will argue that the burgeoning research movement in creativity, with its broad approach and resistance to premature crystallization, is much healthier than was the intelligence-testing movement, especially for long-range research purposes and for avoiding similar pitfalls.

Several relatively large and sustained research programs involving creativity have loosely coordinated their efforts through conferences (C. W. Taylor, 1956, 1958a, 1959c). These research projects have been able to

---

From *Review of Educational Research,* February, 1962, *32* (1), pp. 91–102. Used by permission of the publisher.

219

draw upon a considerable body of basic research findings about human characteristics, especially those findings that have emerged from factorial research studies on intelligence, personality, and motivation. Computers have facilitated the use of large and complex patterns of tests and have made possible large factor-analysis and multiple-correlation studies involving several individual criteria of creativity. Item-alternative analyses of relatively long psychological inventories against creative criteria are becoming relatively routine. But the task of selecting predictors for a particular study from the large number of potentially valid predictors of creative performance must be done by the researcher, not the computer. Consequently, each experimental battery differed from others, but, usually, each involved a small subset of 20 or 30 promising new intellectual tests (not found in the typical intelligence-test composite) plus various nonintellectual tests. Some experimental batteries for creativity have even been entirely nonintellectual in nature. For example, the current unpublished Utah studies of National Aeronautics and Space Administration scientists have used only a long complex biographical inventory as a predictor of each of several criteria.

Traditional Measures of Creativity

Before samples of the most relevant research are reviewed, preliminary comments are in order about certain widely available measures of characteristics of individuals.

If school grades were efficient predictors of creativity, the identification of persons with outstanding creative potential would be simple. Not only certain school grades, but school grades in general, have been shown to have low validity in predicting creative performance (C. W. Taylor, 1958b; C. W. Taylor et al., 1961). If grades are ever to become valid predictors, a significant portion of school activities may have to be changed to demand creative performance and behavior.

Mere accumulation of knowledge does not appear to be sufficient for creative performance; it does not guarantee that the incubation and insight stages of the creative process will occur. One can easily cite examples in the academic world of people who are extremely learned in their fields, but who have demonstrated little creative behavior.

Evidence is gradually accumulating that traditional intelligence tests, at best, reveal only minor variations in creative performance; they do not directly involve the ability to create new ideas or things. In factor-analysis studies by many research workers, the factors involving the ability to sense problem areas, to be flexible in each of several ways, and to produce new and original ideas tend to be unrelated or to have little relation to tests used to measure intelligence (French, 1951; Guilford, 1959c). Chorness (1956) studied civilian Air Force personnel who had suggested ideas that were officially accepted by their organizations. He found that their approximate IQ scores (from the information scales of the Wechsler-Bellevue Intelligence Scale) were spread across the entire range of the IQ's of the sample of civilian personnel.

D. W. Taylor (1958) found that the Terman Concept Mastery Test (designed specifically as an adult-intelligence measure for Terman's follow-up studies) had no significant correlations with supervisory ratings of scientists on creativity, productivity, or originality. Every other intellectual test in this study showed at least some significant validities with these criteria, but it could be argued that there was some restriction of range in the study.

Getzels and Jackson (1959) and Torrance (1959c) reported that if an intelligence test is used to select top-level talent, about 70 percent of the persons with the highest 20 percent of the scores on a "creativity" battery will be missed. Eighty percent, just 10 percent more, would be missed if the intelligence and "creativity" scores were completely unrelated. Torrance has replicated these findings with less restricted groups in yet unpublished studies. The two so-called creativity batteries, however, were not identical in composition, and might more safely be called "divergent-thinking" batteries until they are more adequately validated against suitable external criteria of creativity.

The same type of naming problem still exists for the so-called intelligence tests. Among the nearly 60 dimensions of the mind discovered to date, more than 50 should now be described as *nonintelligence* intellectual dimensions, according to C. W. Taylor (1961), even though intelligence has often been very broadly defined.

Roe (1951, 1953), in studies of eminent scientists, reported that their intelligence scores were all distinctly above average. But this would be expected, since these scientists had been screened through a long, formal, academic program, the grades in which are usually highly correlated with intelligence-test scores. The assumption that this long, formal, academic program (as now constituted) is completely relevant and prerequisite to research and creative work in the sciences (in contrast especially to the arts) is being challenged by researchers who are finding low or negative correlations of academic grades with on-the-job performance in research work (C. W. Taylor, 1958b; Martin & Pachares, 1960; C. W. Taylor et al., 1961). Evidence to support this challenge is found in the unexpected and remarkable readiness of high-school students to do research of publishable quality in the research-participation programs of the National Science Foundation Summer Science Program for Secondary Students; Riley and Overberger (1961) described an example of such readiness.

Guilford and Allen (Guilford, 1959c) selected some 28 dimensions of the mind that they felt were relevant to success in the physical sciences. Using clearly stated descriptions as well as a sample item from a best test for each of these 28 intellectual characteristics, they asked each of a number of scientists of various types to rank these 28 characteristics for importance in his individual job. Nineteen of the top 20 were nonintelligence intellectual characteristics. Rated below the twentieth were several characteristics usually included in commonly used intelligence tests.

The majority of studies suggested that the relation of intelligence tests or components of intelligence tests to creative performance is generally low (.20 to .40) in unselected populations and is zero and even negative for homogeneous samples at high levels of intelligence (MacKinnon, 1959; Holland, 1961; Mullins, 1959; and Yamamoto, 1961). The best conclusion at present is that intelligence, as measured, accounts for only a minor portion of the variation in creative performance and, by itself, is by no means an adequate measure of creativity. In fact, nearly all research attempts to measure and study creativity have focused upon nonintelligence intellectual tests, nonintellectual tests, biographical inventories, and environmental factors.

Multivariable Approaches to Creativity

The forerunners of multivariable approaches to creativity were large factor-analysis studies of well-designed batteries. For example, important pioneering work was accomplished by L. L. Thurstone and his students, who initially analyzed the intelligence-test composites into multiple factors and later extended these efforts into new intellectual areas not covered by intelligence tests. Thurstone (1952) himself wrote a provocative report on creativity.

J. P. Guilford and his colleagues have actively advanced this type of work during the past two decades; their efforts culminated in Guilford's (1956) three-dimensional model of the structure of intellect. Guilford's most relevant study was a factor analysis of a large battery of "creativity" tests (Guilford, Wilson, & Christensen, 1952; Guilford et al., 1951) that formed a main basis for his later statement that some components of memory, cognition, evaluation, convergent production, and especially divergent production are involved in creative work. More specifically, the high-level aptitude (or intellectual) factors most involved are probably originality, adaptive flexibility, spontaneous flexibility, ideational fluency, expressional fluency, associational fluency, word fluency, sensitivity to problems, visualization, judgment, and redefinition (Guilford, 1959c).

Investigations of creative promise have typically emphasized a broad range of assessment variables, an emphasis somewhat in contrast to the identification of the so-called intelligence type of giftedness by means of such a single measure as IQ score. Creativity measures have mainly included new intellectual characteristics not contained in IQ tests—motivational, biographical, sociometric, and other personality characteristics.

Stein (1956) studied forty-six industrial-research chemists who were selected on the basis of composite ratings on creativity by supervisors, colleagues, and subordinates. He subjected them to a two-day individual and group psychometric analysis designed to yield both biographical and self-evaluative information on certain variables. On the basis of biographical data, Stein found that the more creative chemists, in contrast to the less creative ones, came from lower socioeconomic levels, engaged in solitary activities earlier in life, and had parents of lower educational level who were more distant and inconsistent. From the self-evaluations, Stein found that the more creative chemists tended to be more autonomous, strove for more distant goals, had more integrative attitudes, were more cautious and realistic, were more consistent in their desires for rewards, had a more differentiated value hierarchy, and perceived themselves as assertive and authoritative, with leadership ability.

In a study of 103 Navy electronics laboratory scientists by D. W. Taylor (1958), the American Institute for Research Test for Selecting Research Personnel had the most significant, though somewhat low, validities (in the .20's and .30's) against supervisory ratings on creativity, compared with several other tests. This test, consisting of 150 multiple-choice problem situations, attempts to analyze three types of job performances relevant to research: (a) formulating problems and hypotheses, and planning and designing investigations, (b) conducting investigations and interpreting research results, and (c) accepting organizational and personal responsibility. The other tests with less promise or without promise were, in descending order, the *Owens-Bennett Mechanical Comprehension Test,* the *Test of Productive Thinking,* the Terman *Concept Mastery Test,* and the *Strong Vocational Interest Blank* (Engineering key). The study was cross-validated on a second sample of sixty-six Navy scientists.

The creativity research of MacKinnon and staff has continued with good financial support for several years. They invited some 260 highly creative individuals in the areas of writing, architecture, and mathematics, who were nominated by nationally recognized persons in the fields concerned, for a three-day assessment program at the Institute of Personality Assessment and Research. Barron (1959) reported that these subjects were being evaluated on a multiplicity of variables. Qualities such as the following, which Barron reported as appearing in this highly selective group, have been shown to be characteristic by later work, as yet unpublished: an intensity of moral and aesthetic commitment; a component of sexuality in psychic creativity; voluminous production; and diligence, discipline, and total commitment with respect to their work.

Cattell (1959), in a study of 144 leading research physicists, biologists, and psychologists, drew three conclusions. First, the personality profiles of these researchers differed significantly (.01) from that of the average man, particularly as follows: the researchers were more schizothyme, intelligent, dominant, inhibited, emotionally sensitive, and radical, and they were more given to controlling their behavior by an exacting self-concept. Second, the researchers' personality profiles differed from those of persons of equal general intelligence who were outstanding in administration or teaching, specifically as follows: the researchers were more schizothyme, less emotionally stable, more radical, and uniformly lower on all primary personality factors measuring extroversion. Finally, when the researchers' profiles were compared with those of persons eminent in literature and the decorative arts, both groups were shown to be more schizothyme, intelligent, dominant, desurgent, radical, and self-sufficient than average.

Getzels and Jackson (1959) drew twenty-six "highly creative" and twenty-eight "highly intelligent" adolescents from a group of 449 high-school students on the basis of their performances on an IQ measure and of a summated score on five "creative" instruments (Word Association, Uses for Things, Hidden Shapes, Fables, and Makeup Problems). The two groups were then compared on a variety of variables and measures with the following results: the high-IQ subjects used stereotyped meanings, had conventional standards of success, and aspired for conventional careers, whereas the highly creative subjects diverged from stereotyped meanings, had unconventional standards of success, and aspired for unconventional careers. Studies of this type have had an important effect in arousing interest in creativity.

Torrance (1959c), in a series of studies exploring creative thinking in the early school years, developed a tentative battery of measures for identifying creative elementary-school children and comparing them with their classmates on certain variables. Such measures include the inventive manipulation of toys, alternative solutions to frustrating situations in well-known children's stories, the Ask-and-Guess Test, and modified test items for eliciting creative thinking. For example, through sociometric or peer nominations in thirty-three classrooms, Torrance found, with advancing grade levels, a progressive increase in peer sanctions against highly creative children.

The use of creativity-test scores as criteria by Getzels and Jackson and by Torrance has suggested other potential predictors. This plan for investigating appears to be a useful first step; it usually provides a reliable, immediate criterion. The value of such a criterion for discovering and validating predictors lies in the degree to which such devices are equivalent to other more remote or more relevant criteria of creative performance. Such test scores may be useful in defining more explicitly the nature of adult creativity after these scores have also been employed as predictors of creative performance in longitudinal studies.

The Utah studies of Air Force scientists probably are the most extensive example to date of multivariable research in creativity (Taylor et al., 1961). Approximately 50 criterion scores on each scientist were obtained from immediate supervisors, higher-level supervisors, peers, the scientist himself, official records, lists and samples of reports and publications, professional-society membership, college records, and interviews by the project researcher. Almost a year was spent in the research organizations collecting the criterion data and obtaining 130 test scores in five spaced test-administration periods. Shrinkage in sample size occurred during this long, intensive data-collection period, so that complete criterion data were available on 166 of the 210 scientists; test data obtained were complete for 107 of these and almost complete for 33 more. Even this heavy testing program employed only about half the number of the intellectual tests that were deemed promising measures of creative performance. Match Problems, Consequences, Word Association, and Visual Imagery were four of the seven intellectual tests used. The validities of the best individual scores against 14 factored criteria ranged in the .20's to .40's, with more than 30 scores being valid for most criteria. Multiple-correlation analyses showed that approximately half the variance in any of the 14 criteria of creative and other scientific contributions may be overlapped by a linear regression combination of 15 or more valid test predictors. The shrinkage on cross-validation is not yet known.

In summary, there is still uncertainty about the degree to which the foregoing sets of "creativity" tests are valid predictors of important creative performance. The final check of the many concurrent-validity studies will be predictive-validity studies. Nevertheless, these "creativity" tests are, without doubt, measuring intellectual processes and nonintellectual characteristics that are not closely related to those involved in high intelligence-test scores.

Additional References: Bloom (1956); Drevdahl (1954); Harmon (1958); Sprecher (1959).

Single-Test Studies of Creativity

Nearly every study involving even a brief biographical inventory or biographical approach for predicting creativity in scientists has been found to have promising validity in the initial sample studied (Stein, 1956; Knapp, 1956; C. W. Taylor, 1958; Roe, 1958, 1959; Owens, Schumacher, & Clark, 1958; Cattell, 1959; Ellison, 1960; C. W. Taylor et al., 1961; Holland & Astin, 1961; Smith et al., 1961; Mullins, 1959). Mullins did not get good results on cross-validation. Surprisingly high cross-validities (.46 to .56) against creativity criteria have been found in current unpublished studies of four samples of 654 scientists, in which the principal investigators followed up previous biographical studies on Utah scientists (Ellison, 1960) and 107 Air Force scientists (C. W. Taylor et al., 1961). In each of these six studies, item analyses of all responses were made on every sample in an attempt to formulate empirical keys to be cross-validated on other samples. Sizable cross-validities for a biographical inventory were found by Smith and others (1961).

Such special-aptitude tests as the Guilford battery, devised to measure creative ability, have had only modest success. The evidence for the validity of such tests is still incomplete and unclear. In some of these tests, there are evidences of restriction of range which make results unclear when significant validities are not obtained (C. W. Taylor et al., 1961). Chorness and Nottelmann (1957) found that an intelligence measure predicted employee "creativity" as well as did selected tests from the Guilford battery. In such instances, it should be recognized that, in both the academic world and the business world, testees with high intelligence scores probably have an initial advantage, because of current emphasis on such scores, over testees obtaining high scores on creativity-disposing intellectual characteristics. The latter must emerge on their own in competition with those enjoying the initial advantage.

In the majority of studies of creative persons, there has been a strikingly consistent emergence of a sizable number of personal traits relevant to creativity (e.g., independence). These characteristics alone may be of minor significance in their contribution to the total variance in creative performance. But this consistency contrasts sharply with the frequent conflicts in early results in other areas of psychological research.

Ghiselin (1956) described how an approach for obtaining descriptions of the creative process might eventually help in the identification of the creative individual. More recently, Ghiselin developed a Creative Process Check List for the separation of more creative persons from less creative persons. Each subject was asked to check 37 adjectives (items) describing his "states of attention" and 39 adjectives describing "states of feeling," on the basis of whether he experienced them before, during, and/or after problem-solving experiences in his work. The first a priori attempts to score this check list, in C. W. Taylor and others' (1961) study of Air Force scientists, were, in general, not successful.

At the 1955 University of Utah Research Conference on the Identification of Creative Scientific Talent, the Word Association Test, scored for remote associations, appeared to be one of the most promising predictors. The test has since, however, yielded conflicting results, including zero validities and instances where a common-associations score predicted better than did a more-remote-associations score (Hills, 1958; C. W. Taylor et al., 1961). Two-way association tests included in factor studies usually have produced a factor pattern similar to the one-way Word Association Test. How a three-way association test differs enough from these one-way and two-way association tests to yield high validities remains to be determined.

Typical interest inventories, with a few exceptions, generally have been poor predictors. In a battery of 69 predictors including aptitude, personality, and originality scales, self-ratings, and teacher ratings, Holland (1961) found *simple* interest measures to be among the best predictors of creative performance. A complex motivational device, used in a study of Air Force scientists, had very few significant validities against several criteria, whereas a considerably higher percentage of the validities was significant for a brief and simple device measuring minimum aspirational level in several different aspects of scientific work (C. W. Taylor et al., 1961).

The validity of such personality inventories as the *California Personality Inventory, Sixteen Personality Factor Questionnaire,* and Saunders' experimental Personality Research Inventory is generally low, although there is considerable variation according to studies by Holland and Astin (1961) and C. W. Taylor et al. (1961). In the latter study, the Personality Research Inventory yielded valid-appearing scores in self-acceptance, tolerance of ambiguity, self-sufficiency, masculine vigor, artistic ability versus practicality, progressivism versus conservatism, and liking for thinking. However, only 8 percent of the validity coefficients for all 130 criterion tests were significant at the 5-percent level. The evidence for the validity of nonintellectual originality scales falls at about the same level, although there is again a wide range of correlations.

Simple self-ratings in adolescent and adult samples have proved to have moderate validity for a variety of creative performances. Terman's earlier work also showed that ratings of self-confidence, persistence, and integration toward goals were among his most efficient predictors of adult achievement. In C. W. Taylor and others' (1961) study of Air Force scientists, the best overall predictor of all 14 criteria of creativity was a self-rating of creativity, which also was valid for every one of the 6 with creative components out of the 14 factors. Self-ratings on several other characteristics (e.g., resourcefulness, desire for discovery, discrimination of value, and intuition) also had moderate validity for many of the creativity criteria.

Supervisors' ratings appear to be of some value for predicting creative performance, according to Buel (1960). Supervisors' ratings of creativity have also been used with success as rating criteria, and these have been predicted significantly by psychological scores in several studies, including the current Utah biographical study of NASA scientists and the Utah study of Air Force scientists (C. W. Taylor et al., 1961). In the latter study, the supervisory ratings of creativity were significantly correlated with 29 percent of the 130 test scores. Peer nominations and rankings also worked well in the Utah study of Air Force scientists; they were predicted by 35 percent of the test scores. Well-constructed ratings and descriptions by appropriately selected persons may be one of the more promising approaches for predicting creative performance, although, to date, such ratings have usually been used as criteria.

Several investigators have begun work on unique devices and techniques for predicting creative performance, but at present no evidence for their validity is available. A new individual device called Problem-Solving Apparatus, invented by John (1958), is highly complex and interesting and may have potential as a predictor.

A review of the current status of predictors of creative performance suggests the following crude ordering of predictors, by class, with respect to their efficiency: biographical items and past achievements, self-ratings and direct expressions of goals and aspirations, originality and personality inventories, aptitude and intelligence measures (except where restriction-of-range corrections are applicable), and parental attitudes. Any such ordering of promising predictors is admittedly hazardous, since it is subject to unknown biases and errors.

Criteria of Creativity

There is need for exploration and development of multiple criteria of creative performance. The most comprehensive reports now available on the crucial problem of criteria are those of criterion subgroups of the University of Utah creativity conferences of 1955, 1957, and 1959. It is clear from the large criterion study of Taylor, Smith, and Ghiselin (1959) that no single criterion of performance is adequate or desirable, since some criteria are relatively independent of one another. In this study, approximately 50 criterion measures of the creative and other contributions of 166 Air Force scientists were obtained and factor-analyzed to yield 14 meaningful factors. Nearly one-half of these factors included aspects of creativity. One factor involved originality in writing; another entailed supervisory ratings on creativity (as well as on flexibility and independence); a third included two creativity ratings by higher-level supervisors; a fourth showed that the self-rating on creativity had the highest loading. Two other factors included patent rate in their clusters, and another may entail some form of creativity in administrative work, since organizational awards had its highest loading with that factor.

ELIZABETH K. STARKWEATHER

FRIEDA G. COWLING

The Measurement of Conforming
and Nonconforming Behavior
in Preschool Children

Introduction

The present research is seen as a contribution to the study of the nature and development of creative ability. Nonconformity, which is postulated as a motivational characteristic of the creative person, has been chosen for study. Theoretically, the creative person is willing to be a nonconformist, but he is not a compulsive nonconformist. Thus, the problem is one of developing instruments which will discriminate between the child who is a *compulsive* conformist or nonconformist and the child who is *free* to use either conforming or nonconforming behavior. Creative ability is a multi-dimensional quality, and a variety of instruments will be needed for the identification of the potentially creative preschool child.

Taylor (1959b) categorized the characteristics of the creative person as (a) intellectual and (b) motivational-interest. The intellectual characteristics are those which seem to be valid indicators of creative talent, e.g., originality, adaptive flexibility, and the ability to sense problems. Motivational-interest characteristics are those which may facilitate the expression of creative ability, e.g., freedom to be a nonconformist, and willingness to try the difficult. Research findings (Guilford, 1957; Torrance, 1962a; Getzels & Jackson, 1962) indicate that these intellectual and motivational-interest characteristics are inextricably related. In view of this fact, it is possible that the measurement of motivational-interest characteristics may provide the means for identifying young children who are potentially

From *Proceeds of the Oklahoma Academy of Sciences,* 1964, *44,* pp. 168–180. Used by permission of the publisher.

creative. In other words, it may be possible to identify the potentially creative preschool child by his freedom to use conforming and nonconforming behavior, his willingness to try the difficult, and similar characteristics.

Longitudinal studies of creative ability are needed; and the initiation of such studies is dependent upon the availability of instruments which can be used to identify preschool children who are potentially creative. The development of instruments for the measurement of freedom to use conforming and nonconforming behavior is seen as a contribution to this area of study.

Subjects

The subjects were 220 children, boys and girls, ranging in age from two years six months to five years eleven months. The group included community children from their own homes, the majority of whom were in attendance at nursery schools, kindergartens, day care centers, and Bible Schools.

Criteria for the Instrument

An instrument developed for the measurement of conforming and nonconforming behavior should provide the child with an opportunity to make a choice in a situation in which he can follow a model or respond freely according to his own preferences.

A series of pilot studies served to clarify the criteria for the instrument. (a) The compulsive quality and the conforming quality of a child's behavior must be measured independently. The child who is a rigid nonconformist is no more free than the child who is a rigid conformist. (b) Conforming behavior must be studied in a variety of situations. The opportunity to conform to parents or peers, for example, may be more potent than the opportunity to conform in an impersonal situation. (c) The instrument must be adjustable in order that the opportunity to conform be of similar potency for all children. Conforming behavior is common when a child has an opportunity to conform to peers whom he likes, whereas the reverse is true when he dislikes the peers. Similarly, the child's preference for objects used in the task may affect his responses. He will have greater difficulty choosing between two objects when he likes them both than when he likes only one. (d) Sex and age are also factors which should be controlled, inasmuch as studies of older children have indicated sex differences in creative ability (Torrance, 1962).

The Measurement of Social
Conformity and Nonconformity

A color preference task, for the measurement of social conformity, was designed to meet the above criteria. The task consisted of three steps: (a)

Each child indicated his color preferences by ranking thirteen colors. From this ranking, five colors which ranged from first choice to last were chosen for use in the subsequent steps of the research. (b) Each child indicated the strength of his color preferences by selecting the color he preferred when the five colors were presented to him in pairs. (c) Each child then made color selections when there was an opportunity to conform to his friends, and again to his parents. In this last step, a control group of children made color selections with no opportunity to conform.

COLOR PREFERENCES

A color wheel, consisting of thirteen different colored strips of paper attached to a cardboard disc, was presented to each child. He ranked the colors by tearing off the one he liked best, and then repeated this, one color at a time, until all colors had been torn from the wheel. The five colors which a child ranked as 1, 4, 7, 10, and 13, were used for his part in the subsequent steps of the research. In this way, each child could be offered colors which he liked and colors which he disliked when given an opportunity to conform.

The reliability of this method of determining color preferences was tested by administering the color wheel a second time to a group of 29 children. The colors which were high-ranking (#1 and #4) and low-ranking (#10 and #13) during the first session retained their relative positions during the second session ($X^2 = 29.217$; $p < 0.001$).

STRENGTH OF COLOR PREFERENCES

The strength of each child's color preferences was then determined. The assumption was that the child who had strong preferences would be less easily influenced than other children; and therefore, the strength of the color preferences should be considered in the matching of control and experimental groups.

For this step in the research, the five colors designated for each child were arranged in pairs, each color being paired with every other color twice. These paired colors were presented to the child as odd-shaped pieces of gummed paper, ostensibly for making a collage. The sequence was such that no color appeared in two consecutive pairs and no color appeared twice in the same shape. The child chose one color from each pair.

The strength of a child's color preferences was then determined by the number of times that he chose the same color in a given pair both times that it was presented. The possible range of color preference scores was from zero to ten.

CONFORMITY TO PEERS

For this step in the research, the children were assigned to experimental and control groups, matched according to color preference scores, sex, and age (within four months); and each child constructed a small picture booklet of colored pages (2" by 3").

The children in the experimental group were given an opportunity to conform to peers while constructing their booklets. First, each child was asked to name three friends; then three identical pages (e.g., the picture of a cow on a red page) were placed before the child, and he was told that these were for his friends. He was then given his choice between a page identical to those for his friends and a page of a different color (e.g., the picture of a cow on a blue page). As in the previous step of the research, the five colors designated for each child were arranged in pairs, each color being paired with every other color twice, making a total of 20 pairs. These were presented to the child in such a way that he had an opportunity to choose between red and blue, for example, when his friends received red and again when his friends received blue.

The assumption underlying this design was that the child who really preferred one of the two colors, would choose that color on both occasions if he were *free* to use conforming or nonconforming behavior, whereas the *conformist* would choose the preferred color only when his friends received it, and the *nonconformist* would choose the preferred color only when his friends did *not* receive it.

The children in the control group made their choices between the paired booklet pages without an opportunity to conform.

CONFORMITY TO PARENTS

The children in the experimental group repeated the color wheel and the construction of a picture booklet. During this second session, they had an opportunity to conform as booklets were made for their parents.

SCORING

For the experimental group, the scoring consisted of a simple count of the number of conforming and nonconforming responses. For the control group, similar scoring was possible by accepting as a "conforming" response the choice of a color which corresponded to a conforming response for the experimental group.

A D-score, or difference score, was figured by subtracting the number of nonconforming responses from the number of conforming responses. The possible range of D-scores was from +20 to —20 (complete nonconformity).

A task-score was figured by dividing the D-score by the total number of responses. The possible range of task-scores was from +1.00 (complete conformity) to —1.00 (complete nonconformity). This score would be of particular value in a comparison of two or more research instruments which did not offer the same number of opportunities for conforming behavior.

RESULTS

The data for the matched control and experimental groups were analyzed to determine whether the opportunity to conform did influence the responses of the children, and whether the influence was greater in one situation than in another.

If the research instrument provided a valid measure of the influence (positive or negative) of the opportunity to conform, then the children in the experimental group should have larger D-scores than the children in the control group. For the control group, the distribution of conforming and nonconforming responses would be the result of chance; and therefore, the D-scores for this group should approximate zero. In Table 1, the frequency of large and small D-scores is presented for the two groups, the scores for the experimental group being those obtained when there was an opportunity to conform to parents. A chi-square analysis of these data indicated that the children in the experimental group were influenced by the opportunity to conform to their parents ($X^2 = 8.260$; $p < 0.01$).

Similarly, the data obtained when the experimental children had an opportunity to conform to peers (three friends) were analyzed. The responses of the children to this influence were not significantly different from the responses of the children in the control group ($X^2 = 1.020$; n.s.). In this task, the opportunity to conform to parents was more potent than the opportunity to conform to peers.

The reliability of the instrument was then determined by a split-half analysis of the responses of the children when they have an opportunity to conform to parents. The number of conforming responses made by each child during the first and last half of the task were used in this analysis. The Spearman-Brown formula yielded a correlation of $+.779$ ($p < 0.01$). The instrument was accepted as reliable. For this and subsequent analysis, the experimental group was enlarged to include an equal number of boys and girls at each of three age levels: below 4-0; 4-0 to 4-11; 5-0 to 5-11 (N = 120).

The data were further analyzed for age and sex differences. No significant age differences in conforming behavior were apparent; however, there were marked sex differences.

In Table 2, the number of boys and girls responding with large positive and large negative D-scores is presented. Of the 120 children in the experimental group, 41 had large D-scores. Both boys and girls were influenced by the opportunity to conform to parents; however, the girls were the conformists, and the boys were both conformists and nonconformists. A chi-square analysis indicated that this difference between the boys and girls was significant ($X^2 = 9.336$; $p < 0.01$).

In the design of the instrument, the assumption was made that strong likes and dislikes would influence a child's conforming behavior. The validity of this assumption was demonstrated in an analysis of the number of times that the children accepted and rejected their favorite color and their least liked color. When conforming required that the child accept one or the other of these two colors, the favorite color was more frequently accepted ($X^2 = 38.861$; p. < 0.001). When conforming required that the child reject one of these two colors, the least liked color was more frequently rejected ($X^2 = 69.962$; p. < 0.001).

Table 1. FREQUENCY OF LARGE AND SMALL D-SCORES OBTAINED BY CONTROL AND EXPERIMENTAL GROUPS OF PRESCHOOL CHILDREN IN A TASK DESIGNED TO MEASURE SOCIAL CONFORMITY AND NONCONFORMITY (N = 200)

	D-scores*		
	0 to 8	10 to 20	Total
Experimental Group	64	36	100
Control Group	82	18	100

* The D-score is the difference between the number of conforming and nonconforming responses.

Table 2. FREQUENCY OF LARGE POSITIVE AND LARGE NEGATIVE D-SCORES OBTAINED BY PRESCHOOL CHILDREN, BOYS AND GIRLS, IN A TASK DESIGNED TO MEASURE SOCIAL CONFORMITY AND NONCONFORMITY (N = 41)

D-scores	Boys	Girls
+10 to +20	9	20
−10 to −20	10	2
Total	19	22

SUMMARY

A color-preference task, designed to measure social conformity and nonconformity, was developed for use with children of preschool age. The task discriminated between children who were *compulsive* conformists and nonconformists and those who were *free* to use either conforming or nonconforming behavior. The potency of the situation in which conformity was suggested proved to be a major factor in the task; opportunity to conform to parents had a significant influence on the children's responses, whereas opportunity to conform to peers (three friends) had a negligible influence for this preschool group. No age differences in conforming behavior were apparent. Sex differences were marked. Both boys and girls were influenced by the opportunity to conform to parents; however, the girls were the conformists, whereas some boys were conformists and some nonconformists.

The Measurement of Conformity and Nonconformity in an Impersonal Situation

A form board task was designed for the measurement of conformity and nonconformity in an impersonal situation. Four form boards were constructed. The pictures on the form boards were a tree, a house, a playground, and a barnyard. Each form board had five holes, and for each hole there were four different pieces which could be used in completing the picture.

The design of the form board task was similar to that of the color preference task. Picture pieces for the form boards were paired and the child chose the pieces he wanted to use. Two sets of paired pieces were made for each board. For example, in the Tree Form Board, the child first chose between the rabbit and the flowers, and later chose between the ball and the grass, for the hole at the base of the tree. Each child was offered the paired pieces twice, making a total of 80 choices for the four form boards. This was done in two sessions with approximately a one-week interval between the two.

In this task, the opportunity to conform was provided by a line drawing placed behind the form board. In the first session, a line drawing of flowers is shown in the form board, and the child would choose between the flowers and the rabbit. During the next session, a line drawing of the rabbit would be shown, and the child would again choose between the flowers and the rabbit. As in the color preference task, the underlying assumption was that the child who really preferred the rabbit would choose the rabbit during both sessions, if he were free to use conforming and nonconforming behavior; but the child who was a conformist would choose the rabbit only when the line drawing of the rabbit was shown, and the nonconformist would choose the rabbit only when the line drawing of the flowers was shown.

A control group of children was offered the form boards without the line drawings, i.e., without the opportunity to conform.

SCORING

The scoring for the form board task was similar to that for the color preference task. For the experimental group, the number of conforming and nonconforming responses were recorded. A similar score was obtained for the control group by accepting as a "conforming" response the choice of a piece which corresponded to a conforming response for the experimental group.

A D-score was figured by subtracting the number of nonconforming responses from the number of conforming responses; and for this task, the possible range of D-scores was from $+80$ (complete conformity) to -80 (complete nonconformity).

A task-score was figured by dividing the D-score by the total number of responses.

SUBJECTS

The subjects were 156 children, boys and girls, ranging in age from two years seven months to five years eleven months. Children for the experimental and control groups were matched on sex and age (within four months) and were chosen so that there would be at least 24 boys and 24 girls in each of three age groups (below 4-0; 4-0 to 4-11; and 5-0 to 5-11).

RESULTS

The data for the matched control and experimental children were analyzed to determine whether the opportunity to conform did influence their responses. If the research instrument provided a valid measure of this influence, then the children in the experimental group should have larger D-scores than the children in the control group. As with the color preference task, the frequency of conforming and nonconforming responses demonstrated by the control group would be the result of chance; and therefore, the D-scores for this group should approximate zero. In Table 3, the frequency of large and small D-scores is presented for the two groups. A chi-square analysis of these data indicated that the children in the experimental group were influenced by the opportunity to conform ($X^2 = 32.203$; $p < 0.001$).

The reliability of the instrument was determined by a split-half analysis of the responses of the children in the experimental group. The Spearman-Brown formula yielded a correlation of $+.860$ ($p < 0.01$). The instrument was accepted as reliable.

The data for this group were further analyzed for sex and age differences. Neither sex differences nor age differences were apparent.

Table 3. FREQUENCY OF LARGE AND SMALL D-SCORES OBTAINED BY CONTROL AND EXPERIMENTAL GROUPS OF PRESCHOOL CHILDREN IN A TASK DESIGNED TO MEASURE CONFORMITY AND NONCONFORMITY IN AN IMPERSONAL SITUATION (N = 156)

	D-scores		
	0 to 15	16 to 80	Total
Experimental group	33	45	78
Control group	67	11	78

In Table 4, the number of boys and girls responding with large positive and large negative D-scores is presented. Of the 78 children in the experimental group, 45 had large D-scores. Boys and girls alike responded positively to the opportunity to conform (for boys, $X^2 = 6.545$, $p < 0.02$; for girls, $X^2 = 7.304$; $p < 0.01$).

Table 4. FREQUENCY OF LARGE POSITIVE AND LARGE NEGATIVE D-SCORES OBTAINED BY PRESCHOOL CHILDREN, BOYS AND GIRLS, IN A TASK DESIGNED TO MEASURE CONFORMITY AND NONCONFORMITY IN AN IMPERSONAL SITUATION (N = 45)

D-scores	Boys	Girls
+16 to +80	17	18
−16 to −80	5	5
Total	22	23

SUMMARY

A form board task, designed to measure conformity and nonconformity in an impersonal situation, was developed for use with children of preschool age. The task discriminated between children who were *compulsive* conformists or nonconformists and those who were *free* to use either conforming or nonconforming behavior. No age differences or sex differences were apparent. Conforming behavior, rather than nonconforming behavior, was demonstrated by most of the children who were influenced by the opportunity to conform.

Comparison of the Two Tasks

More than one task for the measurement of conforming and nonconforming behavior was developed in order that the influence of different situations be studied. It was possible that the conformity suggestion might be more potent in one situation than in another. In the social conformity task, this proved to be true; parents were a more potent influence than peers.

A comparison of the results of the social conformity tasks (color preferences) and the impersonal conformity task (form boards) indicated a difference in the potency of these two conformity suggestions for individual children. Many of the boys responded negatively to the opportunity to conform to parents, but few responded negatively to the opportunity to conform in an impersonal situation.

Many children who responded freely on one task, as indicated by a task-score below 20, were not free in their responses on the other task. On the form board task, 32 children were free in their use of conforming and nonconforming behavior; and on the color preference task, 22 children responded freely; however, only ten children responded freely on both tasks.

The conclusion to be drawn from this comparison is that conformity-nonconformity must be measured in several different situations, if the child who is free to use conforming and nonconforming behavior is to be identified.

Summary

Two tasks were developed for use with preschool children in the measurement of conforming and nonconforming behavior. One, a color-preference task, was designed to measure social conformity, i.e., conformity to parents or peers. The other, a form board task, was designed to measure conformity in an impersonal situation. Both tasks provided the children with opportunity to follow a model or respond freely according to their own preferences. Both tasks did discriminate between children who were free to use conforming and nonconforming behavior and children who were compulsive conformists or nonconformists.

For individual children, the opportunity to conform was more potent in one situation than in another, indicating that several measures of conformity-nonconformity are necessary for the identification of the young child who responds freely. Of the children who were subjects in this research, only one out of eight was consistently free in his use of conforming and nonconforming behavior.

These tasks will be used in further study of the relationship of conformity-nonconformity to other personality characteristics which may be related to the expression of creative ability.

EUGENE L. GAIER

Creativity, Intelligence, and Achievement in Motor Skills

One of the major by-products of the findings reported on differences between intelligence, per se, and creativity—precipitated in large part by the work of Getzels and Jackson (1962)—has been an intensified effort to isolate and identify the parameters of behavior associated with creativity. The earlier works of Guilford (1956b, 1959a), followed by the isolation and identification of the factors of human intellect by factor analytic techniques, have led to the development of instruments specifically designed to assess abilities associated with creative thinking. That these abilities are not readily identified by the more traditional intelligence tests has been well documented (Getzels & Jackson, 1962). At the same time, these same investigators have presented evidence to support the generalization that creative thinking is associated with academic achievement. These findings, tentative though they may be, have opened areas of exploration into the relationship of these newly identified components of intellect and a variety of aspects of performance and productivity. The literature continues to abound with studies attempting to pinpoint the creative function in terms of four major orientations: (a) the nature and quality of the product created; (b) the actual expression and on-going process during the creation; (c) the nature of the creator; and (d) environmental factors that best lend themselves to foster and support creativity.

The focus of the present paper is the examination of the relationships among motor skill performance, creative thinking ability, and tested intelligence. Four specific aspects will be discussed. First, attention will be given to summarizing the evidence on the relationship between intelligence and motor skills. The second part of the paper will be concerned with the evidence relating to creative thinking ability and motor skills. Suggested personality variables believed associated with creativity and motor skills will be discussed in the third section of the paper. The final section of the paper consists of a summary statement of the present research in the area of motor skills.

Mental Ability and Motor Skill

In summarizing the research on the relationship among measures of intellectual ability and motor skill performance, Thompson (1961) identified three trends that can hardly be viewed as surprising: (a) mental ability and motor skills are dependent; (b) mental ability and motor ability are inversely related; and (c) mental and motor abilities are independent. Even where this relationship has been demonstrated at a variety of age levels, the resulting correlational values have tended to be low, positive, but not statistically significant.

Studying a sample of male college students, DiGiovanna (1937) obtained correlation values of .07 and .08 between IQ determined with the Otis Self-Administering Tests and motor ability and athletic achievement, respectively. With a junior-high sample, Seegars and Postpichal (1936) published similar findings. In a definitive study of more than 1,400 junior high-school girls, Shaffer (1959) investigated the extent to which intelligence (Otis and Binet), age, and physical type were associated with performance on a test to determine minimal muscular fitness. In every instance, the mean IQ score for each pass and fail group for each of the testing periods was higher for the pass group. A positive correlation value was also reported with IQ. Perhaps of greater relevance here were the trend lines reflecting decreases in motor failures with increases in tested intelligence.

With children at the primary and elementary level, low positive correlations have been found among measures of performance involving mental abilities and motor skill *only* when normally distributed populations were involved. With extreme groups, the resulting relationships have tended to be both positive and significantly higher. Thus, Schroeder's investigation (1959) of third-, fourth-, and fifth-grade students yielded no apparent relationship between motor performance and intelligence at any grade level tested. High intelligence groups, however, indicated a preference for sports activities, while low groups preferred games of low organization. Earlier, Seegars and Postpichal (1936) had documented the finding that IQ scores were higher for those doing well in more complicated athletic contests. Where physical measurements involve exercise type tasks, positive relationships have been found with measures of mental ability and success in performance. And measures of strength produced only slightly higher positive findings when related to defined aspects of mental performance (Monohan & Hollingsworth, 1927).

Creative Thinking Ability and Motor Skills

While creative production reflected in the performing arts, architecture, engineering, and the like, has received increasing attention, experimental investigations of the relation between creative thinking ability and motor skills have been minimal and meager. In their discussion of physical performance in terms of creative attitudes, creative acts or processes, and creative products, Latchaw and Brown (1962) observed that opportunities may be present in the physical education context for perfecting skills and freeing the individual to move, making it possible for creativity to arise when a creative and receptive environment is established. Nevertheless, Andrews (1954) emphasized that "creative potentialities in children frequently remain blocked, unnurtured, and untouched." That is, the creative process can be initiated when the individual can develop new forms of new expressions, channelled, of course, with the experiences initially brought to the new situation.

Following their inspection of a number of human abilities with similarities of curves showing ages of winning championships in sports and those for intellectual creativity, Pressey and Kuhlen (1957) were moved to comment that:

perhaps the most striking features of the figures showing achievements is the rather close similarity between profiles for age of outstanding creative work and athletic championships especially in the greatly skilled but not exhaustive sports like target shooting and billiards.

What may be inferred from this observation is that the potential for various outstanding accomplishments may be due more to favorable influences at a particular time rather than individual potential per se. Commenting on the chronological age at which athletes achieved peak performance in differing sports, Lehman (1953) emphasized the similarity between these age curves and success in scientific discoveries and painting—especially marked for painting, golf, and billiards—felt too consistent to be coincidental. Lehman then speculated whether this correspondence was characteristic of human organization in the nature of a fixed order of human development, or was the trend a reflection of motivational factors. In the field of athletic prowess, competition may be the salient motivation. With a very different sample, Torrance (1962a) concluded that there is:

a fairly consistent tendency for children under competitive conditions to excel those under the other conditions. . . . It cannot be denied that such competition is one means by which challenge occurs, and challenge, if not *overwhelming,* is apparently conducive to creative achievement.

Motivation has been delineated an especially strong component of creativity, and various motivating factors have been proposed. From one point of view, motivation for creativity is viewed as a desire to maximize the experiencing of one's own expressive potentials. According to Rogers (1962), the creative individual is attempting to realize and complete himself, and thus "become his potentialities." This view gains support from Golann's study (1962) of highly creative male undergraduates who indicated a preference for activities allowing self-expression, independence, and the use of creative capacity, while low creative males tended to prefer essentially opposite activities.

In a comprehensive investigation designed by Barrett (1965) to examine the relationship between creative thinking ability and achievement in selected motor skills of elementary-school children, 362 students in the fourth, fifth, and sixth grades were given a battery of creative thinking and intelligence instruments, as well as a series of motor skills tests. Specifically, three major questions were raised: (a) What relationship exists between creative thinking abilities and performance in motor skills? (b) If a relationship is demonstrated, does it differ from the relationship between intelligence and performance in motor skills? (c) If a relationship is demonstrated, does it differ between the sexes and/or among the differing grade levels?

In her test battery, intelligence was measured by the Verbal and Nonverbal forms of the *Lorge-Thorndike Intelligence* tests. Creative thinking abilities were assessed with the Verbal and Nonverbal batteries of the *Minnesota Tests of Creative Thinking*. And estimates of performances in selected motor skills were obtained with the *Latchaw Motor Achievement Tests for Fourth, Fifth, and Sixth Grade Boys and Girls*.

Initially, the degree of association between the two measures of intelligence and the two tools of creative thinking was established. This was done to determine the extent of agreement of her sample with results of the studies comparing intelligence and creativity reporting the relationship between the measures as generally low, varying between .20 and .40, in unselected populations. Her results were consistent with previous findings: the correlation coefficients ranged from .128 to .352 for nonverbal intelligence quotients when compared with verbal and nonverbal creative thinking scores, respectively. When verbal IQ was correlated with the scores made on the instruments of creativity, a somewhat greater degree of association emerged, the correlations ranging from .168 to .449, respectively.

Three major conclusions emerged from her analysis: First, a low positive relationship was found between performance on tests of creative thinking and the tests of intelligence employed, indicating, perhaps, that these instruments appeared to measure different types of intellectual ability. Second, there was an apparent lack of relationship between measures of intelligence and achievement in motor skills. None of the correlation values between motor skill performance and intelligence quotients proved significantly different from zero, regardless of the form of the intelligence test administered. These findings were consistent with the earlier works cited and lend support to the view that tested intelligence and tested physical abilities are essentially unrelated. Third, tested creative thinking ability was virtually independent from the ability to perform tasks of the sports types measured by the Latchaw Tests.

Motor Skills and/or Creativity

In the investigation of athletic success, one must assess risk-taking tendencies based on the individual's need to achieve as well as to test limits. McClelland (1963) hypothesized that the creative person has a greater interest in and was more willing to take calculated and long-range risks where his own abilities could make a difference in terms of the estimated odds. Previously, Torrance (1962a) suggested that the creative individual was willing to test limits—whether of his own abilities, or resources, or situational—in his desire for achievement or self-actualization, and thus, take calculated risks. That is, creative children who suggested new ideas and asked unusual questions were actually involved in risk-taking. The creative subjects studied by Getzels and Jackson (1962) manifested risk-taking behaviors by their joining together of two dissimilar elements, their choice of unconventional occupations, and their nonconforming behavior. While some risk-taking may be aroused in the usual tests of motor skills, apparently it is not of the intensity called forth in actual athletic contact. Since creativity is more apt to occur in individuals who are impulsive, aggressive, dominating, and characterized by lack of deliberation, self-control, and restraint, the study of elementary-school children in a laboratory setting may actually serve to eclipse any real assessment of the effect of motor skills and creative thinking ability.

On the basis of responses to the Rorschach, Hersch (1962) offered evidence that artists apparently have a greater capacity for mobile and flexible use of both the relatively mature and relatively primitive processes. They appeared to have more readily accessible control functions and employed their primitive processes for productive expression. That no evidence has been offered to establish any relationship between creativity and motor skill or in athletic prowess may hinge on these findings: First, the samples studied for motor skills have typically been school children who have yet to perfect muscular control through self-discipline and formal practice. By contrast, creative individuals studied in art or architecture or science have typically achieved some agreed upon stature in their respective fields. Second, it may be that success in athletics is dependent upon *not* deviating from the discipline and rigor demanded in training. One might speculate on the success of the athlete who produces new forms of behavior while allowing himself to regress momentarily far into primitive fantasies. Perhaps the kind of *creative behavior* that the successful athlete manifests is the ability to make himself into a culture hero able to attract fans and provide daily drama both with his past struggles and his current triumphs. His productivity may then reflect a combination of successful feats on the playing field, coupled with a flair or charisma that attracts followers. The resulting mystique may be the product created rather than the actual physical feat. Thus, the production of the novel or statistically infrequent response or idea commonly associated with the creative act may not be in the playing aspects of motor skills as much as in the production of a sense of drama or extravaganza or even burlesque.

Carried a step further, what is perceived as creativity with motor skills may be but a function of extra-motor skill activities. Here, the athlete may associate with those who are perceived as "creative" in art or music or politics—who may through their own creativity account for success of a person with mere athletic endowment that in and of itself is not creative.

Outlook

In evaluating the influence of intelligence and creative thinking ability on skill in motor activities, a basic question must be raised: Should one expect to establish a relationship between creativity and proficiency in motor skills? While intelligence and talent in a variety of areas have been shown to be positively related, obviously, not all bright children will have talents in all areas of endeavor. And talent, as such, does *not* necessarily exist in children with lower intelligence. Certainly, the learning of basic skills—be they affective, psychomotor, and/or cognitive—is imperative as an aid both to creative development and its expression. What may be of paramount importance in the area of the development of motor skills may be the thesis posited by Torrance (1962a) when he referred to the under-evaluation by the creative child who feels that his work cannot possibly compare to that of the adults and consequently fails to make any creative attempts. Thus, the creative child may find himself in a situation similar to that of Charlie Brown with Lucy in the world of *Peanuts*. She always wins, though he is right. Eventually, he learns that his behavior just will not make any difference. Since teachers appear to disapprove of the creative child (Getzels & Jackson, 1962), the well-bastioned authority of the teacher or school does its harm. Upon leaving school, the *organization* exercises more subtle controls and pressures to bring nonconforming employees into the line of teamwork and cooperation (Whyte, 1957). More recently, Friedenberg (1965) astutely described the inimical attitude of American society toward intense subjectivity and individualism—both well documented as characteristic of the creative person—with its approval of mediocrity.

The basic generalization here was that the experience of attending school may actually undercut any sense of creativity, particularly those facets of oneself that underlie the individual's attitude to succeed. Extreme situations coupled with these predispositions may culminate in the fragmentation of experience. The too prevalent and inflexible emphasis on teaching, but one approach to problem-solving, may be but an affirmation of the American tradition that no emotional or intellectual or creative undertaking is important enough to be left alone for those undertaking it.

By contrast, there may also be the over-evaluation of the creative child, who, perceiving improvement through practice and denial of impulse satisfaction as meaningless and without challenge, is lost when he must attempt a creative performance without the knowledge of basic skills which he deliberately avoided learning. Ironically, the creative individual may become the very agent responsible for his own difficulties.

After surveying the spate of studies on creativity and the isolated investigations concerned with motor skills, the observer is left—as he might be after a very fruitful seminar—in a state of quandary and speculation. What many research reports choose to tell about creativity is bulky, well documented, and entirely welcome. What still remains to be unraveled is the meaningfulness and application of demonstrated statistical relationships. While creativity appears to be cognitively rooted, perhaps the creative process is ". . . too complex and elusive to be probed effectively in laboratory isolation" (Gaier & White, 1965). This observation is not to imply that creativity must be relegated to the realm of metaphysics but rather that creativity—at least as related to motor skills—appears to be a fusion of variables that, as yet, has not been meaningfully teased apart.

ROBERT BURKHART

The Relation of Intelligence to Art Ability

Introduction

The history of research investigation concerned with intelligence and art ability raises some important questions concerning the present concept of intelligence, as it is represented by the common tests now in use in the grade schools, high schools, and colleges of our nation. These studies have a bearing, because of the research done in the field of art education, on the extent to which tests of intelligence are measuring creativeness.

Early Studies

Practically all the early studies were limited in their measures of intelligence to teachers' estimates of general ability or standing in high-school subjects, since intelligence tests had not yet been developed. Those of Kerchensteiner done in 1905 and of Kir done in 1909 were of this kind.

Not many years afterwards, several studies appeared which included measures of intelligence by standardized tests. However, these studies did not use any objective method for determining the kind and quality of art ability which existed within the group studied. For instance, both Terman (1925) and Manuel (1919) used selected groups for their studies which were formed solely upon the basis of recommendations of the students' art teachers. Terman employed fifteen pupils with "special ability" and Manuel nineteen "talented subjects" in their respective researches. It would seem that they employed too small a sample also to support any strong generalizations on this topic.

Objectivity of Measures
in Studies After 1925

After the year 1925, a number of important researches were done with large populations, and the measures of intelligence and art ability employed

246

appear to be, insofar as it is possible, of an objective nature. The intelligence tests used were established and standardized measures, and the criteria employed in determining art ability were, for the most part, reasonably objective in character. Methods such as counting the number of items which appear in a drawing were often employed, or in the case of aesthetic criteria, a number of qualified judges were used. The extent to which they agreed, regarding the works judged, helped establish the reliability of the evaluations made. In these researches, criteria were employed as well as trained judges. Carefully prepared visual scales were also employed in some of these studies. For the most part, these studies confined themselves to the elementary grades, where the evaluation of the art works could be based upon existing knowledge of the developmental characteristics of child art.

Studies at the Elementary Level
Using Objective Measures

The researches done at the elementary level have been included here because they have a close relationship to the few studies that have been done at the senior high-school level, and beyond. These studies are also important because they tend to show the differences in the various factors of creativity which predominate in childhood as contrasted with those which are dominant during and after adolescence.

Probably the best-known study done with children's drawings is that of Florence Goodenough (1926). Her Draw-a-Man test is still being used. She found close relationship between the conceptual development shown in children's drawings and their general intelligence up to about the age of ten. After this age, there is a sharp decrease in this relationship. She felt the drawings appeared to take on characteristics of special ability in adolescence in which aesthetic considerations might be thought of as becoming increasingly of more importance (1926, pp. 33–34). Her analysis of the characteristics or factors which lead to a high score on her test is of particular interest as it reveals that her test is probably mainly a measure of the child's powers of observation and memory for detail. She states:

Examination of drawings which make unusually high scores on the test leads to the opinion that keener powers of analytic observation, coupled with a good memory for details, are the more potent factors in producing high scores than is artistic ability in the ordinary sense of the term (1926, p. 53).

It has not been sufficiently emphasized that one of Goodenough's important findings in support of the reliability and validity of her intelligence test is that this test is not a measure of art ability. This is stated with some clarity in her conclusions. She states in this connection:

The correlation with teachers' judgments of art ability was found to be .444 within the first three grades, but in grades above the third, the correlations with teachers' judgments was too low to be significant (1926, p. 82).

This is very significant in that later findings tended to show very low correlations of intelligence with art ability after the third-grade level. In order to emphasize this point for all ages, Goodenough (1926, p. 82) also states in her conclusions, "Art ability is a negligible factor at these ages as far as influencing the score is concerned."

An important study which followed that of Goodenough was done by Tiebout and Meier in 1936. They used a sample of a hundred children in each grade from the first through the seventh in their research. Each subject made three paintings to be judged on the basis of aesthetic quality achieved. The judgments were made upon the carefully prepared visual scale developed by Tiebout. They found zero correlations between art ability and intelligence after the third grade. Tiebout and Meier (1936–37a, p. 108) conclude:

Thus while a close relationship does not exist between ability to achieve aesthetic quality in compositions and general intelligence, as is the case with drawings used as a general means of expression at the younger ages, there is a tendency toward some relationship in the lower grades in contrast to the upper where the correlations are approximately zero.

Bird's (1932) study done about the same time tends to confirm these findings, as he finds a drop from .510 to .140 in the correlations with intelligence made on the Dearborn group test after the third grade. His drawings were judged on a more representational basis than Tiebout and Meier, and this may account for a slightly higher correlation which he finds after the third grade. He used three drawings; the first from memory of a cat running after a ball, the second from a model, and the third from memory after the model had been used. These drawings were scored for accuracy of representation and portrayal of action. He states in reference to the findings he made in the early grades that those on the Dearborn test were about half those made with the Goodenough in every case (1932, p. 81). Apparently, no greater relationship to general intelligence exists for ability in representational drawings as analyzed by Bird as exists for achievement in aesthetic quality as it is determined by Tiebout and Meier.

Some clarity is given to these findings by the studies of Hurlock and Thomson (1934), done about the same time. Their research is of particular importance in that they analyzed the drawings in regard to specific kinds of characteristics and ran correlations between each of these characteristics. They studied 2,292 drawings produced by children from four schools. Their drawings were obtained from the kindergartens, the first and second grades. These are the grades in which the very high correlations are found by Goodenough, and in which lower, but significant, correlations were found by Tiebout, Meier, and Bird. The specific value of their findings is that they tend to clarify what specific factors are contributing, and are not contributing, to the significant correlations made in these studies. The first group of their conclusions to be discussed is closely related to the findings of Goodenough and tends to explain their significance as she does in terms of accuracy of observation and memory for detail. Hurlock and Thomson conclude (1934):

The tendency to perceive the specific rather than the general increased with age.

The tendency to perceive details increases with age and to a lesser degree with intelligence.

The accuracy of perception increases with age and to a lesser degree with intelligence.

Between the ages of four and a half and eight and a half years, inclusive, the ability for accurate and detailed perceptions, shows a more constant relationship to chronological age than to intelligence.

This suggests that what Goodenough has tapped is a mainly developmental factor related to the changes which take place in the child's perceptual activities. This would tend to account somewhat for the fact that Goodenough finds that art ability is a "negligible factor" in determining the scores on her tests, for the qualitative differences in children's art abilities cannot be determined by developmental characteristics. For instance, that a base line appears at a certain age for most children is a developmental fact. Certainly, no qualitative distinction in regard to children's art can be made, at an age at which it is normal for a base line to appear, between drawings on the basis that they include the base line. The same distinction holds with regard to the increased accuracy and tendency to perceive the specific, rather than the general, at these age levels. However, this only becomes apparent when a norm is established for the number of details that appear at a given age level. The fact that fewer or more details appear for a particular child at that age level indicates that that child is either advanced or behind his general age group. Still, developmental characteristics are so closely related to general intelligence at early ages, it is difficult to distinguish between them.

Hurlock and Thomson made other findings which tended to explain the lower correlations which Tiebout, Meier, and Bird made at these ages as compared with Goodenough's, which were almost double those reported by these investigators (Goodenough, 1926, p. 137). Hurlock and Thomson state: "The tendency to perceive associated objects and design increases with age, but shows little relationship to intelligence." They conclude, in general: "The ability to give artistic expression through drawing shows little relationship to age or intelligence."

In this respect, they confirm Goodenough's belief that at these levels, art ability is "negligible factor" in determining the relationship between intelligence and the Draw-a-Man test. This suggests that developmental changes account for the relationship of the Draw-a-Man test to intelligence tests.

This tends to explain the reason why low positive correlations are sometimes found as high as the fifth grade, and occasionally beyond, in studies such as McVitty's. McVitty found a correlation of .396 (1954, p.

72). McVitty employed both developmental and aesthetic criteria in the judgment of art works and his correlation may be accounted for on the basis of developmental differences alone, as Goodenough gets a correlation with her criteria at this level of .728 (1926, p. 20) and at age ten of .849. It would be well, if, in the future, developmental criteria were kept separate from aesthetic criteria so that the relationship of intelligence to each of these factors could be determined with greater accuracy.

The studies at this level are summed up well by Lewerenz (1928), who conducted a very comprehensive study concerning the relation of measures of art ability and intelligence. The research extends from the third grade through the twelfth, using criteria for judgment which were largely aesthetic. He employed 939 pupils in this research as a means of evaluating his *Tests in the Fundamental Abilities in Visual Arts*. He found a correlation of .155, which is clearly not significant, between art ability and general intelligence on these measures. His conclusion is very interesting in that it is a good summation of the findings made beyond the third-grade level from 1928, which was the year in which he completed his study to the present day. He states (1928, p. 490):

It is probably true that anyone who succeeds exceptionally well in art will also rank rather high on an intelligence test. However, a high intelligence score does not bring necessarily a corresponding ability in art. The fact is that there are a great number of people whose intelligence quotients range from 85 on up who have equal chances for achieving moderate success in art work. It may be said, therefore, that predicting the success of students in an art class on the basis of intelligence quotients alone probably would yield results little better than a random guess.

Studies at the Senior High-School Level

Perhaps the most extensive study done at the senior high-school level in the 30's was by Tiebout and Meier (1936–37b). In conjunction with their study at the elementary level, for which Tiebout was mainly responsible, Meier conducted the first careful study at the senior high-school level. The subjects were derived from a list made up by the art supervisors and art teachers in the high schools in Milwaukee, Wisconsin (1936–37b, p. 95). They were divided into two groups, those designated as outstanding or unusual, and those regarded as less outstanding but superior. The intelligence test results gave an average IQ on the Kuhlmann-Anderson series of 109.35 in the case of the twenty-four starred or unusual subjects, and of 107.3 for the remaining subjects. These data show that the artistically superior tend to be somewhat superior in intelligence. Meier states that the group average falls at the upper limit of average IQ according to the classifications given by Terman. Yet he concluded:

Rank and intelligence apparently give little indication of the degree of artistic superiority since the starred subjects have only a slightly higher average IQ than the remainder of the group. Within this group of starred subjects, also, the subject indicated as most outstanding had an IQ of 101 on the Kuhlman-Anderson and of 105 on the Stanford series. On the basis of their IQ's one of the group of twenty-four outstanding students would be included in Terman's classification of dull; ten, average; eight, superior; and five, very superior. While there is a slight preponderance of these subjects in the superior and very superior groups, it is obvious that an average IQ does not preclude the possibility of successful artistic performance at the high-school level (1936–37b, p. 111).

The major shortcoming of Meier's study is, of course, that he used a group which was determined on the basis of teacher recommendations, rather than on the basis of criteria judgments.

Winslow (1939) to some extent in his study avoids this problem by using a revised version of the Kline-Carey scale and a special method for evaluating the drawings of ninth graders by compositional arrangement. In studying the relationship of the twenty ranked highest according to their drawings, as compared with the other students included in this study, he concludes:

When all the drawings had been rated and the scores tabulated, the marked superiority of the artistically superior group over the group of pupils of equal intelligence was at once apparent. It was surprising, however, to see how closely the scores of the latter group compared with those of pupils who made the poorest drawings. This would seem to indicate that individuals of approximately the same general intelligence are capable of making drawings of various degrees of artistic excellence, the superior group in art being superior because of certain factors peculiar to art ability (1939, p. 306).

His superior group had an average IQ of 105.5, and the twenty lowest students in drawing ability had an IQ of 103.5. However, Winslow did not correlate the IQ and drawing scores in his study.

If Meier's and Winslow's study, and the other studies done in the upper grades were to have a predictive value, we might expect to find that the outstanding students in art ability found in other researches would have an average IQ of between 105.5 and 109. We would expect that there would be a low correlation found between intelligence and art ability. We might predict that the correlation found would be close to zero, according to their conclusions and those made by other investigators in the upper grades, such as Bird, Tiebout, and Lewerenz.

One hundred and nineteen students were employed in a recent study by the author (Brittain, 1952). This includes those used in the cross-validation. This is a somewhat larger sample than those employed by Meier or Winslow.

The measure for individuality of art expression at the senior high-school level that was developed consisted of ten verbal criteria; these criteria carefully evolved during four revisions and trial runs. Using these criteria, five expert judges scored the works of 80 high-school students from grades

9 through 12, over a 27-week period. Eighteen sample pictures were then selected by score, according to standings from the total range of scores. These were than ranked by 29 art educators on a preference basis. The art educators' preference ranking of the works correlated .89 (significant at the .01 level) with the judgment of the works by the verbal criteria. This acted to establish the lower bound for reliability of this judgment which can be no less than its correlation with another independent measure.

When the IQ scores were correlated with those for the criterion judgment, the result was a .064 correlation, which is interpreted as showing no correlation. This means that IQ as measured by Otis tests had no relationship to achievement in art as judged in this study, and the examination of the mean scores on the IQ tests for the three groups shows them to be only one point apart (note Table 1). The mean for the total group is 106, and the greatest difference from this score is represented by the mean IQ of the outstanding group, which is 107.4. The standard deviation for these scores for the total group is 11.64. All the groups have a standard deviation of around 11. points, which means that 68 percent of the IQ scores in these groups varied from the mean as much as 11 points, this indicating that

Table 1. CORRELATION WITH IQ .064 OR NO CORRELATION WITH CRITERION JUDGMENT

N	Group	Mean for IQ	Standard deviation for IQ
17	Outstanding	107.41	11.05
42	Average	105.28	11.90
21	Low	106.29	11.06
21	Low	106.29	11.06
80	Total	106.00	11.64

there was some real range within the IQ scores of the members of each of these groups.

Since a correlation is usually found between academic average and intelligence at the high-school level, such a correlation was run between these two measures for the students in this group to determine if they were in any way an atypical high-school population in regard to their academic achievements in general. This correlation was .530, which is significant at the .01 level, and, therefore, this group should be considered quite usual in regard to the relation of their academic work to their intelligence quotients.

In order to check further the findings made in this study regarding the relationship of IQ and art achievement, a cross-validation was made, using the scores from another research in this same area. Willard, a graduate student, had recently completed a study at Penn State in which he used the works of 37 students. He had them judged as they were judged for this study; and fortunately, he also had their IQ's measured with the Otis test. The mean score of the group was 100.2, and the standard deviation 10.7. Since both measuring devices were exactly the same as those in the present study, a correlation was made and found to be .067, which is almost exactly the figure reported in this study. The importance of this finding is that it rules IQ out as being a factor in determining individuality of art expression for the students used in these researches. Achievement in art is evidently then the result of intelligence factors other than those measured by standardized tests. It may be that some kind of intelligence, not measured by the usual group IQ test, is involved in creative performance.

Studies Beyond the High-School Level with Findings of Special Value for Further Investigations

INTRODUCTION

Two studies have been done in which special attention has been paid to aspects of this subject not treated extensively in the studies which have been discussed. The findings made are suggestive ones which have important implications and which appear to justify further investigation.

WOODS: THE ROLE OF LANGUAGE HANDICAP IN THE DEVELOPMENT OF ARTISTIC INTEREST

Woods (1948) had several concepts of importance which he investigated by studying with some care a hundred young male veterans for whom he was a special counselor. He believed that "art is a space-relations language" and wanted to determine if "artistic interest is often developed as a result of deficiency in the use of other symbols" (1948, p. 240). The results would give the impression that artistic interest is marked by a low academic intelligence (1948, p. 242). To arrive at this conclusion he used the art interest test from the Kuder Battery and the Army Alpha test of intelligence.

Evidence presented in this study indicates that a negative correlation exists between artistic interest and academic accomplishments measured in terms of school grade completed and ability in the Army Alpha test. The data also tends to indicate that a negative correlation exists between artistic interest and verbal and computational interests, due to an initial handicap in the use of English.

Of course, he is measuring art interest and not art ability, and it may be argued that he deals with a special population. However, Meier and Tiebout found indications of the same thing at both the elementary- and high-school levels. They conclude: "In the light of the oft-expressed opinion that the artist is visually, rather than verbally minded, it is interesting to note that the vocabulary test was more often failed at both levels than any other test" (1936–37b, p. 119). This may be one possible explanation of the way art ability does not apparently correlate with general intelligence.

DeWit: The Block Design Test and Art Ability

In his study, DeWit (1951) used the Kohs Block Design Test to predict the art ability of 63 education students at the college level in introductory courses in art education. This is of particular interest as the Block Design Test has been found to have a strong "space factor" in factor analyses run independently by Kohs (1923), Armitage (1940), Thurstone (1944), and Corter (1949). The study is of additional interest because its findings vary somewhat from those made in previous studies. The difference, however, is mainly that DeWit found what appears to be a somewhat reliable measure of art ability. His findings are very close to all previous findings in regard to the relationship of art ability to intelligence as he reports a correlation coefficient of .097 (1951, p. 23), which is clearly not significant. However, he found a correlation coefficient of .006 between the Block Design Test and drawing ability (1951, p. 23).

The Kohs (1923) Block Design Test has a number of factors other than the spatial one which have been analyzed by means of factor analysis. Kohs himself found two fundamental factors, a synthetic factor and an analytic factor.

Armitage (1946) also found synthetic and analytical factors on the Block Test. Thurstone (1944) found a GG factor which he calls "Changing Gestalts." He defined this factor as the "manipulation of two configurations simultaneously or in succession."

Corter (1949) found several other factors, including those found by other investigators. The first (1949, p. 65) and most important, he names "Mental Productiveness," which he defines as "speed of operation and fluency of expression," or "speed and number of ideas which come to one's mind that pertain to the problem" (1949, p. 65). He also finds a factor that he calls "flexibility," which he defines as "the ability to change one's mental set" (1949, p. 57). In addition to this, he finds a factor that he names "conceptual ability," "the ability to grasp essential similarity between discrete variables, to abstract them and generalize them."

These factors are of particular interest to those in art education, as Guilford's (1952) study of creative ability in science and Brittain's (1952) art education show the presence of eight factors, some of which appear very similar to some found in the Kohs Block Design Test.

The common factors found by Guilford and Brittain which have been demonstrated by factor analysis to be present in the Block Design Test are shown in Table 2.

These findings are of further importance because the Kohs Block Design Test has been shown to correlate .714 with the Wechsler-Bellevue (Wechsler, 1944) test of intelligence. This indicates that the test itself is a good measure of intelligence for a representative population. The factors in it are apparently related to general intelligence. Still, DeWit's study shows the Kohs Block Design Test is not a good predictor of the intelligence

Table 2. THE RELATION OF FACTORS IN CREATIVITY TO THOSE FOUND IN THE BLOCK DESIGN TEST

Guilford	Brittain	Kohs
1. *Fluency* Rapid production of word meeting requirements	*Fluency*	*Mental Productiveness* "Fluency of expression and speed of operation" on "speed and number of ideas which come to mind that pertain to the problem" (found by Corter)
2. *Flexibility* "In easily changed set"	*Flexibility* Definition the same as Guilford	*Flexibility* "The ability to change set" (found by Corter)
3. *Analysis* "Redefinition of organized works"	*Ability to Abstract*	*Analytic Function* (Found by Kohs and Armitage)
4. *Synthesis Ability* (Organizing ideas into large more inclusive patterns)	*Closure*	*Synthetic Functions* (Found by Kohs and Armitage)
5. *Sensitivity to Problems*	*(Same as Guilford)*	*Conceptual Ability* "The ability to grasp the essential similarity between variables, to abstract them and to generalize them (found by Corter)
6. *Redefinition*	*Ability to Rearrange*	*Changing Gestalts* "The manipulation of two configurations simultaneously or in succession (found by Thurstone)
7. *Originality*	*Originality*	(Not found as a factor)
8. *Penetration*	(Not found as a factor)	(Not found as a factor)
9. (Not found as a factor)	*Intuition*	(Not found as a factor)
10. (Not found as a factor)	(Not found as a factor)	*Spatial Factor* Very high—maybe related to art ability (found by Thurstone, Armitage, and Corter)

quotient of people with art ability. The reason is apparently that the people with art ability score much higher on this test than the other students with equivalent intelligence. It is just this that suggests that the Kohs Block Design Test is a good predictor of art ability. However, it is just this that evidently makes it a poor predictor of intelligence for those with art ability. They evidently did not score as high on the other tests included in the total pattern used to measure their intelligence. If they had, the correlations found between intelligence and art ability would have been high and positive rather than near zero.

This suggests that people with art ability have a higher than average level of intelligence in a particular area where the spatial factor is high. This is indicated by the analysis of the Block Design Test. Moreover, on this test a number of other factors have been found that have been demonstrated to be characteristic of creative ability. These implications suggest the need for further extensive researches at all levels using the Kohs Block Design Test so that DeWit's findings can be rejected or supported, confirmed, and extended. Further studies should employ some measures of verbal ability also, so as to determine if verbal deficiencies relate to art achievement.

Summary and Interpretation of Findings

In summary, intelligence tests are not good predictors of art ability beyond the third-grade level. The correlations found beyond the third-grade level were not significant. Groups of students with high art ability usually have a mean IQ which is slightly above average. Highly significant correlations were usually found from kindergarten through the third grade in most investigations. In early investigations, an important factor, which did correlate significantly with intelligence but not art ability, was found by Goodenough. High scores on her tests showed good memory for detail and observational accuracy. Hurlock and Thomson found that an increase in awareness of detail and accuracy of perception took place between the ages of four and a half to eight and a half. Their study showed that this increase correlated more highly with chronological age than with intelligence. This suggests that the increases in accuracy of perception and awareness of details of these ages is a developmental tendency, which reaches its maximum and then levels off about the age of ten. The presence of aesthetic factors in paintings and drawings shows an increase with age but shows little relationship to intelligence even at the first- and second-grade levels, according to Hurlock and Thomson. In general, they are not related to intelligence beyond the third-grade level.

Two relatively distinct factors have then been found to be functioning with different strengths during childhood and adolescence. The first seems to be a developmental one which involves accuracy of perception and memory for detail, and has no apparent relationship to art ability after the third-grade level. The second is a factor which involves aesthetic elements, such as composition and design, manner of handling, originality of ideas, and personal involvement.

An explanation of why significant correlations are found up to the third-grade level and not beyond may be supplied by Jones's (1949) and Thurstone's factor analysis of intelligence tests. Their studies have established the hypothesis that intelligence becomes more differentiated as age increases. Jones (1949) did a factor analysis of the 1937 Stanford-Binet at ages 7, 9, 11, and 13. He concluded that his group factors become more clearly defined and distinct, one from the other, at higher age levels. Thurstone, using 1,154 eighth-grade children and a battery of 10 tests, isolated six factors which he considered primary. These factors appeared to function independently, and he describes them as being number, word fluency, verbal, memory, induction, and spatial. He, Armitage, and Corter found the "spatial" factor to be very high on the Kohs Block Test which supports Woods's belief that art is a "space-relations language." Apparently, in the early grades, the different factors function together more or less as a total unit. This would account for the correlations found with art ability. This correlation would tend to decrease as these apparently separate factors become more distinct and differentiated from each other according to their functions.

Separating the developmental factors from the aesthetic factors helps provide an explanation of the changes in the art activity which occur between childhood and adolescence. Developmental considerations clearly predominate in the early grades and are essential to any evaluation of the art of the child. In the upper grades, aesthetic considerations become increasingly important because developmental tendencies diminish in their importance. However, aesthetic considerations are important at all levels. Apparently, the quality of adolescent art is dependent in a large degree upon the student's ability to take into conscious consideration aesthetic concerns while he works. The aesthetic concerns of the child are not conscious; they may need to be for adolescence. The creative task of the adolescent seems, then, more conscious and less instinctive than that of the child.

These conclusions result in certain questions of importance in this research area. First, are standard measures of adaptability or capacity to succeed in school correlated with the kind of spontaneous flexibility and sensitivity which is intrinsic to art expression? In particular, this research raises doubts about the relatedness of measures such as academic achievement and IQ to measures of creative expression. According to this study, these measurings are not measuring creative ability. In this respect, it may be that the generalized concept of intelligence and creativity fits children better, while a concept involving specific factors and instances of intelligence and creativity is better suited toward the adult level, especially in regard to individuality of art expression in the senior high school. It might also be suggested that intelligence tests, by and large, have not considered factors related to creativity as of any importance to their assessment of intellect.

WILLIAM D. HITT

JOHN R. STOCK

The Relation Between Psychological Characteristics and Creative Behavior

It has been found that research performance can be described meaningfully in terms of two distinctive dimensions: originality and logical reasoning. The purpose of the present study was to investigate the relation between selected psychological characteristics and these two dimensions of research performance. Criteria of job performances were supervisory ratings on the above dimensions. Predictors included measures of creative ability, general intelligence, and personality characteristics. Subjects in the study were 96 scientists and engineers employed by one research laboratory. The results demonstrated that patterns of research behavior can be predicted on the basis of psychological test scores. In addition, further confirmation was given to a "two-factor theory" of creative research.

A recent study of the creative behavior of scientists and engineers identified two distinctive dimensions of creative behavior: originality and logical reasoning (Hitt, 1965). This two-dimensional definition of creative behavior is conceptualized in Figure 1, in which the four quadrants represent four types of behavior. Type I behavior is above-average on both originality and logical reasoning; Type II behavior is above-average on originality, but below-average on logical reasoning; Type III behavior is below-average on both of these dimensions; and Type IV behavior is above-average on logical reasoning, but below-average on originality.

The obvious question that emerged from this study was: What are the characteristics of the researchers who manifest these four types of behavior patterns? To obtain a preliminary answer to this question, a second study was conducted. This paper describes the second study.

From *Psychological Record*, 1965, *15*, pp. 133–140. Used by permission of the publisher.

259

Fig. 1   Four Types of Behavior

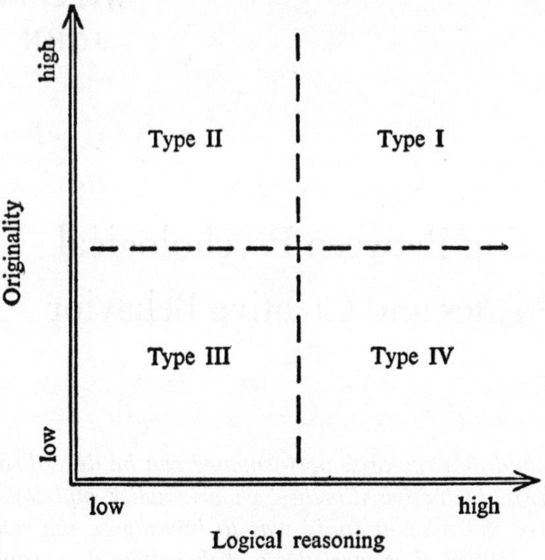

The Hypotheses

A number of hypotheses regarding the characteristics of the four types of researchers were formulated. The hypotheses are phrased in terms of the general intellectual and personality characteristics of the four types of researchers:[1]

Type I (high originality, high logical reasoning)

1. Above the sample average on general intelligence
2. Above the sample average on both convergent and divergent thinking[2]
3. Above the sample average on independence of thought
4. Above the sample average on responsibility

Type II (high originality, low logical reasoning)

1. Above the sample average on divergent thinking
2. Below the sample average on convergent thinking
3. Above the sample average on independence of thought
4. Below the sample average on cautiousness

---

[1] A Type I researcher would be "one who typically manifests Type I behavior."
[2] The terms divergent and convergent thinking as used here imply the definitions developed by J. P. Guilford (1950, 1958).

Type III (low originality, low logical reasoning)
   1. Below the sample average on general intelligence

Type IV (high logical reasoning, low originality)
   1. Above the sample average on convergent thinking
   2. Below the sample average on divergent thinking
   3. Above the sample average on responsibility
   4. Above the sample average on cautiousness

The next step was to test these hypotheses.

Method

DESIGN

Figure 2 shows the general design of the study. The four columns represent the four types of researchers. There are 24 Ss included in each "Type." The rows represent the 19 psychological measures included in the study. The study was designed to permit investigation of differences between "Types of Researchers" on each of the 19 measures.

Fig. 2 Design of the Study

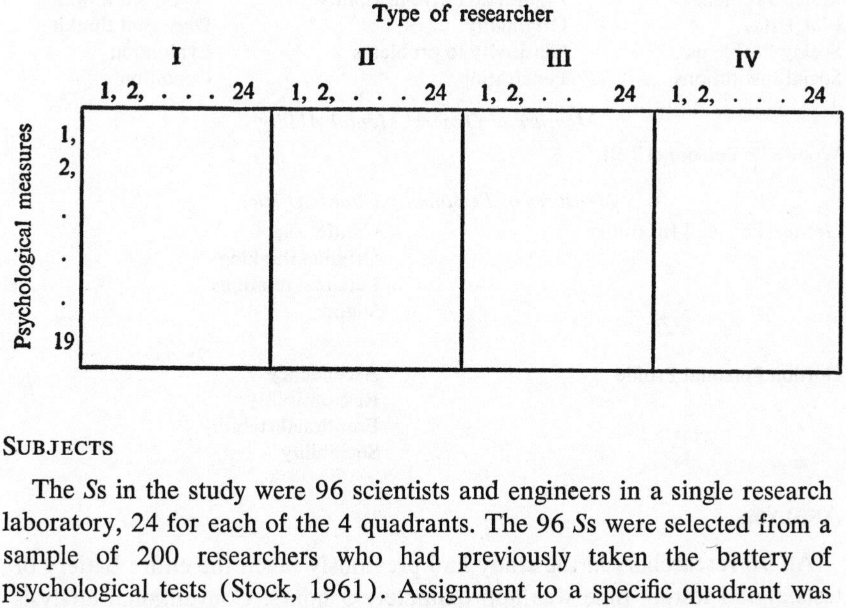

SUBJECTS

The Ss in the study were 96 scientists and engineers in a single research laboratory, 24 for each of the 4 quadrants. The 96 Ss were selected from a sample of 200 researchers who had previously taken the battery of psychological tests (Stock, 1961). Assignment to a specific quadrant was based upon scores obtained on the dimensions of originality and logical reasoning as measured by supervisory ratings. These men were fairly representative of the entire professional research staff employed by the laboratory under study. The requirements for being included in the test sample of 200 were: (1) being a full-time researcher and (2) being employed at the laboratory for a minimum of 12 months. The 96 men were drawn primarily from the physical sciences and engineering. Level of education was approximately as follows: B.A.—50%, M.S.—35%, Ph.D. —15%.

TESTS

The psychological tests included in the battery covered three general classes of characteristics: (1) specific dimensions of intelligence,[3] (2) general mental ability, and (3) personality characteristics. The tests and test factors are listed in Table 1.

Table 1. TESTS AND FACTORS INCLUDED IN PSYCHOLOGICAL TEST BATTERY

Measures of Intellectual Aptitudes (J. P. Guilford)

Test	Factor	Operation
Alternate Uses	Semantic spontaneous flexibility	Divergent thinking
Associational Fluency	Associational fluency	Divergent thinking
Consequences (Remote)	Originality	Divergent thinking
Expressional Fluency	Expressional fluency	Divergent thinking
Gestalt Transformation	Semantic redefinition	Convergent thinking
Ideational Fluency	Ideational fluency	Divergent thinking
Match Problems	Figural adaptive flexibility	Divergent thinking
Plot Titles	Originality	Divergent thinking
Seeing Problems	Sensitivity to problems	Evaluation
Social Institutions	Penetration	Cognition

Measure of General Mental Ability

Wonderlic Personnel Test

Measures of Personality Characteristics

Gordon Personal Inventory	Cautiousness
	Original thinking
	Personal relations
	Vigor
Gordon Personal Profile	Ascendency
	Responsibility
	Emotional stability
	Sociability

ANALYSIS

All 96 researchers in the study had previously taken the entire battery of tests. Total testing time was approximately 3 hours. Conventional analysis

[3] It will be noted that only one test of convergent thinking, Gestalt Transformation, is included in the battery. The hypotheses concerning convergent thinking, therefore, may not have been fairly tested.

of variance techniques were applied to the scores to test for the overall significance of differences between "psychological measures" and "Types of Researcher." The interaction between "Type of Researcher" and "psychological measure" was significant at $p < .01$.

To analyze the profiles for each of the four Types of Researcher, the mean test score on each of the 19 psychological measures was computed for the 24 men representing each of the four types. To permit meaningful comparisons, these mean raw scores were converted to percentiles. The percentile norms for the creativity tests, the Wonderlic Personnel Test, and the Gordon personality tests are based on the scores achieved by the sample of 200 research scientists and engineers.

Results

The results of the analysis are described, first, in terms of the differences between the mean scores for the four types of researchers and, second, in terms of the general profile comparisons of the four types of researchers.

TEST PROFILES

The test performance for the four types of researchers is shown in Table 2. Each score represents the percentile value of the mean score for the 24 researchers included in that type (or quadrant).

Table 2. MEAN TEST SCORES FOR FOUR TYPES OF RESEARCHERS

Test factors	Percentile standings*			
	Type I	Type II	Type III	Type IV
Alternate uses	66	64	41	39
Associational fluency	64	48	39	41
Consequences	69	59	39	52
Expressional fluency	66	53	47	50
Gestalt transformation	56	39	62	46
Ideational fluency	78	62	42	42
Match problems	63	59	52	66
Plot titles	55	41	39	40
Seeing problems	69	48	41	50
Social institutions	53	60	55	52
Wonderlic personnel test	56	49	41	50
Cautiousness	39	32	50	57
Original thinking	56	70	37	49
Personal relations	43	52	54	47
Vigor	65	51	47	59
Ascendency	52	69	41	40
Responsibility	58	37	39	64
Emotional stability	38	36	40	54
Sociability	54	66	43	57

* Mean raw scores computed for each of the four types were converted to percentiles on the basis of the norms established on the original sample of 200 researchers.

The four types of researchers scored on each measure as follows:[4]

1. Alternate uses:
    I and II greater than 60th percentile, III and IV less than 40th percentile
2. Associational fluency:
    I greater than 60th percentile, III and IV less than 40th percentile
3. Consequences:
    I greater than 65th percentile, III less than 40th percentile
4. Expressional fluency:
    I greater than 65th percentile
5. Gestalt transformation:
    III greater than 60th percentile, II less than 40th percentile
6. Ideational fluency:
    I greater than 75th percentile, II greater than 60th percentile
7. Match problems:
    IV greater than 65th percentile, I greater than 60th percentile
8. Plot titles:
    I at the 55th percentile, the other three groups less than 41st percentile
9. Seeing problems:
    I greater than 65th percentile
10. Social institutions:
    II greater than 60th percentile
11. Wonderlic personnel test:
    All groups between 55th and 41st percentiles
12. Cautiousness:[5]
    II less than 35th percentile, I less than 40th percentile
13. Original thinking:
    II greater than 65th percentile, III less than 40th percentile
14. Interpersonal relations:
    All groups between 54th and 43rd percentiles
15. Vigor:
    I greater than 60th percentile
16. Ascendency:
    II greater than 65th percentile, IV less than 40th percentile
17. Responsibility:
    IV greater than 60th percentile, II and III less than 40th percentile
18. Emotional stability:
    I, II, and III less than 40th percentile
19. Sociability:
    II greater than 65th percentile

[4] Groups falling within ten centiles of the 50th percentile for the same of 200 are not mentioned in these summary statements.

[5] Inasmuch as "The Gordon" is a forced-choice test, these group comparisons must be made with some caution.

GENERAL DESCRIPTION

Summary descriptions of the four types of researchers are presented below.

Type I. The Type I researcher is above the sample average in general intelligence. He does well in both divergent and convergent thinking. He is an original thinker, and he is not cautious. He is able to identify problems. He is a responsible person and also is very energetic.

Type II. The Type II researcher does well in divergent thinking. He views himself as an original thinker. He is not cautious. He enjoys mixing with people and asserts himself in a group. He probably is not a very dependable person.

Type III. The Type III researcher is below the average of the entire sample of researchers in general intelligence. He is cautious, he trusts others, and he is not self-assertive.

Type IV. The Type IV researcher is a very responsible person. He is emotionally stable and tends to be cautious. He does not do well in divergent thinking, although he appears to equal the Type II researcher in general intelligence. He does not assert himself in group situations.

The results from only 3 of the 19 tests had "surprisal value" for the authors of this paper. First, the Type II group was the highest of the four types on the Gordon "Sociability" factor. Several studies by other investigators have indicated that there is a positive correlation between originality and introversion (Gruber et al., 1962; Parnes & Harding, 1962; Taylor & Barron, 1963). For researchers at the laboratory studied, however, this sociability finding may be a logical expectation, since in this particular organization the researcher himself plays a major role in selling his own ideas. Hence, it is essential that he be somewhat aggressive and extroverted.

A second finding that was rather surprising concerned the set of four mean scores on the Gestalt Transformation test. The Type III group was slightly higher than Type I and was considerably higher than both the Type II and the Type IV groups. This rather unusual finding might be explained by the nature of the test. It is the only multiple-choice test of all of the Guilford tests used in the study. In pure and simple terms, it appears that many of the brightest researchers who took the tests are in disagreement with the scoring key. This test obviously should be used with caution.

A third finding that was unexpected was the high score of the Type IV group on the Match Problems test. It is important to note, however, that although the test involves *divergent* production, the solutions can be obtained by application of logical reasoning.

Conclusions

The results of the analysis supported nearly all of the hypotheses that were formulated prior to the analysis. It is clear that the Type II researcher does well in divergent thinking and views himself as an original thinker. He can generate a large number of ideas. The Type IV researcher is a responsible person, but tends to be cautious. The Type I researcher is characterized by the desirable attributes of both the Type II and the Type IV researcher. He also has the ability to identify problems, and he is energetic. The Type III researcher is below average in general intelligence. He is cautious and does not assert himself in group situations.

The findings have both theoretical and practical implications. The study provides further support for a two-factor theory of creativity. Furthermore, the results can serve as guidelines in the selection, training, and assignment of research scientists and engineers. Generalizations, however, must be made with caution. The results are based on a sample of only 96 researchers in a single research laboratory.

R. J. GOLDMAN

The Minnesota Tests of Creative Thinking

Background to the Tests

Before 1950, creative ability was a topic on which relatively little research had been undertaken by psychologists. This was pointed out in a paper of that year—the presidential address of J. P. Guilford (1950) to the American Psychological Association. He asserted that tests available at that time covered only a small area of human abilities. His address, and international events such as the Russian Sputnik achievements, stimulated a concern among educators about the aims and methods of American education, and among psychologists for research into creative abilities.

The umbrella term "creativity" was used rather loosely, to describe original, inventive, and novel productions of thought. Defined as such, it was recognized that if creative abilities could be identified by tests and encouraged in education, then the end products of education would help considerably toward the nation's adaptation to international and ideological competition. Much was written of the urgency of this task, a fairly typical title being *The Creative Potential of School Children in the Space Age* (Torrance, 1963a). Immediate concern was voiced for those identified as "the gifted," but no agreed definition for the gifted was reached, especially when some argued for an Intelligence Quotient of 150 and above. The relationship of creative abilities to intelligence was the field for a great deal of research, much of it controversial, for example, Getzels and Jackson (1962).

The Complexity of Creative Abilities

The debate has been somewhat vitiated by lack of agreement about what is meant by creativity. Some have deplored the use of the word as a misleading umbrella term so wide as to mean nothing. There is growing agreement that it is better to use "creative abilities," which may or may not be related

267

to each other, indicating the many complex factors which go to make creative behavior rather than some unitary aptitude.

Not only intellectual factors but personality factors are recognized as central to creative behavior. Some investigators such as Barron (1954b, 1958) and C. W. Taylor (1960) have used the criteria of recognizably successful "creatives" in writing, architecture, science, and medicine, devising personality profiles as a means of identifying latent creative abilities. Such a trait as "tolerance of ambiguity" suggested by Barron is an example of this, where a highly creative may be able to tolerate apparent confusion or ambiguity for a longer period than a poor creative. This suspension of judgment may allow the highly creative person to see greater creative possibilities in a problem situation. Personality factors appear to be an important influence in intellectual achievements, as the first tentative findings of Hudson (1962) seem to show in this country [Britain].

Guilford (1959ab) brought the intellectual aspects of the problem into focus in his theoretical model of the structure of the intellect. He suggests that there are three basic aspects of any ability, the operational, the contents, and the products, which, when seen in a permutative three-dimensional structure, theoretically yield 5 kinds of operations, 4 kinds of contents, and 6 kinds of products, in total producing 5 by 4 by 6 factors— that is, 120 ways of being talented. Guilford conceded that this is a theoretical structure, which will need to be modified in the light of research, as indeed it has been in the last few years. Of the 120 factors hypothesized, Guilford claims that 50 or more can be identified by tests. Commenting upon the factor of verbal comprehension, he remarks that this factor has dominated verbal intelligence tests. "Verbal comprehension is undoubtedly a very important trait in a verbal civilization, but its relatively strong productive power and its obvious role in education has often obscured the importance of other intellectual factors. The overemphasis upon it in testing and in education may have led to serious neglect of other desirable qualities in the general population" (Guilford, 1959b).

Among these "other desirable qualities" he posits creativity, related particularly to the operational aspect of intellect, namely divergent thinking abilities and evaluative thinking abilities. By "divergent" thinking Guilford means thinking which produces differing responses, not the expected or conformist answer demanded by most standardized ability tests. By evaluative thinking, he means an operation which shows, for example, sensitivity to problems unnoticed by less creative persons. To identify these abilities, he devised tests addressed mainly to students in higher education; and factors of fluency, flexibility, and originality emerged, suggesting that these were important intellectual factors in creative production. Other aspects of the model in the "products" dimension are probably related to creative production, transformations and implications, for example. In terms of contents, individuals can be divergent thinkers in any of the four categories posited: figural, symbolic, semantic, or behavioral. This, to some extent, appears to meet the point made by Burt (1962) that we may be mistaken in trying to measure creativity in general, since creativity may be something highly specific to a particular field of interest.

Initial Stages of the Minnesota Tests

Against this theoretical background, we can see the genesis and context of the Minnesota tests of creative thinking. E. P. Torrance, their originator, relied initially upon the Guilford model of the intellect, and began by adapting for younger children some of Guilford's materials. Since 1958, an attempt has been made to devise a set of tasks which can be used from kindergarten through to the graduate school, the emphasis to date being mainly upon children rather than student populations. Alongside Guilford-type tests, other tests were devised based upon reported characteristics of well-known scientific inventors.* One major difference between Guilford and Torrance is that, whereas each of Guilford's tests was designed to identify or represent a single factor, Torrance soon initiated more complex tests each of which could be scored on several factors. Torrance has emphasized that it is the *processes* of creative thinking which demand urgent attention more than the *products* which have so far claimed major consideration. It is interesting, therefore, that he (Torrance, 1962a) has defined creative thinking as "the process of sensing gaps or disturbing, missing elements; forming ideas or hypotheses concerning them; testing these hypotheses; and communicating the results, possibly modifying and retesting the hypotheses."

Among the first tests was an adaptation of Guilford's Unusual Uses test. Whereas he asked his subjects, "Think of as many unusual uses of a brick as you can," Torrence used the same question but substituted "tin cans." Tests asking children to think of impossible situations, and consequences (of a man becoming invisible at will) were added, and many others. The initial batteries of tests were felt to be suitable for fifth grade and above (10 years plus) but not satisfactory for those of a younger age. This led to the development of a variety of nonverbal tests. The earlier ones were in the nature of handling toys and asking children how they would improve them (product improvement) so that they would be "more fun to play with." Since tests of the kind could only be administered to individual children, there developed the need for group nonverbal tests. Through a great deal of experimental pretesting, there has now developed a large battery of varying tests, some 16 or more, with several others awaiting development and further experimentation.

* See ROSSMAN, J. (1931). *The psychology of the inventor.* Washington, D.C.: Inventors Publishing Co. TATON, R. (1957). *Reason and chance in scientific discovery.* New York: Philosophical Library. SCHWARTZ, G., & BISHOP, P. W. (1958). *Moments of discovery.* New York: Basic Books. GOERTZEL, V., & GOERTZEL, M. G. (1962). *Cradles of eminence.* Boston: Little, Brown.

The Varying Types of Tests

A full list of the Minnesota tests, with some description of their content and administration, can be seen in Torrance's *Guiding Creative Talent* (1962a). A very brief account is given here so that scoring, administration, reliability, and validity problems can be discussed.

NONVERBAL TESTS

Incomplete Figures Task

Based upon K. Franck's Drawing Completion Test (Barron, 1958), six incomplete figures are set out (see Fig. 1) and subjects are asked to sketch some objects or design "that no one else in the class will think of." Subjects are asked to write in the names of objects they have sketched, or (for the young) have the titles they suggest written in by the teacher or tester.

Fig. 1   Incomplete Figures Task

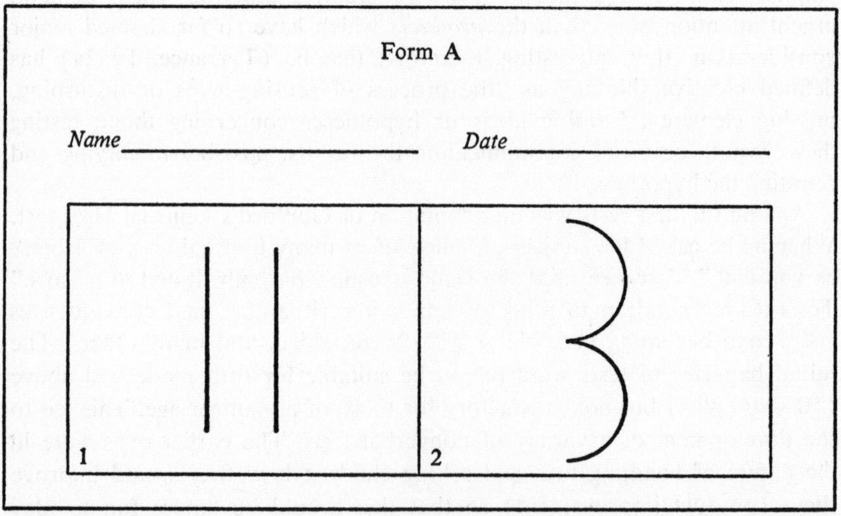

There are two parallel forms, A and B. The task is limited to 10 minutes for each form. Each figure completed is scored for fluency, flexibility, originality, and elaboration. Fluency is scored by the total number of figures completed, one for each figure, e.g., a subject completing all ten will score 10. Flexibility is scored one point for each category used in completing figures, showing a flexible use of ideas. Originality, based upon 1,056 subjects from first grade to high school, is scored 1 point where less than 5 percent of the population have made this response and 2 points where less than 2 percent of the population have responded in this way. Elaboration is scored 1 point for every pertinent detail used in each picture completion.

The Circles Task

Thirty-six small circles (1 in. diameter) are printed on a sheet of paper and the subjects are asked to sketch as many objects as possible which have a circle as a main element in their design. "Add lines to the circles in your picture. Your lines can be inside the circle, outside the circle, or both inside and outside the circle." Titles, indicating the identity of each object should be written in, as in the Figure Completion Task.

A parallel form for the circles task is the Squares Task (35 1-in. squares) with the same timing. Scores for fluency, flexibility, originality, and elaboration are given on similar criteria to the Picture Completion task.

Picture-Construction Task

A blank piece of paper is provided and a piece of glued colored paper, the shapes offering parallel forms of the task, a triangle and a curved "jelly bean" shape. Subjects are asked to think of a picture or object which they can draw with this shape as a part. They are then asked to glue the shape on the paper and add lines to make the picture or object. A title identifying the object is required.

A limit of 10 minutes is imposed. Scoring on fluency, flexibility, originality, and elaboration can be made.

Creative Design Task

Subjects are given circles and strips of various colors and sizes, a four-page booklet, scissors, and glue, and are asked to construct pictures or designs. Scoring and administrative procedures are still being developed for this test.

VERBAL TESTS USING NONVERBAL STIMULI

Product Improvement

A toy dog (alternatively a toy monkey) is shown to the subject with the instruction, "try to think of the cleverest, most interesting and most unusual ways of changing this toy dog so that boys and girls will have more fun playing with it." Individual administration is necessary for younger children so that the tester may write down the responses. The test can be administered to a group where writing skills are developed, and in this case the picture of the toy is projected on to a screen. Later versions of the Product Improvement as a group test have the picture of a toy dog printed in the answer booklets.

The test is limited to 10 minutes. Scoring for fluency, flexibility, and originality is made on a similar basis to the nonverbal tests. An additional score is made on "inventive level" based upon criteria used by the U.S. Patent Office on the basis of such qualities as surprisingness, rarity, challenging nature, and constructiveness.

Unusual Uses

The same toy may be used in conjunction with the Product Improvement test, with similar administration, but altering the instructions to listing "the most unusual uses you can think of for this dog other than as a plaything." A ten-minute limit is made, and scoring is on the same basis as for Product Improvement responses.

The Ask and Guess Test

A picture of a Nursery Rhyme story is shown (the two most used are "Tom, Tom, the Piper's Son" and "Pussy in the Well" and could be used as parallel forms). Subjects are asked to do three things, five minutes being given to each task. They must (a) ask as many questions about the picture as they can think of, (b) state as many possible causes of the events depicted in the picture, and (c) give as many consequences or results as they can of the action depicted. Below fourth grade (9 years), subjects have been tested individually, their oral responses being taken down by the tester. After this age, group administration is possible.

Total time allowed is 15 minutes. Scoring is based upon fluency (number of relevant responses) and adequacy (these scores were different for questions, causes, and consequences and are difficult to summarize).

Sounds and Images

A more recent test, still in its trial stage (Cunnington & Torrance, 1962) involves the use of four auditory stimuli, beginning with an easily recognizable sound (a thunderstorm) and gradually becoming less unified and relatively unfamiliar sounds. Subjects are asked to write down images and ideas associated with each sound in turn. To break down inhibitions the sounds are played three times (in order 1 to 4), and before each round a narrator encourages freer association.

Two forms are being developed, each form taking 30 minutes, allowing for writing responses and listening three times to each of the four sounds. Scoring is 0 to 4 points on originality, taking 544 subject responses as percentage criteria. This means that the greater the percentage of subjects using a response, the lower the score, because it is less original. Conversely, the smaller the percentage using a response, the higher the score awarded, because it is more original. The "Sounds and Images" tape may be used not only as a test but as what is described as a "warm-up for creative activity."

A similar technique is a tape-recorded dramatic episode (e.g., Don Giovanni and the Giant) and where the chief character gets into difficulties, the tape is stopped and the subjects are asked to write down their solutions. Fantasy material is used but reality (historical stories) has also been included (Torrance, 1964, p. 39).

VERBAL TESTS USING VERBAL STIMULI

Unusual Uses

Guilford's Brick-Uses test was adapted, but two other objects were found to be more suitable for children, tin cans and books. The instructions are "Try to think of some unusual uses of tin cans (books)," and subjects are asked to write down as many clever, interesting, or unusual uses as they can think of. For the tin can, for example, use of the can only as a container would indicate some rigidity of thought. Scoring is for fluency, flexibility, and originality. The test is only a group test and a time limit of five minutes is established.

Impossibilities

Another task adapted from Guilford is the asking of subjects simply to "List as many impossibilities as you can think of." A five-minute time limit is imposed, and scoring is for fluency, flexibility, and originality. Use of the Impossiblities Task has been included in the battery of tests mainly for students.

Consequences

Devised originally by Guilford to yield measures of ideational fluency and penetration, Torrance chose situations more suitable for children. There are two forms, A and B, the contents of form A being:

1. What would happen, if man could be invisible at will?
2. What would happen, if a hole could be bored through the earth?
3. What would happen, if the language of birds and animals could be understood by man?

The time limit is five minutes for the three items combined, and responses are scored for fluency, flexibility, and originality.

Other verbal tasks of a similar kind are Just Suppose: Improbable situations (Just suppose, when it is raining all the rain drops stood still in the air and wouldn't move, and they were solid); Situations (How would you handle a friend who likes to kid others but cannot stand to be kidded by them?); Mother Hubbard problem (Think of all the things Mother Hubbard could have done when she found that there were no bones in the cupboard); and the Cow Jumping Problem (similar to Mother Hubbard).

Two other slightly different tests are Common Problems and Imaginative Stories.

Common Problems

Designed to test the factor termed "sensitivity to problems" by asking subjects to write down as many problems that might arise in two situations, taking a bath and doing homework. There are two parallel forms, A and B, each with a time limit of five minutes. The responses are scored for fluency, flexibility, and originality.

Imaginative Stories

Twenty minutes is allowed for writing stories, several topics being given from which the pupils choose, all of them dealing with persons or animals of deviant behavior. Twenty topics, 10 for each, were first used, among them, "The dog that doesn't bark," "The man who cries," "The lion that doesn't roar," and "The flying monkey." Scoring has been devised for originality, interest, and general creativity. In addition, there is a very complex standardized analysis of how children conceive divergency of behavior in their stories. This analysis (Torrance & Tan, 1964) covers how children think of the sources of pressures to conform, the kind of pressures used, the effects of such pressures, how the divergent behavior began, and whether the divergency is seen as a defect or an asset. The scoring is very detailed and complex for what amounts to a story projection device.

Test Batteries

At this stage, batteries of the Minnesota tests are being used to discover what combinations of tests are appropriate for certain age groups in the school and adult population. It is obvious that below a certain age only nonverbal tests should make up a battery. Some nonverbal tests, however, have been combined with verbal ones to cover as wide an age range as possible. Such is the Abbreviated Form VII (Torrance, 1962b) where a battery of four tasks, Figure Completion, Circles, Product Improvement, and Unusual Uses of Tin Cans is being widely used.

Major Problems

The content, administration, and scoring of the Minnesota tests pose various problems, together with questions of sampling and norms and the general reliability and validity of the tests.

CONTENT

Since the contents of the tests are linked with the Guilford concepts of intellectual operations (divergent, convergent, and productive thinking), any criticisms of the contents of the Minnesota tests inevitably involve a criticism of the limitations of factor analysis applied to testing of this kind. This controversy is too technical to enter upon here and is briefly touched upon by P. E. Vernon (1964). Working empirically, Torrance appears to have included stimuli of varied types, verbal and nonverbal, pictorial, physical objects, auditory stimuli, situations, and problems, and to have sampled a diversity of factors about which there is a measure of agreement among those researching on creativity in the U.S.A. On face value alone, fluency of ideas would appear to be an essential ingredient of creative thinking production, as also would ideational flexibility, originality, and elaborative ability. Sensitivity to problems is also sampled in several tests, and the concept of "inventivelevel" corresponds closely to originality. Obviously, the tests cannot claim to sample the entire universe of what is termed creative thinking, but this is not the intention. Torrance in his latest report 725 (1964) states: ". . . We have tried to make the best use of what is known about creativity—the creative process, the creative person, the creative product, and the processes which facilitate creative functioning. We have relied upon the historical accounts of creative achievements, studies of the lives of creative persons, laboratory and field studies designed to affect creative functioning, studies involving the evaluation of creative products and processes, efforts to measure various aspects of man's mental functioning, and the like. We have used these sources in generating ideas and in testing them theoretically to make certain that the instruments developed would have as good face validity as possible." Later he writes: "It may be true that criteria of creative behavior are elusive, but we decided at the outset to define creative thinking as adequately as we could and then to try to remain true to this definition." We shall look at this question of criteria again when we discuss the validity of the Minnesota tests.

A criticism made of some items is that they are rather trivial, e.g., the uses of a tin can, suggesting that one cannot expect subjects to be motivated toward creative production by tests involving trivialities. Such a criticism could be made against most tests, including many items in tests of verbal ability. Yet what many adults would dismiss as trivial in a child's play may be regarded as highly serious by the child himself, and to the discerning observer it may be an indication of creative activity. Children and adolescents observed taking the Minnesota tests were seen to work enthusiastically on items thought of as superficial.

ADMINISTRATION

A major problem faced in the early stages of developing the tests was how to establish rapport with subjects, especially smaller children, by a "warming-up" process which did not involve practice effect or suggestive answers. Initially, instructions included examples such as the beginning of the circles test that they might wish to draw a wheel or in the picture completion test where the first figure was completed by the tester. In the present administrative procedures, examples tend to have disappeared as too suggestive and inhibitive of varied responses.

The problem of timing is a difficult one, since a relevant criticism can be made that in creative production a period of unconscious deliberation over a period of time appears to be necessary. This time lag appears impossible to allow for in test situations, since problems introduced early in a school day and tested a few hours later lead to the introduction of other uncontrolled variables, such as discussion with peers. Similar objections can be made to "take home tests" considered at Minneosta as a means of overcoming the problem of a necessary time lag. In most timed tests, it has been found that a ten-minute time limit is more than most children or adults will use. In the Picture Construction test (A iii above), it was discovered that high elaborators do not have enough time, and those scoring high on fluency kept thinking of additional ideas. Torrance is aware of this problem, and he and his team are experimenting with different time limits for the same tasks. The desirable length of a battery, administered in a single sitting, seems to be less than an hour, since many individuals appear to reduce the quantity and quality of responses toward the end of an hour. On the other hand, many subjects maintain the same pace throughout.

SCORING

Any tests encouraging a variety of divergent responses are bound to involve complex and tedious methods of scoring. Since there is no one correct answer and all responses in the verbal tests are write-in answers, little of the scoring can be reduced to a mechanical or simple clerical task. One or two of Guilford's tests can be scored in this simple way, and fluency scores on the Torrance tests, a numerical count of responses, can be done by unskilled scorers. Other scores such as flexibility, elaboration, and originality can be handled by scorers with a very limited amount of training (a few minutes on a single item). Very detailed instructions, categories and instructions are now available in the form of manuals for all items used, many still subject to revision in the light of experience. The subjective element can be minimized, even in the scoring of imaginative stories (see C v above) by an ingenious but elaborate series of standardized categories. This increases the time of marking but increases interscorer reliabilities. Yamamoto (1962) reports the following coefficients of interscorer reliability, based upon 64 test records scored by independent scorers. *Product Improvement*—Fluency 1.00, Flexibility 0.87, Originality 0.98; *Unusual Uses of Toy Dog*—Fluency 1.00, Flexibility 0.84, Originality 0.92; *Unusual Uses of Tin Cans*—Fluency 1.00, Flexibility 0.87, Originality 0.98; *Circles*—Fluency 1.00, Flexibility 0.91, Originality 0.98; *Ask and Guess* —Fluency 1.00, Adequacy 0.96. Occasional interscorer reliability checks are made from time to time on each scorer.

It appears to be an inescapable feature of these kinds of tests that by maximizing the quality of creative thinking responses, we maximize scoring time, costs, and complexities. To meet this problem the Minnesota tests have become less elaborate since they were begun.

NORMS

The Minnesota tests are still in an experimental and tentative stage, since they are based upon descriptive populations only and not upon random sampling procedures. Whole school populations have been tested in some cities in the Middle West and other areas, but no systematic attempts to typify the samples have yet been made. Some tentative norms have been developed on these descriptive populations for certain grades with several hundred, and in some cases, over a thousand, pupils as the standardizing sample upon which the norms are based.

Norms for creative thinking tests must be developed with great caution because of important cultural variations. Some cultural pressures appear to inhibit creative thinking, as was evident in material produced by Negro children in the state of Georgia, analyzed by the present writer.* This may be true not only of racial groups, but also of certain regional or economic groups within the United States. Certain of the Minnesota nonverbal tests and imaginative story writings have been tried out in Australia, India, the Philippines, Greece, Germany, Malaya, and other countries. Although sampling in these places is based upon descriptive and not random populations, some marked cultural pressures are evident. Differences between what is allowable, the range of exploratory thought, the extent of fantasizing, and "regression in the service of the ego," and other variables within differing cultures make the problem of creative thinking norms extremely difficult. This affects evaluation of responses, since what is an original response, scoring high on an originality scale at less than a 2 percent response in one culture, may be extremely unoriginal or commonplace in another.

It would be possible to use or adapt some of the Minnesota tests for British populations, but separate British norms would have to be established. Torrance (1962a, p. 93) has, for example, suggested that in the U.S.A. a "fourth-grade slump" is evident in creative thinking, when children appear to be less willing to think differently from their peers. It is the growing awareness of peer pressures between 9 and 10 years, which Torrance advances as a hypothesis to explain this apparent phenomenon. To apply, therefore, fourth-grade norms to the responses of British children of this age may have a grossly distorting effect. If there is a temporary decline, or rather recession, of creative thinking in primary schools in Britain, it may not occur at the same age as in the United States.

RELIABILITY

Since a great deal of criticism has been made about the reliability of creative thinking tests, it will be of interest to review the most recent reliability figures on the Minnesota tests. Interscorer reliabilities have been mentioned already. Torrance and Gowan (1963) suggest there are special problems which may contribute to low temporal reliability of some of the tests. Among these are: the shortness of some of the subtests in a battery (e.g., the Figure Completion test is only 10 items long); the difficulties in testing children of tender ages (tests for children tend to become less

* Unpublished report not yet available.

reliable with decreasing age); and the novelty of the tests (a block may be caused first time around when asked for unusual uses for a brick, though later a child may give numerous answers). The latter is an illustration of the time-lag problem in creative thought. A considerable number of test-retests have been done, yielding various coefficients and also split-half reliability coefficients.

On nonverbal tests, the circles split-half reliability is 0.96 for fluency, the highest reported coefficients for temporal stability* are 0.76 for fluency, 0.72 for flexibility, 0.81 for originality, and 0.89 for elaboration. For the figure completion test, the highest reported split-half reliability is 0.97, but there are no reports on temporal stability. For the nonverbal battery as a whole, there is a split-half reliability coefficient of 0.97 for fluency, and there is an 0.75 temporal stability coefficient.

On the verbal tests, temporal stability coefficients for the Ask-and-Guess test are highest at 0.89 for frequency, 0.79 for flexibility, and 0.85 for total score. In the Product Improvement test, the highest temporal stability coefficient is 0.85 for fluency, 0.76 for flexibility, 0.68 for originality, and 0.73 for total score. Unusual Uses tests yield 0.75 for fluency, 0.74 for flexibility, 0.71 for originality, 0.47 for elaboration, and 0.68 for total score. For a battery of four verbal tests, the highest reliabilities reported are 0.85 for fluency, 0.78 for flexibility, 0.83 for originality, 0.85 for elaboration, and 0.87 for total score.

Torrance and Gowan admit many much lower reliability coefficients; but in putting forward the highest coefficients in their summary, they maintain that with further research and experimentation the reliability of the Minnesota tests can be improved. A more recent report by Torrance (1964) appears to support this trend toward better reliability.

Within tests some factors do not correlate highly with other factors, and this has been the subject of some criticism. This may be accounted for by the fact that not only are some persons creative because they are motivated by certain tasks, but also because one individual may be good at producing a large number of ideas (fluency) but poor at elaborating on them, whereas another may have few ideas, but the few he has may be fairly original. Another may be original only in relation to certain categories and outside these categories may be unable or unwilling to apply his powers (poor flexibility).

VALIDITY

Longitudinal studies are planned to test the validity of the Minnesota tests, but the more difficult problem is that of immediate criteria. Torrance claims some face validity in several publications while recognizing the more complex validity problem. Vernon (1964) comments: "Just because

* By temporal stability is meant the requirement of any test that the results will not vary unduly from one test session to another. Cronbach has suggested the term "coefficient of stability" for this kind of reliability.

a set of tests looks as though it involves creativity and gives lowish correlations with g,v, or k tests does not mean that it measures what we recognize as creativity in daily life, unless we can show that they actually differentiate between adults or children *known on other grounds to be creative and noncreative* (my italics), and that they are considerably more valid for this purpose than g or other tests."

Using teacher and peer nominations on various criteria of creative thinking, Torrance found quite uniformly that children nominated by their teachers on such criteria achieved higher scores on his tests than children not nominated. Yamamoto (1962), for example, found significant differences on these criteria with 596 fifth-grade pupils, Sommers (1961) similarly with industrial arts students, and Wallace (1961) with sales assistants in a department store. The reader concerned to evaluate further evidence, based upon sociometric criteria and school achievements, should refer to Torrance (1962a, pp. 47–64; 1964, *Report on Project No. 725*).

Discussion

Since so little is known of Torrance's work in this country, this article has attempted to describe in some detail the Minnesota tests of creative thinking. In evaluating them, it must be borne in mind that these tests are not in their final form, the composition of batteries yielding the highest reliability and validity has not been finally determined, and the assumptions upon which they are based are tentative hypotheses which may be modified in the light of future experimental development. Torrance has moved away from the Guilford type tests to tests of a more complex character, which set out by contrast to test several factors of creative thinking. It is also relevant here to point out that, although Torrance has replicated eight experiments on the Getzels and Jackson procedures to examine the relationship between intelligence and creative thinking, his tests must not be too closely identified with these procedures, which have been, in my view, justly criticized. The value of the Minnesota tests lies in their possible use in identifying creative thinking abilities, in relating to performance in other more conventional tests and to school achievements, and in focusing upon periods in the educational sequence which may be inhibitive periods. Despite the difficulties of scoring, these types of tests should not be too readily dismissed as too cumbersome to use, at least experimentally for the present, in selection for secondary or higher education.

First, however, they must yield better coefficients of reliability and validity than they do at present. Latest research reports indicate improvements in this direction. One important by-product of such tests in post-Plowden developments in Britain could be to make teachers aware of different dimensions to their teaching, help wean them away from the rather depressing dependence upon narrow educational labels and stimulate the application in our secondary schools of principles of learning of a more creative kind, already practiced in our primary schools. Beyond primary school age it is true that the educational climate remains largely formal, demanding convergent performance in most examinable subjects. If tests are successful in diagnosing divergent thinkers of the future, it is evident that our schools, colleges, and universities, as well as society in general, must be educated to adapt more flexibility to the needs of those so identified. This will require educational expectations differing from those evident at the moment, as well as a more appropriate educational climate, which could lead to a greater enrichment of our society and its individual members.

Meanwhile, the Minnesota tests will require much modification and adaptation for use in Britain. This task is already beginning at the University of Reading, where it is also hoped to devise Minnesota-type tests with simplified scoring procedures to facilitate their wider use.

J. P. GUILFORD

Measurement of Creativity

In the context of research, there are two areas in which measurement is important: one is the area of "creative potential" and the other is the area of "creative performance" or "creative production." The general topic will be discussed under these two headings.

"Creative potential" means what an individual brings to a possible creative performance because of his personality structure. "Creative performance" means what an individual actually produces. Actual performance depends both on potentiality and on what the operating situation allows.

The number of qualities that contribute to potential for creativity is large, and the number of spheres of life activity in which creative performance may occur is large. We are faced with multiple dimensions in both domains—multiple dimensions of readiness on the one hand and multiple dimensions of creative output on the other. In either case, we have a problem of taxonomy—questions of what the "real" or operational variables are.

Measurement of Creative Potential

DIMENSIONS OF CREATIVE POTENTIAL

The taxonomic question of what are the relevant variables in creative potential is only a part of the much larger question of the dimensions in human personality. If we knew all the unique dimensions of human personality, we should be completely ready to undertake the problem of relevance. Which of the personality dimensions have any bearing upon readiness for creative production, and how are they weighted in that connection? Experiences of the past twenty years have shown that we have not been ready to raise the question of relevance, for it required further search for personality variables that were suggested by the apparent requirements in fields of creative performance. Search for qualities relevant

281

for creative production has contributed to the more general quest for basic personality variables.

Personality traits in general, including those recognized in the nature of unique dimensions, can be conveniently categorized as motivational, temperamental, and aptitudinal, which is to say that they are in the form of interests and attitudes, emotional dispositions, and abilities. Very likely, traits in all these categories have some possibility of relevance as contributors to potential for creative production. Interests and attitudes should have most to do with whether or not the individual will direct his efforts toward innovative behavior, and if his efforts are so directed, what his choice of area of output will be. Temperamental qualities should determine to some extent whether creative productivity and the directions of that productivity are congenial to the individual's emotional disposition. Aptitude variables should set upper limits to quantity and quality of output on the one hand and should open doors of opportunity for high degrees of performance on the other. Such abilities can be regarded as being within the intellectual domain. Other abilities have more to do with technical aspects of performance.

RELEVANCE OF MOTIVATIONAL AND TEMPERAMENTAL VARIABLES

Different approaches have been utilized in the effort to determine which traits seem to be relevant for creative personalities. At the University of California's Institute for Personality Assessment and Research in Berkeley, the major approach has been the study of groups of recognized creative producers, among them, architects, mathematicians, and writers. The major strategy has been to apply a searching assessment of outstanding groups and to make comparisons of them with people not in such groups, to note any significant differences, in terms of test scores and other variables. The success of such an approach, of course, depends upon the appropriateness of selection of both the experimental and control groups. A supplementary procedure has been to relate scores and other information to rankings of individuals within the outstanding groups on the basis of peer judgments with respect to originality or creativity.

Other investigators have taken the usual route of concurrent-validation studies, correlating trait evaluations with criteria designed to reflect creative performance in groups of scientists, public-relations individuals, advertising copy writers, artists, and the like, not all of whom are distinguished producers. Such groups undoubtedly offer a much greater range of talent than groups selected for outstanding performance. Very little has been done thus far toward conducting predictive-validation studies. Such studies will have more practical utility, for prediction of future creative performance is the ultimate, socially useful, operational goal. We can never be fully confident that concurrent validity indicates also the predictive validity of a measuring device. The validation studies mentioned thus far have pertained to "men on the job," so to speak. There have been some others with students as subjects. In these instances, the criteria have been in the form of ratings by observers of student behavior or of products produced by the students.

It is the confirmed view of this writer that the most meaningful and potentially useful dimensions of personality to use in measurement are those demonstrated to be unique by factor analysis. In the validation studies referred to above, some measuring devices that provide scores for factors have been utilized, but also some standard instruments whose score scales were selected on a priori bases or on the basis of some empirical procedure other than factor analysis. A few of the instruments that have been most productive of positive results and the traits scored with those instruments will be briefly mentioned.

On the *Allport-Vernon-Lindzey Study of Values,* creative performers tend to score higher than controls on the variables called Esthetic and Theoretical (MacKinnon, 1964). On the *Myers-Briggs Type Indicator,* creative performers tend to be higher on scores for the types of introvert (vs. extrovert) and intuition (vs. sensation) (MacKinnon, 1964). The kind of introversion emphasized in this instrument is probably what this writer has called "thinking intoversion," which means an inclination toward reflection rather than action. As for the intuition-vs.-sensation variable, it is apparently a difference in the extent to which things perceived are taken abstractly vs. concretely.

On scales from the Cattell *Sixteen Personality Factors Questionnaire,* the more creative scientists tend to be more emotionally stable (scale C), more self-assertive or dominant (scale E), more restrained or desurgent (scale F), more radically inclined (scale Q1), and more self-sufficient (scale Q2) (Cattell, 1963). There are indications from scattered, but repeated, sources that the more creative individual is more self-confident, more independent, and less sociable than the ordinary run of individuals. Torrance (1962a) reports observations that more creative males tend to score on the feminine side, and more creative females tend to score on the masculine side of the norm central tendencies for those characteristics. Other instruments that measure the same traits as those mentioned from the various sources would presumably have some promise for differentiating between those more-versus-less creative in disposition, so far as nonaptitude qualities are concerned.

Intellectual-Aptitude Variables—Although it has been amply demonstrated that creative performance is related to certain intellectual abilities, traditional intelligence tests, as such, have fallen far short of discriminating among the more and less creative. The obvious reason is that intelligence tests have stayed almost entirely clear of those more relevant abilities.

The latest revision of the *Stanford-Binet Intelligence Scale,* Form LM, for example, includes 140 single tests (counting the alternates), of which only five or six involve ingenuity or cleverness or similar qualities associated with thinking creatively or imaginatively. The reason is historical.

Prior to the development of the first Stanford-Binet scale, Terman did some experimenting with tests. In one study, Terman derived from a population of 500 school children who were rated by their teachers for brightness vs. dullness a selection of the brightest seven and dullest seven (Terman, 1906). He administered to these 14 children a list of tests, one of which he identified as a measure of ingenuity. Because the ingenuity test did not discriminate the two groups as did all the other tests involving intellectual activity, he concluded that it was not a measure of intelligence. The result was a test battery that has excluded measures of the more creative qualities, except for the very few that have slipped in at some time. Thus was the history of intelligence tests determined.

Our knowledge of the kinds of intellectual abilities that are potentially most relevant for the assessment of creative disposition has come almost entirely through factor analysis (Wilson et al., 1964; Guilford & Hoepfner, 1966). These abilities have been recognized as belonging to a few categories: fluency, flexibility, and elaboration. Fluency is a matter of facility with which an individual retrieves items of information from his personal information in storage. There is no source from which a person can generate information that is needed in a creative act other than his memory store or newly acquired information sought in the environment. Most of the needed information comes from his personal memory store. There is a real difference between having the information in storage and being able to retrieve it when it is needed and to use it in new situations, however; hence divergent-production abilities are distinct from memory abilities.

Flexibility is a matter of fluidity of information or a lack of fixedness or rigidity. Novel output automatically implies new and unusual uses of retrieved information and also revisions of that information. Novelty of outcome (novel for the individual) is the sine qua non of creative performance. Flexibility is the basis of originality, ingenuity, and inventiveness.

Elaboration is a facility for adding a variety of details to information that has already been produced. Creative productions very often progress from a vague outline or theme, through development of a more clearly organized structure or system with its essential aspects, then to the more elaborate finished affair, whether it be a poem, a novel, a painting, or a scientific theory. There are implications to be followed up and finishing touches to be added in order to round out the final product.

But the recognition of different kinds of ability in the form of fluency, flexibility, and elaboration is not the whole story. There are three major kinds of fluency and two major kinds of flexibility. One kind of fluency has to do with producing a variety of unitary thoughts or ideas and is known as "ideational fluency." The characteristic test in this category asks the examinee to list rapidly the members of a class that is specified by giving two or three of its attributes, e.g., things that are spherical and edible.

Another kind of fluency pertains to relations and is known as "associational fluency." The typical test asks for a list of things similar to a given idea, e.g., the thought of HARD, the relation being similarity. The third kind asks for the production of a number of complex, organized ideas, as in a test that calls for writing different sentences each containing three given words, e.g., boy, lake, moon. The ability is commonly known as "expressional fluency."

One kind of flexibility has to do with class ideas; a facility for going from one class to another. A test of this quality asks the examinee to list unusual uses for an object, e.g., a newspaper. The emphasis upon *unusual* uses virtually forces the examinee to go from one class of uses to another in every response he gives, e.g., swatting flies, protection from heat, wrapping material, absorbent material, and so on.

Another type of flexibility has to do with shifts of meaning or reinterpretations in the service of problem-solving. It can be tested by asking for clever answers to riddles, clever titles to stories, or to cartoons, or far-reaching consequences to events. All such responses involve reinterpretations or shifts of meaning.

Ability to elaborate may be tested by giving the outline of a plan, as for putting on a school bazaar or carnival, asking the examinee to suggest a number of detailed operations that would be needed for the success of the plan. The different aspects of the plan imply or suggest the operational details.

All the given examples of abilities and tests are in the verbal category. It is well recognized that verbal and nonverbal tests generally do not measure the same abilities. This generalization is very true also of the category of abilities under discussion. Collectively, these abilities have been called divergent-production factors (they have been discovered or demonstrated by means of factor analysis). It is now known that there are two sets of divergent-production abilities parallel to the six verbal or semantic abilities. One set of six pertains to abilities to produce divergent or varied responses where the information is visual-figural (perceived) content. Another set of six involves letters or numbers, the kind of information being given the technical name of "symbolic."

Theoretically, there is a fourth kind of content known as "behavioral," since it concerns the psychological dispositions of observed individuals. With four sets of divergent-production abilities, with six abilities in each set, there are theoretically 24 abilities altogether in this category, of which 16 have been supported by empirical investigation, and tests exist for them. Research is currently proceeding on the hypothesized set of behavioral divergent-production abilities.

Although the divergent-production abilities seem logically most promising for assessing creative potentiality where aptitude is concerned, there are numerous other intellectual abilities in other operation categories—cognition, memory, convergent production, and evaluation, as envisaged by the writer's structure-of-intellect model (Guilford, 1959a; Guilford, 1966b).

Another category of abilities that seems especially pertinent to creativity

has to do with transformations of information. The second kind of flexibility mentioned above deals with the divergent production of transformations. Abilities for dealing with transformations in the other operation
categories undoubtedly contribute to insights, intuitions, and inspirations
that are often characteristic of creative thinking. Beyond the two categories
emphasized here, many other abilities may well become significant contributors, depending upon the particular problem or incident in connection
with which creative production occurs.

Some general points should be emphasized. One follows from the
immediately preceding trend in the discussion. Specific acts or kinds of acts
of creative production draw upon their own collections or pattern of
abilities. For the purposes of predictive validity, therefore, no one factor
test can be expected to have substantial predictive validity in any one
situation. Nor would it be in order to attempt to derive a single composite
score and say that it is *the* measure of creative potential. Such a composite
score could have almost zero predictive validity in connection with any one
criterion of creative performance because it would contain so many
irrelevant components.

Another point is that, with divergent-production tests, it is necessary to
ask the examinee to *produce* something, which means responses of the
completion type. Answer-sheet tests cannot be appropriately used, and any
test of multiple-choice type that is proposed as a measure of creative ability
should be looked upon with suspicion.

A third point may be added. Tests of divergent-production abilities tend
to have relatively low reliability. This is probably in large part a reflection
of the general instability of the level of functioning of individuals in
creative ways, and will probably be found to apply to criterion measurements of creative output as well as to test scores. High levels of predictive
validity should, therefore, not be expected, unless the criterion clearly
emphasizes a certain combination of contributing traits, and the predictor
instrument emphasizes the same kind of composite.

RELEVANCE OF THE APTITUDE TRAITS

Space does not permit a review of the evidence for the construct validity
and the predictive validity of measures of the abilities just discussed. The
writer has assembled much of the evidence elsewhere (Guilford, 1967b).

Measurement of Creative Performance

There is space for only a few general comments regarding the measurement
of creative output in daily life. Lehman (1953) faced this problem when
he investigated the relation of creativity to age. He adopted a solution with
respect to the measurement of *quantity* of output that called for counting
units, such as poems, novels, inventions, scientific contributions, and the
like, without attempting to weight such products for importance. For

evaluation of *quality* of output, he used judgments of historians, biographers, and others in positions to have valid ideas about each contributor's best work.

Other interests in evaluations of creative production are very much centered about the criterion problem, the crucial problem encountered in validation studies. The most common criteria have been subjective in that they depend upon judgments of observers who make ratings; judgments made by peers or by superiors (C. W. Taylor et al., 1963). Such criterion measures have appeared to be more predictable than most.

In some instances the ratings have been made of products of the individuals, such as samples of drawings or of creative writing (C. A. Jones, 1960). Purely objective criteria, such as numbers of patents of industrial scientists and engineers, have not served so well, probably because they are multiply determined by many irrelevant circumstances. Holland (1964), however, has used a survey of incidents that reflect creative efforts, to indicate creative output of high-school graduates.

Nothing more can be said here regarding the evaluation of creative-performance level of individuals except to say that whatever type of evaluation is used, the variable of measurement is probably a composite psychologically, and differs in its component variables depending upon the area of production, whether it is in music, painting, science, writing, inventing, or politics, for example. Like the intellectual abilities, the areas of life within which creative performance shows itself make different demands upon individuals' psychological resources. Here, again, one must render unto Caesar.

KAORU YAMAMOTO

Validation of Tests of Creative Thinking: A Review of Some Studies

Abstract: A substantive review of some of the recent validation studies in the area of creative thinking suggested that (a) investigators have not come to an agreement as to the most meaningful and practical immediate criteria of creative thinking; (b) every one of the easily obtainable measures including school grades, supervisor and teacher ratings, peer nominations, production records, and psychiatric diagnosis, has shortcomings as a suitable criterion; and (c) more validation studies are urgently needed to establish both empirical and conceptual validities of the current instruments.

As is in any burgeoning fields of inquiry, recent studies in creative thinking have been beset by ambiguities in definitions, by difficulties in selection of criteria, and by scarcity of reliable and valid instruments of measurement (Yamamoto, 1964a). Criteria of creativity have received little, if any, consideration from investigators and validation studies are few. This paper attempts to review some of the criterial aspects of recent creativity research.

Criterion of Creative Thinking

The criterion problem is indeed a difficult one, and no easy consensus is to be expected from various authors. Wilson (1958), for one, has argued that creativity as a process should be inferred from the product. He also raised a point about the individual-social criterion dilemma in the studies of creativity. He stated: "Creativity in adults is usually evaluated in terms of

From *Exceptional Children*, February, 1965, pp. 281–290. Used by permission of the publisher.

a social criterion. The evaluation of the newness is usually based on the alternative of new to our society or at least new to the group doing the evaluation. In evaluating creativity in children it is more customary to adopt a psychological criterion in which major emphasis is placed on the newness of an idea or object to the individual who produced it. . . . In making a deliberate effort to develop creativity in children, it is generally *assumed* that activities which promote self-expression or doing things which have not been done before are likely to produce adults who will be regarded as creative" (1958, pp. 110–111). This assumption should be examined carefully in the future, but, meanwhile, the problem will keep bothering those who try to evaluate children's "products" for their creative quality.

McPherson (1963) proposed a multidimensional approach to the problem of criteria. He presented a scheme in which three sets of evaluations were collected on the same people: (a) ratings by judges (quick judgment), (b) a numerical count of products, and (c) a qualitative analysis of each product of each man. These three rankings were then subjected to an analysis to find the relationships among them. McPherson believed that an examination of the products of research workers was one of the best sources for ultimate criteria of creativity and suggested the concept of "inventivelevel" of products (employed originally in evaluation of patents) as a useful starting point. A product is said to rise to inventivelevel when it represents (a) creative strength in problem-solving with considerable prior experimentation, (b) overcoming of a history of failure, special difficulties, and/or general skepticism, and (c) technical and business usefulness, novelty, and pertinence. This notion of "inventivelevel" was extended into a measure of creative thinking ability by Torrance and his staff (Torrance, Palm, Palamutulu, & Radig, 1959).

The Criterion Committee of the 1955 University of Utah Research Conference on the Identification of Creative Scientific Talent arrived at a conceptual scheme (Harmon, 1956) in which a backward movement is made from some agreed upon ultimate criterion to some more immediate and feasible working criterion which can serve as an reasonably good substitute. The ultimate criterion is a measure of the indivdiual scientist's total creative scientific accomplishment, and the assessment is made by a panel of scientists for each field of specialization. Some intermediate, substitute criterion which correlates highly with the ultimate criterion is then defined. A wide representation of specialists in the panel and multiple judgments are to be expected to curtail individual and subcultural biases. Finally, a criterion must be developed which comes earliest in one's career, and so meets one of the most important practical requirements. This consists of judgment of performance, of behavior related to scientific activity. At about this point of the backward movement, criterion behavior fades into test behavior or predictors.

Creativity in Terms of Products

Ghiselin (1963), while recognizing advantages in using many substitute criteria together to offset whatever biases there are, insisted that the basic difficulty is that these intermediate criteria represent some form or refinement of human judgment ungoverned by ultimate criteria and, hence, their validity remains undetermined. He, therefore, tried to pinpoint once and for all what the epithet "creative" stands for in terms of products. According to Ghiselin, "a creative product is intrinsically a configuration of the mind, a presentation of constellated meaning, which at the time of its appearance in the mind was new in the sense of being unique, without specific precedent" (1963, p. 36). He emphasized the importance of the initial act as a creative product and agreed that this, and this alone, adds something to the structure of the mind and brings into being some spiritual increment. All repetitions of the association are no more than the use of that increment and, therefore, resourcefulness is not the same thing as creativity. The important thing is not originality in the sense of statistical rarity, which indicates only a degree of unusualness, but originality in the absolute sense of priority in the time of their introduction into the sphere of human thought. The question is not of what is unusual in a product of the mind, but of what is unique in the constitution of the product at the time of its production.

Ghiselin differentiated two modes or levels of creativity. The higher, primary sort of creative action alters the universe of meaning itself, by introducing into it some new element of meaning or some new order of significance, or both. Such actions then transcend existing order, and the mind moves independently of it. The lower, secondary sort of creative actions gives further development to an established body of meaning through initiating some advance in its use. Here the mind moves in dependence upon existing order, but moves more expansively than uncreative minds.

Ghiselin's point is well taken and his contention that the ultimate criterion of creativity should be the extent to which a creative product restructures our universe of understanding is a very stimulating one. It is true that, without some clearly defined ultimate standard against which intermediate criteria are checked and corrected, no meaningful progress can be achieved. It is, however, equally true that the final validation with an ultimate criterion is practically impossible unless we constantly define substitute criteria and conduct provisional validation studies with them. Whether a product really added some new meaning to our universe of understanding can only be decided retrospectively, and only when adequate and exhaustive data are available to judge its meaning at the point of its first introduction to the sphere of our understanding, and when numerous intermediate criteria convey this information on the impact of the product.

Evaluation of Creativity

The Criterion Committee of the 1957 University of Utah Research Conference of the Identification of Creative Scientific Talent (Lacklen & Harmon, 1958) gave favorable comments on both Ghiselin's and Lacklen's formulations that a measure of creativity of a contribution might be made in terms of the extent of the area of science which such a contribution underlies. The committee further presented a series of hypotheses. It should be noted here that the committee, after Ghiselin and Lacklen, defined a product in terms of an idea rather than a concrete object.

The hypotheses were: (a) a positive relationship between the level of creativity exhibited by an individual scientist and the amount of his creative productivity; (b) a positive relationship between the level of creativity of products and diversity of an individual's contributions; (c) the reliability of the creativity level of product scale over various fields of specialty and over various scorers; (d) a positive relationship between the Ghiselin-Lacklen measure and subjective judgment of creativity; (e) a possibility of construction of abbreviated but valid procedures to evaluate journal articles; (f) the usefulness of official records in evaluation of creativity; (g) a possibility to evaluate the leadership creativity through subordinates' productivity; and (h) a possibility to evaluate the teaching ability of a teacher through the products of his students.

The Criterion Committee of the 1959 University of Utah Research Conference on the Identification of Creative Scientific Talent (Sprecher, 1959) extended the trend toward a clearer operational definition of criteria and evaluation of creativity. After having presented an outline of variables and dimensions potentially involved in criteria of creativity, the committee adopted several suggestions for future research. These were: (a) products of creative behavior to be the first object of study; (b) the necessity to rely, at present, on the professional judgment of contemporaries; (c) the selection of a criterion group to be primarily in terms of products or contributions and not in terms of characteristics or individuals; (d) two primary bases of evaluation to be the "novelty" (in social sense) and the "breadth of applicability" (generation of additional creative activities); and (e) the heaviest, if not exclusive, weight to be placed on each individual's best contribution.

In all of the foregoing papers, the society is more or less regarded as a receiving end of the creative impact. In reality, however, the society not only receives what creative individuals offer but also gives back important means and resources to these people. If we are interested in the identification and cultivation of talent in our society, such interactions between environment and individual had better be taken into consideration. In discussing the criterion problem of creativity, it seems insufficient to depend solely upon products, because some undesirable environmental variables might be inflicting some inequity upon those potentially creative but unlucky individuals whose products would thus never be considered for their impact upon the society and upon the universe of understanding. Evaluation of products is necessary so far as we regard our society as a passive recipient of benefits, but it is not sufficient from the society's standpoint as an active provider for the tomorrow.

In this connection, Stein's paper (1959) is thought provoking. He pointed out that prediction of creativity involves two basic problems: (a) a better understanding of the psychological criteria of creativity, and (b) a better understanding of the environment. He argued that the more we learn about an individual, his environment, and their interrelationships, the closer we will come to solving the prediction problem, because creative behavior, as all other forms of human behavior, is a function of the trans-actional relationships between the individual and his environment. He then mentioned various subtle problems involved in our consideration, including the typologies of creative individuals, styles of creativity, and variations in psychological factors in different areas of creativity, and those involved in our consideration of environmental factors. These would include the environmental characteristics necessary for a new breakthrough and for maintenance and expansion of the field thereafter, value system of the environment, characteristics of organization of institutional framework, and the relationship between the period of prediction and the period of validation.

Empirical Validation Studies:
School Grades as a Criterion

Empirical studies on criterion and/or predictor validation are not large in number at the moment nor are they very sophisticated in technique. Without claiming any comprehensiveness nor representativeness, some of these studies are summarized herein.

Various intermediate criteria have been employed in validation studies, one of them being the school grade. For example, Guilford (1956a) presented some results of his factor analytic validation studies with course grades as criteria. The course grades were chosen not because of any belief that they reflected creative performance, but largely because they were readily available. A University of Washington study (Lower Division, N = 91 to 894), U.S. Coast Guard Academy studies (1957 freshman, N = 110; 1958 freshman, N = 116), John Hills' study in three Los Angeles institutions of higher learning (N = 10 to 83), and Lockheed Aircraft Corporation studies (aircraft engineers, N = 52 to 65; operations analysts, N = 19 to 20) gave quite variable validity coefficients for each of the numerous Guilford factors such as originality, ideational fluency, logical evaluation, and verbal comprehension. The highest coefficient reached .60 but, on the average, coefficients were the size of .20–.30 even when they were significant. When multiple correlation coefficients were computed, it was found that a composite of factor score tests gave better prediction (R = .40, approximately) than did achievement tests (R = .20 to .40). When a composite of these two kinds of tests was used, the result was better (R = .40 to .50). The observed variability of validity coefficients, varying from institution to institution, curriculum to curriculum, and criterion to criterion, could, at least partially, be attributed to differences in policies and practices in teaching, examining, marking, and other sampling error sources.

Jex (1963) reported a negative correlation of −.09 between the first-quarter grade point averages of 52 entering freshman students at the University of Utah and their performance on a revised version of Flanagan's Ingenuity Test.

Supervisory Ratings: A Criterion
in Validation Studies

In the same paper, Jex (1963) also reported negative correlations between scores on two ingenuity tests and supervisor ratings. Of 54 teachers participating in a mathematics-science institute at the University of Utah, average principal-supervisor ratings gave a correlation of −.19 with their performance on the revised Flanagan Ingenuity Test and one of −.25 with their average achievement on a Cooperative battery of achievement tests in the mathematics-science area.

In the course of the institute, one of the participants constructed another ingenuity test consisting of eight items, correlating .20 with the revised Flanagan. When the 54 teachers' performances on this test were correlated with supervisor ratings, it was found that seven out of the eight items gave negative coefficients (−.07 to −.37). When the test results were correlated with each of the ten components of the average principal-supervisor ratings (all-around ability and effectiveness, enthusiasm and interest, knowledge of subject matter, and the like), all ten correlated negatively (−.01 to −.43), eight of these were statistically significant. The largest negative correlation (−.43) was with a personality criterion. It was thus suggested by Jex that the ability to score high on ingenuity might be somewhat antagonistic to whatever is involved in high ratings of teachers by their principals or supervisors. He wondered whether ingenuity is more apt to be penalized than rewarded in formal academic programs. No discussion was presented, however, on the reliability of these ingenuity tests themselves.

Harmon (1963) reported an analysis of supervisor (expert) judgment in the selection process of the National Science Foundation Fellowship Program. A mail follow-up of the candidates in this program in 1949 yielded data on 504 scientists, 347 in physical sciences and 157 in biological sciences. These questionnaires were then subjected to expert judgment and, at the same time, various objective reference variables (number of publications, income, and the like) were extracted from the questionnaires to be correlated with the judgmental ratings. The results showed that the heaviest rating weight was given to publications, the correlation between ratings and publication criteria being .61 for the physical scientists, and .76 for the biological scientists. When multiple correlation coefficients were computed for predicting the rating criterion from publications, income, and supervisory level, the values were .65 in physical sciences and .78 in biological sciences. Validities of the predictors (verbal test, quantitative test, advanced achievement test, undergraduate science grade point average, confidential reports, graphic and descriptive ratings) against the ratings on achievement as of 1955–56 were quite low (r ranging from $-.32$ to $-.27$, most of them negligible).

Harris (1960) constructed two forms (20 items each) of a test of creativity in engineering and three scores, flexibility (number of different response categories), originality (derived by weighting different categories of the flexibility score), and fluency (number of different responses) were derived from questions on mechanical parts and geometric forms. When these two forms were administered to two groups of engineers (N = 33 and 29) at a large automotive accessories manufacturing company, correlation coefficients (ranging from .10 to .57) were obtained between these scores and rankings by three supervisors. It was concluded that the test had significant concurrent validity. Internal consistency by Spearman-Brown formula gave coefficients of .80–.93, while interscorer agreement between two independent judges ranged from .87 to 1.00 on those three scores.

The creativity scores correlated .28–.63 with the AC Test of Creative Ability developed by Harris earlier, but correlations were negligible with the Wonderlic Personnel Test and with the Bennett Mechanical Comprehension Test. The test had a reasonable face validity when tested by a question, "Do you think that the test you have just taken can measure creativity in engineering?" It was found with the Harris test, unfortunately, that the flexibility score is correlated .95 with the originality score and, hence, there is little value in the extra effort required to obtain the originality score. The fluency score was correlated .56 with the flexibility score and .49 with the originality score.

Taylor (1958b) also used supervisor ratings to examine the relationship of scientists' undergraduate grades to success in research. At an engineering research center, he gathered both grade point averages (GPA's) and supervisor ratings for 239 research scientists. If a GPA was predictive of future success as a research scientist, fairly large differences would be expected in mean GPA's of the top, second, and third groups on the merit rating. This, however, was not the case (mean GPA's 2.73, 2.60, 2.69, respectively). Further, if college grades were predictive of research success, the GPA of the 239 successful scientists would be substantially higher than that of the graduating engineering class used as a control. This again was not the case (mean GPA's, 2.66 for scientists and 2.68 for students). It was, therefore, concluded that there is no relationship between GPA and merit rating, and that the GPA should be given preferably no weight in selecting engineers for the type of research carried out at this particular center.

Taylor and his colleagues reported another study (Taylor, Smith, & Ghiselin, 1963) in which nearly 150 scores were obtained on 166 scientists. After numerous small studies, 52 of these 150 were retained for a major criterion study. The criteria included immediate supervisor ratings, laboratory chief ratings, peer ratings, official records, reports and publications, professional membership, project researcher ratings, and self-ratings. The correlation coefficients among scores from supervisor ratings, peer ratings, and laboratory chief ratings were usually low, though often significant (no figures are given). The coefficients between scores subjectively obtained and those obtained from objective records were generally negligible. Scores either from supervisors or from peers generally correlated zero with scores on research reports or publications. The control variables such as age, education, and experience were generally quite independent from the criterion scores.

As a result, two very important observations were made. The first was that the data on contributions of scientists tend to be relatively independent when obtained from different sources. The second was that, although the typical correlation is low, the range of correlations often varies widely between different pairs of scores from any two sources of information.

Teacher Nominations: A Criterion in Validation Studies

In educational institutions, teacher ratings or teacher nominations take the place of supervisor ratings. Drevdahl (1954) studied 65 volunteers from among advanced undergraduate and graduate students in the various science and arts departments at the University of Nebraska. Several of Guilford's creativity factor tests, Thurstone's Primary Mental Abilities Test, and Cattell's Sixteen Personality Factor Questionnaire were administered to these students. Two groups were identified on the basis of teacher ratings, and they were compared with each other on various variables measured by the objective tests. The results showed, among other things, that the creative group was superior to the noncreative group in their verbal fluency, flexibility, and originality. This, then, was interpreted as an indirect validation of the creativity tests involved.

A similar differentiation was obtained by Torrance and his colleagues (Torrance, DeYoung, Ghei, & Michie, 1958) in their study of 157 graduate students enrolled in a course of mental hygiene at the University of Minnesota. Three judges independently rated projects in which the students had been asked to develop original ideas, theories, or hypotheses concerning personality development. The High Creative and Low Creative groups each had thirty-six projects represented. When these two groups were compared on various measures of personality and achievement, it was found, among other things, that the High Creativity group scored significantly higher on the Creativity scale of the Personal Attitude Inventory developed by Torrance (a 107-item questionnaire on which the subject marks each item true or false with reference to himself). On Criticalness, it was seen that strongly critical tendencies interfered with the development of creative ideas. In addition, it was found that the scores on the Miller Analogies tests differentiated the two groups (the High Creative higher than the Low Creative), while scores on the Cooperative English and Cooperative Mathematics tests did not.

Getzels and Jackson (1962) also used teacher nominations as a part of their study of 449 high-school students in which it was shown that the High Creative group, in spite of a mean difference of 23 less IQ points, did as well on standardized achievement tests as did the High Intelligent group. Ratings by teachers of these subjects clearly showed that the High IQ group stood out as being more "desirable" than the average students, while the High Creative group did not. Even though their academic performance was equal, the High Intelligent students were preferred to the High Creative ones.

Torrance (1959a) replicated the Getzels-Jackson study at the elementary level and found essentially the same results. In rankings by teachers, the clearest difference occurred in relation to the greater desirability of the highly intelligent group as pupils. Teachers stated that they knew the highly intelligent pupils better than they knew the highly creative pupils.

The foregoing two studies raised some question about the validity of ratings by teachers of their students. Holland (1959) studied limitations of teacher ratings as predictors of creativity, using 783 boys and 394 girls randomly chosen out of 7,500 high-school students who were the finalists in the 1958 National Merit Scholarship program. These 1,177 subjects were administered Cattell's Sixteen Personality Factor Questionnaire, the National Merit Student Survey, and Holland's Vocational Preference Inventory. Teachers and principals, independently of these measures, filled out part of an extensive information blank including 12 graphic rating scales for each student. When intercorrelations of the rating scales were obtained, it was clear that the ratings were closely related (average r, .64 for boys and .59 for girls) despite the diversity of the personal qualities rated. The high intercorrelations suggested that there was a strong halo effect working. As a result, Holland chose one scale which correlated highest with the remaining 11 scales as the most representative rating.

High and low ratings on this scale, Maturity, were then correlated with scores on the various measures mentioned. It was observed that the student rated high by his teachers appeared to be a bright, persistent, conscientious academic achiever and student leader. His personal adjustment was characterized by self-control, sense of security, and freedom from anxiety. As a whole, teacher ratings were potentially more useful as predictors of academic achievement and leadership potential rather than as predictors of creativity. Therefore, opined Holland, only a limited reliance on teacher ratings as predictors of creativity appears desirable.

Nevertheless, in actual studies of creative thinking, ratings by informed teachers who have been given enough time to get acquainted with their children would seem to be able to distinguish the creative pupils from the less creative ones when asked to nominate them on specific criteria such as "coming up with most ideas" (fluency), "finding a new way of meeting problems" (flexibility), and "best at thinking of all the details" (elaboration). Thus, Yamamoto (1963) reported that, among 461 fifth-grade children, those nominated by teachers obtained a significantly (at the .05 level) higher mean than nonnominated ones on fluency, flexibility, originality, and total creativity scores on a pencil and paper battery, and almost significantly (p < .10) higher mean on elaboration. In this group of 461 children, incidentally, the correlation coefficient between IQ and total creativity score was .14.

In still another study, not yet published, the author replicated this finding among 825 fifth-grade children whose IQ's correlated .22 with total creativity scores. In this study, teachers nominated those both "high" and "low" on separate criteria of creative thinking (fluency, flexibility, adequacy, originality, elaboration) and the mean scores on a pencil and paper battery of tests of creative thinking for the three resultant groups, Nominated-as-High, Nonnominated, and Nominated-as-Low, were compared. Without exception, the means were different among themselves to a statistically significant extent (p < .001) and to the expected direction.

Peer Nominations: A Criterion
in Validation Studies

Peer nominations are another source of information which could be used as a criterion of creativity. Torrance (1959a) administered a six-item peer nomination questionnaire to 150 subjects, 25 in each grade from the first through sixth. These items were: (a) Who are your best friends in your room? (b) Who does the most talking? (c) Who thinks of the most good ideas? (d) Who thinks up the most ideas for being naughty? (e) Who thinks of the most silly, wild, or fantastic ideas? and (f) Who doesn't speak up their ideas? When the High Creativity group (top 20 percent on the Minnesota creativity battery, but not in the top 20 percent on IQ) was compared with the High IQ group (top 20 percent on the Wechsler Intelligence Scale for Children but not in the top 20 percent on creativity), there were no differences between these two groups in received nominations except for a significant difference in relation to the superiority of the High IQ group on the "best friends" criterion.

The same set of peer nominations was administered by the same author, Torrance (1959b), to 485 children from grades one through six. Three groups, (a) a highly talkative group, (b) a nontalkative group receiving no nominations as "most talkative," and (c) a nontalkative group perceived as "not speaking out" their ideas, were identified and compared on various measures (Minnesota battery) of creative thinking, nonverbal intelligence and ideation, and psychological accessibility. In the first grade, those perceived as "not speaking out" their ideas tended to be more frequently perceived as having good ideas, more frequently chosen as friends, higher on a measure of spontaneous flexibility, more intelligent, and higher on a nonverbal measure of creativity. This pattern seemed to shift gradually from the second grade up and, by the fourth grade, the highly talkative group established their influence rather firmly. They were more frequently perceived as having good ideas and received friendship choices. This tendency persisted through the sixth grade but, at this level, the highly talkative individuals were no more creative than the nontalkative group receiving no nominations as "most talkative." On the other hand, the child who was seen as "not speaking out his ideas" had become increasingly more neglected by his peers and became less creative and less accessible. At all grade levels, the most talkative group was perceived more frequently than either of the other two groups as having a lot of ideas for being naughty and a lot of wild and silly ideas.

Yamamoto (1964c) administered the Minnesota battery of tests of creative thinking and a sociometric test to 428 high school students in the seventh through twelfth grades. According to the scores on the creativity tests, subjects were divided into three groups—High Creativity, Middle Creativity, and Low Creativity. The sociometric tests consisted of six items: (a) Who in this group (your class) comes up with the most ideas? (b) Who has the most original or unusual ideas? (c) If the situation changed or if a solution to a problem would not work, who in your group would be the first to find a new way of meeting the problem? (d) Who in your group does the most inventing and developing of new ideas, gadgets, and the like? (e) Who in the group are best at thinking of all the details involved in working out a new idea and thinking of all of the consequences? and (f) Who are your best friends in the group? The results, on the whole, showed that at the junior-high level, the peer nominations tended to support the groupings based on the creativity tests but, at the senior-high level, the same was true only for boys and not for girls.

When the fluency, flexibility, and inventive-level scores on the battery were further correlated with the nomination scores from, respectively, the first, third, and fourth questions, correlation coefficients ranging from $-.18$ to $.65$ were obtained (Yamamoto, 1964b). Marked variations from measure to measure and grade to grade were observed, although sex differences were not significant. For the entire group, the correlations were .24 (Fluency), .22 (Flexibility), and .15 (Inventivelevel).

Performance Record and Psychiatric Diagnoses: Criteria in Validation Studies

Wallace (1961), in an interesting study of 61 elderly saleswomen in a department store, used their sales production in terms of the dollar value of sales per hour of employment as a criterion. High sales producers were identified as belonging in the top third in sales production within their departments; low sales producers were in the bottom third. In addition, those departments requiring creative customer service were differentiated on the basis of the personnel director's judgment from those not requiring creative customer service. Together with the distinction in terms of production, this resulted in a 2 (production level) by 2 (creative service) classification. These groups were then compared on their performance on the Minnesota battery of creativity tests. It was found that high sales producers scored significantly higher than low sales producers and that those in creative customer service departments scored significantly higher than those in less creative customer service departments. No interaction was detected between these two dimensions.

Interesting features of this study were (a) that even in the departments where little customer service was required, the creative thinking ability of the saleswomen seemed to affect sales production to a significant degree and (b) that the creativity of the low sales producers in creative departments was almost the same as those who were high sales producers in noncreative departments. Seemingly, the supervisor ratings of required creative ability were not as sharp as the creative battery in differentiating adequate personnel to be distributed among various departments.

The final study reviewed herein is the one by Hebeisen (1959) on a group of hospitalized schizophrenic patients. She compared the performance of 68 schizophrenic (majority of them being paranoid) patients of ages under 45 in a Minnesota State Hospital with that of 100 normal college freshmen on the Minnesota battery of creativity tests. As a whole, the sample group of schizophrenic subjects revealed a marked impoverishment of imagination or creative thinking. Differences in quality appeared to be even greater than differences in quantity or fluency. Schizophrenic patients gave fewer responses (less than two-thirds of the normal students), more irrelevant responses (30 percent compared to only three percent in the normal population), more inflexible responses (more than twice those of normal), and showed more blocking. The creativity tests seemed to be tapping some very important function of the mind which is characteristically impaired in schizophrenics.

Summary

It is obvious that some evidence could be gleaned from here and there for the validity of various measures of creative thinking but also that well-planned, straight-forward validation studies are badly needed to attain a stronger foothold for further progress. For the moment, we cannot afford to be too particular about what specific intermediate criteria to use. The major task would appear to be in gathering as much dependable information about as many carefully defined criteria as possible.

Even when some external criteria such as school grades, number of publications, and amount of production, are used, additional qualitative analysis is recommended. Evidently, we cannot totally exclude some subjective evaluation at this stage of the development and, therefore, it seems quite necessary to check back and forth among various means of evaluation.

In the case of ratings by supervisors and/or teachers, more attention should be given to the definition of what to be looked for and evaluated. Unless dimensions of creativity are clearly formulated and meticulously defined so as to avoid personal interpretations and biases, judgment tends to be overshadowed by traditional consideration of the "brightness" in terms of intelligence, of the "good personality" in terms of interpersonal relations, and even of "active participation" stemming from some defensive attitudes. Peer nominations have more or less the same weak points as those of supervisor and teacher ratings. Therefore, some concurrent ratings by experienced and trained observers who belong to the third party had better be obtained to check dependability of teacher, supervisor, or peer ratings. Until it becomes clear that judges are, in fact, rating the same traits using the same frame of reference, subjective ratings should not be used exclusively as adequate intermediate criteria. Multicriterion approach seems to be the logical one to be adopted.

In many studies, reliabilities of instruments are more or less assumed when their validities are examined. It would seem obvious that satisfactory validities are not obtainable until and unless stable and consistent measures are first developed. Intercorrelations between creativity measures and other more traditional measures of aptitudes, achievement, interests, values, beliefs, and personality, including both the pencil and paper and miniature situation varieties, should also be studied intensively to provide a larger and tighter nomological net around this concept of creative thinking. Last but not least, longitudinal inquiries must be undertaken, both to examine the adequacy of various intermediate criteria against the ultimate criterion of one kind or another, and also to study the relevance of numerous implicit assumptions involved in measurement of creativity, especially among children and adolescents.

TAHER A. RAZIK

Psychometric Measurement of Creativity

When one considers the developments of recent years in the study of creativity, one can see that grounds are gradually being laid for progress in the development of educational programs for creativity. Thus far, the major effort has had to go into reconceiving the nature, nurture, and measurement of creativity. Major conceptual blocks have stood in the way.

One block has been the culturally inherited conception of creativity as being that property of the genius which mysteriously accounts for his uncommon ability and which, by definition, the common man cannot understand or possess. Assumably, genius is where one finds it; creativity is where one finds it, and little can be done through education to affect it.

This conception was common in America, even through the nineteen-thirties when Progressive Education was a fairly widespread movement and focused attention on creative qualities in children. When teachers and parents observed that young children were naturally curious, exploratory, experimental, and capable of fresh responses to their world, and the term "creative" was often used to summarize such observations, the connection was not made between such behaviors in children and those of a similar nature in adults of genius caliber. The child's world and the world of the genius were taken as worlds apart.

Both were assumed to be something granted by nature, much like the weather, and about which one could comment, but actually do little. Against this prevailing view, the Progressive Education Movement was discounted as romantic, sentimental, and soft. In the struggle of World War II, creativity was forgotten.

In the postwar world, the subject came into prominence again, this time with a new orientation. The atomic bomb, closing the war, dramatized the power which science and technology had gained in setting new conditions for the further existence and development of men. Progress had gone so far in harnessing the powers of nature that man was clearly seen to be

301

arranging for his own fate by the creative work of his own hands. Genius might account for the basic ideas on which new developments were possible, but thousands of men were involved in the further innovations necessary to deliver that power as it reached the people.

The atomic bomb had been created by a massive effort of many men, and the whole fabric of modern life was, in fact, being drastically altered by extensive efforts of organized institutions of government and industry. Sputnik catalyzed the realization for Americans that further life and development would depend on having many creative men at work in a constant effort to transcend what had already been done with accomplishments still more novel and powerful. However creative our scientists and engineers had been previous to Sputnik, they would need to be more creative in the future; their numbers would have to be greatly increased. Ways would have to be found to identify such people, to support them, and to cultivate them. Young men showing the capability of being creative would need to be recruited.

In the presence of the Russian threat, "creativity" could no longer be left to the chance occurrence of the genius; neither could it be left in the realm of the wholly mysterious and the untouchable. Men *had* to be able to do something about it; creativity *had* to be a property in many men; it *had* to be something identifiable; it *had* to be subject to the effects of efforts to gain more of it. Through necessity, the basic concept of creativity thus changed from something heretofore soft and sentimental to something hard and realistic, closely connected with hardware and survival, as are the machines of war and industrial production. Research on creativity became legitimized as a properly serious concern of the military, government, and industry.

As work progressed in defining and identifying aspects of creative behavior in adults, the words and conceptions coming to be used could be recognized by educators as those commonly used to characterize the behavior of young children. The similarity was too obvious to be missed and, this time, there was need to see the connection. If children came endowed with creative capacities, then the role of education, in serving the national need, would be to recognize these capacities, and to develop them through the students' growing years into adulthood. In this way, cultivating creativity might be possible to provide for the vast numbers of people needed in the creative developments of the future. This could now be the vision of those educators who wanted to see education in this new role.

In a few years, the climate of public opinion thus changed with respect to creativity so that it could now be seen as a potential property of all men, potentially identifiable and subject to nurture through suitable education. Arriving here, however, there was another conceptual block standing in the way of educators who wanted to see education take on its new role as cultivator of creativity in the masses of students. This blockage centered, ultimately, in the measurements which educators used to guide their efforts.

What finally controls an institution are the values it holds for itself and the means which are used to determine whether or not the values are being attained through the efforts of the institution. This boils down, in the concrete world, to the specification of observables which denote the values desired and the degree of their achievement. This means, in baldest terms, the measurements which are used, for it is measurement which supplies the concrete specifications of the behaviors desired and also the means by which to judge their attainment. Schools are controlled, finally, by the measures they want to make, can make, and do, in fact, make.

The basic measurements on which schools have come to depend are not measurements which include the new dimensions of creativity. These basic measures are those provided by the intelligence tests and the achievement tests, the former to judge the capacity of students for schoolwork and the latter to judge the progress students make on their way through the school program.

These tests have been developed in an era when the main focus of educators has been on the formation of the school as a social system. In the need to get our society organized into consistent institutional forms, the efforts of educators have been centered on organizing the school as a working, social assemblage. The development of the child has been less important than the development of a smoothly operating social mechanism. Narrow definitions of targets were helpful in such a situation. Intelligence came to be operationally defined as what the intelligence tests measure, these tests being largely validated on school success. Achievement tests came to be defined as what students could do on tasks set for them by the school system—tasks for which there were single, predetermined, and "right" answers.

Both intelligence and achievement tests have thus been tied to the narrow limits of those abilities which the school establishment values for its operation as a given social system. Divergent and creative responses and abilities not fitting to the school norm have not been measured, operationally valued, nor rewarded in systematic ways. The development of the student as a growing creative creature has been neglected.

Educators who have wanted to promote education for creativity have, therefore, come face to face with a formidable problem. Traditional measurements are deeply rooted in school practice, as are the narrow concepts on which they are based. New measures and concepts, sufficiently strong to compete with the old, are required. Tests are needed which include the new dimensions and which are pragmatically useful to classroom teachers in spotting creative behaviors in students and in judging the progress of students (and hence the effectiveness of the teaching) in the development of creative abilities. Apart from the creation of such measures, it is highly improbable that any general progress can be made in reordering education so that it serves the needs of the nation in cultivating the creativity of its general population.

Understandably, progress at this basic level has been slow. Nevertheless, progress has been made in some of the most essential matters. The following serves to highlight some of the major accomplishments to date.

J. P. Guilford (1950), who opened the present era of research on creativity with his 1950 presidential address to the American Psychological Association, has effectively redefined intelligence so as to include creative behaviors. In seventeen years of consistent and cumulative effort since that date, he has evolved a battery of tests which operationally specify dimensions of intelligence that go far beyond what traditional tests of intelligence have included. Using factor analysis, he has isolated 120 separate, measurable abilities. Present intelligence tests measure six to eight of these abilities. By 1962 Guilford (Taylor, 1963) was able to operationally specify 61 of the total 120.

Especially useful in clarifying creativity has been the distinction Guilford has made between abilities for divergent thinking and abilities for convergent thinking. Divergent thinking moves away, as it were, from responses already known and expected. Convergent thinking moves toward responses that fit to the known and the specified. The experimental tests used to measure creativity emphasize divergent thinking—originality, fluency of ideas, flexibility, sensitivity to defects and missing elements, and the ability to elaborate and redefine. Traditional measures of intelligence emphasize convergent thinking—logical reasoning toward single, "right" answers. Measures of creativity call for new ideas, an original or unconventional response, and breaking away from the beaten path.

Supported largely by Air Force grants and focusing on adults in military establishments, Guilford has demonstrated that concern for creativity in the national interest is a hard core concern that can be productively pursued. Having opened the field to the adult world, he has also opened the field to the world of children and youth, since his tests and his concepts are and have been directly usable by educators in devising further tests for use in school situations. His work has been the fountainhead for the work of many others, and his concepts, operationally displayed in the tests he provides, now make it quite impossible for educators or others to assume that they have measured intelligence when they have used traditional intelligence tests alone.

J. W. Getzels and P. W. Jackson, in their study of creative adolescents at the University of Chicago Laboratory School (1962), have directly assaulted the bastions of complacency in school practice by bringing into plain view the operational consequences of judging students on the basis of intelligence tests alone. Benefiting from Guilford's breakthrough and devising tests for creativity, they contrasted the abilities of students who scored high on IQ (but not on creativity) with students who scored high on creativity (but not on IQ). They were able to show that the cream of the student crop in creativity would have been missed if traditional measures of intelligence had alone been used to reveal the "able students." Creative students have something else and something more than the intelligence tests show. Sizable porportions of students have these abilities, but can go undetected, if reliance is placed on the traditional tests alone.

Getzels and Jackson (1962) also showed that it is not only the intelligence tests that are biased against the highly creative child, but also the teachers. When asked to rate students on the degree to which they would like to have them in class, teachers clearly preferred the high-IQ over the highly creative pupil, and this in spite of the fact that, in this particular study, the high-IQ students and the highly creative students were equally superior to other students in school achievement. The study also showed that the high-IQ child tends to hold a self-image consistent with what he feels the teacher would approve, seeking to conform to the projected values of the teacher; the creative pupil, on the other hand, tends to hold to a self-image consistent with his own projected values, often not conforming to the teacher's values. He considers high marks and goals that projectively lead to adult success in life less important than does a member of the high-IQ group. He has a much greater interest in unconventional careers than his less creative peers.

Much of what Getzels and Jackson discovered has been subsequently confirmed; some has been modified. Educational circles have finally realized that reliance cannot be placed on testing as usual and teaching as usual, if creativity is to be valued in education. What Guilford showed to be intellectually wrong in conceiving of intelligence in narrow terms, Getzels and Jackson showed to be also educationally wrong. The usual practices in school not only neglect creativity; they damage it.

Knowing the negative effects of the traditional with respect to creativity is not enough to produce the positive programs that are needed. Extensive pioneering work needs to be done to lay out the lines along which the new, and the more encompassing, can be built. Guilford, Getzels, and Jackson had necessarily opened the positive to illuminate the negative, but it remained to E. Paul Torrance to carry the direct and visible attack significantly into the positive domain in educational practice.

Through extensive work done at the University of Minnesota, Torrance created measures and methods that are usable by teachers in classroom settings. His aim has been to serve the profession as widely as possible by giving to classroom teachers in the public schools the tools they need to be able to cultivate creativity in children through their daily teaching practices. Beginning his work with studies which confirmed and built from the contributions of Guilford, Getzels, and Jackson, he constructed tests of creativity usable at several levels of education, but focused mainly on the elementary school. Involved in field contacts, workshops, and training programs for teachers, he developed programs both for classroom teaching and for teacher training.

Whereas Getzels and Jackson had done their research on students in the upper range of the IQ scale and in a university laboratory school, Torrance worked with children of various levels of ability and in the public schools. Getzels and Jackson had demonstrated some correlation between IQ and creativity scores up to a certain level of IQ, but had found no correlation beyond that point. Torrance, in comparable studies (1962a), confirmed the finding and also discovered that above a 120 IQ there was no correlation between IQ and creativity. Torrance estimates that we miss about 70 percent of our more creative youth when we depend solely on IQ tests to measure ability. Some type of creative talent may be found all along the "normal" IQ range, even in children in the below-average group.

Confirming Getzels and Jackson on the attitudes of teachers toward the high-IQ student as compared to the high-creative, Torrance (1963d) also found that teachers rate the high-IQ students as more desirable students, more ambitious and hardworking, less unruly, and more friendly. A study, using sixty-two characteristics as measuring factors, was made by Torrance (1963c) to obtain teachers' concepts of the ideal pupil. The study indicated that the teachers had a great deal of ambivalence toward the kind of pupil who could be described as highly creative. Among the sixty-two characteristics, the teachers rated independence in thinking second, independence in judgment nineteenth, and courage twenty-ninth. It was far more important to teachers that children be courteous than that they be courageous. It was also more important that children do their work on time, be industrious, be obedient, be popular among their peers, and have other traits of this kind than that they be courageous. Because of a limited concept of giftedness and an emphasis on academic prowess, it is quite natural that the child who answers questions correctly, produces what he is told, and knows what the textbook says, is considered by teachers to be superior. The creative child often fails to fit this model.

Torrance's tests (1962c) have no single, predetermined "right" answers; several answers are possible, and, usually, the more (and the more unique) the better. Complex tasks are called for: for example, the Product Improvement Test calls for novel ideas for improving objects such as children's toys. Generally, during the test the objects are available for the child's manipulation. The Ask-and-Guess Test calls for questions and hypotheses about causes and results related to a picture. The Just Suppose Test presents improbable situations accompanied by drawings and requires imaginative solutions. To get the most information from a minimum of testing time, the measures have been constructed to allow responses to be scored for more than one dimension of creativity.

Substantial as the beginnings have been, Torrance regards these tests as *only* a beginning. How many tasks, of what length, of what variety of stimuli, how modified for diverse ages and cultural backgrounds, how scored, etc.—these are continuing and pressing problems if educators, generally, are to have what they need for identifying and developing creative behaviors in their daily teaching. But, without question, educators can now concretely sense the positive meanings of creative measurements.

Torrance has assembled and presented ample illustrations. Directions for progress are indicated. Teachers can take hold of the testing task at their levels of operation; the problem now focuses on helping teachers develop the conceptions and the skills which enable them to teach effectively for the kind of behaviors the tests test. Much help is needed if teachers throughout the country are to get what they need for effectively influencing masses of students.

The citadels for primary help in educating and reeducating teachers for creative education are the universities and the upper echelons of the teaching profession. Here, the requirements for granting help are that creativity be thoroughly understood and appreciated. The intellectuals want intellectual grounding for what they do. This calls for research in depth and an integral understanding of the phenomenon of the creative human being.

Donald W. MacKinnon and Frank Barron of the Institute for Personality Assessment, University of California at Berkeley, undertook extensive studies (Brown, 1962; New York State Education, 1963) focused on the personality structure and experience pattern of highly creative adults who had become valuable creative producers for society. Outstanding creative architects, writers, and scientists were given intensive testing. A wide variety of tests, test situations, depth interviews and observations were used. "Intelligence," as measured by IQ, and formal education were but a few of many considerations. The basic question studied was "What factors contribute to creativity?" Psychoanalytic, psychological, and humanistic frames of reference were used in interpreting the data.

In accord with the findings of Getzels and Jackson, and Torrance, MacKinnon and Barron found no simple relation between IQ and creativity. (Most of their subjects were above the "breaking point" of relationship, i.e., 120 IQ.) On school grades, MacKinnon and Barron's data showed that the creative person rarely was a straight-A student; averages on grades ranged around B for the architects, and somewhere between C and B for research scientists. Many of the subjects had grades that would not admit them to graduate study today.

MacKinnon and Barron's subjects were men who had had their education in a period when admission requirements and grading standards were less stringent, and insistence on institutionalized education as a prerequisite to responsible positions was less emphasized than it is today. Complexity of knowledge and rapidity of change now require more years of preparation, and educational institutions now get a tighter and tighter hold on the channels of opportunity. The inference of MacKinnon and Barron's findings is inescapable—that our present identification methods may be keeping many of our potentially creative producers out of colleges and graduate schools, and, among those admitted, grading practices may well be failing or discouraging many so that, though admitted, they do not graduate.

The measurements used in higher education to identify and evaluate students would appear to be as misleading and damaging to creative development as Getzels and Jackson, and Torrance, found them to be at elementary and secondary levels of education. The studies of MacKinnon and Barron make this clear for educators to see; reform is needed throughout the whole range of institutionalized education.

MacKinnon and Barron's studies also make clear the complexity of the task. The creative person is a many faceted creature who is difficult to serve through preset systems. Such persons are original, independent, self-assertive, imaginative, and sensitive. Their needs can be served only through practices that value, focus on, and flexibly modify to honor their individual uniqueness. Professors who help them must be persons who can listen as well as talk, who enjoy being challenged as well as to challenge, who gain joy in life from the new structures of thought that form in their students' minds, as well as from new structures that form in their own minds.

Much opportunity needs be allowed for student expression. The curriculum can only be a tentative approximation for what, in fact, is required as students become engaged in it. The heart of the system can only be the active communication of creative minds that resonate to one another's needs and challenges. Creative learning requires creative teaching, and there is no substitute or shortcut.

MacKinnon and Barron's studies do not amplify these points, but their findings make such points clear to those educators who are looking for the inferences. Creative practices are needed in all areas of university life. Certainly they are needed in those areas responsible for the education and reeducation of teachers in the public schools. Here, in the universities and the upper echelons of educational leadership, lies the staging area for any further significant advances in evolving the people needed for contemporary life.

Obviously, education in the universities, or elsewhere, is not going to develop in significant proportions apart from the interlocked efforts of many men, supplying strength from many different directions. A vehicle is needed to invite cooperation, sharing of perspectives, research findings, and resources.

One such vehicle of central importance has been the series of conferences organized by Calvin W. Taylor of the University of Utah. Five of these conferences (1955, 1957, 1959, 1961, 1962) were focused primarily on problems connected with identifying creative talent for the sciences and were supported by the National Science Foundation. The sixth (1964) was focused on the use of educational media as a means for creative education and was supported by the U.S. Office of Education. Seeking empirical and operational grounds on which to research creativity, these conferences (and publications from them) have established the researchability of the subject. They have effectively moved conceptions of creativity from vague abstractions to concrete referents which are visibly significant for guiding action in the selection and cultivation of creative personnel.

Oriented chiefly to needs for creative personnel at the upper echelons, i.e., in science, these concrete referents have, nevertheless, led naturally and easily to the connected concern for creativity in the education of youth. Designed primarily for research men, they serve the interests of university men who want an intellectual and research base for what they do. Educators at the university level who want to develop educational programs to cultivate creativity in their students may now do so, knowing that they have a substantial base from which to build.

Gradually, then, the groundwork is being laid for significant advances in the development of creative education. Unmentioned have been many notable conferences, agencies, and programs, and many research contributions which should surely be included if we were attempting a broad survey. The purpose, however, has been to sketch a perspective of what has been accomplished to date by citing the most evident developments and the core of need which lies in the realm of measurements and methods by which educators can guide their daily activity.

Development at this level requires the active work of a community of research men; Taylor's conferences have helped to establish such a community. Movement in depth and breadth of understanding of creative persons is required; MacKinnon and Barron have opened up that domain. Instruments and correlative methods of teaching are required in forms usable and used by classroom teachers in the field; Torrance has met this need. Clear-cut recognition that traditional measurements and methods are not adequate is required; Getzels and Jackson have effectively dramatized this fact. Reconception of basic intelligence is required; Guilford has supplied this reconception.

These are substantial contributions. Because of them creative education has a source for its further development which is far ahead of the sources available to educators in any prior period of our history. These developments have charted out the field and secured the anchorages for the contributions of many others, present and future. American education is far from being effective in the development of creativity in the masses of students, but the solid beginnings are there.

References

ADAMSON, R. E., & TAYLOR, D. W. Functional fixedness as related to elapsed time and to set. *J. exp. Psychol.*, 1954, *47:* 122–126.

ALLPORT, G. W. *Personality*. New York: Holt, 1937.

ALLPORT, G. W. *Becoming*. New Haven: Yale Univer. Press, 1955.

ALSCHULER, ROSE H., & HATTWICK, LA BERTZ WEISS. *Painting and personality. Vol. I.* Univer. of Chicago Press, 1947.

ANDERSON, H. H. Creativity as personality development. In H. H. Anderson (Ed.), *Creativity and its cultivation.* New York: Harper, 1959, 119–141.

ANDREWS, GLADYS. *Creative rhythmic movement for children.* Englewood Cliffs, N. J.: Prentice-Hall, 1954.

ARMITAGE, S. An analysis of certain psychological tests used for evaluation of brain injury. *Psychol. Monogr.*, 1946, *60* (1).

ARNOLD, J. W. Useful creative techniques. In S. J. Parnes & H. F. Harding (Eds.), *A source book for creative thinking.* New York: Scribners, 1962, 252–268.

BARRETT, JEAN A. Creative thinking ability and performance in selected motor skills for fourth, fifth, and sixth grade boys and girls. Unpublished Ed. D. dissertation, State Univer. of N. Y. at Buffalo, 1965.

BARRON, F. *Personal soundness in university graduate students: an experimental study of young men in the sciences and professions.* Univer. of Calif. Publications in Personality Assessment and Research, No. 1. Berkeley: Univer. of Calif. Press, 1954a.

BARRON, F. Some relationships between originality and style of personality. *Amer. Psychologist,* 1954b, *9:* 326.

BARRON, F. The psychology of imagination. *Sci. Amer.*, Sept., 1958, *199:* 151–166.

BARRON, F. Current work at the Institute of Personality Assessment Research. In C. W. Taylor (Ed.), *The Third (1959) Univer. of Utah Research Conference on the Identification of Creative Scientific Talent.* Salt Lake City: Univer. of Utah Press, 1959, 72–76.

BAVINK, B. *Ergebnisse und Probleme der Naturwissenschaften.* Zurich: Hirzel, 1949.

BERGLER, E. Psychoanalysis of writers and literary productivity. In G. Roheim (Ed.), *Psychoanalysis and the social sciences,* Vol. 1. New York: International Universities Press, 1947, 247–296.

311

312 : REFERENCES

BERGSON, H. *Creative evolution.* New York: Holt, 1911.

BERTALANFFY, L. 'Open systems' in physics and biology. *Nature,* 1949, London, *163:* 384.

BERTALANFFY, L. *Problems of life.* London: Watts, 1952.

BIRD, M. H. A study in aesthetics. *Harvard Monogr. in Educ.,* 1932, *11:* 370–426.

BLOCK, J. The Q-sort method in personality assessment and psychiatric research. To be published.

BLOOM, B. S. (Ed.) *Taxonomy of educational objectives: the classification of educational goals. Handbook I: cognitive domain.* New York: David McKay, 1956.

BOESEN, SISTER MARY THEODORE. An analysis of the question-asking behavior of teachers in a parochial school. Unpublished research paper, Univer. of Minnesota, Minneapolis, 1966.

BOND, N. A. An experimental study of transfer effects in human problem solving. Unpublished doctoral dissertation, Univer. of Southern Calif., 1955.

BOUTWELL, W. D. What's happening in education? *PTA Magazine,* June, 1964.

BOWERS, J. B. *Explorations of creative thinking in the early school years: XIV. A preliminary factor-analytic study of the creative thinking abilities of children,* Res. Memorandum Ber 60–15. Bureau of Educational Res., Univer. of Minnesota, 1960.

BRITTAIN, W. L. Experiments for a possible test to determine some aspects of creativity in the visual arts. Unpublished doctor's thesis, Pennsylvania State College, 1952.

BRODY, S. *Biogenetics and growth.* New York: Reinhold, 1945.

BROOKS, F. D. The relative accuracy of ratings assigned with and without use of drawing scales. *School and Soc.,* 1928, *27:* 518–520.

BROWN, E. J. Highly intelligent but not necessarily highly creative. *Sch. and Community,* Nov., 1962.

BRUNER, J. S. *The process of education.* Cambridge, Mass.: Harvard Univer. Press, 1960.

BUEL, W. D. The validity of behavioral rating scale items for the assessment of individual creativity. *J. appl. Psychol.,* Dec., 1960, *44:* 407–412.

BUHLER, C. Maturation and motivation. *Personality,* 1951, *1:* 184–211.

BUHLER, C. The reality principle. *Amer. J. Psychother.,* 1954, *8:* 626–647.

BURKHART, R. C. An analysis of individuality of art expression at the senior high school level. Unpublished doctoral thesis, Pennsylvania State Univer., Univer. Park, 1957.

BURKHART, R. C., & BERNHEIM, G. *Object question test manual.* Univer. Park, Pa.: Dept. of Art Educ. Res., Pennsylvania State Univer., 1963. (Mimeo.)

BURT, C. Critical notice *Creativity and intelligence* by J. W. Getzels and P. W. Jackson. *Brit. J. educ. Psychol.,* 1962, *32:* 292–298.

CANNON, W. *The wisdom of the body.* New York: Norton, 1939.

CATTELL, R. B. The personality and motivation of the researcher from measurements of contemporaries and from biography. In C. W. Taylor (Ed.), *The Third (1959) Univer. of Utah Research Conference on the Identification of Creative Scientific Talent.* Salt Lake City: Univer. of Utah Press, 1959, 77–93.

CATTELL, R. B. The personality and motivation of the researcher from measurements of contemporaries and from biography. In C. W. Taylor & F. Barron (Eds.), *Scientific creativity: its recognition and development.* New York: Wiley, 1963, 119–131.

CHORNESS, M. An interim report on creativity research. In C. W. Taylor (Ed.), *The 1955 Univer. of Utah Research Conference on the Identification of Creative Scientific Talent.* Salt Lake City: Univer. of Utah Press, 1956.

CHORNESS, M., & NOTTELMANN, D. N. *The prediction of creativity among Air Force civilian employees.* Technical Note, AFPTRC–TN–57–36, ASTIA Documents No. 126366. Lackland Air Force Base, Texas: Air Force Personnel Training Res. Center, Air Res. and Develpm. Command, March, 1957.

COGHILL, G. E. *Anatomy and the problem of behavior.* Cambridge: Univer. Press, 1929.

CORTER, H. M. A factor analysis of some individually administered reasoning tests. Unpublished doctor's thesis, Pennsylvania State College, 1949.

Creativity can be cultivated. *N. Y. State Educ.,* April, 1963.

CRICK, F. H. C. The structure of the hereditary material. *Sci. Amer.,* 1954, *191:* 54–61.

CRUTCHFIELD, R. S. Assessment of persons through a quasi group-interaction technique. *J. abnorm. soc. Psychol.,* Oct., 1951, *46:* 577–588.

CRUTCHFIELD, R. S., & WOODWORTH, D. G. Effective functioning of officer personnel in a quasi group-interaction situation. *Res. Bull.,* Univer. of Calif., Berkeley, Institute of Personality Assessment and Research, 1954, 6.

CRUTCHFIELD, R. S., WOODWORTH, D. G., & ALBRECHT, R. E. *Perceptual performance and the effective person.* Technical Note WADC–TN–58–60, ASTIA Document No. AD 151 039. Lackland Air Force Base, Texas: Wright Air Development Center, Personnel Laboratory, 1958.

CUNNINGTON, B. P., & TORRANCE, E. P. *Sounds and images.* Bureau of Educational Res., Univer. of Minnesota, 1962.

DAVIDS, A. Generality and consistency of relations between the alienation syndrome and cognitive processes. *J. abnorm. soc. Psychol.,* 1955, *51:* 61–67.

DEWEY, J. *How we think.* Boston: Heath, 1933.

DEWIT, F. The Block Design Test and drawing ability. Unpublished master's thesis, Pennsylvania State College, 1951.

DICKENS, C. M'Choakumchild's schoolroom. In B. Johnston (Ed.), *Issues in education.* Boston: Houghton Mifflin, 1964.

DIGIOVANNA, D. G. A comparison of the intelligence and athletic ability of college men. *Res. Quart.,* 1937, *8:* 96–106.

DILTHEY, W. *Dichterische Einbildungskraft und Wahnsinn.* Leipzig: Duncker & Humblat, 1886.

DOBZHANSKY, T. Heredity, environment, and evolution. *Science,* 1950, *111:* 161–166.

DOBZHANSKY, T., & ASHLEY-MONTAGU, M. F. Natural selection and the mental capacities of mankind. *Science,* 1947, *105:* 587–590.

DREIKURS, R. Causality versus indeterminism. *Indiv. Psychol. Bull.,* 1951, *9:* 108–117.

DREVDAHL, J. E. An exploratory study of creativity in terms of its relationships to various personality and intellectual factors. *Dissertation Abstracts,* 1954, *142:* 1256.

DREVDAHL, J. E. Factors of importance for creativity. *J. clin. Psychol.,* 1956, *12:* 23–26.

DREWS, ELIZABETH M. Profile of creativity. *NEA J.,* Jan., 1963.

DUKE, R. L., & McGUIRE, C. Intellectual and personality structure of lower-class adolescents in small cities. Invited paper, Amer. Psychological Assn., Convention Reports Duplication Service, 1201 Worton Blvd., Cleveland 24, Ohio, 1961.

DUNCKER, K. A qualitative (experimental and theoretical) study of productive thinking (solving of comprehensible problems). *Ped. Sem.,* 1926, *33:* 642–708.

DUNCKER, K. *Zur Psychologie des Producktiven Denkens.* Berlin: Springer, 1935.

DUNCKER, K. On problem solving. *Psychol. Monogr.,* 1945, *58:* Whole No. 270.

EHRENZWEIG, A. *Psychoanalysis of artistic vision and hearing.* London, 1953.

EISNER, E. W. Research and creativity: some findings and conceptions. *Childh. Educ.,* April, 1963.

ELKISH, PAULA. Children's drawings in a projective technique. *Psychol. Monogr.,* 1945, *58* (1): 1–31.

ELLISON, R. L. The relationship of certain biographical information to success in science. Master's thesis, Univer. of Utah, Salt Lake City, 1960.

FLEMING, E. S., & WEINTRAUB, S. Attitudinal rigidity as a measure of creativity in gifted children. *J. educ. Psychol.,* 1962, *53:* 81–85.

FRANK, L. K. The teacher as communicator. *Wheelock Alumnae Quart.,* Fall, 1963, *34* (4).

FRANKL, V. E. *From death camp to existentialism.* Boston: Beacon Press, 1960.

FRENCH, J. W. *The description of aptitude and achievement tests in terms of rotated factors.* Psychometric Monograph No. 5. Chicago: Univer. of Chicago Press, 1951.

FRENKEL-BRUNSWIK, E. Intolerance of ambiguity as an emotional and perceptual personality variable. In J. S. Bruner & D. Krech (Eds.), *Perception and personality.* Durham: Duke Univer. Press, 1949.

FREUD, S. *The basic writings of . . . .* (Brill, A. A., Ed.) New York: Random House, 1938.

FRIEDENBERG, E. Z. *Coming of age in America: growth and acquiescence.* New York: Random House, 1965.

FRIEDMAN, H. Perceptual regression in scizophrenia: an hypothesis suggested by the use of the Rorschach test. *J. proj. Tech.,* 1953, *17:* 171–186.

GAIER, E. L., & WHITE, W. F. Trends in the measurement of personality. *Rev. educ. Res.,* 1965, *35* (2): 66–67.

GALTON, F. *Inquiries into human faculty and its development.* New York: Macmillan, 1883.

GETZELS, J. W., & JACKSON, P. W. The meaning of giftedness: an examination of an expanding concept. *Phi Delta Kappan,* Nov., 1959, *40:* 75–78.

GETZELS, J. W., & JACKSON, P. W. The highly intelligent and the highly creative adolescent: a summary of some research findings. In C. W. Taylor (Ed.), *The Third (1959) Univer. of Utah Research Conference on the Identification of Creative Scientific Talent.* Salt Lake City: Univer. of Utah Press, 1959, 46–57.

GETZELS, J. W., & JACKSON, P. W. Occupational choice and cognitive functioning: career aspirations of highly intelligent and of highly creative adolescents. *J. abnorm. soc. Psychol.*, July, 1960, *61:* 119–123.

GETZELS, J. W., & JACKSON, P. W. The study of giftedness: a multidimensional approach. In Cooperative Res. Monogr. No. 2 of the U. S. Office of Educ., *The gifted student.* Washington, D. C.: U. S. Office of Educ., 1960, 1–18.

GETZELS, J. W. & JACKSON, P. W. The meaning of 'giftedness.' *Education,* April, 1962.

GETZELS, J. W., & JACKSON, P. W. *Creativity and intelligence: explorations with gifted students.* New York: Wiley, 1962.

GHISELIN, B. *The creative process.* Berkeley: Univer. of Calif. Press, 1952.

GHISELIN, B. The creative process and its relation to the identification of creative talent. In C. W. Taylor (Ed.), *The 1955 Univer. of Utah Research Conference on the Identification of Creative Scientific Talent.* Salt Lake City: Univer. of Utah Press, 1956, 195–203.

GHISELIN, B. Ultimate criteria for two levels of creativity. In C. W. Taylor & F. Barron (Eds.), *Scientific creativity.* New York: Wiley, 1963.

GIBSON, W. C. *Young endeavour.* Springfield, Ill.: Charles C. Thomas, 1958.

GIEDION, S. *Mechanization takes command.* New York: Oxford Univer. Press, 1948.

GIVENS, P. R. Identifying and encouraging creative processes. *J. Higher Educ.,* June, 1962.

GOLANN, S. E. The creativity motive. *J. Pers.,* 1962, *30* (4): 588–600.

GOLDMAN, R. J. *A basic reading list in creative thinking for British readers.* (Duplicated bibliography.) Dept. of Educ., Univer. of Reading, 1964.

GOODENOUGH, FLORENCE. *Measurement of intelligence by drawings.* New York: World Book, 1926.

GOODY, MARJORIE. Painting with words. Unpublished poems, Fifth Grade, Alamo School, San Francisco, Calif.

GORDON, W. J. J. *Synectics.* New York: Harpers, 1961.

GOUGH, H. Mentioned in review by Putney, W. W. Characteristics of creative drawings of stutterers. Unpublished doctor's thesis, 1955, 51–80.

GRINKER, R. R. (Ed.), *Toward a unified theory of human behavior.* New York: Basic Books, 1956.

GROTJAHN, M. Creativity and freedom in art and analysis. In M. Grotjahn, *Beyond laughter.* New York: McGraw-Hill, 1957, 121–137.

GRUBER, H. E., TERRELL, G., & WERTHEIMER, M. *Contemporary approaches to creative thinking.* New York: Prentice-Hall, 1962.

GUILFORD, J. P. Creativity. *Amer. Psychologist,* 1950, *5:* 444–454.

GUILFORD, J. P., WILSON, R. C., CHRISTENSEN, P. R., & LEWIS, D. J. *A factor-analytic study of creative thinking I. Hypotheses and description of tests.* Reports from the Psychological Laboratory, No. 4. Los Angeles: Univer. of Southern Calif., 1951. (Offset.)

GUILFORD, J. P. *A factor analytic study of creative thinking.* Univer. of Southern Calif. Press, July, 1952.

GUILFORD, J. P. The nature of creativity. *Res. Bull.,* Eastern Arts Assn., 1954.

GUILFORD, J. P. The relation of intellectual factors to creative thinking in science. In C. W. Taylor (Ed.), *The First Univer. of Utah Research Conference on the Identification of Creative Scientific Talent.* Salt Lake City: Univer. of Utah Press, 1956a, 69–95.

316 : REFERENCES

GUILFORD, J. P. The structure of intellect. *Psychol. Bull.*, 1956b, *53:* 267–293.

GUILFORD, J. P. *A revised structure of intellect.* Reports from the Psychological Laboratory, No. 19. Los Angeles: Univer. of Southern Calif., April, 1957.

GUILFORD, J. P. Creative activities in the arts. *Psychol. Rev.*, 1957, *64:* 110–118.

GUILFORD, J. P. Basic traits in intellectual performance. In C. W. Taylor (Ed.), *The Second (1957) Research Conference on the Identification of Creative Scientific Talent.* Salt Lake City: Univer. of Utah Press, 1958, 66–81.

GUILFORD, J. P. Three faces of intellect. *Amer. Psychologist*, 1959a, *14:* 469–479.

GUILFORD, J. P. The dimensions of aptitude. *Personality.* New York, London: McGraw-Hill, 1959b.

GUILFORD, J. P. Intellectual resources and their values as seen by scientists. In C. W. Taylor (Ed.), *The Third (1959) Univer. of Utah Research Conference on the Identification of Creative Scientific Talent.* Salt Lake City: Univer. of Utah Press, 1959c, 128–149.

GUILFORD, J. P. An emerging view of learning theory. In *Intelligence, creativity, and learning.* Bellingham, Wash.: Western Washington College, 1960.

GUILFORD, J. P. Factorial angles to psychology. *Psychol. Rev.*, 1961a, *68:* 1–20.

GUILFORD, J. P. An informational view of mind. *J. Psychol. Researches*, 1961b, *6:* 1–10.

GUILFORD, J. P. Basic problems in teaching for creativity. In C. W. Taylor & F. E. Williams (Eds.), *Instructional media and creativity.* New York: Wiley, 1966a, 71–103.

GUILFORD, J. P. Intelligence: 1965 model. *Amer. Psychologist*, 1966b, *21:* 20–26.

GUILFORD, J. P. Some new views of creativity. In H. Helson, *Theory and data in psychology.* Princeton, N. J.: D. Van Nostrand, in press—a.

GUILFORD, J. P. *The nature of human intelligence.* New York: McGraw-Hill, 1967 (in press)—b.

GUILFORD, J. P., CHRISTENSEN, P. R., FRICK, J. W., & MERRIFIELD, P. R. *The relations of creative-thinking aptitudes to nonaptitude personality traits.* Rep. Psychol. Lab., No. 20. Los Angeles: Univer. of Southern Calif., 1957.

GUILFORD, J. P., & HOEPFNER, R. Sixteen divergent-production abilities at the ninth-grade level. *Multiv. Beh. Res.*, 1966, *1:* 43–66.

GUILFORD, J. P., & MERRIFIELD, P. R. The structure-of-intellect model: its uses and applications. *Rep. psychol. Lab.*, No. 24, 1960. Los Angeles: Univer. of Southern Calif.

GUILFORD, J. P., WILSON, R. C., & CHRISTENSEN, P. R. *A factor-analytic study of creative thinking. II. Administration of tests and analysis of results.* Reports from the Psychological Laboratory, No. 8. Los Angeles: Univer. of Southern Calif., 1952. (Offset.)

GUILFORD, J. P., WILSON, R. C., CHRISTENSEN, P. R., AND LEWIS, D. J. *A factor analytic study of creative thinking: I. Hypotheses and description of tests.* Los Angeles: Univer. of Southern Calif. Press, 1951.

HADAMARD, J. *An essay on the psychology of invention in the mathematical field.* Princeton: Princeton Univer. Press, 1949.

HARMON, L. R. Criterion Committee report. In C. W. Taylor (Ed.), *The First Univer. of Utah Research Conference on the Identification of Creative Scientific Talent*. Salt Lake City: Univer. of Utah Press, 1956, 251–259.

HARMON, L. R. The development of a criterion of scientific competence. In C. W. Taylor & F. Barron (Eds.), *Scientific creativity*. New York: Wiley, 1963, 44–52.

HARRIS, D. The development and validation of a test of creativity in engineering. *J. appl. Psychol.*, 1960, *44:* 254–257.

HARTMAN, R. S. The individual in management. Lecture presented to The Nationwide Management Center, Columbus, Ohio, November 7, 1962.

HAWKINS, D. The informed vision: an essay on science education. *Daedalus,* Summer, 1965, 538–552.

HEALY, W., & BRONNER, Λ. F. *The structure and meaning of psychoanalysis.* New York: Knopf, 1930.

HEBEISEN, ARDYTH A. The performance of a group of schizophrenic patients on a test of creative thinking. In E. P. Torrance (Ed.), *Creativity: proceedings of the Second Minnesota Conference on Gifted Children*. Minneapolis: Center for Continuation Study, Univer. of Minnesota, 1959, 125–129.

HERSCH, C. The cognitive functioning of the creative person: a developmental analysis by means of the Rorschach test. Unpublished doctoral dissertation, Clark Univer., 1957.

HERSCH, C. The cognitive functioning of the creative person: a developmental analysis. *J. proj. Tech.*, 1962, *26* (2): 193–200.

HILLS, J. R. Recent creativity studies at educational testing service. In C. W. Taylor (Ed.), *The Second (1957) Univer. of Utah Research Conference on the Identification of Creative Scientific Talent*. Salt Lake City: Univer. of Utah Press, 1958, 181–191.

HITT, W. D. Toward a two-factor theory of creativity. *Psychol. Rec.*, 1965, *15:* 127–132.

HOCH, O. Improving the present status of the creative student. *High School J.,* October, 1962.

HOLLAND, J. L. Some limitations of teacher ratings as predictors of creativity. *J. educ. Psychol.*, 1959, *50:* 219–223.

HOLLAND, J. L. Creative and academic performance among talented adolescents. *J. educ. Psychol.*, June, 1961, *52:* 136–147.

HOLLAND, J. L. The assessment and prediction of creative performance of high-aptitude youth. In C. W. Taylor (Ed.), *Widening horizons in creativity*. New York: Wiley, 1964, 298–315.

HOLLAND, J. L., & ASTIN, A. W. *The prediction of academic, artistic, scientific, and special achievement among undergraduates of superior scholastic aptitude*. Evanston, Ill.: National Merit Scholarship Corp., 1961. (Mimeo.)

HORNEY, K. *Neurosis and human growth.* New York: Norton, 1950.

HOROWITZ, N. H. The gene. *Sci. Amer.*, 1956, *195:* 79–90.

HOUSTON, J. P., & MEDNICK, S. A. Creativity and the need for novelty. *J. abnorm. soc. Psychol.*, 1963, *66:* 137–141.

HUDSON, L. Intelligence, divergence and potential originality. *Nature,* 1962, *196:* 601.

HULL, C. L. *Principles of behavior*. New York: Appleton-Century-Crofts, 1943.

HURLOCK, ELIZABETH B., & THOMSON, J. L. Children's drawings: an experimental study of perception. *Child Developm.*, 1934, *5* (2): 127–138.

JACKSON, P. W. New dimensions in creativity. *Bull. of the National Assn. of Secondary-Sch. Principals,* Oct., 1962.

JEX, F. B. Negative validities for two different ingenuity tests. In C. W. Taylor & F. Barron (Eds.), *Scientific creativity.* New York: Wiley, 1963, 299–301.

JOHN, E. R. *Contributions to the study of the problem-solving process.* Psychological Monographs: General and Applied, *71* (18) (Whole No. 447), 1958.

JOHNSON, R. T. The growth of creative thinking abilities in Western Samoa. Doctoral dissertation, Univer. of Minnesota, Minneapolis, 1963.

JONES, C. A. Some relationships between creative writing and creative drawing of sixth grade children. Doctor's thesis, Pennsylvania State Univer., 1960.

JONES, L. V. A factor analysis of the Stanford-Binet at four age levels. *Psychometrika,* 1949, *14* (4).

KLAUSMEIER, H. J., HARRIS, C. W., & ETHNATHIOS, Z. Relationships between divergent thinking abilities and teacher ratings of high school students. *J. educ. Psychol.,* 1962, *53:* 72–75.

KLINE, L. W., & CAREY, C. L. *A measuring scale for free-hand drawings.* Baltimore: Johns Hopkins Press, 1922.

KNAPP, R. H. Demographic cultural and personality attributes of scientists. In C. W. Taylor (Ed.), *The 1955 Univer. of Utah Research Conference on the Identification of Creative Scientific Talent.* Salt Lake City: Univer. of Utah Press, 1956, 204–212.

KNELLER, G. F. *The art and science of creativity.* New York: Holt, Rinehart, and Winston, 1965.

KOHS, S. C. *Intelligence measurement.* New York: Macmillan, 1923.

KRIS, E. Psychoanalysis and the study of creative imagination. *Bull. N. Y. Acad. Med.,* 1953, 334–351.

KUBIE, L. S. *Neurotic distortion of the creative process.* Lawrence: Univer. of Kansas Press, 1958.

LACKLEN, R., & HARMON, L. R. Criterion Committee report. In C. W. Taylor (Ed.), *The Second Univer. of Utah Research Conference on the Identification of Creative Scientific Talent.* Salt Lake City: Univer. of Utah Press, 1958, 243–248.

LANSING, K. M. The effect of class size and room size upon the creative drawings of fifth grade children. Unpublished doctor's thesis, Pennsylvania State Univer., 1956.

LANSING, K. M. The effect of class size and room size upon the creative drawings of fifth grade children. *Res. in Art Educ.,* National Art Educ. Assn., 9th Yearbook, 1959.

LASKI, M. *Ecstasy.* London: Cresset Press, 1961.

LATCHAW, MARJORIE, & BROWN, CAMILLE. *The evaluation process on physical education and recreation.* Englewood Cliffs, N. J.: Prentice-Hall, 1962.

LEHMAN, H. C. *Age and achievement.* Princeton, N. J.: Princeton Univer. Press, 1953.

LEWERENZ, A. S. IQ and ability in art. *Sch. and Soc.,* 1928, *27:* 489–490.

LIGON, E. M. The co-scientist and his potential. *Charact. Potential,* 1965, *3:* 1–26.

LORGE, I. *Semantic count of the 570 commonest English words.* New York: Bureau of Publications, Teachers College, Columbia Univer., 1949.

LOWENFELD, V. *Creative and mental growth.* New York: Macmillan, 1952.

LOWENFELD, V., & BEITTEL, K. Interdisciplinary criteria of creativity in the arts and sciences: a progress report. *Res. in Art Educ.,* National Art Educ. Assn., 9th Yearbook, 1959.

MACKINNON, D. W. What do we mean by talent and how do we test for it? In *The search for talent,* College Admissions, No. 7. New York: College Entrance Examination Board, 1959, 20–29.

MACKINNON, D. W. The nature and nurture of creative talent. *Amer. Psychologist,* 1962, *17:* 484–495.

MACKINNON, D. W. The creativity of architects. In C. W. Taylor (Ed.), *Widening horizons in creativity.* New York: Wiley, 1964, 359–378.

MCCELLAND, D. C. The calculated risk: an aspect of scientific performance. In C. W. Taylor & F. Barron (Eds.), *Scientific creativity: its recognition and development.* New York: Wiley, 1963, 184–192.

MCGEOCH, J. A., & IRION, A. L. *The psychology of human learning.* New York: David McKay, 1952.

MCGUIRE, C. The Textown study of adolescence. *Texas J. of Sci.,* 1956a, *8:* 264–274.

MCGUIRE, C. Factors influencing individual mental health. *Rev. educ. Res.,* 1956b, *26:* 451–478.

MCGUIRE, C. Personality. In C. W. Harris (Ed.), *Encyclopedia of educational research.* New York: Macmillan, 1960a, 945–957.

MCGUIRE, C. Foundations of emotional development. *Texas State J. of Med.,* 1960b, *56:* 723–725.

MCGUIRE, C. The prediction of talented behavior in junior high schools. *Proceedings of the 1960 invitational conference on testing problems.* Princeton, N. J.: Educational Testing Service, 1961a, 46–73.

MCGUIRE, C. Sex role and community variability in test performance. *J. educ. Psychol.,* 1961b, *52:* 61–73.

MCGUIRE, C., HINDSMAN, E., KING, F. J., & JENNINGS, E. Dimensions of talented behavior. *Educ. psychol. Measmt.,* 1961, *21:* 3–38.

MCGUIRE, C., & WHITE, G. Social-class influences on discipline at school. *Educational Leadership,* 1957, *14:* 229–236.

MCPHERSON, J. H. A proposal for establishing ultimate criteria for measuring creative output. In C. W. Taylor & F. Barron (Eds.), *Scientific creativity.* New York: Wiley, 1963, 24–29.

MCVITTY, L. An experimental study on various methods in art motivation at the fifth grade level. Unpublished doctor's thesis, Pennsylvania State Univer., 1954.

MAIER, N. R. F. Reasoning in humans. Part I. On direction. *J. comp. physiol. Psychol.,* 1930, *10:* 115–143.

MAIER, N. R. F. Reasoning and learning. *Psychol. Rev.,* 1931a, *38:* 332–346.

MAIER, N. R. F. Reasoning in humans: II. The solution of a problem and its appearance in consciousness. *J. comp. Psychol.,* 1931b, *12:* 181–194.

MAIER, N. R. F. An aspect of human reasoning. *Brit. J. Psychol.,* 1933, *24:* 144–155.

MALTZMAN, I., BROOKS, L. O., BOGARTZ, W., & SUMMERS, S. S. The facilitation of problem-solving by prior exposure to uncommon responses. *J. exp. Psychol.*, 1958, *56:* 339–406.

MANUEL, H. T. *Talent in drawing*. Bloomington, Ill.: Pub. Sch. Pub. Co., 1919.

MARTIN, R. A., & PACHARES, J. *Evaluating engineers and scientists for a research and development activity*. Calvin City, Calif.: Hughes Aircraft Co., 1960. (Multilithed.)

MASLOW, A. H. *Motivation and personality*. New York: Harper, 1954.

MASLOW, A. H. Defense and growth. *Merrill-Palmer Quart.*, 1956, *3:* 37–38.

MASLOW, A. H. Creativity in self actualizing people. Lecture for Creativity Symposium, Mich. State Univer., East Lansing, Feb. 28, 1958.

MASLOW, A. H. Emotional blocks to creativity. *Humanist*, 1958, *18:* 325–332.

MASLOW, A. H. Emotional blocks to creativity. *J. indiv. Psychol.*, 1958, *14:* 51–56.

MASLOW, A. H. *Toward a psychology of being*. New York: Van Nostrand, 1962a.

MASLOW, A. H. Lessons from the peak-experiences. *J. humanistic Psychol.*, 1962b, *2:* 9–18.

MASLOW, A. H. Notes on a psychology of being. *J. humanistic Psychol.*, 1962c.

MATTIL, E. L. A study to determine the relationship between the creative products of children, age 11 to 14, and their adjustment. Unpublished doctor's thesis, Pennsylvania State Univer., 1953.

MAY, R. (Ed.), *Existential psychology*. New York: Random House, 1961.

MEER, M., & STEIN, M. I. Measures of intelligence and creativity. *J. Psychol.*, 1955, *39:* 117–126.

MICHAEL, J. The effects of award, adult standard, and peer standard upon the creativeness in art of high school pupils. Unpublished doctoral thesis, Pennsylvania State Univer., Univer. Park, 1959.

MILLER, J. G. Toward a general theory for the behavioral sciences. *Amer. Psychologist*, 1955, *10:* 513–531.

MILLER, J. G. General behavior systems theory and summary. *J. counsel. Psychol.*, 1956, *3:* 120–124.

MILLER, G. A., GALANTER, E., & PRIBRAM, K. H. *Plans and the structure of behavior*. New York: Holt, 1960.

MONOHAN, JANE E., & HOLLINGSWORTH, LETA S. Neuromuscular capacity of children who test above 135 I.Q. Stanford Binet. *J. educ. Psychol.*, 1927, *18:* 88–96.

MOONEY, R. L. A conceptual model for integrating four approaches to the identification of creative talent. In C. W. Taylor & F. Barron, *Scientific creativity: its recognition and development*. New York: Wiley, 1963.

MORGAN, C. L. *Emergent evolution*. London: Williams & Norgate, 1923.

MORGAN, J. J. *Child psychology* (revised ed.). New York: Farrar and Rinehart, 1937.

MOUSTAKAS, C. *The authentic teacher*. Cambridge, Mass.: Howard Doyle Publishing Co., 1966.

MOUSTAKAS, C. Confrontation and encounter. In *Creativity and conformity*. New Jersey: D. Van Nostrand, in press—a.

MOUSTAKAS, C. Education, alienation, and existential life. In H. Winthrop (Ed.), *Essays towards a humanistic psychology,* in press—b.

MULLINS, C. J. *The prediction of creativity in a sample of research scientists.* Technical Note, WADC–TN–59–36, ASTIA Documents No. AD 211039. Lackland Air Force Base, Texas: Personnel Laboratory, Wright Air Development Center, Air Res. and Develpm. Command, Feb., 1959.

NAUMBURG, MARGARET. *Studies of the "free" art expression of behavior problem children and adolescents as a means of diagnosis and therapy.* New York: Coolidge Foundation, 1946.

OJEMANN, R. H. Research in planned learning programs and the science of behavior. *J. educ. Res.,* 1948, *42:* 96–104.

OJEMANN, R. H., & PRITCHETT, K. Piaget and the role of guided experiences in human development. *Percept. mot. Skills,* 1963, *17:* 927–939.

OJEMANN, R. H., MAXEY, E. J., & SNIDER, B. C. F. The effect of a program of guided learning experiences in developing probability concepts at the third grade level. *J. exp. Educ.,* 1965, *33:* 321–330.

ORZECK, A. A., McGUIRE, C., & LONGENECKER, D. Multiple self concepts as effected by mood states. *Amer. J. Psychiat.,* 1958, *115:* 349–353.

OSBORN, A. F. *Applied imagination.* Rev. ed. New York: Scribners, 1957.

OSBORN, A. F. *Creative imagination.* (Third rev.) New York: Scribners, 1963.

OWENS, W. A., SCHUMACHER, C. F., & CLARK, J. B. The measurement of creativity in machine design. In C. W. Taylor (Ed.), *The Second (1957) Univer. of Utah Research Conference on the Identification of Creative Scientific Talent.* Salt Lake City: Univer. of Utah Press, 1958, 129–140.

PARNES, S. J., & HARDING, H. F. (Eds.), *A source book of creative thinking.* New York: Scribners, 1962.

PECK, R. F. Family patterns correlated with adolescent personality structure. *J. abnorm. soc. Psychol.,* 1958, *57:* 347–350.

PECK, R. F. Personality patterns of prospective teachers. *J. exp. Educ.,* 1960, *29:* 169–175.

PECK, R. F. Student mental health; the range of personality patterns in a college population. In R. L. Sutherland et al. (Eds.), *Personality factors on the college campus.* Austin, Tex.: Hogg Foundation for Mental Health, Univer. of Texas, 1962, 161–199.

PECK, R. F., & GALLIANI, C. Intelligence, ethnicity, and social roles in adolescent society. *Sociometry,* 1962, *25:* 64–71.

PECK, R. F., & HAVIGHURST, R. J. *The psychology of character development.* New York: Wiley, 1960.

PETERSON, H. (Ed.), *Great teachers.* New York: Vintage Books, 1946.

PILLSBURY, W. B. *The psychology of reasoning.* New York: Appleton, 1910.

PILLSBURY, W. B. Recent naturalistic theories of reasoning. *Scientia,* 1924, *36:* 23–32.

PRAKASH, A. O. Understanding the fourth grade slump: a study of the creative thinking abilities of Indian children. Master's research paper, Univer. of Minnesota, Minneapolis, 1966.

PRESSEY, S. L., & KUHLEN, R. G. *Psychological development through the life span.* New York: Harper, 1957.

RAINA, M. K. A study of sex differences in creativity. Research paper, Regional College of Educ., Ajmer, India, 1966.

RANK, O. *Das Trauma der Geburt.* Leipzig: Internationaler Psychoanalytischer Verlag, 1924.

RAZIK, TAHER A. *Bibliography of Creativity Studies and Related Areas*, Creative Education Foundation and State University of New York at Buffalo, 1965, 451.

READ, H. E. *Education through art*. London: Faber & Faber, 1943.

READ, H. E. *Art now*. New York: Pitman, 1948.

REYNOLDS, M. C. Nurturing talents. Paper presented at Elementary Leaders Conference, Iowa State Teachers College, Jan. 31, 1958.

RIBOT, T. A. *The evolution of general ideas*. Chicago: Open Court, 1899.

RIBOT, T. A. *Essay on creative imagination*. Chicago: Open Court, 1906.

RILEY, R. F., & OVERBERGER, C. G. A summer research participation program for high school students. *J. chem. Educ.*, Aug., 1961, *38:* 424–427.

ROE, ANNE. Psychological tests of research scientists. *J. consult. Psychol.*, 1951, *15:* 492–495.

ROE, ANNE. *The making of a scientist*. New York: Dodd, Mead, & Co., 1953.

ROE, ANNE. Early differentiation of interests. In C. W. Taylor (Ed.), *The Second (1957) Univer. of Utah Research Conference on the Identification of Creative Scientific Talent*. Salt Lake City: Univer. of Utah Press, 1958, 98–108.

ROE, ANNE. Personal problems and science. In C. W. Taylor (Ed.), *The Third (1959) Univer. of Utah Research Conference on the Identification of Creative Scientific Talent*. Salt Lake City: Univer. of Utah Press, 1959, 202–212.

ROGERS, C. R. *Counseling and psychotherapy*. Boston: Houghton Mifflin, 1942.

ROGERS, C. R. Significant aspects of client-centered therapy. *Amer. Psychologist*, 1946, *1:* 415–422.

ROGERS, C. R. *Client-centered therapy*. Boston: Houghton Mifflin, 1951.

ROGERS, C. R. Toward a theory of creativity. *ETC: A review of general semantics*, Summer, 1954.

ROGERS, C. R. Toward a theory of creativity. In S. J. Parnes and H. F. Harding (Eds.), *A source book for creative thinking*. New York: Scribners, 1962, 63–72.

ROGERS, C. Learning to be free. *Pastoral psychology,* Part I, *13* (128), 47–54; Part II, *13* (129), 43–51.

ROGERS, MARY JUNE. An attempt to find drawing criteria specific to the junior high level. Unpublished master's thesis, 1955.

ROSSMAN, J. *The psychology of the inventor*. Washington, D. C.: Inventors Publishing Co., 1931.

RUSSELL, E. S. The study of behavior. *Rep. Brit. Assn.*, 1934, 83–98.

RUSSELL, E. S. *The directiveness of organic activities*. Cambridge: Cambridge Univer. Press, 1945.

SACHS, C. *The history of musical instruments*. New York: Norton, 1940.

SALINGER, J. D. *Nine stories*. Boston: Little, Brown and Co., 1953.

SANDERS, N. M. *Classroom questions: what kinds?* New York: Harper and Row, 1966.

SARASON, S. B., DAVIDSON, K. S., LIGHTHALL, F. F., WAITE, R. R., & RUEBUSH, B. K. *Anxiety in elementary school children*. New York: Wiley, 1960.

SCHILDER, P. *The image and appearance of the human body*. New York: International Universities Press, 1950.

SCHROEDER, GEORGIA E. The relationship of social acceptance, motor performance and intelligence to children's activity choices. Unpublished M. A. thesis, State Univer. of Iowa, 1959.

SEEGARS, J. C. & POSTPICHAL, O. Relation between intelligence and certain aspects of physical ability. *J. educ. Res.*, 1936, *30:* 104–109.

SHAFFER, G. K. Variables affecting Kraus-Weber failures among junior high school girls. *Res. Quart.*, 1959, *30:* 75–86.

SINNOTT, E. W. *The biology of the spirit.* New York: Viking, 1955.

SINNOTT, E. W. *Matter, mind and man.* New York: Harper, 1957.

SMITH, R. M. *The relationship of creativity to social class.* (USOE Cooperative Res. Project 2250.) Pittsburgh: Univer. of Pittsburgh, 1965.

SMITH, W. J., ET AL. The prediction of research competence and creativity from personal history. *J. appl. Psychol.,* Feb., 1961, *45:* 59–62.

SNYGG, D., & COMBS, A. W. *Individual behavior.* New York: Harper, 1949.

SOMMERS, W. S. *The influence of selected teaching methods on the development of creative thinking.* Ann Arbor, Mich.: Dissertation Abstracts, 1961.

STOCK, J. R. Test prediction of scientific research performance factors. Paper presented at APA Convention, Sept., 1961.

SPRECHER, T. B. Committee report on criteria of creativity. In C. W. Taylor (Ed.), *The Third Univer. of Utah Research Conference on the Identification of Creative Scientific Talent.* Salt Lake City: Univer. of Utah Press, 1959, 287–297.

STARKWEATHER, J. A., & CRUTCHFIELD, R. S. Introversion and perceptual accuracy. *Amer. Psychologist,* Sept., 1954, *9:* 560.

STEIN, M. I. A transactional approach to creativity. In C. W. Taylor (Ed.), *The 1955 Univer. of Utah Research Conference on the Identification of Creative Scientific Talent.* Salt Lake City: Univer. of Utah Press, 1956, 171–181.

STEIN, M. I. Problems involved in predictors of creativity. In C. W. Taylor (Ed.), *The Third Univer. of Utah Research Conference on the Identification of Creative Scientific Talent.* Salt Lake City: Univer. of Utah Press, 1959, 178–186.

STERN, W. *Person und Sache. Bd. I: Ableitung und Grundlehre.* Leipzig: Barth, 1906.

STERN, W. *Person und Sache. Bd. II: Die Menschliche Persoenlichkeit.* Leipzig: Barth, 1918.

STERN, W. *Person und Sache. Bd. III: Wertphilosophie.* Leipzig: Barth, 1924.

SULLIVAN, H. S. Conceptions of modern psychiatry. *Psychiatry,* 1940, *3,* and 1945, *8.*

TABA, HILDA. Opportunities for creativity in education for exceptional children. *Except. Child.,* Feb., 1963.

TAYLOR, C. W. (Ed.), *The 1955 Univer. of Utah Research Conference on the Identification of Creative Scientific Talent.* Salt Lake City: Univer. of Utah Press, 1956.

TAYLOR, C. W. (Ed.), *The Second (1957) Univer. of Utah Research Conference on the Identification of Creative Scientific Talent.* Salt Lake City: Univer. of Utah Press, 1958a.

TAYLOR, C. W. Some variables functioning in productivity and creativity. In C. W. Taylor (Ed.), *The Second (1957) Univer. of Utah Research Confer-

ence on the Identification of Creative Scientific Talent. Salt Lake City: Univer. of Utah Press, 1958b, 3–19.

TAYLOR, C. W. The identification of creative scientific talent. *Amer. Psychologist,* 1959a, *14:* 100–102.

TAYLOR, C. W. Identifying the creative individual. In E. P. Torrance (Ed.), *Creativity: Second Minnesota Conference on Gifted Children.* Minneapolis: Center for Continuation Study, Univer. of Minnesota, 1959b, 3–21.

TAYLOR, C. W. (Ed.), *The Third (1959) Univer. of Utah Research Conference on the Identification of Creative Scientific Talent.* Salt Lake City: Univer. of Utah Press, 1959c.

TAYLOR, C. W. The creative individual: a new portrait in giftedness. *Educational Leadership,* 1960, *8* (1): 7–12.

TAYLOR, C. W. A tentative description of the creative individual. In *Human variability and learning.* Washington, D. C.: Assn. for Supervision and Curriculum Develpm. of the NEA, 1961, 62–79.

TAYLOR, C. W. Many-sided intelligence. *Childh. Educ.,* April, 1963.

TAYLOR, C. W. Who are the exceptionally creative? *Except. Child.,* April, 1962.

TAYLOR, C. W., SMITH, W. R., GHISELIN, B., & ELLISON, R. *Explorations in the measurement and prediction of contributions of one sample of scientists.* Technical Report ASD–TR–61–96. Lackland Air Force Base, Texas: Personnel Laboratory, Aeronautical Systems Div., Air Force Systems Command, April, 1961.

TAYLOR, C. W., & BARRON, F. *Scientific creativity: its recognition and development.* New York: Wiley, 1963.

TAYLOR, C. W., SMITH, W. R., & GHISELIN, B. Analyses of multiple criteria of creativity and productivity of scientists. In C. W. Taylor (Ed.), *The Third (1959) Univer. of Utah Research Conference on the Identification of Creative Scientific Talent.* Salt Lake City: Univer. of Utah Press, 1959, 5–28.

TAYLOR, C. W., SMITH, W., & GHISELIN, B. The creative and other contributions of one sample of research scientists. In C. W. Taylor & F. Barron (Eds.), *Scientific creativity.* New York: Wiley, 1963, 53–76.

TAYLOR, D. W. Variables related to creativity and productivity among men in two research laboratories. In C. W. Taylor (Ed.), *The Second (1957) Univer. of Utah Research Conference on the Identification of Creative Scientific Talent.* Salt Lake City: Univer. of Utah Press, 1958, 20–54.

TERMAN, L. M. Genius and stupidity: a study of some of the intellectual processes of seven 'bright' and seven 'stupid' boys. *Ped. Sem.,* 1906, *13:* 307–373.

TERMAN, L. M., ET AL. Genetic studies of genius, vol. I. In *Mental and physical traits of a thousand gifted children.* Stanford Univer. Press, 1925, 37.

THOMPSON, MARGARET M. A study in the relationship between selected motor skills and mental achievement of children of elementary school age. Unpublished doctor's thesis, State Univer. of Iowa, 1961.

THORNDIKE, E. L. The measurement of achievement in drawing. *Teachers College Rec.,* 1913, *14* (5): 1–38.

THORNDIKE, E. L. *The psychology of arithmetic.* New York: Macmillan, 1922.

THORNDIKE, E. L. *Human learning.* New York: Century, 1931.

THORNDIKE, R. L. The measurement of creativity. *Teachers Coll. Rec.,* 1963, *64:* 422–424.

THURSTONE, L. L. *Factoral study of perception.* Univer. of Chicago Press, 1944.

THURSTONE, L. L. Creative talent. In L. L. Thurstone (Ed.), *Applications of psychology.* New York: Harper, 1952, Chap. 2, 18–37.

TIEBOUT, C. E. The measurement of quality in children's paintings by the scale method. *Psychol. Monogr.,* 1936–37a, *48:* 85–94.

TIEBOUT, C. E., & MEIER, N. C. Artistic ability and general intelligence. *Psychol. Monogr.,* 1936–37b, *48:* 95–125. (Review of studies of intelligence before 1925).

TORRANCE, E. P. *Explorations in creative thinking in the early school years:* VI. *Highly intelligent and highly creative children in a laboratory school.* Minneapolis: Bureau of Educational Res., Univer. of Minnesota, 1959a.

TORRANCE, E. P. *Explorations in creative thinking in the early school years:* VII. *Talkativeness and creative thinking.* Minneapolis: Bureau of Educational Res., Univer. of Minnesota, 1959b.

TORRANCE, E. P. Explorations in creative thinking in the early school years: a progress report. In C. W. Taylor (Ed.), *The Third (1959) Univer. of Utah Research Conference on the Identification of Creative Scientific Talent.* Salt Lake City: Univer. of Utah Press, 1959c, 58–71.

TORRANCE, E. P. Educational achievement of the highly intelligent and the highly creative: eight partial replications of the Getzels-Jackson study. *Res. Memorandum,* BER–60–18, Bureau of Educational Research, Univer. of Minnesota.

TORRANCE, E. P. Problems of highly creative children. *Educ. Digest,* Nov., 1961.

TORRANCE, E. P. Testing and creative talent. *Educational Leadership,* Oct., 1962c.

TORRANCE, E. P. *Guiding creative talent.* Englewood Cliffs, N. J.: Prentice-Hall, 1962a.

TORRANCE, E. P. *Administration and scoring manual for abbreviated form VII Minnesota tests of creative thinking.* Bureau of Educational Res., Univer. of Minnesota, 1962b.

TORRANCE, E. P. Are there tops in our cages? *Amer. Voc. J.,* March, 1963d.

TORRANCE, E. P. Essay review: creativity and intelligence. *Sch. Rev.,* Spring, 1963c.

TORRANCE, E. P. The creative potential of school children in the space age. In *Education and the creative potential.* Minneapolis: Univer. of Minnesota Press, 1963a.

TORRANCE, E. P. *Education and the creative potential.* Minneapolis: Univer. of Minnesota Press, 1963b.

TORRANCE, E. P. *Role of evaluation in creative thinking.* Report on Project No. 725. Bureau of Educational Res., Univer. of Minnesota, 1964.

TORRANCE, E. P. *Rewarding creative behavior.* Englewood Cliffs, N. J.: Prentice-Hall, 1965a.

TORRANCE, E. P. *Gifted children in the classroom.* New York: Macmillan, 1965b.

TORRANCE, E. P., & GOLDMAN, R. J. *Creative development in a segregated Negro school.* Minneapolis: Dept. of Educational Psychol., Univer. of Minnesota, 1966.

TORRANCE, E. P., & GOWAN, J. C. *The reliability of the Minnesota tests of creative thinking.* Memorandum BER–63–4. Bureau of Educational Res., Univer. of Minnesota, 1963.

TORRANCE, E. P., & GUPTA, R. *Development and evaluation of recorded programmed experiences in creative thinking in the fourth grade.* Minneapolis: Bureau of Educational Res., Univer. of Minnesota, 1964.

TORRANCE, E. P., & HANSEN, E. The question-asking behavior of highly creative and less creative basic business teachers identified by a paper-and-pencil test. *Psychol. Reports,* 1965, *17:* 815–818.

TORRANCE, E. P., & MICHIE, H. W. *Explorations in creative thinking in the early school years: I. Scoring manual for "how good is your imagination,"* Res. Memorandum Ber 59–1. Bureau of Educational Res., Univer. of Minnesota, 1959.

TORRANCE, E. P., & RADIG, H. J. *The ask-and-guess test; scoring manual and rationale,* Res. Memorandum Ber 59–6. Bureau of Educational Res., Univer. of Minnesota, 1959.

TORRANCE, E. P., & TAN, C. A. *Revised scoring guide for analyzing attitudes concerning divergency in imaginative stories.* Univer. of Minnesota, 1964.

TORRANCE, E. P., DEYOUNG, K. N., GHEI, S. N., & MICHIE, H. W. *Explorations in creative thinking in mental hygiene: II. Some characteristics of the more creative individuals.* Minneapolis: Bureau of Educational Res., Univer. of Minnesota, 1958.

TORRANCE, E. P., PALM, H. J., PALAMUTULU, N., & RADIG, H. J. *Scoring manual for a measure of inventive level.* Minneapolis: Bureau of Educational Res., Univer. of Minnesota, 1959.

VANDENBERG, D. Experimentalism in the aesthetic society. *Harvard educ. Rev.,* Spring, 1962, *32* (2): 155–187.

VELDMAN, D. J., PECK, R. F., & McGUIRE, C. Measuring the value systems of education professors. *J. educ. Psychol.,* 1961, *52:* 330–334.

VERNON, P. E. Creativity and intelligence. *Educ. Res.,* 1964, vi, *3:* 163–169.

WACHNER, TRUDE S. Formal criteria for the analysis of children's drawings. *Amer. J. Orthopsychiat.,* 1942, *12* (1): 95–103.

WALLACE, H. R. Creative thinking: a factor in sales productivity. *Voc. Guidance Quart.,* 1961, *9:* 223–226.

WALLAS, G. *The art of thought.* New York: Harcourt & Brace, 1926.

WALLAS, G. *The art of thought.* London: C. A. Watts, 1945.

WECHSLER, D. *The measurement of adult intelligence.* Baltimore: Williams & Wilkins Co., 1944.

WERTHEIMER, M. *Productive thinking.* New York: Harper, 1945.

WHITE, R. W. Motivation reconsidered: the concept of competence. *Psychol. Rev.,* 1961, *66:* 297–333.

WHYTE, W. H. *The organization man.* Garden City, N. Y.: Doubleday, 1957.

WILSON, R. C. Creativity. In N. B. Henry (Ed.), *Education for the gifted,* Yearbook of the National Soc. for the Study of Educ., 1958, *57,* Part II, 108–126.

WILSON, R. C., GUILFORD, J. P., CHRISTENSEN, P. R., & LEWIS, D. J. A factor-analytic study of creative-thinking abilities. *Psychometrika,* 1954, *19:* 297–311.

WINSLOW, L. L. *The integrated school art program.* New York, London: McGraw-Hill, 1939.

WITTY, P. A. The gifted and the creative pupil. *Education,* April, 1962.

WODKE, K. A study of the reliability and validity of creative tests at the elementary school level. Doctor's thesis, Univer. of Utah. Ann Arbor, Mich.: Univer. Microfilms, 1963.

WOODRUFF, A. D. *The psychology of teaching.* New York: Longmans Green and Co., 1946.

WOODS, W. A. The role of language handicap in the development of artistic interest. *J. consult. Psychol.,* 1948, *12:* 240–245.

WOODWORTH, D. G., & MACKINNON, D. W. *The use of trait ratings in an assessment of 100 Air Force captains.* Technical Note WADC–TN–58–64, ASTIA Document No. AD 202 845. Lackland Air Force Base, Tex.: Wright Air Develpm. Center, Personnel Laboratory, 1958.

YAMAMOTO, K. *Scoring manual for the non-verbal tasks of creative thinking,* first draft. Bureau of Educational Res., Univer. of Minnesota, 1960.

YAMAMOTO, K. *Creativity and intellect: review of current research and projection.* Paper presented to the Minnesota Psychological Assn. Minneapolis: Univer. of Minnesota, April, 1961. (Mimeo.)

YAMAMOTO, K. A study of the relationships between creative thinking abilities of fifth grade teachers and academic achievement. Doctor's thesis. Ann Arbor, Mich.: Univer. Microfilms, 1962.

YAMAMOTO, K. Relationships between creative thinking abilities of teachers and achievement and adjustment of pupils. *J. exp. Educ.,* 1963, *32:* 3–25.

YAMAMOTO, K. Creative thinking: some thoughts on research. *Except. Child.,* 1964a, *30:* 403–410.

YAMAMOTO, K. Evaluation of some creativity measures in a high school with peer nominations as criteria. *J. Psychol.,* 1964b, *58:* 285–293.

YAMAMOTO, K. Creativity and sociometric choice among adolescents. *J. soc. Psychol.,* 1964c, *64:* 249–261.

Index